D3.js in Action

ELIJAH MEEKS

MANNING

SHELTER ISLAND

For online information and ordering of this and other Manning books, please visit
www.manning.com. The publisher offers discounts on this book when ordered in quantity.
For more information, please contact

> Special Sales Department
> Manning Publications Co.
> 20 Baldwin Road
> PO Box 761
> Shelter Island, NY 11964
> Email: orders@manning.com

Manning Publications Co.	Development editor: Susanna Kline
20 Baldwin Road	Technical development editor: Valentin Crettaz
PO Box 761	Copyeditor: Tara Walsh
Shelter Island, NY 11964	Proofreader: Katie Tennant
	Technical Proofreader: Jon Borgman
	Typesetter: Dennis Dalinnik
	Cover designer: Marija Tudor

ISBN: 9781617292118
Printed in the United States of America
1 2 3 4 5 6 7 8 9 10 – EBM – 20 19 18 17 16 15

brief contents

contents

8   *Traditional DOM manipulation with D3   240*

PART 3   ADVANCED TECHNIQUES 259

9   *Composing interactive applications   261*

preface

I've always loved making games. Board games, role-playing games, computer games—I just love abstracting things into rules, numbers, and categories. As a natural consequence, I've always loved data visualization. Damage represented as a bar, spells represented with icons, territory broken down into hexes, treasure charted out in a variety of ways. But it wasn't until I started working with maps in grad school that I became aware of the immeasurable time and energy people have invested in understanding how to best represent data.

I started learning D3 after having worked with databases, map data, and network data in a number of different desktop packages, and also coding in Flash. So I was naturally excited when I was introduced to D3, a JavaScript library that deals not only with information visualization generally, but also with the very specific domains of geospatial data and network data. The fact that it lives in the DOM and follows web standards was a bonus, especially because I'd been working with Flash, which wasn't known for that kind of thing.

Since then, I've used D3 for everything, including the creation of UI elements that you'd normally associate with jQuery. When I was approached by Manning to write this book, I thought it would be the perfect opportunity for me to look deeply at D3 and make sure I knew how every little piece of the library worked, while writing a book that didn't just introduce D3 but really dived into the different pieces of the library that I found so exciting, like mapping and networks, and tied them together.

As a result, the book ended up being much longer than I expected and covers everything from the basics of generating lines and areas to using most of the layouts that come to mind when you think of data visualization. It also devotes some space to maps, networks, mobile, and optimization.

In the end, I tried to give readers a broad approach to data visualization tools, whether that means maps or networks or pie charts.

acknowledgments

I'd like to thank my wife, Hajra, for giving me the support and inspiration and the keen editorial eye necessary for a book like this.

I'd also like to thank Manning Publications for the chance to write this book. The exercise of writing a book like this serves as a finishing school for learning about a library, and as a result of writing *D3.js in Action*, I feel more confident with D3 than I would have had I simply created applications. I'd like to especially thank my editor, Susanna Kline, for her patience and hard work at turning my prose into something worth buying. Also, thanks to the production team and everyone else at Manning who worked on the book behind the scenes.

The following reviewers provided feedback on the manuscript at various stages of its development, and I thank them for their time and effort: Prashanth Babu V V, Dwight Barry, Margriet Bruggeman, Nikander Bruggeman, Matthew Faulkner, Jim Frohnhofer, Ntino Krampis, Andrea Mostosi, Arun Noronha, Alvin Raj, Adam Tolley, and Stephen Wakely. Thanks also to technical editor Valentin Crettaz and technical proofreader Jon Borgman for lending their expertise and making this a much better book.

Finally, I'd like to thank Stanford University Library and all the people there, but especially the head of that library, Mike Keller, for giving me the opportunity to use D3 to create amazing new research and applications in a number of exciting projects.

about this book

People come to data visualization, and D3 particularly, from three different areas. The first is traditional web development, where they assume D3 is a charting library or, less commonly, a mapping library. The second is more traditional software development, like Java, where D3 is part of the transition into HTML5 development. The last area is a trajectory that involves statistical analysis using R, Python, or desktop apps.

In each case, D3 represents two major transitions for folks: modern web development and data visualization. I touch on aspects of both that may give a reader more grounding in what I expect to be new and strange fields. Someone who's intimately familiar with JavaScript may find that some of these subjects (like function chaining) are already well understood, and others who know data visualization well may feel the same way about some of the general principles, like graphical primitives.

Although I do provide an introduction to D3, the focus of this book is on a more exhaustive explanation of key principles of the library. Whether you're just getting started with D3, or you're looking to develop more advanced skills, this book provides you with the tools you need to create whatever data visualization you can think of.

Roadmap

This book is split into three parts. The first three chapters focus on the fundamentals of D3. You'll see data-binding, loading data, and creating graphical elements from data in a variety of different ways. It also deals with scales, color, and other important aspects of data visualization that you might already know well. Some of the core technologies used by D3, like JavaScript, CSS, and SVG, are explained throughout these chapters.

The next five chapters use D3 in the ways we typically think of. Chapter 4 teaches you how to create simple graphics from data, such as line charts, axes, and boxplots. Chapter 5 gives an in-depth exploration of various traditional data visualization layouts like pie charts, tree layouts, and word clouds. Chapter 6 is devoted to network visualization, which might seem exotic, but network visualization is being used more and more in a variety of domains. Chapter 7 dives into the rich mapping capabilities in D3, and includes leveraging TopoJSON to do interesting geodata manipulation in the browser. Chapter 8 is devoted to manipulating traditional HTML elements, like paragraphs and lists, to demonstrate that D3 is not tied to SVG.

The last three chapters and chapter 12 (online only) cover topics that can be considered deep diving into D3. I've found that each has become an important part of my own practice. This includes principles for wiring up your own data dashboard, creating your own D3 layouts and components, optimizing data visualization for large datasets, and writing data visualization for mobile. Even if you don't think you'll ever be using D3 in these ways, each of these chapters still touches on key aspects of using D3.

How to use this book

If you're just getting started with D3, I suggest going through chapters 1 through 4 in order. Each chapter builds on the last and establishes the basic principles not only of D3 but also of data visualization. After that, it depends on what you plan to use D3 for. If your data is mostly geographic, then you can jump to chapter 7, and similarly, if your data is mostly network data, you can jump to chapter 6. If you're doing traditional data visualization, then I suggest going to chapter 5 and then on to chapter 9 to start thinking about dashboards, which are a key component of traditional data visualization.

If you've been using D3 for a while and want to improve your skills, I suggest skimming the first three chapters. The parts that I think might be of particular interest are in chapter 3, and deal with color and loading external resources like SVG icons or HTML content. You might also want to review generators and components in chapter 4 to fill in any gaps you might have dealing with these common, but often underexamined, parts of D3. After that, it depends on what you see as your strengths and what you see as your goals for using D3. If you want to maximize traditional data visualization, take a look at chapter 5 to see the layouts, and then look at chapter 9 for dashboards. You're probably familiar with most of the content there, but these chapters deal with it more exhaustively than you likely have experienced. After that, look at chapter 11 and see if there are any optimization techniques you might want to bring into your data visualization, or look at chapter 8 and think about how you might use the D3 tricks you know to build UI elements and otherwise do traditional web development.

Much of the value of this book comes in chapters 6 and 7, which go into great detail about using D3 for two major areas of data visualization: networks and maps. Along those lines, the use of HTML5 canvas in chapters 8 and 11 is an area that even experienced D3 developers might not be familiar with.

Regardless of your level of experience with D3, I recommend you really spend some time with chapter 10, which deals with the structure of layouts and components while showing you how to build your own. Beginning to build modular, reusable components and layouts will allow you to create not only effective data visualization, but also an effective career in visualizing data.

Chapter 12 is available online only from the publisher's website at www.manning .com/D3.jsinAction and is a fun read that will expand your horizons.

Online graphics

Most of the graphics in this book were created in color and are meant to be viewed in color. The eBook versions do include color graphics, but the print book is printed in grayscale. To view the color graphics, please refer to the eBook versions in PDF, ePub, and Kindle formats, which are available to pBook owners for free after they register their print book at www.manning.com/D3.jsinAction.

About one third of the graphics in this book also have an online component. To see the online graphic and the code that was used to generate it, please look for this icon in the captions of certain figures: .

In the eBook versions, clicking on the icon will take you to the interactive graphic online. For print book readers, please go to the publisher's website at www.manning .com/D3.jsinAction where you will find the interactive graphics listed by figure number. By clicking on the URLs for those figures, you will be able to view the graphics online on your computer or tablet as you read the print book.

Code conventions

Initial code examples in chapters are complete, with later code examples that extend an initial example only showing the code that has changed. It's best to use the source code and online examples alongside the text. The line lengths of some of the examples exceed the page width, and in cases like these, the ➡ marker is used to indicate that a line has been wrapped for formatting.

All source code in listings or in text is in a `fixed-width font like this` to separate it from ordinary text. Code annotations accompany many of the listings, highlighting important concepts.

Source code downloads

The source code for the examples in this book is available online from the publisher's website at www.manning.com/D3.jsinAction, and a list of all interactive versions is hosted on GitHub and can be found at emeeks.github.io/d3ia/.

Software requirements

D3.js requires a browser to run, and you should have a local web server installed on your computer to host your code.

about the cover illustration

The figure on the cover of *D3.js in Action* is captioned "Habit of a Moorish Pilgrim Returning from Mecca in 1586." The illustration is taken from Thomas Jefferys' *A Collection of the Dresses of Different Nations, Ancient and Modern* (four volumes), London, published between 1757 and 1772. The title page states that these are hand-colored copperplate engravings, heightened with gum arabic. Thomas Jefferys (1719–1771) was called "Geographer to King George III." He was an English cartographer who was the leading map supplier of his day. He engraved and printed maps for government and other official bodies and produced a wide range of commercial maps and atlases, especially of North America. His work as a mapmaker sparked an interest in local dress customs of the lands he surveyed and mapped, an interest that is brilliantly displayed in this four-volume collection.

Fascination with faraway lands and travel for pleasure were relatively new phenomena in the late eighteenth century, and collections such as this one were popular, introducing both the tourist as well as the armchair traveler to the inhabitants of other countries. The diversity of the drawings in Jefferys' volumes speaks vividly of the uniqueness and individuality of the world's nations some 200 years ago. Dress codes have changed since then, and the diversity by region and country, so rich at the time, has faded away. It is now often hard to tell the inhabitant of one continent from another. Perhaps, trying to view it optimistically, we have traded a cultural and visual diversity for a more varied personal life, or a more varied and interesting intellectual and technical life.

At a time when it is hard to tell one computer book from another, Manning celebrates the inventiveness and initiative of the computer business with book covers based on the rich diversity of regional life of two centuries ago, brought back to life by Jeffreys' pictures.

Part 1

D3.js fundamentals

The first three chapters introduce you to the fundamental aspects of D3 and get you started with creating graphical elements in SVG using data. Chapter 1 lays out how D3 relates to the DOM, HTML, CSS, and JavaScript, and provides a few examples of how to use D3 to create elements on a web page. Chapter 2 focuses on loading, measuring, processing, and changing your data in preparation for data visualization using the various functions D3 includes for data manipulation. Chapter 3 turns toward design and explains how you can use D3 color functions for more effective data visualization, as well as load external elements such as HTML for modal dialogs or icons in raster and vector formats. In all, part 1 shows you how to load, process, and visually represent data in SVG without relying on built-in layouts or components, which is critical for using and extending those layouts and components.

An introduction to D3.js

This chapter covers

- The basics of HTML, CSS, and the Document Object Model (DOM)
- The principles of Scalable Vector Graphics (SVG)
- Data-binding and selections with D3
- Different data types and their data visualization methods

Note to print book readers: Many graphics in this book are meant to be viewed in color. The eBook versions display the color graphics, so they should be referred to as you read. To get your free eBook in PDF, ePub, and Kindle formats, go to manning.com/D3.jsinAction to register your print book.

D3 stands for *data-driven documents*. It's a brand name, but also a class of applications that have been offered on the web in one form or another for years. For quite some time we've been building and working with data-driven documents such as interactive dashboards, rich internet applications, and dynamically driven content. In one sense, the D3.js library is an iterative step in a chain of technologies used for data-driven documents, but in another sense, it's a radical step.

1.1   What is D3.js?

D3.js was created to fill a pressing need for web-accessible, sophisticated data visualization. Because of the library's robust design, it does more than make charts. And that's a good thing, because *data visualization* no longer refers to pie charts and line graphs. It now means maps and interactive diagrams and other tools and content integrated into news stories, data dashboards, reports, and everything else you see on the web.

D3.js's creator, Mike Bostock, helped develop an earlier data visualization library, Protovis, and also developed Polymaps, a JavaScript library that provides vector- and tile-mapping capability in a lightweight form. These earlier endeavors would inform the creation of D3.js, which focuses on modern standards and modern browsers. As Bostock describes it, "This avoids proprietary representation and affords extraordinary flexibility, exposing the full capabilities of web standards such as CSS3, HTML5 and SVG" (http://d3js.org/). This is the radical nature of D3.js. Although it won't run on Internet Explorer 6, the widespread adoption of standards on modern browsers has finally allowed web developers to deliver dynamic and interactive content seamlessly in the browser.

Until recently, you couldn't build high-performance, rich internet applications in the browser unless you built them in Flash or as a Java applet. Flash and Java are still around on the internet, and especially for internal web apps, for this reason. D3.js provides the same performance, but integrated into web standards and the Document Object Model (DOM) at the core of HTML. D3 provides developers with the ability to create rich interactive and animated content based on data and tie that content to existing web page elements. It gives you the tools to create high-performance data dashboards and sophisticated data visualization, and to dynamically update traditional web content.

But D3 isn't easy for people to pick up, because they often expect it to be a simple charting library. A case in point is the pie chart layout, which you'll see in chapter 5. D3 doesn't have one single function to create a pie chart. Rather, it has a function that processes your dataset with the necessary angles so that, if you pass the dataset to D3's arc function, you get the drawing code necessary to represent those angles. And you need to use yet another function to create the paths necessary for that code. It's a much longer process than using dedicated charting libraries, but the D3 process is also its strength. Although other charting libraries conveniently allow you to make line graphs and pie charts, they quickly break down when you want to make something more than that. Not D3, which allows you to build whatever data-driven graphics and interactivity you can imagine, and that's why D3 is behind much of the most innovative and exciting information visualization on the web today.

1.2   How D3 works

Let's take a look at the principles of data visualization, as well as how D3 works in general. In figure 1.1 you see a rough map of how you might start with data and use D3 to process and represent that data, as well as add interactivity and optimize the data visualization you've created. In this chapter we'll start by establishing the principles of how D3 selections and data-binding work and learning how D3 interacts with SVG and

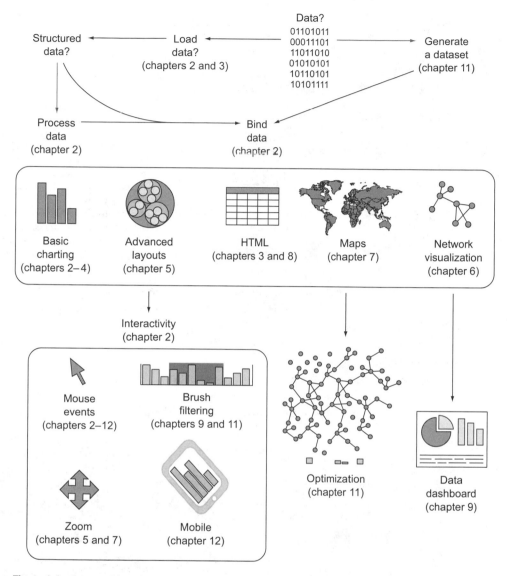

Figure 1.1 A map of how to approach data visualization with D3.js that highlights the approach in this book. Start at the top with data, and then follow the path depending on the type of data and the needs you're addressing.

the DOM. Then we'll look at data types that you'll commonly encounter. Finally, we'll use D3 to create simple DOM and SVG elements.

1.2.1 Data visualization is more than data visualization

You may think of data visualization as limited to pie charts, line charts, and the variety of charting methods popularized by Tufte and deployed in research. It's much more than that. One of the core strengths of D3.js is that it allows for the creation of vector

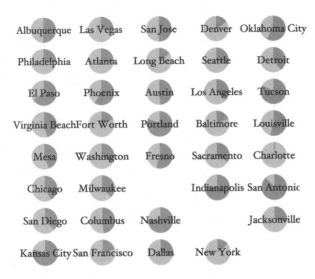

Albuquerque Las Vegas   San Jose   Denver Oklahoma City

Philadelphia Atlanta   Long Beach   Seattle   Detroit

El Paso   Phoenix   Austin   Los Angeles   Tucson

Virginia Beach Fort Worth Portland   Baltimore   Louisville

Mesa   Washington   Fresno   Sacramento   Charlotte

Chicago   Milwaukee   Indianapolis San Antonic

San Diego   Columbus   Nashville   Jacksonville

Kansas City San Francisco Dallas   New York

Figure 1.2   D3 can be used for simple charts, such as this set of multiple pie charts (explained in chapter 5) used to represent the differences in the use of language about nature in major US city planning (from the City Nature project at citynature.stanford.edu). Each pie shows the ratio of language referring to parks and open space (green) versus habitat (red) in city plans.

graphics for traditional charting, but also the creation of geospatial and network visualizations, as well as traditional HTML elements like tables, lists, and paragraphs. This broad-based approach to data visualization, where a map or a network graph or a table is just another kind of representation of data, is the core of the D3.js library's appeal for application development.

Figures 1.2 through 1.8 show data visualization pieces that I've created with D3. They include maps and networks, along with more traditional pie charts and completely custom data visualization layouts based on the specific needs of my clients.

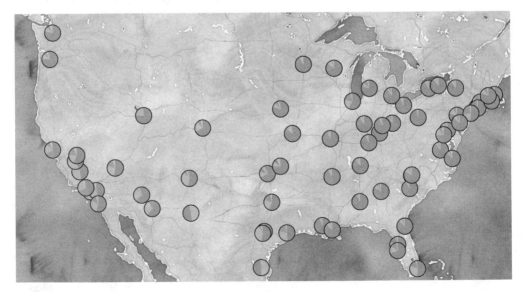

Figure 1.3   D3 can also be used to create web maps (see chapter 7), such as this map showing the ethnic makeup of major metropolitan areas in the United States.

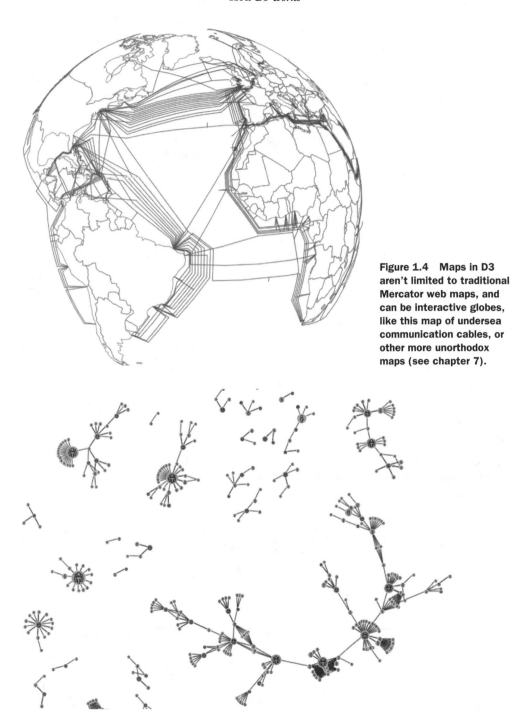

Figure 1.4   Maps in D3 aren't limited to traditional Mercator web maps, and can be interactive globes, like this map of undersea communication cables, or other more unorthodox maps (see chapter 7).

Figure 1.5   D3 also provides robust capacities to create interactive network visualizations (see chapter 6). Here you see the social and coauthorship network of archaeologists working at the same dig for nearly 25 years.

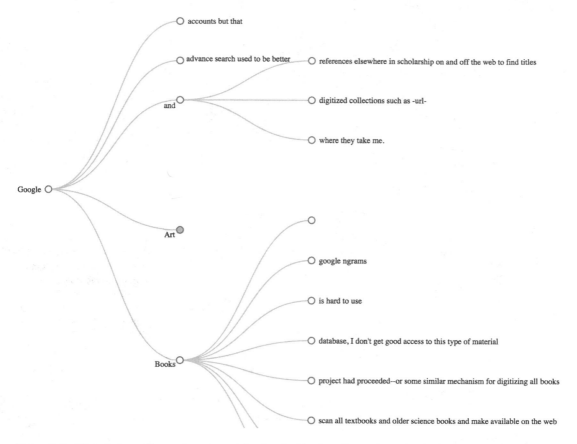

Figure 1.6   D3 includes a library of common data visualization layouts, such as the dendrogram (explained in chapter 5), that let you represent data such as this word tree.

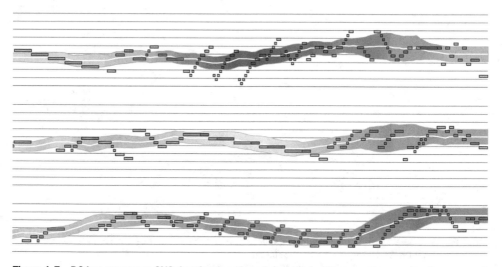

Figure 1.7   D3 has numerous SVG drawing functions (see chapter 4) so you can create your own custom visualizations, such as this representation of musical scores.

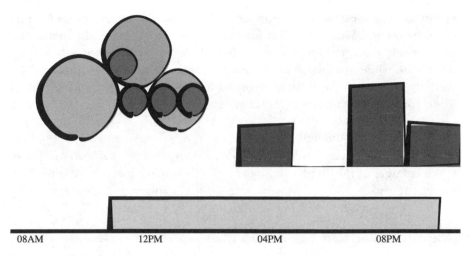

Figure 1.8   You can combine these layouts and functions to create a data dashboard like we'll do in chapter 9. You can also use the drawing functions to make your bar charts look distinctive, such as this "sketchy" style.

Although the ability to create rich and varied graphics is one of D3's strong points, more important for modern web development is the ability to embed the high level of interactivity that users expect. With D3, every element of every chart, from a spinning globe to a single, thin slice of a pie chart, is made interactive in the same way. And because D3 was written by someone well versed in data visualization practice, it includes a number of interactive components and behaviors that are standard in data visualization and web development.

You don't invest your time learning D3 so that you can deploy Excel-style charts on the web. For that, there are easier, more convenient libraries. You learn D3 because it gives you the ability to implement almost every major data visualization technique. It also gives you the power to create *your own* data visualization techniques, something a more general library can't do.

For more examples of the variety of different data visualization techniques realized with D3, take a look at Christophe Viau's gallery of over 2,000 D3 examples here: http://christopheviau.com/d3list/gallery.html.

By requiring a break with the practice of supporting long-obsolete browsers, D3.js affords developers the capacity to make not only richly interactive applications but also applications that are styled and served like traditional web content. This makes them more portable, more amenable to the growing, linked data web, and more easily maintained by large teams.

The decision on Bostock's part to deal broadly with data, and to create a library capable of presenting maps as easily as charts, as easily as networks, as easily as ordered lists, also means that a developer doesn't need to try to understand the abstractions and syntax of one library for maps, and another for dynamic text content, and another for data visualization. Instead, the code for running an interactive, force-directed network layout is very close to pure JavaScript and also similar to the code representing dynamic points of interest (POIs) on a D3.js map. Not only are the methods the same, but the very data could be the same, formulated in one way for lists and paragraphs and spans, while formulated in another way for geospatial representation. The class of data-driven documents is already broad and becomes even more all-encompassing when you also treat images and text as data.

1.2.2 *D3 is about selecting and binding*

Throughout this chapter, you'll see code snippets that you can run in your browser to make changes to the graphical appearance of elements on your website. At the end of the chapter is an application written in D3 that explains the basics of the code we're running in JavaScript. But before that we'll explore the principles of web development using D3, and you'll see this pattern of code over and over again: selecting.

Imagine we have a set of data, such as the price and size of a few houses, and a set of web page elements, whether graphics or traditional <div> elements, and that we want to represent the dataset, whether with text or through size and color. A *selection* is the group of all of them together, and we perform actions on the elements in the group, such as moving them, changing their color, or updating the values in the data. We work with the data and the web page elements separately, but the real power of D3 comes from using selections to combine data and web page elements.

Here's a selection without any data:

```
d3.selectAll("circle.a").style("fill", "red").attr("cx", 100);
```

This takes every circle on our page with the class of "a" and turns it red and moves it so that its center is 100 pixels to the right of the left side of our <svg> canvas. Likewise, this code turns every div on our web page red and changes its class to "b":

```
d3.selectAll("div").style("background", "red").attr("class", "b");
```

But before we can change our circles and divs, we'll need to create them, and before we do that, it's best to understand what's happening in this pattern.

The first part of that line of code, d3.selectAll(), is part of the core functionality necessary for understanding D3: selections. Selections can be made with d3.select(), which selects the first single element found, but more often you'll use d3.select-All(), which can be used to select multiple elements. Selections are a group of one or more web page elements that may be associated with a set of data, like the following code, which binds the elements in the array [1,5,11,3] to <div> elements with the class of "market":

```
d3.selectAll("div.market").data([1,5,11,3])
```

This association is known in D3 as *binding data,* and you can think of a selection as a set of web page elements and a corresponding, associated set of data. Sometimes there are more data elements than DOM elements, or vice versa, in which case D3 has functions designed to create or remove elements that you can use to generate content. We'll cover selections and data-binding in detail in chapter 2. Selections might not include any data-binding, and won't for most of the examples in this chapter, but the inclusion allows the powerful information visualization techniques of D3. You can make a selection on any elements in a web page, including items in a list, circles, or even regions on a map of Africa. Just as the elements can take a number of shapes, the data associated with those elements (where applicable) can take many forms.

1.2.3 *D3 is about deriving the appearance of web page elements from bound data*

After you have a selection, you can then use D3 to modify the appearance of web page elements to reflect differences in the data. You may want to make the length of a line equal to the value of the data, or change the color to a particular color that corresponds to a class of data. You may want to hide or show elements as they correspond to a user's navigation of a dataset. As you can see in figure 1.9, after the page has loaded, you use D3 to select elements and bind data for the purpose of creating, removing, or changing DOM elements. You continue to use this process in response to user interaction.

You modify the appearance of elements by using selections to reference the data bound to an element in a selection. D3 iterates through the elements in your selection and performs the same action using the bound data, which results in different graphical

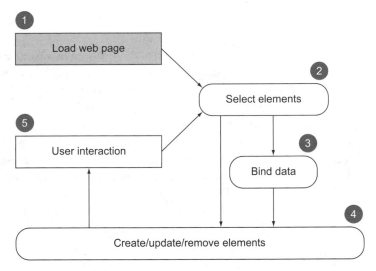

Figure 1.9 A page utilizing D3 is typically built in such a way that the page loads with styles, data, and content as defined in traditional HTML development ❶ with its initial display using D3 selections of HTML elements ❷, either with data-binding ❸ or without it, to modify the structure and appearance of the page ❹. The changes in structure prompt user interaction ❺, which causes new selections with and without data-binding to further alter the page. Step 1 is shown differently because it only happens once (when you load the page), whereas every other step may happen multiple times, depending on user interaction.

effects. Although the action you perform is the same, the effect is different because it's based on the variation in the data. You'll see data-binding first at the end of this chapter, and in much more detail throughout this book.

1.2.4   *Web page elements can now be divs, countries, and flowcharts*

We've grown accustomed to thinking of web pages as consisting of text elements with containers for pictures, videos, or embedded applications. But as you grow more familiar with D3, you'll begin to recognize that every element on the page can be treated with the same high-level abstractions. The most basic element on a web page, a `<div>` that represents a rectangle into which you can drop paragraphs, lists, and tables, can be selected and modified in the same way you can select and modify a country on a web map, or individual circles and lines that make up a complex data visualization.

To be able to select items on a web page, you have to ensure that they're built in a manner that makes them a part of the traditional structure of a web page. You can't select items in a Java applet, or in a Flash runtime, nor can you select the labels on an embedded Google map, but if you create these elements so that they exist as elements in your web page, then you give yourself tremendous flexibility. To get a taste of this, look at chapter 7, where we'll build robust mapping applications in D3, and we'll use the `d3.select()` syntax to update the appearance of a mapping application in the same manner as it's being used here and elsewhere to create and move circles or `<div>` elements.

1.3   *Using HTML5*

We've come a long way from the days when animated GIFs and frames were the pinnacle of dynamic content on the web. In figure 1.10, you can see why GIFs never caught on for robust data visualization on the web. GIFs, like the infoviz libraries designed to use VML, are still necessary for earlier browsers, but D3 is designed for modern browsers that don't need the helper libraries necessary for backward compatibility. D3 development isn't for everyone, but if your audience can be assumed to have access to a modern web browser, D3 also brings a significant reduction in the cost necessary not only to code for older browsers but also to learn and keep updated on the various libraries that support backward compatibility with those older browsers.

A modern browser typically can not only display SVG graphics and obey CSS3 rules, but also has great performance. Along with Cascading Style Sheets (CSS) and Scalable Vector Graphics (SVG), we can break down HTML5 into the DOM and JavaScript. The following sections treat each of them and include code you can run to see how D3 uses their functionality to create interactive and dynamic web content.

1.3.1   *The DOM*

A web page is structured according to the DOM. You need a passing familiarity with the DOM to do web development, so we'll take a quick look at DOM elements and structure in a simple web page in your browser and touch on the basics of the DOM. To get started, you'll need a web server that you can access from the computer that

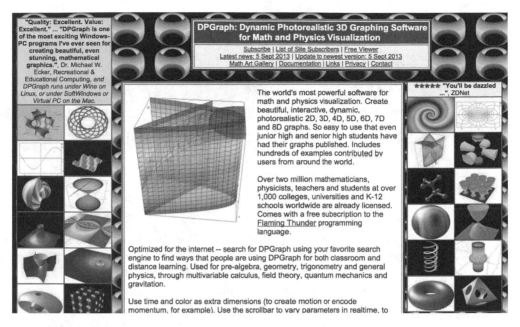

Figure 1.10 Before GIFs were weaponized to share cute animal behavior, they were your only hope for animated data visualization on the web. Few examples from the 1990s like dpgraph.com exist, but this page has more than enough GIFs to remind us of their dangers.

you're using to code. With that in place, you can download the D3 library from d3js.org (d3.js or d3.min.js for the minified version) and place that in the directory where you'll make your web page. You'll create a page called d3ia.html in the text editor with the following contents.

Listing 1.1   A simple web page demonstrating the DOM

```
<!doctype html>
<html>
<head>
  <script src="d3.v3.min.js" type="text/JavaScript"></script>     ⟵┐ A child element
</head>                                                              of <html>
<body>
  <div id="someDiv" style="width:200px;height:100px;border:black 1px solid;">  ⟵
<input id="someCheckbox" type="checkbox" />     ⟵┐ A child element         A child element
  </div>                                            of <div>                 of <body>
</body>
</html>
```

A child element of `<html>`

Basic HTML like this follows the DOM. It defines a set of nested elements, starting with an `<html>` element with all its child elements and their child elements and so on. In this example, the `<script>` and `<body>` elements are children of the `<html>` element, and the `<div>` element is a child of the `<body>` element. The `<script>` element loads the D3 library here, or it can have inline JavaScript code, whereas any content in the `<body>` element shows up onscreen when you navigate to this page.

UTF-8 and D3.js

D3 utilizes UTF-8 characters in its code, which means that you can do one of three things to make sure you don't have any errors.

You can set your document to UTF-8:

```
<!DOCTYPE html><meta charset="utf-8">
```

Or you can set the charset of the script to UTF-8:

```
<script charset="utf-8" src="d3.js"></script>
```

Or you can use the minified script, which shouldn't have any UTF-8 characters in it:

```
<script src="d3.min.js"></script>
```

Three categories of information about each element determine its behavior and appearance: styles, attributes, and properties. *Styles* can determine transparency, color, size, borders, and so on. *Attributes* typically refer to classes, IDs, and interactive behavior, though some attributes can also determine appearance, depending on which type of element you're dealing with. *Properties* typically refer to states, such as the "checked" property of a check box, which is `true` if the box is checked and `false` if the box is unchecked. D3 has three corresponding functions to modify these values. If we wanted to modify the HTML elements in the previous example, we could use D3 functions that abstract this process:

```
d3.select("#someDiv").style("border", "5px darkgray dashed");
d3.select("#someDiv").attr("id", "newID");
d3.select("#someCheckbox").property("checked", true);
```

Like many D3 functions of this kind, if you don't signify a new value, then the function returns the existing value. You'll see this in action throughout this book, and later in the chapter as you write more code, but for now remember that these three functions allow you to change how an element appears and interacts.

The DOM also determines the onscreen drawing order of elements, with child elements drawn after and inside parent elements. Although you have some control over drawing elements above or below each other with traditional HTML using `z-index`, this isn't available for SVG elements (though it might be implemented at some point using the `render-order` attribute).

EXAMINING THE DOM IN THE CONSOLE

Navigate to d3ia.html, and you can get exposure to how D3 works. The page isn't very impressive, with just a single, black-outlined rectangle. You could modify the look and feel of this web page by updating d3ia.html, but you'll find that it's easy to modify the page by using your web browser's developer console. This is useful for testing changes to classes or elements before implementing them in your code. Open up the developer console, and you'll have two useful screens, shown in figures 1.11 and 1.12, which we'll go back to again and again.

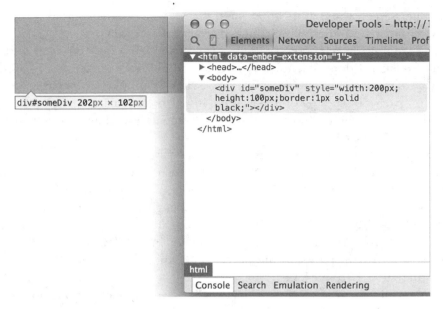

Figure 1.11 **The developer tools in Chrome place the JavaScript console on the rightmost tab, labeled "Console," with the element inspector available using the hourglass on the bottom left or by browsing the DOM in the Elements tab.**

NOTE You'll see the console in this first chapter, but in chapter 2, once you're familiar with it, I'll show only the output.

The element inspector allows you to look at the elements that make up your web page by navigating through the DOM (represented as nested text, where each child element is shown indented). You can also select an element onscreen graphically, typically represented as a magnifying glass or cursor icon.

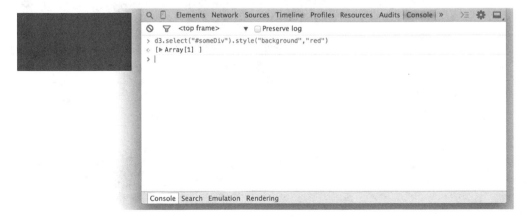

Figure 1.12 **You can run JavaScript code in the console and also call global variables or declare new ones as necessary. Any code you write in the console and changes made to the web page are lost as soon as you reload the page.**

The other screen you'll want to use quite often is the console (figure 1.12), which allows you to write and run JavaScript code right on your web page.

The examples in this book use Google Chrome and its developer console, but you could use Safari's developer tools or Firebug in Firefox, or whatever developer console you're most comfortable with. You can see and manipulate DOM elements such as <div> or <body> by clicking on the element inspector or looking at the DOM as represented in HTML. You can click one of these elements and change its appearance by modifying it in the console.

You can even delete elements in the console. Give it a try: select the div either in the DOM or visually, and press Delete. Now your web page is very lonely. Press Refresh so that your page reloads the HTML and your div comes back. You can adjust the size and color of your div by adding new styles or changing the existing one, so you can increase the width of the border and make it dashed by changing the border style to Black 5px Dashed. You can add content to the div in the form of other elements, or you can add text by right-clicking on the element and selecting Edit as HTML, as shown in figures 1.13 and 1.14.

You can then write whatever you'd like in between the opening and closing HTML.

Any changes you make, regardless of whether they're well structured or not, will be reflected on the web page. In figure 1.15 you see the results of modifying the HTML, which is rendered immediately on your page.

In this way, you could slowly and painstakingly create a web page in the console. We're not going to do that. Instead, we'll use D3 to create elements on the fly with size, position, shape, and content based on our data.

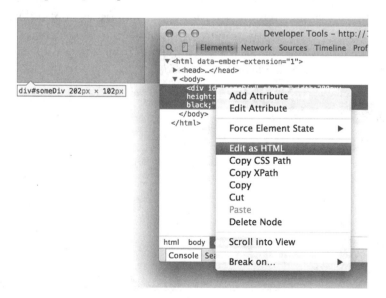

Figure 1.13   Rather than adding or modifying individual styles and attributes, you have the ability to rewrite the HTML code as you would in a text editor. As with any changes, these only last until you reload the page.

```
▶ <head>…</head>
▼ <body>
    <div id="someDiv"
    style="width:200px;height:100px;border
    :1px solid black;">Here's some text to
    put into my div</div>
    </body>
</html>
```

Figure 1.14 Changing the content of a DOM element is as simple as adding text between the opening and ending brackets of the element.

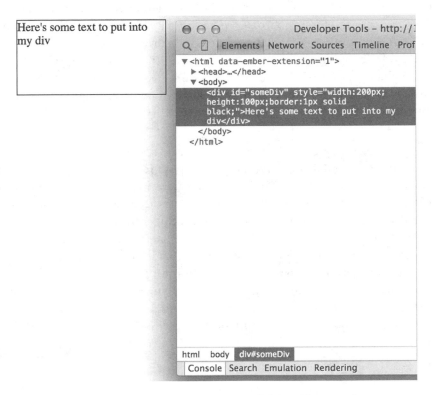

Figure 1.15 The page is updated as soon as you finish making your changes. Writing HTML manually in this way is only useful for planning how you might want to dynamically update the content.

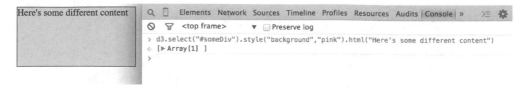

Figure 1.16   The D3 `select` syntax modifies style using the `.style()` function, and traditional HTML content using the `.html()` function.

1.3.2   Coding in the console

You'll do a lot of your coding in the IDE of your choice, but one of the great things about web development is that you can test JavaScript code changes by using your console. Later you'll focus on writing JavaScript, but for now, to demonstrate how the console works, copy the following code into your console and press Enter:

```
d3.select("div").style("background","lightblue").style("border", "solid black
    1px").html("Something else maybe");
```

You should see the effect shown in figure 1.16.

You'll see a few more uses of traditional HTML elements in this chapter, and then again in chapter 3, but then you won't see traditional DOM elements again until chapter 8, where we'll use D3 to create complex, data-driven spreadsheets and galleries using <div>, <table>, and <select> elements. If all D3 could do was select HTML elements and change their style and content like this, then it wouldn't be that useful for data visualization. To do more, we have to move away from traditional HTML and focus on a special type of element in the DOM: SVG.

1.3.3   SVG

A major value of HTML5 is the integrated support for SVG. SVG allows for simple mathematical representation of images that scale and are amenable to animation and interaction. Part of the attractiveness of D3 is that it provides an abstraction layer for drawing SVG. This is because SVG drawing can be a little confusing. SVG drawing instructions for complex shapes, known as <path> elements, are written a bit like the old LOGO programming language. You start at a point on a canvas and draw a line from that point to another. If you want it to curve, you can give the SVG drawing code coordinates on which to make that curve. So if you want to draw the line on the left, you'd create a <path> element in an <svg> canvas element in your web page, and you'd set the d attribute of that <path> element equal to the text on the right:

```
M50,485.714857L58.3332,473.809238C66.66666,4
61.90487,83.33331,438.09381,99.9999,433.3333
3C116.66,428.57142857142856,133.34,442.85714
285714283,150,445.22C166.669,447.61904761904
76,183.3331,438.0952380952381,199.9997,421.4
285714285714C216.663,404.7619047619047,233.3
31,380.9523809523809,250,383.33C266.667,385.
71428571428567,283.337,414.2857142857143,300
,430.95238095238096C316.6674,447.61904761904
76,333.337,452.3809523809524,350,450C366.667
,447.6190476190476,383.33,438.0952380952381,
400,442.85714285714283C416.663,447.619047619
0476,433.33,466.6663,449.994,469.049C466.666
63,471.42857142857144,483.3333333,457.142857
1,491.663,450L500,442.8571429
```

But you'd almost never want to create SVG by manually writing drawing instructions like this. Instead, you'll want to use D3 to do the drawing with a variety of helper functions, or rely on other SVG elements that represent simple shapes (known as geometric or graphical primitives) using more readable attributes. You'll start doing that in chapter 4, where you'll use d3.svg.line and d3.svg.area to create line and area charts. For now, you'll update d3ia.html to look like the following listing, which includes the necessary code for displaying SVG, as well as examples of the various shapes you might use.

Listing 1.2 A sample web page with SVG elements

```
<!doctype html>
<html>
    <script src="d3.v3.min.js" type="text/JavaScript">
</script>
<body>
  <div id="infovizDiv">
  <svg style="width:500px;height:500px;border:1px lightgray solid;">
    <path d="M 10,60 40,30 50,50 60,30 70,80"
       style="fill:black;stroke:gray;stroke-width:4px;" />
    <polygon style="fill:gray;"
       points="80,400 120,400 160,440 120,480 60,460" />
  <g>
  <line x1="200" y1-"100" x2="450" y2="225"
  style="stroke:black;stroke-width:2px;"/>
  <circle cy="100" cx="200" r="30"/>
  <rect x="410" y="200" width="100" height="50"
       style="fill:pink;stroke:black;stroke-width:1px;" />
  </g>
  </svg>
  </div>
</body>
</html>
```

You can inspect the elements like you would the traditional elements we looked at earlier, as you can see in figure 1.17, and you can manipulate these elements using

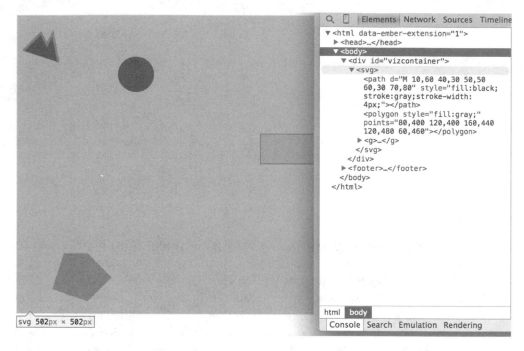

Figure 1.17   Inspecting the DOM of a web page with an SVG canvas reveals the nested graphical elements as well as the style and attributes that determine their position. Notice that the circle and rectangle exist as child elements of a group.

traditional JavaScript selectors like `document.getElementById` or with D3, removing them or changing the style like so:

```
d3.select("circle").remove()              ⟵┐ Deletes the circle
d3.select("rect").style("fill", "purple")     ⟵┐ Changes the rectangle
                                                 color to purple
```

Now refresh your page and let's take a look at the new elements. You're familiar with divs, and it's useful to put an SVG canvas in a div so you can access the parent container for layout and styling. Let's take a look at each of the elements we've added.

<SVG>

This is your canvas on which everything is drawn. The top-left corner is 0,0, and the canvas clips anything drawn beyond its defined height and width of 500,500 (the rectangle in our example). An <svg> element can be styled with CSS to have different borders and backgrounds. The <svg> element can also be dynamically resized using the viewBox attribute, which is more complex and beyond the scope of the overview here.

You can use CSS (which we'll touch on later in this chapter) to style your SVG canvas or use D3 to add inline styles like so:

```
d3.select("svg").style("background", "darkgray");
```
◁— **Infoviz is always cooler on a dark background.**

NOTE The x-axis is drawn left-to-right, but the y-axis is drawn top-to-bottom, so you'll see that the circle is set 200 pixels to the right and 100 pixels down.

\<canvas\>

There's a second mode of drawing available with HTML5 using \<canvas\> elements to draw bitmaps. We won't go into detail here, but you'll see this method used in chapter 8 and again in chapter 11. The \<canvas\> element creates static graphics drawn in a manner similar to SVG that can then be saved as images. There are four main reasons to use canvas:

- *Compatibility*—We won't worry about this because if you're using D3, then you're coding for a modern browser.
- *Creating static images*—You can draw your data visualization with canvas to save views as snapshots for thumbnail and gallery views (this is what we'll do in chapter 8).
- *Large amounts of data*—SVG creates individual elements in the DOM, and although this is great for attaching events and styling, it can overwhelm a browser and cause significant slowdown (this is what we'll use canvas for in chapter 11).
- *WebGL*—The \<canvas\> element allows you to use WebGL to draw, so that you can create 3D objects. You can also create 3D objects like globes and polyhedrons using SVG, which we'll get into a bit in chapter 7 as we examine geospatial information visualization.

\<CIRCLE\>, \<RECT\>, \<LINE\>, \<POLYGON\>

SVG óprovides a set of common shapes, each of which has *attributes* that determine their size and position to make them easier to deal with than the generic d attribute you saw earlier. These attributes vary depending on the element that you're dealing with, so that \<rect\> has x and y attributes that determine the shape's top-left corner, as well as height and width attributes that determine its overall form. In comparison, the \<circle\> element has cx and cy attributes that determine the center of the circle, and an r attribute that determines the radius of the circle. The \<line\> element has x1 and y1 attributes that determine the starting point of the line and x2 and y2 attributes that determine its end point. There are other simple shapes that are similar to these, such as the \<ellipse\>, and there are more complex shapes, like the \<polygon\> with a points attribute that holds a set of comma-separated xy coordinates, in clockwise order, that determines the area bounded by the polygon.

Each of these attributes can be hand-edited in HTML to adjust its size, form, and position. Open up your element inspector, and click the \<rect\>. Change its width to 25 and its height to 25, as shown in figure 1.18.

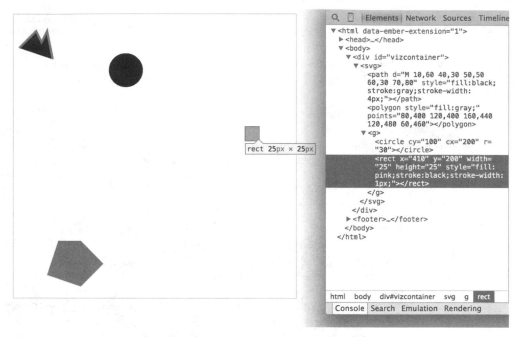

Figure 1.18   Modifying the height and width attributes of a `<rect>` element changes the appearance of that element. Inspecting the element also shows how the stroke adds to the computed size of the element.[1]

Infoviz term: geometric primitive

Accomplished artists can draw anything with vector graphics, but you're probably not looking at D3 because you're an artist. Instead, you're dealing with graphics and have more pragmatic goals in mind. From that perspective, it's important to understand the concept of geometric primitives (also known as graphical primitives). Geometric primitives are simple shapes such as points, lines, circles, and rectangles. These shapes, which can be combined to make more complex graphics, are particularly useful for visually displaying information.

Primitives are also useful for understanding complex information visualizations that you see out in the real world. Dendrograms like the one shown in figure 1.20 are far less intimidating when you realize they're just circles and lines. Interactive timelines are easier to understand and create when you think of them as collections of rectangles and points. Even geographic data, which primarily comes in the form of polygons, points, and lines, is less confusing when you break it down into its most basic graphical structures.

---

[1]   Figures that have a picture icon at the end of the caption, like figure 1.18, have an online example that you can work with interactively or download to run locally. Click on the icon in the eBook version of the book, or go to manning.com/meeks to find all interactive examples online.

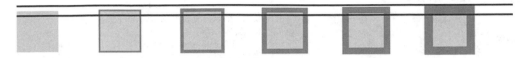

Figure 1.19 **The same 25 x 25 `<rect>` with no, 1-px, 2-px, 3-px, 4-px, and 5-px strokes. Though these are drawn on a retina screen using half-pixels, the second and third report the same width and height (27 px x 27 px) as the fourth and fifth (29 px x 29 px).**

Now you've learned why there's no SVG `<square>`. The color, stroke, and transparency of any shape can be changed by adjusting the style of the shape, with `"fill"` determining the color of the area of the shape and `"stroke"`, `"stroke-width"`, `"stroke-dasharray"` determining its outline.

Notice, though, that the inspected element has a measurement of 27 px x 27 px. That's because the 1-px stroke is drawn on the outside of the shape. That makes sense, once you know the rule, but if you change the `"stroke-width"` to `"2px"` it will still be 27 px x 27 px. That's because the stroke is drawn evenly over the inside and outside borders as seen in figure 1.19. This may not seem too big a deal, but it's something to remember when you're trying to line up your shapes later on.

Change the style parameters of the rectangle to the following:

```
"fill:purple;stroke-width:5px;stroke:cornflowerblue;"
```

Congratulations! You've now successfully visualized the complex and ambiguous phenomenon known as "ugly."

`<TEXT>`

SVG provides the capacity to write text as well as shapes. SVG text, though, doesn't have the formatting support found in HTML elements, and so it's primarily used for labels. If you do want to do basic formatting, you can nest `<tspan>` elements in `<text>` elements.

`<G>`

The `<g>` or group element is distinct from the SVG elements we've discussed in that it has no graphical representation and doesn't exist as a bounded space. Instead, it's a logical grouping of elements. You'll want to use `<g>` elements extensively when creating graphical objects that are made up of several shapes and text. For instance, if you wanted to have a circle with a label above it and move the label and the circle at the same time, then you'd place them inside a `<g>` element:

```
<g>
<circle r="2"/>
<text>This circle's Label</text>
</g>
```

Moving a `<g>` around your canvas requires you to adjust the `transform` attribute of the `<g>` element. The `transform` attribute is more intimidating than the various xy attributes of shapes, because it accepts a structured description in text of how you want to transform a shape. One of those structures is `translate()`, which accepts a pair of coordinates that

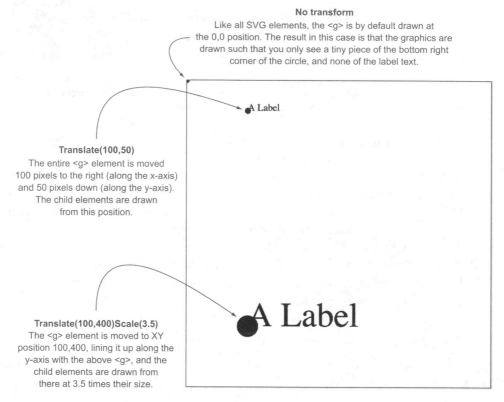

No transform
Like all SVG elements, the <g> is by default drawn at the 0,0 position. The result in this case is that the graphics are drawn such that you only see a tiny piece of the bottom right corner of the circle, and none of the label text.

Translate(100,50)
The entire <g> element is moved 100 pixels to the right (along the x-axis) and 50 pixels down (along the y-axis). The child elements are drawn from this position.

Translate(100,400)Scale(3.5)
The <g> element is moved to XY position 100,400, lining it up along the y-axis with the above <g>, and the child elements are drawn from there at 3.5 times their size.

A Label

Figure 1.20   All SVG elements can be affected by the `transform` **attribute, but this is particularly salient when working with** <g> **elements, which require this approach to adjust their position. The child elements are drawn by using the position of their parent** <g> **as their relative 0,0 position. The** `scale()` **setting in the** `transform` **attribute then affects the scale of any of the size and position attributes of the child elements.**

move the element to the xy position defined by the values in `translate(x,y)`. So if you want to move a <g> element 100 pixels to the right and 50 pixels down, then you need to set its `transform` attribute to `transform="translate(100,50)"`. The transform attribute also accepts a `scale()` setting so you can change the rendered scale of the shape. You can see these settings in action by modifying the previous example with the results shown in figure 1.20.

Listing 1.3   Grouping SVG elements

```
<g>
    <circle r="2"/>
    <text>This circle's Label</text>
</g>
<g transform="translate(100,50)">
    <circle r="2" />
    <text>This circle's Label</text>
</g>
```

```
<g transform="translate(100,400) scale(2.5)">
   <circle r="2"/>
   <text>This circle's Label</text>
</g>
```

<PATH>

A path is an area determined by its d attribute. Paths can be open or closed, meaning the last point connects to the first if closed and doesn't if open. The open or closed nature of a path is determined by the absence or presence of the letter *Z* at the end of the text string in the d attribute. It can still be filled either way. You can see the difference in figure 1.21.

Listing 1.4 SVG path fill and closing

```
<path style="fill:none;stroke:gray;stroke-width:4px;"
    d="M 10,60 40,30 50,50 60,30 70,80" transform="translate(0,0)" />
<path style="fill:black;stroke:gray;stroke-width:4px;"
    d="M 10,60 40,30 50,50 60,30 70,80" transform="translate(0,100)" />
<path style="fill:none;stroke:gray;stroke-width:4px;"
    d="M 10,60 40,30 50,50 60,30 70,80Z" transform="translate(0,200)" />
<path style="fill:black;stroke:gray;stroke-width:4px;"
    d="M 10,60 40,30 50,50 60,30 70,80Z" transform="translate(0,300)" />
```

Open – unfilled
Path elements are by default filled with no stroke. You need to set the fill style to "none" and stroke and stroke-width style if you want to draw it as a line.

```
<path style="fill:none;stroke:gray;stroke-width:4px;"
d="M 10,60 40,30 50,50 60,30 70,80"
transform="translate(0,0)" />
```

Open – filled
An open path can be filled just like a closed path, with the fill area defined by the same area that would be bounded if the path were closed.

```
<path style="fill:black;stroke:gray;stroke-width:4px;"
d="M 10,60 40,30 50,50 60,30 70,80"
transform="translate(0,100)" />
```

Closed – unfilled
A path will always close by drawing a line from the end point to the start point.

```
<path style="fill:none;stroke:gray;stroke-width:4px;"
d="M 10,60 40,30 50,50 60,30 70,80Z"
transform="translate(0,200)" />
```

Closed – filled
Notice the stroke overlaps the fill area slightly.

```
<path style="fill:black;stroke:gray;stroke-width:4px;"
d="M 10,60 40,30 50,50 60,30 70,80Z"
transform="translate(0,300)" />
```

Figure 1.21 Each path shown here uses the same coordinates in its d attribute, with the only differences between them being the presence or absence of the letter Z at the end of the text string defining the d attribute, the settings for fill and stroke, and the position via the transform attribute.

Although sometimes you may want to write that d attribute yourself, it's more likely that your experience crafting SVG will come in one of three ways: using geometric primitives like circles, rectangles, or polygons; drawing SVG using a vector graphics editor like Adobe Illustrator or Inkscape; or drawing SVG parametrically using hand-written constructors or built-in constructors in D3. Most of this book focuses on using D3 to create SVG, but don't overlook the possibility of creating SVG using an external application or another library and then manipulating them using D3 like we'll do using d3.html in chapter 3.

1.3.4   CSS

CSS are used to style the elements in the DOM. A style sheet can exist as a separate .css file that you include in your HTML page or can be embedded directly in the HTML page. Style sheets refer to an ID, class, or type of element and determine the appearance of that element. The terminology used to define the style is a *CSS selector* and is the same type of selector used in the d3.select() syntax. You can set inline styles (that are applied to only a single element) by using d3.select("#someElement") .style("opacity", .5) to set the opacity of an element to 50%. Let's update your d3ia.html to include a style sheet.

> **Listing 1.5   A sample web page with a style sheet**

```
<!doctype html>
<html>
<script src="d3.v3.min.js" type="text/JavaScript"></script>
<style>
.inactive, .tentative {
  stroke: darkgray;
  stroke-width: 2px;
  stroke-dasharray: 5 5;
}

.tentative {
  opacity: .5;
}

.active {
  stroke: black;
  stroke-width: 4px;
  stroke-dasharray: 1;
}

circle {
  fill: red;
}

rect {
  fill: darkgray;
```

```
}
</style>
<body>
  <div id="infovizDiv">
  <svg style="width:500px;height:500px;border:1px lightgray solid;">
    <path d="M 10,60 40,30 50,50 60,30 70,80" />
    <polygon class="inactive" points="80,400 120,400 160,440 120,480 60,460" />
  <g>
  <circle class="active tentative" cy="100" cx="200" r="30"/>
  <rect class="active" x="410" y="200" width="100" height="50" />
  </g>
  </svg>
  </div>
</body>
</html>
```

The results stack on each other, so when you examine the rectangle element, as shown in figure 1.22, you see that its style is set by the reference to `rect` in the style sheet as well as the class attribute of `active`.

Style sheets can also refer to a state of the element, so with `:hover` you can change the way an element looks when the user mouses over that element. You can learn

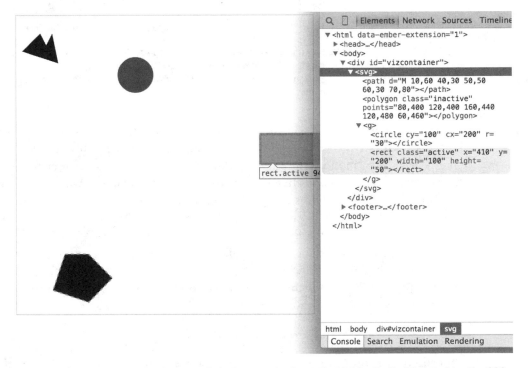

Figure 1.22 Examining an SVG rectangle in the console shows that it inherits its fill style from the CSS style applied to `<rect>` types and its stroke style from the `.active` class.

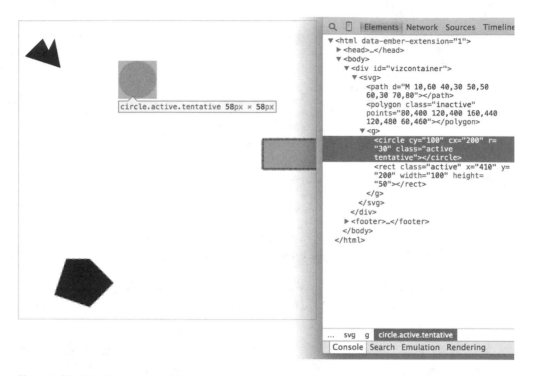

Figure 1.23   The SVG circle has its fill value set by its type in the style sheet, with its opacity set by its membership in the `.tentative` **class and its stroke set by its membership in the** `.active` **class. Notice that the stroke settings from the** `.tentative` **class are overwritten by the stroke settings in the later declared** `.active` **class.**

about other complex CSS selectors in more detail in a book devoted to that subject. For this book, we'll focus mostly on using CSS classes and IDs for selection and to change style. The most useful way to do this is to have CSS classes associated with particular stylistic changes and then change the class of an element. You can change the class of an element, which is an attribute of an element, by selecting and modifying the class attribute. The circle shown in figure 1.23 is affected by two overlapping classes: `.active` and `.tentative`.

In listing 1.5 we see a couple of possibly overlapping classes, with tentative, active, and inactive all applying different style changes to your shape (such as the highlighted circle in figure 1.23). When an element needs only be assigned to one of these classes, you can overwrite the class attribute entirely:

```
d3.select("circle").attr("class", "tentative");
```

The results, as shown in figure 1.24, are what we would expect. This overwrites the entire class attribute to the value you set. But elements can have multiple classes, and sometimes an element is both active and tentative or inactive and tentative, so let's

Figure 1.24 An SVG circle with fill style determined by its type and its opacity and stroke settings determined by its membership in the `tentative` class.

reload the page and take advantage of the helper function `d3.classed()`, which allows you to add or remove a class from the classes in an element:

```
d3.select("circle").classed("active", true);
```

By using `.classed()`, you don't overwrite the existing attribute, but rather append or remove the named class from the list. You can see the results of two classes with conflicting styles defined. The active style overwrites the tentative style because it occurs later in the style sheet. Another rule to remember is that more specific rules overwrite more general rules. There's more to CSS, but this book won't go into that.

By defining style in your style sheet and changing appearance based on class membership, you create code that's more maintainable and readable. You'll need to use inline styles to set the graphical appearance of a set of elements to a variety of different values, for example, changing the fill color to correspond to a color ramp based on the data bound to that set of elements. You'll see that functionality in action later when you deal with bound data. But as a general rule, setting inline styles should only be used when you can't use traditional classes and states defined in a style sheet.

1.3.5 JavaScript

D3, like many information visualization libraries in JavaScript, provides functions to abstract the process of creating and modifying web page elements. On top of that, it provides mechanisms to link data and web page elements in a way that makes the drawing and updating of these SVG elements reusable and maintainable. But these mechanisms are also applicable to more traditional HTML elements like paragraphs and divs.

As a result, a web application written in D3 can accomplish much of the UI functionality that users expect without relying on libraries like jQuery. This is because the latest version of JavaScript has built-in functionality that used to be available only with jQuery. If you read the solutions on Stack Overflow, you may think that being a JavaScript developer requires being a jQuery developer, but unless you're developing for an audience that uses a browser that won't support the key features of D3, or you need to use a plugin that requires jQuery, then you might just as easily write the same functionality in JavaScript.

When writing JavaScript with D3, you should familiarize yourself with two subjects: method chaining and arrays.

METHOD CHAINING

D3 examples, like many examples written in JavaScript, use method chaining extensively. Method chaining, also known as function chaining, is facilitated by returning the method itself with the successful completion of functions associated with a method. One way to think of method chaining is to think of how we talk and refer to each other. Imagine you were talking to someone at a party, and you asked about another guest:

"What's her name?"
"Her name is Lindsay."
"Where does she work?"
"She works at Tesla."
"Where does she live?"
"She lives in Cupertino."
"Does she have any children?"
"Yes, she has a daughter."
"What's her name?"

Do you think the answer to that last question would be "Lindsay"? Of course not. You'd expect the answer to refer to Lindsay's daughter, even though all the previous questions referred to Lindsay. Method chaining is like that. It returns the same function as long as you use getter and setter methods of that function, and returns the new function when you call a method that creates something new. Method chaining is used a lot in D3 examples, which means you'll see something like this written on one line or formatted (but functionally identical) to something written on multiple lines:

```
d3.selectAll("div").data(someData).enter().append("div").html("Wow").append("
    span").html("Even More Wow").style("font-weight", "900");
```

That line is the same as the following code. The only change is in the use of line breaks, which JavaScript ignores:

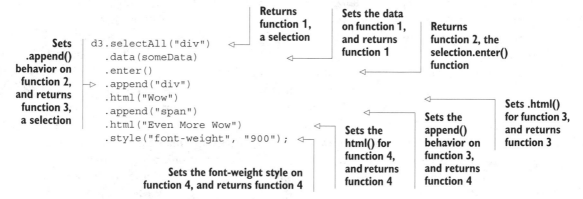

You could write each line separately, declaring the different variables as you go, and achieve the same effect. That might make more sense if you haven't been exposed to method chaining before.

```
var function1 = d3.selectAll("div");
var function1withData = function1.data(someData);
var function2 = function1withData.enter();
var function3 = function2.append("div");
function3.html("Wow");
var function4 = function3.append("span");
function4.html("Even More Wow");
function4.style("font-weight", "900");
```

You can see this when you run the code in your console. This is the first time you've used the .data() function, which along with .select() is at the core of developing with D3. When you use .data(), you bind each element in your selection to each item in an array. If you have more items in your array than elements in your selection, then you can use the .enter() function to define what to do with each extra element. In the previous function, you select all the <div> elements in the <body> and the .enter() function tells D3 to .append() a new div when there are more elements in the array than elements in the selection. Given that your d3ia.html page already has one div, if you bind an array with more than one value, D3 appends, or adds, a div for each value in the array beyond the first.

A corresponding .exit() function defines how to respond when an array has fewer values than a selection. For now, you'll run the code as it appears in the examples, and in later chapters we'll get into much more detail on the way selections and binding work.

With this example, you're not doing anything with the data in the array and only creating elements based on the size of the array (one <div> for each element in the array). This example assumes that you already have a <div> in your html with a black border (as seen in figure 1.25). Here's the HTML that would get that done:

```
<!doctype html>
<html>
<script src="d3.v3.min.js" type="text/JavaScript"></script>
<style>
#borderdiv {
width: 200px;
height: 50px;
border: 1px solid gray;
}
</style>
<body>
  <div id="borderdiv"></div>
  </body>
</html>
```

For this to work, you need to give someData a value. With that in place, you can run your code:

```
var someData = ["filler", "filler", "filler", "filler"];
d3.select("body").selectAll("div")
  .data(someData)
  .enter()
  .append("div")
  .html("Wow")
```

```
.append("span")
.html("Even More Wow")
.style("font-weight", "900");
```

The result, as shown in figure 1.25, is the addition of three lines of text. It might surprise you that this code is three lines, given that the array has four values. Although the data was bound to the existing <div> element on the page, the actions that changed the contents were only applied to the .enter() function. They were only applied to the newly created <div> elements that were "entering" the DOM for the first time.

When you inspect the DOM, as shown in figure 1.26, you see that the method chaining operated in the manner just described. A <div> was added, and its HTML

Figure 1.25   By binding an array of four values to a selection of <div> elements on the page, the .enter() function created three new <div> elements to reflect the size mismatch between the data array and the selection.

Figure 1.26   Inspecting the DOM shows that the new <div> elements have been created with unformatted content followed by the child <span> element with style and content set by your code.

content was set to "Wow". A <span> element with a different style was appended to the <div>, and its HTML content was set to "Even More Wow". There's more you can do, but first you need to examine the array object you're binding, and focus on JavaScript arrays and array functions.

ARRAYS AND ARRAY FUNCTIONS

D3 is all about arrays, and so it's important to understand the structure of arrays and the options available to you to prepare those arrays for binding to data. Your array might be an array of string or number literals, such as this:

```
someNumbers = [17, 82, 9, 500, 40];
someColors = ["blue", "red", "chartreuse", "orange"];
```

Or it may be an array of JSON objects, which will become more common as you do more interesting things with D3:

```
somePeople = [{name: "Peter", age: 27}, {name: "Sulayman", age: 24},
{name: "K.C.", age: 49}];
```

One example of a useful array function is .filter(), which returns an array whose elements satisfy a test you provide. For instance, here's how to create an array out of someNumbers that had values greater than 40:

```
someNumbers.filter(function(el) {return el >= 40});
```

Likewise, here's how you could create an array out of someColors with names shorter than five letters:

```
someColors.filter(function(el) {return el.length < 5});
```

The function .filter() is a method of an array and accepts a function that iterates through the array with the variable you've named. In this function, you name that variable el, and the function runs a test on each value by testing on el. When that test evaluates true, the element is kept in our new array.

The result of this .filter() function, which you can see in figure 1.27, returns either the element or nothing (depending on if it satisfies the test), building a new array consisting only of the elements that do.

```
smallerNumbers = someNumbers.filter(
  function(el) {return el <= 40 ? this : null});
d3.select("body").selectAll("div")
  .data(smallerNumbers)
  .enter()
  .append("div")
  .html(function (d) {return d});
```

The resulting code creates two new divs from your three-value array smallerNumbers. (Remember that one div already exists, and so the .enter() function doesn't trigger even though data is bound to that existing div.) The contents of the div are the values in your array. This is done through an anonymous function (sometimes referred to in D3 examples as an *accessor*) in your .html() function and is another key aspect of D3. Any

```
17
9
40
```

```
   Q  🔲    Elements  Network  Sources  Timeline  Profiles  Resources  Audits | Console |
   🚫   🔻   <top frame>  ▼  ☐ Preserve log
 > d3.selectAll("div").remove()
 < [▶ Array[2] ]
 > someNumbers = [17, 82, 9, 500, 40];
 < [17, 82, 9, 500, 40]
 > smallerNumbers = someNumbers.filter(
   function(el) {return el <= 40 ? this : null});

   d3.select("body").selectAll("div")
   .data(smallerNumbers)
   .enter()
   .append("div")
   .html(function (d) {return d});
 < [▶ Array[3] ]
```

Figure 1.27   Running JavaScript in the console allows you to test your code. Here you've created a new array called `smallerNumbers` that consists of only three values, which you can then use as your data in a selection to update and create new elements. 🔳

anonymous function called when setting the `.style()`, `.attr()`, `.property()`, `.html()`, or other function of a selection can provide you with the data bound to that selection. As you explore examples, you'll see this function deployed again and again:

```
.style("background", function(d,i) {return d})
.attr("cx", function(d,i) {return i})
.html(function(d,i) {return d})
```

In every case, the first variable (typically represented with the letter *d*, but you can declare it as whatever you want) contains the data value bound to that element, and the second variable returns the array position (known as an index, hence the variable name *i*) of the value bound to that element. This may seem a bit strange, but you'll get used to it as you see it used in a variety of ways in the upcoming chapters.

JavaScript has many other array functions, and you can do much more than we covered here, but that's the subject of several other books. It's time to look at the kinds of data you'll work with.

1.4   *Data standards*

Standardization of methods of displaying data has been fed by and feeds into standardization of methods of formatting that data. Data can be formatted in a variety of manners for a variety of purposes, but it tends to fall into a few recognizable classes: tabular data, nested data, network data, geographic data, raw data, and objects.

1.4.1   *Tabular data*

Tabular data appears in columns and rows typically found in a spreadsheet or a table in a database. Although you invariably end up creating arrays of objects in D3, it's often more efficient and easier to pull in data in tabular format. Tabular data is delimited with a particular character, and that delimiter determines its format. You can have Comma-Separated Values (CSV), where the delimiter is a comma, or tab-delimited values, or a semicolon or a pipe symbol acting as the delimiter. For instance, you may have a spreadsheet of user information that includes age and salary. If you export it in a delimited form, it will look like table 1.1.

Table 1.1 Delimited data can be expressed in different forms. Here a dataset stores name, age, and salary of two people using commas, spaces, or the bar symbol to delimit the different fields.

name,age,salary	name age salary	name|age|salary
Sal,34,50000	Sal 34 50000	Sal|34|50000
Nan,22,75000	Nan 22 75000	Nan|22|75000

D3 provides three different functions to pull in tabular data: d3.csv(), d3.tsv(), and d3.dsv(). The only difference between them is that d3.csv() is built for comma-delimited files, d3.tsv() is built for tab-delimited files, and d3.dsv() allows you to declare the delimiter. You'll see them in action throughout the book.

1.4.2   Nested data

Data that is nested, with objects existing as children of objects recursively, is very common. Many of the most intuitive layouts in D3 are based on nested data, which can be represented as trees, such as the one in figure 1.28, or packed in circles or boxes. Data isn't often output in such a format, and requires a bit of scripting to organize it as

Figure 1.28   Nested data represents parent/child relationships of objects, typically with each object having an array of child objects, and is represented in a number of forms, such as this dendrogram. Notice that each object can have only one parent.

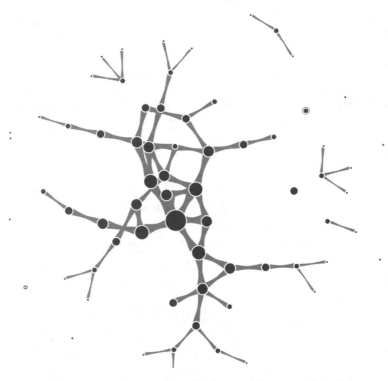

Figure 1.29   Network data consists of objects and the connections between them. The objects are typically referred to as nodes or vertices, while the connections are referred to as edges or links. Networks are often represented using force-directed algorithms, such as the example here, that arrange the network in such a way as to pull connected nodes toward each other.

such, but the flexibility of this representation is worth the effort. You'll see hierarchical data in detail in chapter 5 when we look at various popular D3 layouts.

1.4.3   Network data

Networks are everywhere. Whether they're the raw output of social networking streams, transportation networks, or a flowchart, networks are a powerful method of delivering an understanding of complex systems. Networks are often represented as node-link diagrams, as shown in figure 1.29. Like geographic data, network data has many standards, but this text focuses only on two forms: node/edge lists and connected arrays. Network data can also be easily transformed into these data types by using a freely available network analysis tool like Gephi (available at gephi.org). We'll examine network data and network data standards when we deal with network visualization in chapter 6.

1.4.4   Geographic data

Geographic data refers to locations either as points or shapes, and is used to create the variety of online maps seen on the web today, such as the map of the United States in figure 1.30. The incredible popularity of web mapping means that you can get access

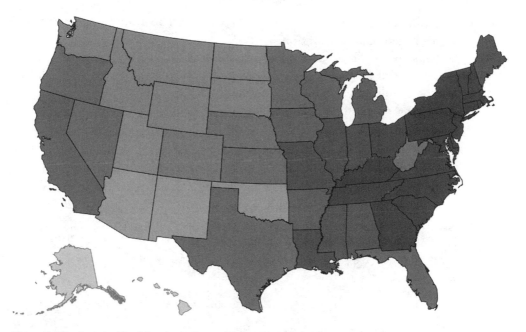

Figure 1.30 Geographic data stores the spatial geometry of objects, such as states. Each of the states in this image is represented as a separate feature with an array of values indicating its shape. Geographic data can also consist of points, such as for cities, or lines, such as for roads.

to a massive amount of publicly accessible geodata for any project. Geographic data has a few standards, but the focus in this book is on two: the GeoJSON and TopoJSON standards. Although geodata may come in many forms, readily available geographic information systems (GIS) tools like Quantum GIS allow developers to transform it into GIS format for ready delivery to the web. We'll look at geographic data closely in chapter 7.

1.4.5 Raw data

As you'll see in chapter 2, everything is data, including images or blocks of text. Although information visualization typically uses shapes encoded by color and size to represent data, sometimes the best way to represent it in D3 is with linear narrative text, an image, or a video. If you develop applications for an audience that needs to understand complex systems, but you consider the manipulation of text or images to be somehow separate from the representation of numerical or categorical data as shapes, then you arbitrarily reduce your capability to communicate. The layouts and formatting used when dealing with text and images, typically tied to older modes of web publication, are possible in D3, and we'll deal with that throughout this book, but especially in chapter 8.

1.4.6 Objects

You'll use two types of data points with D3: literals and objects. A literal, such as a string literal like `"Apple"` or `"beer"` or a number literal like `64273` or `5.44`, is straightforward. A JavaScript object, expressed using JavaScript Object Notation (JSON), isn't so straightforward, but is something that you need to understand if you plan to do sophisticated data visualization.

Let's say you have a dataset that consists of individuals from an insurance database, and you need to know how old someone is, whether they're employed, their name, and their children, if any. A JSON object that represents each individual in such a database would be expressed as follows:

```
{name: "Charlie", age: 55, employed: true, childrenNames: ["Ruth", "Charlie
Jr."]}
```

Each object is surround by braces,{}, and has attributes that have a string, number, array, boolean, or object as their value. You can assign an object to a variable and access its attributes by referring to them, like so:

```
var person = {name: "Charlie", age: 55, employed: true, childrenNames:
["Ruth", "Charlie Jr."]};

person.name // Charlie
person["name"] // Charlie
person.name = "Charles" // Sets name to Charles
person["name"] = "Charles" // Sets name to Charles
person.age < 65 // true
person.childrenNames // ["Ruth", "Charlie Jr."]
person.childrenNames[0] // "Ruth"
```

Objects can be stored in arrays and associated with elements using d3.select() syntax. But objects can also be iterated through like arrays using a for loop:

```
for (x in person) {console.log(x); console.log(person[x]);}
```

The x in the loop represents each attribute in the person object. Each x will be one of the attributes such as name, age, and so on This allows you to iterate through the attributes using person[x] to show the value of that attribute of the object.

If your data is stored as JSON, then you can import it using d3.json(), which you'll see many times in later chapters. But remember that whenever you use d3.csv(), D3 imports the data as an array of JSON objects. We'll look at objects more extensively as we use them later.

1.5   *Infoviz standards expressed in D3*

Information visualization has never been so popular as it is today. The wealth of maps, charts, and complex representations of systems and datasets isn't just present in the workplace, but also in our entertainment and everyday lives. With this popularity comes a growing library of classes and subclasses of representation of data and information using visual means, as well as aesthetic rules to promote legibility and comprehension. Your audience, whether the general public, academics, or decision makers, has grown accustomed to what we once considered incredibly abstract and complicated representations of trends in data. This is why libraries like D3 are popular not only among data scientists, but also among journalists, artists, scholars, IT professionals, and even fan communities.

But the wealth of options can seem overwhelming, and the relative ease of modifying a dataset to appear in a streamgraph, treemap, or histogram tends to promote the idea that information visualization is more about style than substance. Fortunately, well-established rules dictate what charts and methods to use for different types of data from different systems. Although we can't cover every rule in the book, we'll touch on ones that are useful to consider as we create more complicated information visualizations. Although some developers use D3 to revolutionize the use of color and layout, most simply want to create visual representations of data that support practical concerns. Because D3 is being developed in this mature information visualization environment, it contains numerous helper functions to let developers worry about interface and design rather than color and axes.

Still, to properly deploy information visualization, you should know what to do and what not to do. The best way to learn this is to review the work of established designers and information visualization practitioners, and you need to have a firm understanding not only of your data but of your audience. Although an entire library of works deals with these issues, here are a few that I've found useful and can get you oriented on the basics:

- *The Visual Display of Quantitative Information Envisioning Information*, Edward Tufte
- *Designing for Information*, Isabel Meirelles
- *Pattern Recognition*, Christian Swinehart

These are by no means the only or most applicable texts for learning data visualization, but I've found them useful for getting started. You should pare down and establish fundamental, even basic, data visualization practices that clearly represent the trends that are salient to your audience. When in doubt, simplify—it's often better to present a histogram than a streamgraph, or a hierarchical network layout (like a dendrogram) than a force-directed one. The more visually complex methods of displaying data tend to inspire more excitement, but can also lead an audience to see what they want to see or focus on the aesthetics of the graphics rather than the data.

> ### Infoviz tip: kill your darlings
> One of the best pieces of advice when it comes to working in information visualization comes from the practice of writing: "Kill your darlings." Just as writers may become enamored of certain scenes or characters, you can become enamored of a particularly elegant or sophisticated-looking graphic. Your love of a cool chart or animation can distract you from the goal of communicating the structure and patterns in the data. Remember to save your harshest criticism for your most beloved pieces, because you may find, much to your chagrin, that they're not as useful and informative as you think they are.

One thing to keep in mind while reading about data visualization is that the literature is often focused on static charts. With D3 you'll be making interactive and dynamic visualizations and not just static ones. You'll make a dynamic (or animated) data visualization before you finish this chapter, and using D3 to make a chart interactive is incredibly simple. A few interactive touches can make a visualization not only more readable but significantly more engaging. Users who feel like they're exploring rather than reading, even if only with a few mouseover events or a simple click to zoom, will find the content of the visualization more compelling than in a static page. But this added complexity requires an investment in learning principles of interface design and user experience. We'll get into this in more detail in chapters 9 and 12.

1.6   *Your first D3 app*

Throughout this chapter, you've seen various lines of code and the effect of those lines of code on the growing d3ia.html sample page you've been building. But I've avoided explaining the code in too much detail so that you could concentrate on the principles at work in D3. It's simple to build an application from scratch that uses D3 to create and modify elements. Let's put it all together and see how it works. First, let's start with a clean HTML page that doesn't have any defined styles or existing divs.

Listing 1.6   A simple webpage

```
<!doctype html>
<html>
<head>
    <script src="d3.v3.min.js" type="text/JavaScript"></script>
</head>
<body>
</body>
</html>
```

1.6.1   *Hello world with divs*

We can use D3 as an abstraction layer for adding traditional content to the page. Although we can write JavaScript inside our .html file or in its own .js file, let's put code in the console and see how it works. Later, we'll focus on the various commands in more detail for layouts and interfaces. We can get started with a piece of code that uses D3 to write to our web page.

Listing 1.7   Using d3.select to set style and HTML content

```
d3.select("body").append("div")
  .style("border", "1px black solid")
  .html("hello world");
```

We can adjust the element on the page and give it interactivity with the inclusion of the .on() function.

Listing 1.8   Using d3.select to set attributes and event listeners

```
d3.select("div")
  .style("background-color", "pink")
```

```
    .style("font-size", "24px")
    .attr("id", "newDiv")
    .attr("class", "d3div")
    .on("click", function() {console.log("You clicked a div")});
```

The .on() function allows us to create an event listener for the currently selected element or set of elements. It accepts the variety of events that can happen to an element, such as click, mouseover, mouseout, and so on. If you click your div, you'll notice that it gives a response in your console, as shown in figure 1.31.

1.6.2 Hello World with circles

You didn't pick up this book to learn how to add divs to a web page, but you likely want to deal with graphics like lines and circles. To append shapes to a page with D3, you need to have an SVG canvas element somewhere in your page's DOM. You could either add this SVG canvas to the page as you write the HTML, or you could append it using the D3 syntax you've learned:

```
d3.select("body").append("svg");
```

Let's adjust our d3ia.html page to start with an SVG canvas.

Listing 1.9 A simple web page with an SVG canvas

```
<!doctype html>
<html>
<head>
    <script src="d3.v3.min.js" type="text/JavaScript"></script>
</head>
<body>
    <div id="vizcontainer">
    <svg style="width:500px;height:500px;border:1px lightgray solid;" />
    </div>
</body>
</html>
```

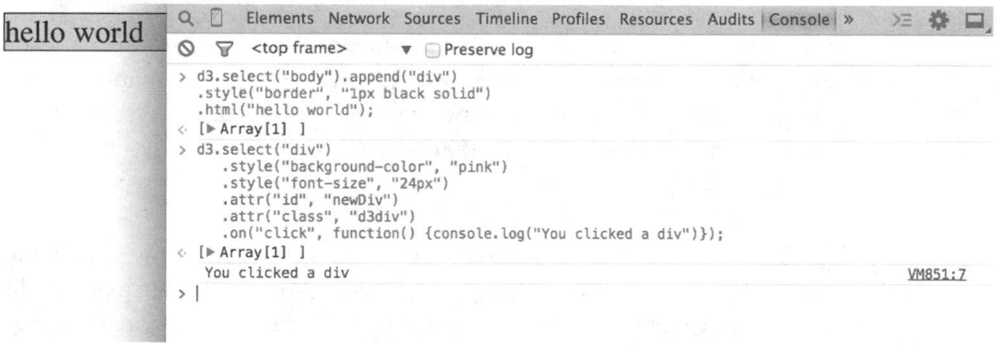

Figure 1.31 Using `console.log()`**, you can test to see if an event is properly firing. Here you create a** `<div>` **and assign an onclick event handler using the** `.on()` **syntax. When you click that element and fire the event, the action is noted in the console.**

After we have an SVG canvas on our page, we can append various shapes to it using the same `select()` and `append()` syntax we've been using in section 1.6.1 for `<div>` elements.

Listing 1.10   Creating lines and circles with select and append

```
d3.select("svg")
  .append("line")
  .attr("x1", 20)
  .attr("y1", 20)
  .attr("x2",400)
  .attr("y2",400)
  .style("stroke", "black")
  .style("stroke-width","2px");

d3.select("svg")
  .append("text")
  .attr("x",20)
  .attr("y",20)
  .text("HELLO");

d3.select("svg")
  .append("circle")
  .attr("r", 20)
  .attr("cx",20)
  .attr("cy",20)
  .style("fill","red");

d3.select("svg")
  .append("circle")
  .attr("r", 100)
  .attr("cx",400)
  .attr("cy",400)
  .style("fill","lightblue");

d3.select("svg")
  .append("text")
  .attr("x",400)
  .attr("y",400)
  .text("WORLD");
```

Notice that your circles are drawn over the line and the text is drawn above or below the circle, depending on the order in which you run your commands, as you can see in figure 1.32. This is because the draw order of SVG is based on its DOM order. Later you'll learn some methods to adjust that order.

1.6.3   *A conversation with D3*

Writing Hello World with languages is such a common example that I thought we should give the world a chance to respond. Let's add the same big circle and little circle from before, but this time, when we add text, we'll include the `.style ("opacity")` setting that makes our text invisible. We'll also give each text element a `.attr("id")` setting so that the text near the small circle has an `id` attribute with the value of `"a"`, and the text near the large circle has an `id` attribute with the value of `"b"`.

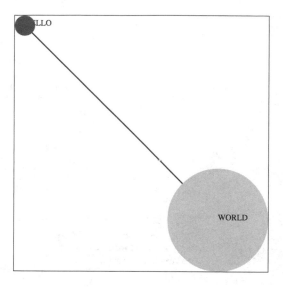

Figure 1.32 The result of running listing 1.10 in the console is the creation of two circles, a line, and two text elements. The order in which these elements are drawn results in the first label covered by the circle drawn later.

Listing 1.11 SVG elements with IDs and transparency

```
d3.select("svg")
  .append("circle")
  .attr("r", 20)
  .attr("cx",20)
  .attr("cy",20)
  .style("fill","red");

d3.select("svg")
  .append("text")
  .attr("id", "a")
  .attr("x",20)
  .attr("y",20)
  .style("opacity", 0)
  .text("HELLO WORLD");

d3.select("svg")
  .append("circle")
  .attr("r", 100)
  .attr("cx",400)
  .attr("cy",400)
  .style("fill","lightblue");

d3.select("svg")
  .append("text")
  .attr("id", "b")
  .attr("x",400)
  .attr("y",400)
  .style("opacity", 0)
  .text("Uh, hi.");
```

Two circles, no line, and no text. Now you make the text appear using the `.transition()` method with the `.delay()` method, and you should have an end state like the one shown in figure 1.33:

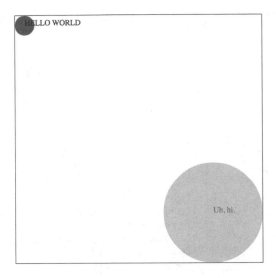

Figure 1.33   Transition behavior when associated with a delay results in a pause before the application of the attribute or style.

```
d3.select("#a").transition().delay(1000).style("opacity", 1);
d3.select("#b").transition().delay(3000).style("opacity", .75);
```

Congratulations! You've made your first dynamic data visualization. The `.transition()` method indicates that you don't want your change to be instantaneous. By chaining it with the `.delay()` method, you indicate how many milliseconds to wait before implementing the style or attribute changes that appear in the chain after that `.delay()` setting.

We'll get a bit more ambitious later on, but before we finish here, let's look at another `.transition()` setting. You can set a `.delay()` before applying the new style or attribute, but you can also set a `.duration()` over which the change is applied. The results in your browser should move the shapes in the direction of the arrows in figure 1.34:

```
d3.selectAll("circle").transition().duration(2000).attr("cy", 200);
```

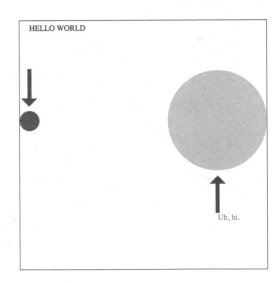

Figure 1.34   Transition behavior when associated with position makes the shape graphically move to its new position over the course of the assigned duration. Because you used the same y position for both circles, the first circle moves down and the second circle moves up to the y position you set, which is between the two circles.

The .duration() method, as you can see, adjusts the setting over the course of the amount of time (again, in milliseconds) that you set it for.

That covers the basics of how D3 works and how it's designed, and these fundamental concepts will surface again and again throughout the following chapters, where you'll learn more complicated variations on representing and manipulating data.

1.7 Summary

In this chapter you've had an overview of D3 with a focus on how well suited it is for developers building web applications for the modern browser. I've highlighted the standardizations and advances that allow this to happen:

- A few examples of the kinds of data visualization you can create with D3
- A process map to show how to go from data to data visualization to interactivity, noting where you can find each step in this book
- An overview of the DOM, SVG, and CSS
- A first look at data-binding and selection to create and change elements on the page
- An overview of the different types of data you'll encounter when planning and creating your data visualizations
- Some simple animations using D3 transitions

D3.js is another JavaScript library, one of thousands, but it's also indicative of a change in our expectations of what a web page can do. Although you may initially use it to build one-off data visualizations, D3 has much more power and functionality than that. Throughout this book, we'll explore the ways that you can use D3 to create rich, data-driven documents that will enthrall and impress.

Information
visualization data flow

This chapter covers

- Loading data from external files of various formats
- Working with D3 scales
- Formatting data for analysis and display
- Creating graphics with visual attributes based on data attributes
- Animating and changing the appearance of graphics

Toy examples and online demos sometimes present data in the format of a JavaScript-defined array, the same way we did in chapter 1. But in the real world, your data is going to come from an API or a database and you're going to need to load it, format it, and transform it before you start creating web elements based on that data. This chapter describes this process of getting data into a suitable form and touches on the basic structures that you'll use again and again in D3: loading data from an external source; formatting that data; and creating graphical representations of that data, like you see in figure 2.1.

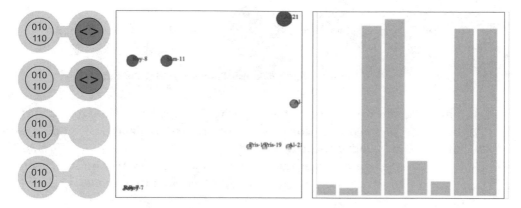

Figure 2.1 Examples from this chapter, including a diagram of how data-binding works (left) from section 2.3.3, a scatterplot with labels (center) from section 2.3, and the bar chart (right) we'll build in section 2.2

2.1 Working with data

We'll deal with two small datasets in this chapter and take them through a simplified five-step process (figure 2.2) that will touch on everything you need to do with and to data to turn it into a data visualization with D3. One dataset consists of a few cities and their geographic location and population. The other is a few fictional tweets with information about who made them and who reacted to them. This is the kind of data you're often presented with. You're tasked with finding out which tweets have more of an impact than others, or which cities are more susceptible to natural disasters than others. In this chapter you'll learn how to measure data in D3 in a number of ways, and how to use those methods to create charts.

Out in the real world, you'll deal with much larger datasets, with hundreds of cities and thousands of tweets, but you'll use the same principles outlined in this chapter. This chapter doesn't teach you how to create complex data visualizations, but it does explain in detail some of the most important core processes in D3 that you'll need to do so.

2.1.1 Loading data

As we touched on in chapter 1, our data will typically be formatted in various but standardized ways. Regardless of the source of the data, it will likely be formatted as single-document data files in XML, CSV, or JSON format. D3 provides several functions for

Figure 2.2 The data visualization process that we'll explore in this chapter assumes we begin with a set of data and want to create (and update) an interactive or dynamic data visualization.

Figure 2.3   The first step in creating a data visualization is getting the data.

importing and working with this data (the first step shown in figure 2.3). One core difference between these formats is how they model data. JSON and XML provide the capacity to encode nested relationships in a way that delimited formats like CSV don't. Another difference is that `d3.csv()` and `d3.json()` produce an array of JSON objects, whereas `d3.xml()` creates an XML document that needs to be accessed in a different manner.

FILE FORMATS

D3 has five functions for loading data that correspond to the five types of files you'll likely encounter: `d3.text()`, `d3.xml()`, `d3.json()`, `d3.csv()`, and `d3.html()`. We'll spend most of our time working with `d3.csv()` and `d3.json()`. You'll see `d3.html()` in the next chapter, where we'll use it to create complex DOM elements that are written as prototypes. You may find `d3.xml()` and `d3.text()` more useful depending on how you typically deal with data. You may be comfortable with XML rather than JSON, in which case you can rely on `d3.xml()` and format your data functions accordingly. If you prefer working with text strings, then you can use `d3.text()` to pull in the data and process it using another library or code.

Both `d3.csv()` and `d3.json()` use the same format when calling the function, by declaring the path to the file being loaded and defining the callback function:

```
d3.csv("cities.csv",function(error,data) {console.log(error,data)});
```

The error variable is optional, and if we only declare a single variable with the callback function, it will be the data:

```
d3.csv("cities.csv",function(d) {console.log(d)});
```

You first get access to the data in the callback function, and you may want to declare the data as a global variable so that you can use it elsewhere. To get started, you need a data file. For this chapter we'll be working with two data files: a CSV file that contains data about cities and a JSON file that contains data about tweets, as shown in the following listings.

Listing 2.1   File contents of cities.csv

```
"label","population","country","x","y"
"San Francisco", 750000,"USA",122,-37
"Fresno", 500000,"USA",119,-36
"Lahore",12500000,"Pakistan",74,31
"Karachi",13000000,"Pakistan",67,24
"Rome",2500000,"Italy",12,41
```

```
"Naples",1000000,"Italy",14,40
"Rio",12300000,"Brazil",-43,-22
"Sao Paolo",12300000,"Brazil",-46,-23
```

Listing 2.2   File contents of tweets.json

```
{
"tweets": [
{"user": "Al", "content": "I really love seafood.",
   "timestamp": " Mon Dec 23 2013 21:30 GMT-0800 (PST)",
   "retweets": ["Raj","Pris","Roy"], "favorites": ["Sam"]},
{"user": "Al", "content": "I take that back, this doesn't taste so good.",
   "timestamp": "Mon Dec 23 2013 21:55 GMT-0800 (PST)",
   "retweets": ["Roy"], "favorites": []},
{"user": "Al",
   "content": "From now on, I'm only eating cheese sandwiches.",
   "timestamp": "Mon Dec 23 2013 22:22 GMT-0800 (PST)",
   "retweets": [],"favorites": ["Roy","Sam"]},
{"user": "Roy", "content": "Great workout!",
   "timestamp": " Mon Dec 23 2013 7:20 GMT-0800 (PST)",
   "retweets": [],"favorites": []},
{"user": "Roy", "content": "Spectacular oatmeal!",
   "timestamp": " Mon Dec 23 2013 7:23 GMT-0800 (PST)",
   "retweets: [],"favorites": []},
{"user": "Roy", "content": "Amazing traffic!",
   "timestamp": " Mon Dec 23 2013 7:47  GMT-0800 (PST)",
   "retweets": [],"favorites": []},
{"user": "Roy", "content": "Just got a ticket for texting and driving!",
   "timestamp": " Mon Dec 23 2013 8:05 GMT-0800 (PST)",
   "retweets": [],"favorites": ["Sam", "Sally", "Pris"]},
{"user": "Pris", "content": "Going to have some boiled eggs.",
   "timestamp": " Mon Dec 23 2013 18:23 GMT-0800 (PST)",
   "retweets": [],"favorites": ["Sally"]},
{"user": "Pris", "content": "Maybe practice some gymnastics.",
   "timestamp": " Mon Dec 23 2013 19:47  GMT-0800 (PST)",
   "retweets": [],"favorites": ["Sally"]},
{"user": "Sam", "content": "@Roy Let's get lunch",
   "timestamp": " Mon Dec 23 2013 11:05 GMT-0800 (PST)",
   "retweets": ["Pris"], "favorites": ["Sally", "Pris"]}
]
}
```

With these two files, we can access the data by using the appropriate function to load them:

```
d3.csv("cities.csv",function(data) {console.log(data)});
d3.json("tweets.json",function(data) {console.log(data)});
```

Prints "Object {tweets: Array[10]}" in the console

In both cases, the data file is loaded as an array of JSON objects. For tweets.json, this array is found at data.tweets, whereas for cities.csv, this array is data. The function d3.json() allows you to load a JSON-formatted file, which can have objects and attributes in a way that a loaded CSV can't. When you load a CSV, it returns an array of objects, which in this case is initialized as data. When you load a JSON file, it could return an object with several name/value pairs. In this case, the object that's initialized as `data` has a name/value pair of `tweets: [Array of Data]`. That's why we need to refer to `data.tweets` after we've loaded tweets.json, but refer to `data` when we load cities.csv. The structure of tweets.json highlights this distinction.

Both d3.csv and d3.json are asynchronous, and will return after the request to open the file and not after processing the file. Loading a file, which is typically an operation that takes more time than most other functions, won't be complete by the time other functions are called. If you call functions that require the loaded data before it's loaded, then they'll fail. You can get around this asynchronous behavior in two ways. You can nest the functions operating on the data in the data-loading function:

```
d3.csv("somefiles.csv", function(data) {doSomethingWithData(data)});
```

Or you can use a helper library like queue.js (which we'll use in chapter 7) to trigger events upon completion of the loading of one or more files. You'll see queue.js in action in later chapters. Note that `d3.csv()` has a method `.parse()` that you can use on a block of text rather than an external file. If you need more direct control over getting data, you should review the documentation for `d3.xhr()`, which allows for more fine-grained control of sending and receiving data.

2.1.2 Formatting data

After you load the datasets, you'll need to define methods so that the attributes of the data directly relate to settings for color, size, and position graphical elements. If you want to display the cities in the CSV, you probably want to use circles, size those circles based on population, and then place them according to their geographic coordinates. We have long-established conventions for representing cities on maps graphically, but the same can't be said about tweets. What graphical symbol to use to represent a single tweet, how to size it, and where to place it are all open questions. To answer these questions, you need to understand the forms of data you'll encounter when doing data visualization. Programming languages and ontologies define numerous datatypes, but it's useful to think of them as quantitative, categorical, geometric, temporal, topological, or raw.

QUANTITATIVE
Numerical or quantitative data is the most common type in data visualization. Quantitative data can be effectively represented with size, position, or color. You'll typically need to normalize quantitative data (the second step in creating data visualization shown in figure 2.4) by defining scales using `d3.scale()`, as explained in section 2.1.3,

Figure 2.4   After loading data, you need to make sure that it's formatted in such a way that it can be used by various JavaScript functions to create graphics.

or by transforming your quantitative data into categorical data using techniques like quantiles, which group numeric values.

For one of our datasets, we have readily accessible quantitative data: the population figures in the cities.csv table. For the tweets dataset, though, it seems like we don't have any quantitative data available, which is why we'll spend time in section 2.1.3 looking at how to transform data.

CATEGORICAL

Categorical data falls into discrete groups, typically represented by text, such as nationality or gender. Categorical data is often represented using shape or color. You map the categories to distinct colors or shapes to identify the pattern of the groups of elements positioned according to other attributes.

The tweets data has categorical data in the form of the user data, which you can recognize by intuitively thinking of coloring the tweets by the user who made them. Later, we'll discuss methods to derive categorical data.

TOPOLOGICAL

Topological data describes the relationship of one piece of data with another, which can also be another form of location data. The genealogical connection between two people or the distance of a shop from a train station each represent a way of defining relationships between objects. Topological attributes can be represented with text referring to unique ID values or with pointers to the other objects. Later in this chapter we'll create topological data in the form of nested hierarchies.

For the cities data, it seems like we don't have topological data. However, we could easily produce it by designating one city, such as San Francisco, to be our frame of reference. We could then create a distance-to-San-Francisco measure that would give us topological data if we needed it. The tweets data has its topological component in the `favorites` and `retweets` arrays, which provide the basis for a social network.

GEOMETRIC

Geometric data is most commonly associated with the boundaries and tracks of geographic data, such as countries, rivers, cities, and roads. Geometric data might also be the SVG code to draw a particular icon that you want to use, the text for a class of shape, or a numerical value indicating the size of the shape. Geometric data is, not surprisingly, most often represented using shape and size, but can also be transformed like other data, for example, into quantitative data by measuring area and perimeter.

The cities data has obvious geometric data in the form of traditional latitude and longitude coordinates that allow the points to be placed on a map. The tweets data, on the other hand, has no readily accessible geometric data.

TEMPORAL

Dates and time can be represented using numbers for days, years, or months, or with specific date-time encoding for more complex calculations. The most common format is ISO 8601, and if your data comes formatted that way as a string, it's easy to turn it into a date datatype in JavaScript, as you'll see in section 2.1.4. You'll work with dates and times often. Fortunately, both the built-in functions in JavaScript and a few helper functions in D3 are available to handle data that's tricky to measure and represent.

Although the cities dataset has no temporal data, keep in mind that temporal data for common entities like cities and countries is often available. In situations where you can easily expand your dataset like this, you need to ask yourself if it makes sense given the scope of your project. In contrast, the tweets data has a string that conforms to RFC 2822 (supported by JavaScript for representing dates along with ISO 8601) and can easily be turned into a date datatype in JavaScript.

RAW
Raw, free, or unstructured data is typically text and image content. Raw data can be transformed by measuring it or using sophisticated text and image analysis to derive attributes more suited to data visualization. In its unaltered form, raw data is used in the content fields of graphical elements, such as in labels or snippets.

The city names provide convenient labels for that dataset, but how would we label the individual tweets? One way is to use the entire content of the tweet as a label, as we'll do in chapter 5, but when dealing with raw data, the most difficult and important task is coming up with ways of summarizing and measuring it effectively.

2.1.3 *Transforming data*

As you deal with different forms of data, you'll change data from one type to another to better represent it. You can transform data in many ways. Here we'll look at casting, normalizing (or scaling), binning (or grouping), and nesting data.

CASTING: CHANGING DATATYPES
The act of casting data refers to turning one datatype into another from the perspective of your programming language, which in this case is JavaScript. When you load data, it will often be in a string format, even if it's a date, integer, floating-point number, or array. The date string in the tweets data, for instance, needs to be changed from a string into a date datatype if you want to work with the date methods available in JavaScript. You should familiarize yourself with the JavaScript functions that allow you to transform data. Here are a few:

> **Casts the string 77 into the number 77 with no decimal places**

> **Casts the string 3.14 into the number 3.14 with decimal places**

```
parseInt("77");
parseFloat("3.14");
Date.parse("Sun, 22 Dec 2013 08:00:00 GMT");
text = "alpha,beta,gamma"; text.split(",");
```

> **Casts an ISO 8601– or RFC 2822–compliant string into a date datatype**

> **Splits the comma-delimited string into an array, which isn't strictly speaking a casting operation, but changes the type of data**

NOTE JavaScript defaults to type conversion when using the == test, whereas it forces no type conversion when using === and the like, so you'll find your code will often work fine without casting. But this will come back to haunt you in situations where it doesn't default to the type you expect, for example, when you try to sort an array and JavaScript sorts your numbers alphabetically.

SCALES AND SCALING

Numerical data rarely corresponds directly to the position and size of graphical elements onscreen. You can use d3.scale() functions to normalize your data for presentation on a screen (among other things). The first scale we'll look at is d3.scale().linear(), which makes a direct relationship between one range of numbers and another. Scales have a domain setting and a range setting that accept arrays, with the domain determining the ramp of values being transformed and the range referring to the ramp to which those values are being transformed. For example, if you take the smallest population figure in cities.csv and the largest population figure, you can create a ramp that scales from the smallest to the largest so that you can display the difference between them easily on a 500-px canvas. In figure 2.5 and the code that follows, you can see that the same linear rate of change from 500,000 to 13,000,000 maps to a linear rate of change from 0 to 500.

You create this ramp by instantiating a new scale object and setting its domain and range values:

```
var newRamp = d3.scale.linear().domain([500000,13000000]).range([0, 500]);
newRamp(1000000);
newRamp(9000000);
newRamp.invert(313);
```

Returns 20, allowing you to place a country with population 10,000,000 at 20 px

Returns 340

The invert function reverses the transformation, in this case returning 8325000.

You can also create a color ramp by referencing CSS color names, RGB colors, or hex colors in the range field. The effect is a linear mapping of a band of colors to the band of values defined in the domain, as shown in figure 2.6.

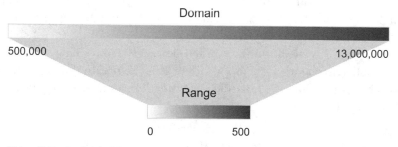

Domain

500,000   13,000,000

Range

0   500

Figure 2.5 Scales in D3 map one set of values (the domain) to another set of values (the range) in a relationship determined by the type of scale you create.

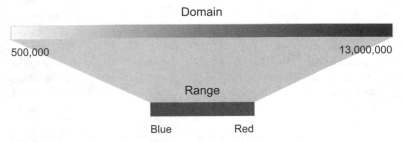

Figure 2.6   Scales can also be used to map numerical values to color bands, to make it easier to denote values using a color scale.

The code to create this ramp is the same, except for the reference to colors in the range array:

```
var newRamp = d3.scale.linear().domain([500000,13000000]).range(["blue",
"red"]);
newRamp(1000000);
newRamp(9000000);
newRamp.invert("#ad0052");
```

Returns "#ad0052"

The invert function only works with a numeric range, so inverting in this case returns NaN.

Returns "#0a00f5", allowing you to draw a city with population 1,000,000 as dark purple

You can also use d3.scale.log(), d3.scale.pow(), d3.scale.ordinal(), and other less common scales to map data where these scales are more appropriate to your dataset. You'll see these in action later on in the book as we deal with those kinds of datasets. Finally, d3.time.scale() provides a linear scale that's designed to deal with date datatypes, as you'll see later in this chapter.

BINNING: CATEGORIZING DATA

It's useful to sort quantitative data into categories, placing the values in a range or "bin" to group them together. One method is to use quantiles, by splitting the array into equal-sized parts. The quantile scale in D3 is, not surprisingly, called d3.scale.quantile(), and it has the same settings as other scales. The number of parts and their labels are determined by the .range() setting. Unlike other scales, it gives no error if there's a mismatch between the number of .domain() values and the number of .range() values in a quantile scale, because it automatically sorts and bins the values in the domain into a smaller number of values in the range.

The scale sorts the array of numbers in its .domain() from smallest to largest and automatically splits the values at the appropriate point to create the necessary categories. Any number passed into the quantile scale function returns one of the set categories based on these break points.

```
var sampleArray = [423,124,66,424,58,10,900,44,1];
var qScale = d3.scale.quantile().domain(sampleArray).range([0,1,2]);
qScale(423);
qScale(20);
qScale(10000);
```

Returns 2

Returns 0

Returns 2

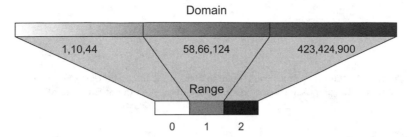

Figure 2.7 Quantile scales take a range of values and reassign them into a set of equally sized bins.

Notice that the range values in figure 2.7 are fixed, and can accept text that may correspond to a particular CSS class, color, or other arbitrary value.

```
var qScaleName =
d3.scale.quantile().domain(sampleArray).range(["small","medium","large"]);
qScaleName (68);                                    Returns "medium"
qScaleName (20);                        Returns "small"
qScaleName (10000);            Returns "large"
```

NESTING

Hierarchical representations of data are useful, and aren't limited to data with more traditional or explicit hierarchies, such as a dataset of parents and their children. We'll get into hierarchical data and representation in more detail in chapters 4 and 5, but in this chapter we'll use the D3 nesting function, which you can probably guess is called d3.nest().

The concept behind nesting is that shared attributes of data can be used to sort them into discrete categories and subcategories. For instance, if we want to group tweets by the user who made them, then we'd use nesting:

```
d3.json("tweets.json",function(data) {
  var tweetData = data.tweets;
  var nestedTweets = d3.nest()
    .key(function(el) {return el.user})
    .entries(tweetData);
});
```

This nesting function combines the tweets into arrays under new objects labeled by the unique user attribute values, as shown in figure 2.8.

```
nestedTweets
[▼ Object           , ▼ Object           , ▼ Object           , ▼ Object                    ]
    key: "Al"            key: "Roy"            key: "Pris"            key: "Sam"
  ▼ values: Array[3]   ▼ values: Array[4]   ▼ values: Array[2]   ▼ values: Array[1]
    ▶ 0: Object          ▶ 0: Object          ▶ 0: Object          ▶ 0: Object
    ▶ 1: Object          ▶ 1: Object          ▶ 1: Object            length: 1
    ▶ 2: Object          ▶ 2: Object            length: 2           ▶ __proto__: Array[0]
      length: 3          ▶ 3: Object          ▶ __proto__: Array[0] ▶ __proto__: Object
    ▶ __proto__: Array[0]  length: 4          ▶ __proto__: Object
  ▶ __proto__: Object    ▶ __proto__: Array[0]
                         ▶ __proto__: Object
```

Figure 2.8 Objects nested into a new array are now child elements of a values array of newly created objects that have a key attribute set to the value used in the d3.nest.key function.

Figure 2.9   After formatting your data, you'll need to measure it to ensure that the graphics you create are appropriately sized and positioned based on the parameters of the dataset.

Now that we've loaded our data and transformed it into types that are accessible, we'll investigate the patterns of that data by measuring the data (the third step shown in figure 2.9).

2.1.4   *Measuring data*

After loading your data array, one of the first things you should do is measure and sort it. It's particularly important to know the distribution of values of particular attributes, as well as the minimum and maximum values and the names of the attributes. D3 provides a set of array functions that can help you understand your data.

You'll always have arrays filled with data that you'll want to size and position based on the relative value of an attribute compared to the distribution of the values in the array. You should therefore familiarize yourself with the ways to determine the distributions of values in an array in D3. You'll work with an array of numbers first before you see these functions in operation with more complex and more data-rich JSON object arrays:

```
var testArray =  [88,10000,1,75,12,35];
```

Nearly all the D3 measuring functions follow the same pattern. First, you need to designate the array and an accessor function for the value that you want to measure. In our case, we're working with an array of numbers and not an array of objects, so the accessor only needs to point at the element itself.

```
d3.min(testArray, function (el) {return el});
d3.max(testArray, function (el) {return el});
d3.mean(testArray, function (el) {return el});
```

Returns the minimum value in the array, 1

Returns the maximum value in the array, 10000

Returns the average of values in the array, 1701.8333333333335

If you're dealing with a more complex JSON object array, then you'll need to designate the attribute you want to measure. For instance, if we're working with the array of JSON objects from cities.csv, we may want to derive the minimum, maximum, and average populations:

Returns the minimum value of the population attribute of each object in the array, 500000

Returns the maximum value of the population attribute of each object in the array, 1300000

```
d3.csv("cities.csv", function(data) {
d3.min(data, function (el) {return +el.population});
d3.max(data, function (el) {return +el.population });
```

```
d3.mean(data, function (el) {return +el.population });    ◁─┐  Returns the average
});                                                            value of the population
                                                              attribute of each object
                                                              in the array, 6856250
```

Finally, because dealing with minimum and maximum values is a common occurrence, d3.extent() conveniently returns d3.min() and d3.max() in a two-piece array:

```
d3.extent(data, function (el) {return +el.population});    ◁─┤  Returns
                                                              [500000, 1300000]
```

You can also measure nonnumerical data like text by using the JavaScript .length() function for strings and arrays. When dealing with topological data, you need more robust mechanisms to measure network structure like centrality and clustering. When dealing with geometric data, you can calculate the area and perimeter of shapes mathematically, which can become rather difficult with complex shapes.

Now that we've loaded, formatted, and measured our data, we can create data visualizations. This requires us to use selections and the functions that come with them, which we'll examine in more detail in the next section.

2.2 Data-binding

We touched on data-binding in chapter 1, but here we'll go into it in more detail, explaining how selections work with data-binding to create elements (the fourth step shown in figure 2.10) and also to change those elements after they've been created. Our first example uses the data from cities.csv. After that we'll see the process using this data as well as simple numerical arrays, and later we'll do more interesting things with the tweets data.

2.2.1 Selections and binding

You use selections to make changes to the structure and appearance of your web page with D3. Remember that a selection consists of one or more elements in the DOM as well as the data, if any, associated with them. You can also create or delete elements using selections, and change the style and content. You've seen how to use d3.select() to change a DOM element, and now we'll focus on creating and removing elements based on data. For this example, we'll use cities.csv as our data source, and so we'll need to load cities.csv and trigger our data visualization function in the callback to create a set of new <div> elements on the page using this code, with the results shown in figure 2.11.

Figure 2.10 To create graphics in D3, you use selections that bind data to DOM elements.

Figure 2.11   When our selection binds the cities.csv data to our web page, it creates eight new divs, each of which is classed with "cities" and with content drawn from our data.

```
d3.csv("cities.csv",function(error,data) {dataViz(data);});
function dataViz(incomingData) {
  d3.select("body").selectAll("div.cities")
    .data(incomingData)
    .enter()
    .append("div")
    .attr("class","cities")
    .html(function(d,i) { return d.label; });
}
```

Binds the data to your selection

Creates an element in the current selection

An empty selection because there are no <div> elements in <body> with class of "cities"

Defines how to respond when there's more data than DOM elements in a selection

Sets the content of the created <div>

Sets the class of each newly created element

The selection and binding procedure shown here is a common pattern throughout the rest of this book. A subselection is created when you first select one element and then select the elements underneath it, which you'll see in more detail later. First, let's take a look at each individual part of this example.

D3.SELECTALL()

The first part of any selection is d3.select() or d3.selectAll() with a CSS identifier that corresponds to a part of the DOM. Often no elements match the identifier, which is referred to as an *empty selection*, because you want to create new elements on the page using the .enter() function. You can make a selection on a selection to designate how to create and modify child elements of a specific DOM element. Note that a subselection won't automatically generate a parent. The parent must already exist, or you'll need to create one using .append().

.DATA()

Here you associate an array with the DOM elements you selected. Each city in our dataset is associated with a DOM element in the selection, and that associated data is stored in a `data` attribute of the element. We could access these values manually using JavaScript like so:

```
document.getElementsByClassName("cities")[0].__data__
```
   ◁—— **Returns a pointer to the object representing San Francisco**

Later in this chapter we'll work with those values in a more sophisticated way using D3.

.ENTER() AND .EXIT()

When binding data to selections, there will be either more, less, or the same number of DOM elements as there are data values. When you have more data values than DOM elements in the selection, you trigger the `.enter()` function, which allows you to define behavior to perform for every value that doesn't have a corresponding DOM element in the selection. In our case, `.enter()` fires four times, because no DOM elements correspond to `"div.cities"` and our `incomingData` array contains eight values. When there are fewer data elements, then `.exit()` behavior is triggered, and when there are equal data values and DOM elements in a selection, then neither `.exit()` nor `.enter()` is fired.

.APPEND() AND .INSERT()

You'll almost always want to add elements to the DOM when there are more data values than DOM elements. The `.append()` function allows you to add more elements and define which elements to add. In our example, we add `<div>` elements, but later in this chapter we'll add SVG shapes, and in other chapters we'll add tables and buttons and any other element type supported in HTML. The `.insert()` function is a sister function to `.append()`, but `.insert()` gives you control over where in the DOM you add the new element. You can also perform an append or insert directly on a selection, which adds one DOM element of the kind you specify for each DOM element in your selection.

.ATTR()

You're familiar with changing styles and attributes using D3 syntax. The only thing to note is that each of the functions you define here will be applied to each new element added to the page. In our example, each of our four new `<div>` elements will be created with `class="cities"`. Remember that even though our selection referenced `"div.cities"`, we still have to manually declare that we're creating `<div>` elements and also manually set their class to `"cities"`.

.HTML()

For traditional DOM elements, you set the content with a `.html()` function. In the next section, you'll see how to set content based on the data bound to the particular DOM element.

2.2.2 *Accessing data with inline functions*

If you ran the code in the previous example, you saw that each `<div>` element was set with different content derived from the data array that you bound to the selection. You did this using an inline anonymous function in your selection that automatically provides access to two variables that are critical to representing data graphically: the data value itself and the array position of the data. In most examples you'll see these represented as d for data and i for array index, but they could be declared using any available variable name.

The best way to see this in action is to use our data to create a simple data visualization. We'll keep working with d3ia.html, which we created in chapter 1, and which is a simple HTML page with minimal DOM elements and styles. A histogram or bar chart is one of the most simple and effective ways of expressing numerical data broken down by category. We'll avoid the more complex datasets for now and start with a simple array of numbers:

```
[15, 50, 22, 8, 100, 10]
```

If we bind this array to a selection, we can use the values to determine the height of the rectangles (our bars in a bar chart). We need to set a width based on the space available for the chart, and we'll start by setting it to 10 px:

```
d3.select("svg")
  .selectAll("rect")
  .data([15, 50, 22, 8, 100, 10])
  .enter()
  .append("rect")
  .attr("width", 10)
  .attr("height", function(d) {return d;});
```

Sets the width of the rectangles to a fixed value

Sets the height equal to the value of the data associated with each element

When we used the label values of our array to create <div> content with labels in section 2.2.1, we pointed to the object's label attribute. Here, because we're dealing with an array of number literals, we use the inline function to point directly at the value in the array to determine the height of our rectangles. The result, shown in figure 2.12, isn't nearly as interesting as you might expect.

Figure 2.12 The default setting for any shape in SVG is black fill with no stroke, which makes it hard to tell when the shapes overlap each other.

All the rectangles overlap each other—they have the same default x and y positions. The drawing is easier to see if the outline, or stroke, of your rectangles is different from their fill. We can also make them transparent by adjusting their opacity style, as shown in figure 2.13.

Figure 2.13 By changing the fill, stroke, and opacity settings, you can see the overlapping rectangles.

```
d3.select("svg")
  .selectAll("rect")
  .data([15, 50, 22, 8, 100, 10])
  .enter()
  .append("rect")
  .attr("width", 10)
  .attr("height", function(d) {return d;})
  .style("fill", "blue")
  .style("stroke", "red")
  .style("stroke-width", "1px")
  .style("opacity", .25);
```

You may wonder about practical use of the second variable in the inline function, typically represented as i. One use of the array position of a data value is to place visual elements. If we set the x position of each rectangle based on the i value (multiplied by the width of the rectangle), then we get a step closer to a bar chart:

```
d3.select("svg")
  .selectAll("rect")
  .data([15, 50, 22, 8, 100, 10])
  .enter()
  .append("rect")
  .attr("width", 10)
  .attr("height", function(d) {return d;})
  .style("fill", "blue")
  .style("stroke", "red")
  .style("stroke-width", "1px")
  .style("opacity", .25)
  .attr("x", function(d,i) {return i * 10});
```

Our histogram seems to be drawn from top to bottom, as seen in figure 2.14, because SVG draws rectangles down and to the right from the 0,0 point that we specify. To adjust this, we need to move each rectangle so that its y position corresponds to a position that is offset based on its height. We know that the tallest rectangle will be 100. The y position is measured based on the distance from the top left of the canvas, so if we set the y attribute of each rectangle equal to its length minus 100, then the histogram is drawn in the manner we'd expect, as shown in figure 2.15.

Figure 2.14 SVG rectangles are drawn from top to bottom.

```
d3.select("svg")
  .selectAll("rect")
  .data([15, 50, 22, 8, 100, 10])
  .enter()
  .append("rect")
  .attr("width", 10)
  .attr("height", function(d) {return d;})
  .style("fill", "blue")
  .style("stroke", "red")
  .style("stroke-width", "1px")
  .style("opacity", .25)
  .attr("x", function(d,i) {return i * 10;})
  .attr("y", function(d) {return 100 - d;});
```

2.2.3 Integrating scales

This way of building a chart works fine if you're dealing with an array of values that correspond directly to the height of the rectangles relative to the height and width of your <svg> element. But if you have real data, then it tends to have widely divergent values that don't correspond directly to the size of the shape you want to draw. The previous code doesn't deal with an array of values like this:

```
[14, 68, 24500, 430, 19, 1000, 5555]
```

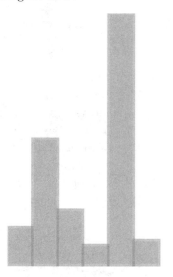

Figure 2.15 When we set the y position of the rectangle to the desired y position minus the height of the rectangle, the rectangle is drawn from bottom to top from that y position.

You can see how poorly it works in figure 2.16.

```
d3.select("svg")
  .selectAll("rect")
  .data([14, 68, 24500, 430, 19, 1000, 5555])
  .enter()
  .append("rect")
  .attr("width", 10)
  .attr("height", function(d) {return d})
  .style("fill", "blue")
  .style("stroke", "red")
  .style("stroke-width", "1px")
  .style("opacity", .25)
  .attr("x", function(d,i) {return i * 10;})
  .attr("y", function(d) {return 100 - d;});
```

And it works no better if you set a y offset equal to the maximum:

```
d3.select("svg")
  .selectAll("rect")
  .data([14, 68, 24500, 430, 19, 1000, 5555])
  .enter()
  .append("rect")
  .attr("width", 10)
  .attr("height", function(d) {return d})
  .style("fill", "blue")
  .style("stroke", "red")
  .style("stroke-width", "1px")
  .style("opacity", .25)
  .attr("x", function(d,i) {return i * 10;})
  .attr("y", function(d) {return 24500 - d;});
```

Figure 2.16   **SVG shapes will continue to be drawn offscreen.**

There's no need to bother with a screenshot. It's just a single bar running vertically across your canvas. In this case, it's best to use D3's scaling functions to normalize the values for display. We'll use the relatively straightforward `d3.scale.linear()` for this bar chart. A D3 scale has two primary functions: `.domain()` and `.range()`, both of which expect arrays and which must have arrays of the same length to get the right results. The array in `.domain()` indicates the series of values being mapped to `.range()`, which will make more sense in practice. First, we make a scale for the y-axis:

```
var yScale = d3.scale.linear().domain([0,24500]).range([0,100]);
yScale(0);                                                          ⎯  Returns 0
yScale(100);                                              ⎯  Returns
yScale(24000);      ⎯  Returns                               0.40816326530612246
                       97.95918367346938
```

As you can see, `yScale` now allows us to map the values in a way suitable for display. If we then use `yScale` to determine the height and y position of the rectangles, we end up with a bar chart that's more legible, as shown in figure 2.17.

```
var yScale = d3.scale.linear() .domain([0,24500]).range([0,100]);

d3.select("svg")
  .selectAll("rect")
  .data([14, 68, 24500, 430, 19, 1000, 5555])
  .enter()
  .append("rect")
  .attr("width", 10)
  .attr("height", function(d) {return yScale(d);})
  .style("fill", "blue")
  .style("stroke", "red")
  .style("stroke-width", "1px")
  .style("opacity", .25)
  .attr("x", function(d,i) {return i * 10;})
  .attr("y", function(d) {return 100 - yScale(d);});
```

When you deal with such widely diverging values, it often makes more sense to use a polylinear scale. A polylinear scale is a linear scale with multiple points in the domain and range. Let's suppose that for our dataset, we're particularly interested in values between 1 and 100, while recognizing that sometimes we get interesting values between 100 and 1000, and occasionally we get outliers that can be quite large. We could express this in a polylinear scale as follows:

```
var yScale =
d3.scale.linear().domain([0,100,1000,24500]).range([0,50,75,100]);
```

The previous draw code produces a different chart with this scale, as shown in figure 2.18.

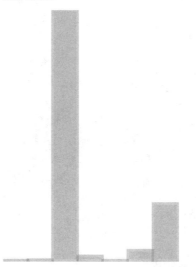

Figure 2.17 A bar chart drawn using a linear scale

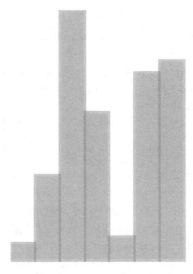

Figure 2.18 The same bar chart from figure 2.17 drawn with a polylinear scale

There may be a cutoff value, after which it isn't so important to express how large a datapoint is. For instance, let's say these datapoints represent the number of responses for a survey, and it's deemed a success if there are more than 500 responses. We may only want to show the range of the data values between 0 and 500, while emphasizing the variation at the 0 to 100 level with a scale like this:

```
var yScale = d3.scale.linear()
.domain([0,100,500]).range([0,50,100]);
```

You may think that's enough to draw a new chart that caps the bars at a maximum height of 100 if the datapoint has a value over 500. This isn't the default behavior for scales in D3, though. In figure 2.19 you can see what would happen running the draw code with that scale.

Figure 2.19 A bar chart drawn with a linear scale where the maximum value in the domain is lower than the maximum value in the dataset

Notice the rectangles are still drawn above the canvas, as evidenced by the lack of a border on the top of the four rectangles with values over 500. We can confirm this is happening by putting a value greater than 500 into the scale function we've created:

```
yScale(1000);     ⟵  Returns 162.5
```

By default, a D3 scale continues to extrapolate values greater than the maximum domain value and less than the minimum domain value. If we want it to set all such values to the maximum (for greater) or minimum (for lesser) range value, then we need to use the .clamp() function:

```
var yScale = d3.scale.linear()
            .domain([0,100,500])
            .range([0,50,100])
            .clamp(true);
```

Running the draw code now produces rectangles that have a maximum value of 100 for height and position, as shown in figure 2.20.

We can confirm this by plugging a value into yScale() that's greater than 500:

```
yScale(1000);    ⟵  Returns 100
```

Scale functions are key to determining position, size, and color of elements in data visualization. As

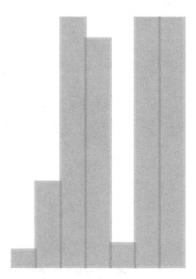

Figure 2.20 A bar chart drawn with values in the dataset greater than the maximum value of the domain of the scale, but with the clamp() function set to true

you'll see later in this chapter and throughout the book, this is the basic process for using scales in D3.

2.3 Data presentation style, attributes, and content

Next, we'll work with the cities and tweets data to create a second bar chart combining the techniques you've learned in this chapter and chapter 1. After that, we'll deal with the more complicated methods necessary to represent the tweets data in a simple data visualization. Along the way, you'll learn how to set styles and attributes based on the data bound to the elements, and explore how D3 creates, removes, and changes elements based on changes in the data.

2.3.1 Visualization from loaded data

A bar chart based on the cities.csv data is straightforward, requiring only a scale based on the maximum population value, which we can determine using d3.max(), as shown in the following listing. This bar chart (shown annotated in figure 2.21) shows you the distribution of population sizes of the cities in our dataset.

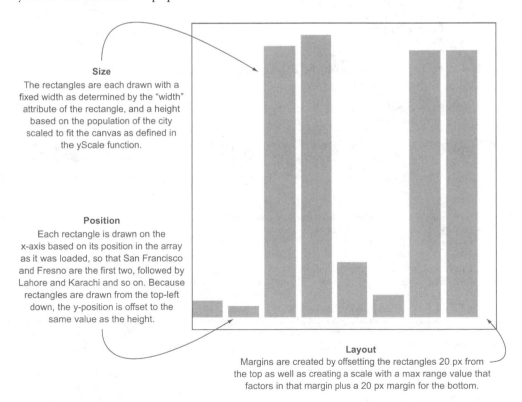

Size
The rectangles are each drawn with a fixed width as determined by the "width" attribute of the rectangle, and a height based on the population of the city scaled to fit the canvas as defined in the yScale function.

Position
Each rectangle is drawn on the x-axis based on its position in the array as it was loaded, so that San Francisco and Fresno are the first two, followed by Lahore and Karachi and so on. Because rectangles are drawn from the top-left down, the y-position is offset to the same value as the height.

Layout
Margins are created by offsetting the rectangles 20 px from the top as well as creating a scale with a max range value that factors in that margin plus a 20 px margin for the bottom.

Figure 2.21 The cities.csv data drawn as a bar chart using the maximum value of the population attribute in the domain setting of the scale

Listing 2.3   Loading data, casting it, measuring it, and displaying it as a bar chart

```
d3.csv("cities.csv",function(error,data) {dataViz(data);});

function dataViz(incomingData) {

 var maxPopulation = d3.max(incomingData, function(el) {
     return parseInt(el.population);}
 );
 var yScale = d3.scale.linear().domain([0,maxPopulation]).range([0,460]);
 d3.select("svg").attr("style","height: 480px; width: 600px;");
 d3.select("svg")
   .selectAll("rect")
   .data(incomingData)
   .enter()
   .append("rect")
   .attr("width", 50)
   .attr("height", function(d) {return yScale(parseInt(d.population));})
   .attr("x", function(d,i) {return i * 60;})
   .attr("y", function(d) {return 480 - yScale(parseInt(d.population));})
   .style("fill", "blue")
   .style("stroke", "red")
   .style("stroke-width", "1px")
   .style("opacity", .25);
}
```

> Transforms the population value into an integer

Creating a bar chart out of the Twitter data requires a bit more transformation. As shown in the following listing, we use d3.nest() to gather the tweets under the person making them, and then use the length of that array to create a bar chart of the number of tweets (shown annotated in figure 2.22).

Listing 2.4   Loading, nesting, measuring, and representing data

```
d3.json("tweets.json",function(error,data) {dataViz(data.tweets)});
function dataViz(incomingData) {

var nestedTweets = d3.nest()
.key(function (el) {return el.user;})
.entries(incomingData);

nestedTweets.forEach(function (el) {
el.numTweets = el.values.length;
})

var maxTweets = d3.max(nestedTweets, function(el) {return el.numTweets;});

var yScale = d3.scale.linear().domain([0,maxTweets]).range([0,100]);

d3.select("svg")
  .selectAll("rect")
  .data(nestedTweets)
  .enter()
  .append("rect")
  .attr("width", 50)
```

> Specifies data.tweets, where your data array is located

> Creates a new attribute based on the number of tweets

```
      .attr("height", function(d) {return yScale(d.numTweets);})
      .attr("x", function(d,i) {return i * 60;})
      .attr("y", function(d) {return 100 - yScale(d.numTweets);})
      .style("fill", "blue")
      .style("stroke", "red")
      .style("stroke-width", "1px").style("opacity", .25);
}
```

2.3.2 Setting channels

So far, we've only used the height of a rectangle to correspond to a point of data, and in cases where you're dealing with one piece of quantitative data, that's all you need. That's why bar charts are so popular in spreadsheet applications. But most of the time you'll use multivariate data, such as census data for counties or medical data for patients.

"Multivariate" is another way of saying that each datapoint has multiple data characteristics. For instance, your medical history isn't a single score between 0 and 100. Instead, it consists of multiple measures that explain different aspects of your health. In cases with multivariate data like that, you need to develop techniques to represent multiple data points in the same shape. The technical term for how a shape visually expresses data is *channel*, and depending on the data you're working with, different channels are better suited to express data graphically.

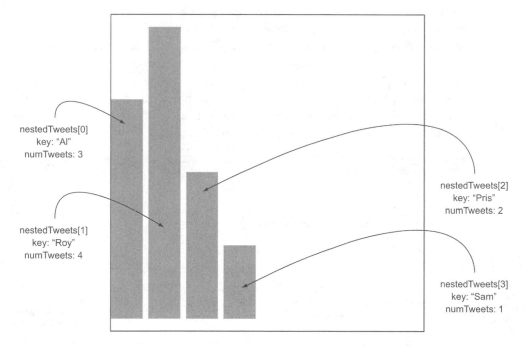

Figure 2.22 By nesting data and counting the objects that are nested, we can create a bar chart out of hierarchical data.

Infoviz term: channels

When you represent data using graphics, you need to consider the best visual methods to represent the types of data you're working with. Each graphical object, as well as the whole display, can be broken down into component channels that relay information visually. These channels, such as height, width, area, color, position, and shape, are particularly well suited to represent different classes of information. For instance, if you represent magnitude by changing the size of a circle, and if you create a direct correspondence between radius and magnitude, then your readers will be confused, because we tend to recognize the area of a circle rather than its radius. Channels also exist at multiple levels, and some techniques use hue, saturation, and value to represent three different pieces of information, rather than just using color more generically.

The important thing here is to avoid using too many channels, and instead focus on using the channels most suitable to your data. If you aren't varying shape, for instance, if you're using a bar chart where all the shapes are rectangles, then you can use color for category and value (lightness) to represent magnitude.

Going back to the tweets.json data, it may seem like there's not much data available to put on a chart, but depending on what factors we want to measure and display, we can take a couple different approaches. Let's imagine we want to measure the impact factor of tweets, treating tweets that are favorited or retweeted as more important than tweets that aren't. This time, instead of a bar chart, we'll create a scatterplot, and instead of using array position to place it along the x-axis, let's use time, because there's good evidence that tweets made at certain times are more likely to be favorited or retweeted. We'll place each tweet along the y-axis using a scale based on the maximum impact factor of our set of tweets. From this point on, we'll focus on the data-Viz() function as in the following listing, because you should be familiar now with getting your data in and sending it to such a function.

Listing 2.5 Creating a scatterplot

```
function dataViz(incomingData) {

  incomingData.forEach(function (el) {
    el.impact = el.favorites.length + el.retweets.length;
    el.tweetTime = new Date(el.timestamp);
  })

  var maxImpact = d3.max(incomingData, function(el) {return el.impact;});
  var startEnd = d3.extent(incomingData, function(el) {
    return el.tweetTime;
  });
  var timeRamp = d3.time.scale().domain(startEnd).range([20,480]);
  var yScale = d3.scale.linear().domain([0,maxImpact]).range([0,460]);
  var radiusScale = d3.scale.linear()
                    .domain([0,maxImpact]).range([1,20]);
```

Annotations:
- Transforms the ISO 8906–compliant string into a date datatype → `el.tweetTime = new Date(el.timestamp);`
- Creates an impact score by totaling the number of favorites and retweets → `el.impact = el.favorites.length + el.retweets.length;`
- Returns the earliest and latest times for a scale
- startEnd is an array.

```
var colorScale = d3.scale.linear()
                     .domain([0,maxImpact]).range(["white","#990000"]);
d3.select("svg")
  .selectAll("circle")
  .data(incomingData)
  .enter()
  .append("circle")
  .attr("r", function(d) {return radiusScale(d.impact);})
  .attr("cx", function(d,i) {return timeRamp(d.tweetTime);})
  .attr("cy", function(d) {return 480 - yScale(d.impact);})
  .style("fill", function(d) {return colorScale(d.impact);})
  .style("stroke", "black")
  .style("stroke-width", "1px");
};
```

Builds a scale that maps impact to a ramp from white to dark red ⟶

⟵ **Size, color, and vertical position will all be based on impact**

As shown in figure 2.23, each tweet is positioned vertically based on impact and horizontally based on time. Each tweet is also sized by impact and colored darker red based on impact. Later on we'll want to use color, size, and position for different attributes of the data, but for now we'll tie most of them to impact.

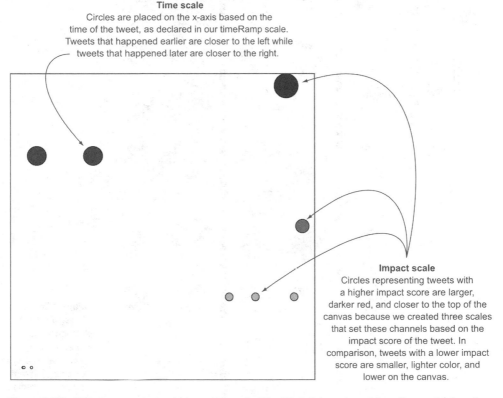

Time scale
Circles are placed on the x-axis based on the time of the tweet, as declared in our timeRamp scale. Tweets that happened earlier are closer to the left while tweets that happened later are closer to the right.

Impact scale
Circles representing tweets with a higher impact score are larger, darker red, and closer to the top of the canvas because we created three scales that set these channels based on the impact score of the tweet. In comparison, tweets with a lower impact score are smaller, lighter color, and lower on the canvas.

Figure 2.23 Tweets are represented as circles sized by the total number of favorites and retweets, and are placed on the canvas along the x-axis based on the time of the tweet and along the y-axis according to the same impact factor used to size the circles. Two tweets with the same impact factor that were made at nearly the same time are shown overlapping at the bottom left.

2.3.3   *Enter, update, and exit*

You've used the `.enter()` behavior of a selection many times already. Now let's take a closer look at it and its counterpart, `.exit()`. Both of these functions operate when there's a mismatch between the number of data values bound to a selection and the number of DOM elements in the selection. If there are more data values than DOM elements, then `.enter()` fires, whereas if there are fewer data values than DOM elements, then `.exit()` fires, as in figure 2.24. You use `selection.enter()` to define how you want to create new elements based on the data you're working with, and you use `selection.exit()` to define how you want to remove existing elements in a selection when the data that corresponds to them has been deleted. Updating data, as

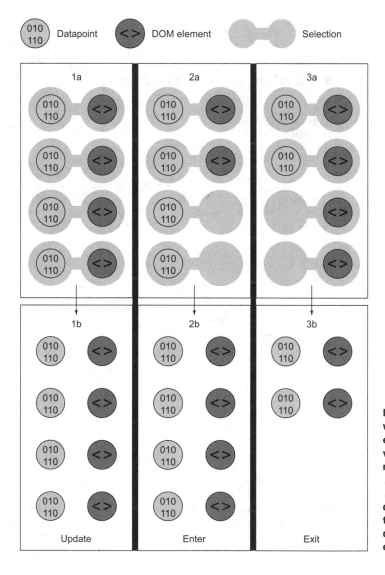

Figure 2.24   Selections where the number of DOM elements and number of values in an array don't match will fire either an `.enter()` event or an `.exit()` event, depending on whether there are more or fewer data values than DOM elements, respectively.

you'll see in the next example, is accomplished through reapplying the functions you used to create the graphical elements based on your data.

Each .enter() or .exit() event can include actions taken on child elements. This is mostly useful with .enter() events, where you use the .append() function to add new elements. If you declare this new appended element as a variable, and if that element is amenable to child elements, like a <g> element is, then you can include any number of child elements. In the case of SVG elements, only <svg>, <g>, and <text> can have child elements, but if you're using D3 with traditional DOM manipulation, then you can use this method to add <p> elements to <div> elements and so on.

For example, let's say we want to show a bar chart based on our newly measured impact score, and we want the bars on the bar chart to have labels. We need to append <g> elements, and not shapes, to the <svg> canvas in our initial selection. Because the data is bound to these elements, we can use the same syntax when we add child elements. Because we're using <g> elements, we need to set the position using the transform attribute. We add child elements to the .append() function, and we need to declare it as a variable tweetG. This allows tweetG to stand in for d3.select("svg").selectAll("g") so we don't have to retype it throughout the example. The following listing uses all the same scales to determine size and position as the previous example.

Listing 2.6 Creating labels on <g> elements

```
var tweetG = d3.select("svg")
  .selectAll("g")
  .data(incomingData)
  .enter()
  .append("g")
  .attr("transform", function(d) {
  return "translate(" +
    timeRamp(d.tweetTime) + "," + (480 - yScale(d.impact))
    + ")";
  });
```
<g> requires a transform, which takes a constructed string.

```
tweetG.append("circle")
  .attr("r", function(d) {return radiusScale(d.impact);})
  .style("fill", "#990000")
  .style("stroke", "black")
  .style("stroke-width", "1px");
```
Uses .getHours() to make the label a bit more legible

```
tweetG.append("text")
  .text(function(d) {return d.user + "-" + d.tweetTime.getHours();});
```

In figure 2.25 you can see the result of our code, along with some annotation. The same circles in the same position show that translate works much like changing cx and cy for circles, but now we can add other SVG elements, like <text> for labels.

The labels are illegible in the bottom left, but they're not much better for the rest. Later on, you'll learn how to make better labels. The inline functions such as .text(function(d) {return d.user + "-" + d.tweetTime.getHours()}) set the label

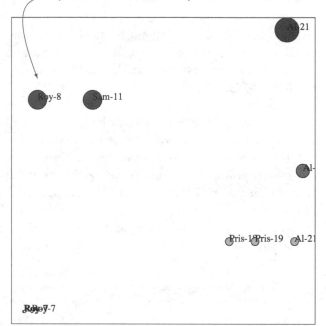

Text anchoring
By default, SVG text is anchored at the start
of the text, meaning that the text will be drawn to the
right of the initial position. If you want to draw it differently,
you can set the "text-anchor" style to "end" or "middle".

Child elements
Each datapoint is represented by a
complex graphic consisting of a <g>,
a <circle>, and a <text> element. Each
child element gains its initial position
from its parent, but is drawn from the
position according to the rules for
that element. So, text is anchored,
circles are centered, and rectangles are
drawn from a 0,0 position determined
by the parent <g>.

Figure 2.25   Each tweet is a <g> element with a circle and a label appended to it. The various tweets by Roy at 7 A.M. happen so close to each other that they're difficult to label.

to be the name of the person making the tweet, followed by a dash, followed by the hour of the tweet. These functions all refer to the same data elements, because the child elements inherit their parents' data functions. If one of your data elements is an array, you may think you could bind it to a selection on the child element, and you'd be right. You'll see that in the next chapter and later in the book.

EXIT

Corresponding to the .append() function is the .remove() function available with .exit(). To see .exit() in action, you need to have some elements in the DOM, which could already exist, depending on what you put in your HTML, or which could have been added with D3. Let's stick with the state that the previous code creates, which provides us with ample opportunity to test the .exit() function. DOM element styles and attributes aren't updated if we make a change to the array unless we call the necessary .style() and .attr() functions. If we bind any array to the existing <g> elements in your DOM, then we can use .exit() to remove them:

```
d3.selectAll("g").data([1,2,3,4]).exit().remove();
```

This code deleted all but four of our <g> elements, because there are only four values in our array. In most of the explanations of D3's .enter() and .exit() behavior, you won't see this kind of binding of an entirely different array to a selection. Instead, you'll see a rebinding of the initial data array after it's been filtered to represent a change via user interaction or other behavior. You'll see an example like this next, and throughout the book. But it's important to understand the difference between your data, your selection, and your DOM elements. The data that's bound to our DOM elements has been overwritten, so our data-rich objects from tweets.csv have now been replaced with boring numbers. But the only change to the visual representation is that the number has been reduced to reflect the size of the array we've bound. D3 doesn't follow the convention that when the data changes, the corresponding display is updated; you need to build that functionality yourself. Because it doesn't follow that convention, it gives you greater flexibility that we'll explore in later chapters.

UPDATING

You can see how the visual attributes of an element can change to reflect changes in data by updating the <text> elements in each g to reflect the newly bound data:

```
d3.selectAll("g").select("text").text(function(d) {return d});
```

Figure 2.26 shows our long labels replaced by the numbers we bound to the data.

In this example we had to .selectAll() the parent elements and then subselect the child elements to re-initialize the data-binding for the child elements. Whenever you bind new data to a selection that utilizes child elements, you'll need to follow this pattern. You can see that, because we didn't update the <circle> elements, they still have the old data bound to each element:

Figure 2.26 Only four <g> elements remain, corresponding to the four data values in the new array, with their <text> labels reset to match the new values in the array. But when you inspect the <g> element, you see that its __data__ property, where D3 stores the bound data, is different from that of its <circle> child element, which still has the JSON object we bound when we first created the visualization.

**Returns values from
the newly bound array**

**Returns values
from the newly
bound array,
because we used
a subselect**

```
d3.selectAll("g").each(function(d) {console.log(d)});
d3.selectAll("text").each(function(d) {console.log(d)});
d3.selectAll("circle").each(function(d) {console.log(d)});
```

**Returns values from the old tweetData
array, because we haven't specified
overwriting with a subselect**

The .exit() function isn't intended to be used for binding a new array of completely
different values like this. Instead, it's meant to update the page based on the removal
of elements from the array that's been bound to the selection. But if you plan to do
this, you need to specify how the .data() function binds data to your selected elements. By default, .data() binds based on the array position of the data value. This
means, in the previous example, that the first four elements in our selection are maintained and bound to the new data, while the rest are subject to the .exit() function.
In general, though, you don't want to rely on array position as your binding key.
Rather, you should use something meaningful, such as the value of the data object
itself. The key requires a string or number, so if you pass a JSON object without using
JSON.stringify, it treats all objects as "[object object]" and only returns one unique
value. To manually set the binding key, we use the second setting in the .data() function and use the inline syntax typical in D3.

Listing 2.7   Setting the key value in data-binding

```
function dataViz(incomingData) {

incomingData.forEach(function(el) {
    el.impact = el.favorites.length + el.retweets.length;
    el.tweetTime = new Date(el.timestamp);
})

var maxImpact = d3.max(incomingData, function(el) {
    return el.impact
});

var startEnd = d3.extent(incomingData, function(el) {
    return el.tweetTime
});

var timeRamp = d3.time.scale().domain(startEnd).range([ 50, 450 ]);
var yScale = d3.scale.linear().domain([ 0, maxImpact ]).range([ 0, 460 ]);
var radiusScale = d3.scale.linear()
    .domain([ 0, maxImpact ])
    .range([ 1, 20 ]);

d3.select("svg").selectAll("circle")
.data(incomingData, function(d) {
    return JSON.stringify(d)
}).enter().append("circle").attr("r", function(d) {
    return radiusScale(d.impact)
```

**We could use any unique attribute as
the key, but using the entire object
works if we don't have a unique value,
though we have to stringify it first.**

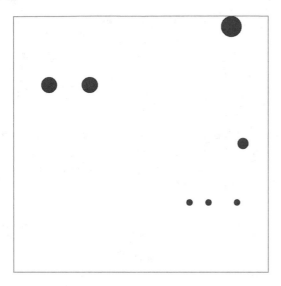

Figure 2.27 All elements corresponding to tweets that were not favorited and not retweeted were removed.

```
}).attr("cx", function(d, i) {
    return timeRamp(d.tweetTime)
}).attr("cy", function(d) {
    return 480 - yScale(d.impact)
}).style("fill", "#990000")
  .style("stroke", "black")
  .style("stroke-width", "1px");
}
```

The visual results are the same as our earlier scatterplot with the same settings, but now if we filter the array we used for the data, and bind that to the selection, we can get to the state shown in figure 2.27 by defining some useful .exit() behavior:

```
var filteredData = incomingData.filter(
    function(el) {return el.impact > 0}
);
d3.selectAll("circle")
  .data(filteredData, function(d) {return JSON.stringify(d)})
  .exit()
  .remove();
```

Using the stringified object won't work if you change the data in the object, because then it no longer corresponds with the original binding string. If you plan to do significant changing and updating, then you'll need a unique ID of some sort for your objects to use as your binding key.

2.4 Summary

In this chapter we looked closely at the core elements for building data visualizations using D3:

- Loading data from external files in CSV and JSON format
- Formatting and transforming data using D3 scales and built-in JavaScript functions

- Measuring data to build graphically useful visualizations
- Binding data to create graphics based on the attributes of the data
- Using subselections to create complex graphical objects made of multiple shapes using the <g> element
- Understanding how to create, change, and move elements using enter(), exit(), and selections

Almost all the code you'll write using D3 is a variation of or elaboration on the material covered in this chapter. In the next chapter we'll focus on the design details necessary for a successful D3 project, while exploring how D3 implements interaction, animation, and the use of pregenerated content.

Data-driven design and interaction

This chapter covers

- Enabling interactivity for graphical elements
- Working with color effectively
- Loading traditional HTML for use as pop-ups
- Loading external SVG icons into charts

Data visualization frameworks have existed in a form that separates them from the rest of web development. Flash or Java apps are dropped into a web page, and the only design necessary is to make sure the `<div>` is big enough or to take into account that it may be resized. D3 changes that, and gives you the opportunity to integrate the design of your data visualization with the design of your more traditional web elements.

You can and should style content you generate with D3 with all the same CSS settings as traditional HTML content. You can easily maintain those styles and have a consistent look and feel. This can be done by using the same style sheet classes for what you create with D3 as the ones you use with your traditional page elements when possible, and by following thoughtful use of color and interactivity with the graphics you create using D3.

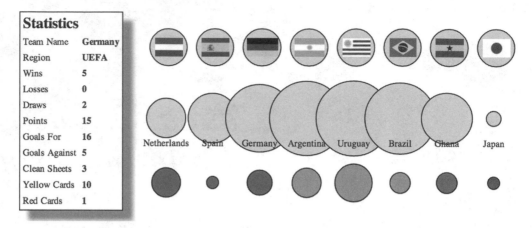

Statistics	
Team Name	Germany
Region	UEFA
Wins	5
Losses	0
Draws	2
Points	15
Goals For	16
Goals Against	5
Clean Sheets	3
Yellow Cards	10
Red Cards	1

Figure 3.1   This chapter covers loading HTML from an external file and updating it (section 3.3.2), as well as loading external images for icons (section 3.3.1), animating transitions (section 3.2.2), and working with color (section 3.2.4).

This chapter deals with design broadly speaking, and it touches not only on graphical design but on interaction design, project architecture, and the integration of pregenerated content. It highlights the connections between D3 and other methods of development, whether we're identifying libraries typically used alongside D3 or integrating HTML and SVG resources created using other tools. We can't cover all the principles of design (which isn't one field but many). Instead, we'll focus on how to use particular D3 functionality to follow the best practices established by design professionals to create some simple data visualization based on the statistics associated with the 2010 World Cup, as seen in figure 3.1.

3.1   Project architecture

When you create a single web page with an interesting information visualization on it, you don't need to think too much about where all your files are going to live. But if you build an application that provides multiple points of interaction and different states, then you should identify the resources that you need and plan your project accordingly.

3.1.1   Data

Your data will tend to come in one of two forms: either dynamically delivered via server/API or in static files. If you're pulling data dynamically from a server or API, it's possible that you'll have static files as well. A good example of this is building maps, where the base data layer (such as a map of countries) is from a static file and the dynamic data layer (such as the places where tweets are made) comes from a server. For this chapter, we'll use the file worldcup.csv to represent statistics for the 2010 World Cup:

```
"team","region","win","loss","draw","points","gf","ga","cs","yc","rc"
"Netherlands","UEFA",6,0,1,18,12,6,2,23,1
"Spain","UEFA",6,0,1,18,8,2,5,8,0
"Germany","UEFA",5,0,2,15,16,5,3,10,1
"Argentina","CONMEBOL",4,0,1,12,10,6,2,8,0
"Uruguay","CONMEBOL",3,2,2,11,11,8,3,13,2
"Brazil","CONMEBOL",3,1,1,10,9,4,2,9,2
"Ghana","CAF",2,2,1,8,5,4,1,12,0
"Japan","AFC",2,1,1,7,4,2,2,4,0
```

That's a lot of data for each team. We could try to come up with a graphical object that encodes all nine data points simultaneously (plus labels), but instead we'll use interactive and dynamic methods to provide access to the data.

3.1.2 Resources

Pregenerated content, like hand-drawn SVG and HTML components, comes as an external file that you'll need to know how to load. You'll see examples of these later on in the chapter. Each file contains enough code to draw the shape or traditional DOM elements we'll add to our page. We'll spend more time with the contents of this folder later on in sections 3.3.2 and 3.3.3 when we deal with loading pregenerated content.

3.1.3 Images

Later on, we'll use a set of Portable Network Graphics (PNGs) with the flags of each team represented in your dataset. We'll name the PNGs the same as the teams, so that it's easier to use the images with D3, as you'll see later. Every digital file consists of code, but we think of images as fundamentally different. This distinction breaks down when you work with SVG and you're accustomed to treating SVG as images. If you're working with SVG images as images and not as code that you want to manipulate in D3, then you should put them in your image directory and keep the SVG files that you intend to deal with as code in your resources directory.

3.1.4 Style sheets

Although we won't focus on CSS in this chapter too much, you should be aware that you can use CSS compilers to support variables in CSS and other improved functionality. Our style sheet shown in listing 3.1 has classes for the different states of the SVG elements we're dealing with, including SVG text elements that use a different syntax than traditional DOM elements for font.

Listing 3.1 d3ia.css

```
text {
font-size: 10px;
}

g > text.active {
font-size: 30px;
}
```

```
circle {
fill: pink;
stroke: black;
stroke-width: 1px;
}

circle.active {
fill: red;
}

circle.inactive {
fill: gray;
}
```

3.1.5   *External libraries*

For the example in this chapter, we'll use two more .js files besides d3.min.js, which is the minified D3 library. The first is soccerviz.js, which stores the functions we'll build and use in this chapter. The second is colorbrewer.js, which also comes bundled with D3 and provides a set of predefined color palettes that we'll find useful.

We reference these files in the much cleaner d3ia_2.html.

Listing 3.2   d3ia_2.html

```html
<html>
<head>
  <title>D3 in Action Examples</title>
  <meta charset="utf-8" />
  <link type="text/css" rel="stylesheet" href="d3ia.css" />
</head>
<script src="d3.v3.min.js" type="text/javascript"></script>
<script src="colorbrewer.js" type="text/javascript"></script>
<script src="soccerviz.js" type="text/javascript"></script>
<body onload="createSoccerViz()">
<div id="viz">
<svg style="width:500px;height:500px;border:1px lightgray solid;" />
</div>
<div id="controls" />
</body>
</html>
```

The <body> has two <div> elements, one with the ID viz and the other with the ID controls. Notice that the <body> element has an onload property that runs create-SoccerViz(), one of our functions in soccerviz.js (shown in the following listing). This loads the data and binds it to create a labeled circle for each team. It's not much, as you can see in figure 3.2, but it's a start.

Listing 3.3   soccerviz.js

```
function createSoccerViz() {
  d3.csv("worldcup.csv", function(data) {        ◁─┤ Loads the data and
    overallTeamViz(data);                              runs createSoccerViz
  })                                                    with the loaded data
```

```
function overallTeamViz(incomingData) {
  d3.select("svg")
    .append("g")
    .attr("id", "teamsG")
    .attr("transform", "translate(50,300)")
    .selectAll("g")
    .data(incomingData)
    .enter()
    .append("g")
    .attr("class", "overallG")
    .attr("transform",
       function (d,i) {return "translate(" + (i * 50) + ", 0)"}
       );

  var teamG = d3.selectAll("g.overallG");

  teamG
    .append("circle")
    .attr("r", 20)
    .style("fill", "pink")
    .style("stroke", "black")
    .style("stroke-width", "1px");

  teamG
    .append("text")
    .style("text-anchor", "middle")
    .attr("y", 30)
    .style("font-size", "10px")
    .text(function(d) {return d.team;});
  }
}
```

Appends a \<g\> to the \<svg\> canvas to move it and center its contents more easily

Creates a \<g\> for each team to add labels or other elements as we get more ambitious

Assigns the selection to a variable to refer to it without typing out d3.selectAll() every time

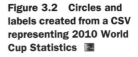

Figure 3.2 Circles and labels created from a CSV representing 2010 World Cup Statistics

Although you might write an application entirely with D3 and your own custom code, for large-scale sustainable projects you'll have to integrate more external libraries. We'll only use one of those, colorbrewer.js, which isn't intimidating. The colorbrewer library is a set of arrays of colors, which are useful in information visualization and mapping. You'll see this library in action in section 3.3.2.

3.2   *Interactive style and DOM*

Creating interactive information visualization is necessary for your users to deal with large and complex datasets. And the key to building interactivity into your D3 projects is the use of events, which define behaviors based on user activity. After you learn how to make your elements interactive, you'll need to understand D3 transitions, which allow you to animate the change from one color or size to another. With that in place, you'll turn to learning how to make changes to an element's position in the DOM so that you can draw your graphics properly. Finally, we'll look more closely at color, which you'll use often in response to user interaction.

3.2.1   *Events*

To get started, let's update our visualization to add buttons that change the appearance of our graphics to correspond with different data. We could handcode the buttons in HTML and tie them to functions as in traditional web development, but we can also use D3 to discover and examine the attributes in the data and create buttons dynamically. This has the added benefit of scaling to the data, so that if we add more attributes to our dataset, then this function automatically creates the necessary buttons.

```
var dataKeys = d3.keys(incomingData[0]).filter(function(el) {
        return el != "team" && el != "region";
    });

d3.select("#controls").selectAll("button.teams")
        .data(dataKeys).enter()
        .append("button")
        .on("click", buttonClick)
.html(function(d) {return d;});

function buttonClick(datapoint) {
    var maxValue = d3.max(incomingData, function(d) {
        return parseFloat(d[datapoint]);
    });

var radiusScale = d3.scale.linear()
    .domain([ 0, maxValue ]).range([ 2, 20 ]);

d3.selectAll("g.overallG").select("circle")
        .attr("r", function(d) {
            return radiusScale(d[datapoint]);
        });
};
```

Remember that dataKeys consists of an array of attribute names, so the *d* corresponds to one of those names and makes a good button title.

Builds buttons based on the data that's numerical, so we want all the attributes except the team and region attributes, which store strings

Registers an onclick behavior for each button, with a wrapper that gives access to the data that was bound to it when it was created

The function each button is calling on click, with the bound data sent automatically as the first argument

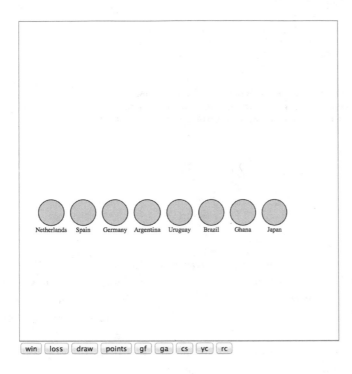

Figure 3.3   **Buttons for each numerical attribute are appended to the** `controls` **div behind the** `viz` **div. When a button is clicked, the code runs** `buttonClick`.

We use d3.keys and pass it one of the objects from our array. The d3.keys function returns the names of the attributes of an object as an array. We've filtered this array to remove the team and region attributes because these have nonnumerical data and won't be suitable for the buttonClick functionality we define. Obviously, in a larger or more complex system, we'll want to have more robust methods for designating attributes than listing them by hand like this. You'll see that later when we deal with more complex datasets. In this case, we bind this filtered array to a selection to create buttons for all the remaining attributes, and give the buttons labels for each of the attributes, as shown in figure 3.3.

The .on function is a wrapper for the traditional HTML mouse events, and accepts "click", "mouseover", "mouseout", and so on. We can also access those same events using .attr, for example, using .attr("onclick", "console.log('click')"), but notice that we're passing a string in the same way we would using traditional HTML. There's a D3-specific reason to use the .on function: it sends the bound data to the function automatically and in the same format as the anonymous inline functions we've been using to set style and attribute.

We can create buttons based on the attributes of the data and dynamically measure the data based on the attribute bound to the button. Then we can resize the circles representing each team to reflect the teams with the highest and lowest values in each category, as shown in figure 3.4.

We can use .on() to tie events to any object, so let's add interactivity to the circles by having them indicate whether teams are in the same FIFA region:

Figure 3.4   Our initial `buttonClick` function resizes the circles based on the numerical value of the associated attribute. The radius of each circle reflects the number of goals scored against each team, kept in the `ga` attribute of each datapoint.

```
teamG.on("mouseover", highlightRegion);
function highlightRegion(d) {
    d3.selectAll("g.overallG").select("circle")
        .style("fill", function(p) {
            return p.region == d.region ? "red" : "gray";
        });
};
```

This time we used d as our variable, which is typical in the examples you'll see online for D3 functionality. As a result, we changed the inline function variable to p, so that it wouldn't conflict. Here you see an "ifsie," which is an inline `if` statement that compares the region of each element in the selection to the region of the element that you moused over, with results like those in figure 3.5.

Restoring the circles to their initial color on `mouseout` is simple enough that the function can be declared inline with the `.on` function:

```
teamG.on("mouseout", function() {
    d3.selectAll("g.overallG").select("circle").style("fill", "pink");
});
```

If you want to define custom event handling, you use `d3.dispatch`, which you'll see in action in chapter 9.

3.2.2   *Graphical transitions*

One of the challenges of highly interactive, graphics-rich web pages is to ensure that the experience of graphical change isn't jarring. The instantaneous change in size or color that we've implemented doesn't just look clumsy, it can actually prevent a reader from understanding the information we're trying to relay. To smooth things out a bit, I'll introduce transitions, which you saw briefly at the end of chapter 1.

Transitions are defined for a selection, and can be set to occur after a certain delay using `delay()` or to occur over a set period of time using `duration()`. We can easily implement a transition in our `buttonClick` function:

Figure 3.5   The effect of our initial `highlightRegion` selects elements with the same region attribute and colors them red, while coloring gray those that aren't in the same region.

```
d3.selectAll("g.overallG").select("circle").transition().duration(1000)
          .attr("r", function(p) {
              return radiusScale(d[datapoint]);
          });
```

Now when we click our buttons, the sizes of the circles change, and the change is also animated. This isn't just for show. We're encoding new data, indicating the change between two datapoints using animation. When there was no animation, the reader had to remember if there was a difference between the ranking in draws and wins for Germany. Now the reader has an animated indication that shows Germany visibly shrink or grow to indicate the difference between these two datapoints.

The use of transitions also allows us to delay the change through the .delay() function. Like the .duration() function, .delay() is set with the wait in milliseconds before implementing the change. Slight delays in the firing of an event from an inter-action can be useful to improve the legibility of information visualization, allowing users a moment to reorient themselves to shift from interaction to reading. But long delays will usually be misinterpreted as poor web performance.

Why else would you delay the firing of an animation? Delays can also draw attention to visual elements when they first appear. By making the elements pulse when they arrive onscreen, you let users know that these are dynamic objects and tempt users to click or otherwise interact with them. Delays, like duration, can be dynamically set based on the bound data for each element. You can use delays with another feature: transition chaining. This sets multiple transitions one after another, and each is activated after the last transition has finished. If we amend the code in overall-TeamViz() that first appends the <circle> elements to our <g> elements, we can see transitions of the kind that produce the screenshot in figure 3.6:

```
teamG
.append("circle").attr("r", 0)
.transition()
.delay(function(d,i) {return i * 100})
.duration(500)
.attr("r", 40)
.transition()
.duration(500)
.attr("r", 20);
```

This causes a pulse because it uses transition chaining to set one transition, followed by a second after the completion of the first. You start by drawing the circles with a

Figure 3.6   A screenshot of your data visualization in the middle of its initial drawing, showing the individual circles growing to an exaggerated size and then shrinking to their final size in the order in which they appear in the bound dataset.

radius of 0, so they're invisible. Each element has a delay set to its array position i times 0.1 seconds (100 ms), after which the transition causes the circle to grow to a radius of 40 px. After each circle grows to that size, a second transition shrinks the circles to 20 px. The effect, which isn't easy to present with a screenshot, causes the circles to pulse sequentially.

3.2.3 *DOM manipulation*

Because these visual elements and buttons are all living in the DOM, it's important to know how to access and work with them both with D3 and using built-in JavaScript functionality.

Although D3 selections are extremely powerful, you sometimes want to deal specifically with the DOM element that's bound to the data. These DOM elements come with a rich set of built-in functionality in JavaScript. Getting access to the actual DOM element in the selection can be accomplished in one of two ways:

1 Using this in the inline functions
2 Using the .node() function

Inline functions always have access to the DOM element along with the datapoint and array position of that datapoint in the bound data. The DOM element, in this case, is represented by this. We can see it in action using the .each() function of a selection, which performs the same code for each element in a selection. We'll make a selection of one of our circles and then use .each() to send d, i, and this to the console to see what each corresponds to (which should look similar to the results in figure 3.7):

```
d3.select("circle").each(function(d,i) {
    console.log(d);console.log(i);console.log(this);
});
```

Unpacking this a bit, we can see the first thing echoed, d, is the data bound to the circle, which is a JSON object representing the Netherlands team. The second thing echoed, i, is the array position of that object in the array we used to create these elements, which in this case is 0 and means that incomingData[0] is the Netherlands JSON object. The last thing echoed to the console, this, is the <circle> DOM element itself.

We can also access this DOM element using the .node() function of a selection:

```
d3.select("circle").node();
```

```
> d3.select("circle").each(function(d,i) {console.log(d);console.log(i);console.log(this)})
  ▶ Object {team: "Netherlands", region: "UEFA", win: "6", loss: "0", draw: "1"…}
  0
  <circle r="20" style="fill: #ffc0cb; stroke: #000000; stroke-width: 1px;"></circle>
```

Figure 3.7   The console results of inspecting a selected element, which show first the datapoint in the selection, then its position in the array, and then the SVG element itself.

```
d3.select("circle").node()
<circle r="20" style="fill: #ffc0cb; stroke: #000000; stroke-width: 1px;"></circle>
```

Figure 3.8   **The results of running the `node` function of a selection in the console, which is the DOM element itself—in this case, an SVG `<circle>` element.**

Getting to the DOM element, as shown in figure 3.8, lets you take advantage of built-in JavaScript functionality to do things like measure the length of a `<path>` element or clone an element. One of the most useful built-in functions of nodes when working with SVG is the ability to re-append a child element. Remember that SVG has no Z-levels, which means that the drawing order of elements is determined by their DOM order. Drawing order is important because you don't want the graphical objects you interact with to look like they're behind the objects that you don't interact with. To see what this means, let's first adjust our highlighting function so that it increases the size of the label when we mouse over each element:

```
function highlightRegion2(d,i) {
    d3.select(this).select("text").classed("active", true).attr("y", 10);
    d3.selectAll("g.overallG").select("circle").each(function(p,i) {
     p.region == d.region ?
        d3.select(this).classed("active",true)  :
        d3.select(this).classed("inactive",true);
   });
};
```

> By turning on "active" class for the `<g>` that we hover over, we take advantage of the "g > text.active" rule in CSS that makes any text elements in that `<g>` increase their font size.

Because we're doing a bit more, we should change the `mouseout` event to point to a function, which we'll call `unHighlight`:

```
teamG.on("mouseout", unHighlight)

function unHighlight() {
 d3.selectAll("g.overallG").select("circle").attr("class", "");
 d3.selectAll("g.overallG").select("text")
.classed("highlight", false).attr("y", 30);
};
```

As shown in figure 3.9, Germany was appended to the DOM before Argentina. As a result, when we increase the size of the graphics associated with Germany, those graphics remain behind any graphics for Argentina, creating a visual artifact that looks unfinished and distracting. We can rectify this by re-appending the node to the parent `<g>` during that same highlighting event, which results in the label being displayed above the other elements, as shown in figure 3.10:

Figure 3.9   **The `<text>` element "Germany" is drawn at the same DOM level as the parent `<g>`, which, in this case, is behind the element to its right.**

Netherlands   Spain   Argentina   Uruguay   Brazil   Ghana   Japan

Figure 3.10   Re-appending the `<g>` element for Germany to the `<svg>` element moves it to the end of that DOM region and therefore it's drawn above the other `<g>` elements.

```
function highlightRegion2(d,i) {
  d3.select(this).select("text").classed("highlight", true).attr("y", 10);
    d3.selectAll("g.overallG").select("circle")
      .each(function(p, i) {
        p.region == d.region ?
            d3.select(this).classed("active", true) :
            d3.select(this).classed("inactive", true);
      });
  this.parentElement.appendChild(this);
};
```

You'll see in this example that the `mouseout` event becomes less intuitive because the event is attached to the `<g>` element, which includes not only the circle but the text as well. As a result, mousing over the circle or the text fires the event. When you increase the size of the text, and it overlaps a neighboring circle, it doesn't trigger a `mouseout` event. We'll get into event propagation later, but one thing we can do to easily disable mouse events on elements is to set the style property `"pointer-events"` of those elements to `"none"`:

```
teamG.select("text").style("pointer-events","none");
```

3.2.4   *Using color wisely*

Color seems like a small and dull subject, but when you're representing data with graphics, color selection is of primary importance. There's a lot of good research on the use of color in cognitive science and design, but that's an entire library. Here, we'll deal with a few fundamental issues: mixing colors in color ramps, using discrete colors for categorical data, and designing for accessibility factors related to colorblindness.

> **Infoviz term: color theory**
>
> Artists, scholars, and psychologists have been thinking critically about the use of color for centuries. Among them, Josef Albers—who has influenced modern information visualization leaders like Edward Tufte—noted that in the visual realm, one plus one can equal three. The study of color, referred to as *color theory*, has proved that placing certain colors and shapes next to each other has optical consequences, resulting in simultaneous and successive contrast as well as accidental color.

(continued)

It's worth studying the properties of color—hue, value, intensity, and temperature—to ensure the most harmonious color relationships in a visualization. Leonardo da Vinci organized colors into psychological primaries, the colors the eye sees unmixed, but the modern exploration of color theory, as with many other phenomena in physics, can be attributed to Sir Isaac Newton. Newton observed the separation of sunlight into bands of color via a prism in 1666 and called it a color spectrum. Newton also devised a color circle of seven hues, a precursor to the many future visualizations that would organize colors and their relationships. About a century later, J. C. Le Blon identified the primary colors as red, yellow, and blue, and their mixes as the secondaries. The work of other more modern color theoreticians like Josef Albers, who emphasized the effects of color juxtaposition, influences the standards for presentation in print and on the web.

Color is typically represented on the web in red, green, and blue, or RGB, using one of three formats: hex, RGB, or CSS color name. The first two represent the same information, the level of red, green, and blue in the color, but do so with either hexadecimal or comma-delimited decimal notation. CSS color names use vernacular names for its 140 colors (you can read all about them at http://en.wikipedia.org/wiki/Web_colors#X11_color_names). Red, for instance, can be represented as

```
"rgb(255,0,0)"
"#ff0000"
"red"
```

RGB, or red-green-blue, encoded color

Hex, or hexadecimal, formatted RGB

CSS3 web color name

D3 has a few helper functions for working with colors. The first is d3.rgb(), which allows us to create a more feature-rich color object suitable for data visualization. To use d3.rgb(), we need to give it the red, green, and blue values of our color:

```
teamColor = d3.rgb("red");
teamColor = d3.rgb("#ff0000");
teamColor = d3.rgb("rgb(255,0,0)");
teamColor = d3.rgb(255,0,0);
```

These color objects have two useful methods, .darker() and .brighter(). They do exactly what you'd expect: return a color that's darker or brighter than the color you started with. In our case, we can replace the gray and red that we've been using to highlight similar teams with darker and brighter versions of pink, the color we started with:

Argentina
Netherlands
Spain
Germany
Uruguay
Brazil
Ghana
Japan

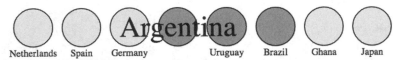

Figure 3.11 Using the darker and brighter functions of a `d3.rgb` object in the highlighting function produces a darker version of the set color for teams from the same region and lighter colors for teams from different regions.

```
function highlightRegion2(d,i) {
 var teamColor = d3.rgb("pink")
 d3.select(this).select("text").classed("highlight", true).attr("y", 10)
 d3.selectAll("g.overallG").select("circle")
       .style("fill", function(p) {return p.region == d.region ?
               teamColor.darker(.75) : teamColor.brighter(.5)})
 this.parentElement.appendChild(this);
}
```

Notice that you can set the intensity for how much brighter or darker you want the color to be. Our new version (shown in figure 3.11) now maintains the palette during highlighting, with darker colors coming to the foreground and lighter colors receding. Unfortunately, you lose the ability to style with CSS because you're back to using inline styles. As a rule, you should use CSS whenever you can, but if you want access to things like dynamic colors and transparency using D3 functions, then you'll need to use inline styling.

You can represent color in other ways with various benefits, but we'll only deal with HSL, which stands for hue, saturation, and lightness. The corresponding `d3.hsl()` allows you to create HSL color objects in the same way that you would with `d3.rgb()`. The reason why you may want to use HSL is to avoid the muddying when you darken pink, which can also happen when you build color ramps and mix colors using D3 functions.

COLOR MIXING

In chapter 2, we mapped a color ramp to numerical data to generate a spectrum of color representing our datapoints. But the interpolated values for colors created by these ramps can be quite poor. As a result, a ramp that includes, say, yellow, can end up interpolating values that are muddy and hard to distinguish. You may think this isn't important, but when you're using a color ramp to indicate a value and your color ramp doesn't interpolate the color in a way that your reader expects, then you can end up showing wrong information to your users. Let's add a color ramp to our `buttonClick` function and use the color ramp to show the same information we did with the radius.

```
var ybRamp = d3.scale.linear()
  .domain([0,maxValue]).range(["yellow", "blue"]);
```

This is the same kind of color ramp we built in chapter 2, using the maxValue we calculated for our circle radius scale.

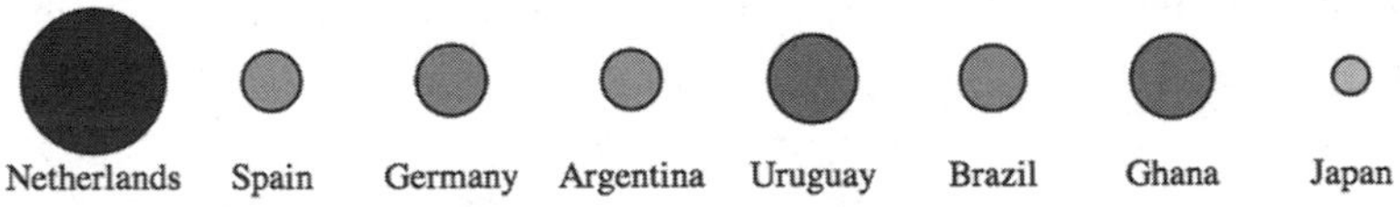
Netherlands
Spain
Germany
Argentina
Uruguay
Brazil
Ghana
Japan

Figure 3.12 Color mixing between yellow and blue in the RGB scale results in muddy, grayish colors displayed for the values between yellow and blue.

Figure 3.13 Interpolation of yellow to blue based on hue, saturation, and lightness (HSL) results in a different set of intermediary colors from the same two starting values.

You'd be forgiven if you expected the colors in figure 3.12 to range from yellow to green to blue. The problem is that the default interpolator in the scale we used is mixing the red, green, and blue channels numerically. We can change the interpolator in the scale by designating one specifically, for instance, using the HSL representation of color (figure 3.13) that we looked at earlier:

```
var ybRamp = d3.scale.linear()
  .interpolate(d3.interpolateHsl)
  .domain([0,maxValue]).range(["yellow", "blue"]);
```

> Setting the interpolation method for a scale is necessary when we don't want it to use its default behavior, such as when we want to create a color scale with a method other than interpolating the RGB values.

D3 supports two other color interpolators, HCL (figure 3.14) and LAB (figure 3.15), which each deal in a different manner with the question of what colors are between blue and yellow. First, the HCL ramp:

```
var ybRamp = d3.scale.linear()
  .interpolate(d3.interpolateHcl)
  .domain([0,maxValue]).range(["yellow", "blue"]);
```

Finally, the LAB ramp:

```
var ybRamp = d3.scale.linear()
  .interpolate(d3.interpolateLab)
  .domain([0,maxValue]).range(["yellow", "blue"]);
```

Figure 3.14 Interpolation of color based on hue, chroma, and luminosity (HCL) provides a different set of intermediary colors between yellow and blue.

Netherlands   Spain   Germany   Argentina   Uruguay   Brazil   Ghana   Japan

Figure 3.15 Interpolation of color based on lightness and color-opponent space (known as LAB; L stands for *lightness* and A-B stands for the color-opponent space) provides yet another set of intermediary colors between yellow and blue.

As a general rule, you'll find that the colors interpolated in RGB tend toward muddy and gray, unless you break the color ramp into multiple stops. You can experiment with different color ramps, or stick to ramps that emphasize hue or saturation (by using HSL). Or you can rely on experts by using the built-in D3 functions for color ramps that are proven to be easier for a reader to distinguish, which we'll look at now.

DISCRETE COLORS

Oftentimes, we use color ramps to try to map colors to categorical elements. It's better to use the discrete color scales available in D3 for this purpose. The popularity of these scales is the reason why so many D3 examples have the same palette. To get started, we need to use a new D3 scale, d3.scale.category10, which is built to map categorical values to particular colors. It works like a quantizing scale where you can't change the domain, because the domain is already defined as 10 highly distinct colors. Instead, you instantiate your scale with the values you want mapped to those colors. In our case, we want to distinguish the various regions in our dataset, which consists of the top eight FIFA teams from the 2010 World Cup, representing four global regions. We want to represent these as different colors, and to do so, we need to create a scale with those values in an array.

```
function buttonClick(datapoint) {
    var maxValue = d3.max(incomingData, function(el) {
        return parseFloat(el[datapoint ]);
    });
    var tenColorScale = d3.scale.category10(
        ["UEFA", "CONMEBOL", "CAF",  "AFC"]);
    var radiusScale = d3.scale.linear().domain([0,maxValue]).range([2,20]);
    d3.selectAll("g.overallG").select("circle").transition().duration(1000)
        .style("fill", function(p) {return tenColorScale(p.region) })
        .attr("r", function(p) {return radiusScale(p[datapoint ])});
};
```

The application of this scale is visible when we click one of our buttons, which now resizes the circles as it always has, but also applies one of these distinct colors to each team (figure 3.16).

COLOR RAMPS FOR NUMERICAL DATA

Another option is to use color schemes based on the work of Cynthia Brewer, who has led the way in defining effective color use in cartography. Helpfully, d3js.org provides

Netherlands   Spain   Germany   Argentina   Uruguay   Brazil   Ghana   Japan

Figure 3.16   Application of the category10 **scale in D3 assigns distinct colors to each class applied, in this case, the four regions in your dataset.**

colorbrewer.js and colorbrewer.css for this purpose. Each array in colorbrewer.js corresponds to one of Brewer's color schemes, designed for a set number of colors. For instance, the reds scale looks like this:

```
Reds: {
3: ["#fee0d2","#fc9272","#de2d26"],
4: ["#fee5d9","#fcae91","#fb6a4a","#cb181d"],
5: ["#fee5d9","#fcae91","#fb6a4a","#de2d26","#a50f15"],
6: ["#fee5d9","#fcbba1","#fc9272","#fb6a4a","#de2d26","#a50f15"],
7: ["#fee5d9","#fcbba1","#fc9272","#fb6a4a","#ef3b2c","#cb181d","#99000d"],
8: ["#fff5f0","#fee0d2","#fcbba1","#fc9272",
    "#fb6a4a","#ef3b2c","#cb181d","#99000d"],
9: ["#fff5f0","#fee0d2","#fcbba1","#fc9272","#fb6a4a",
    "#ef3b2c","#cb181d","#a50f15","#67000d"]
}
```

This provides high-legibility, discrete colors in the red spectrum for our elements. Again, we'll color your circles by region, but this time, we'll color them by their magnitude using our buttonClick function. We need to use the quantize scale that you saw earlier in chapter 2, because the colorbrewer scales, despite being discrete scales, are designed for quantitative data that has been separated into categories. In other words, they're built for numerical data, but numerical data that has been sorted into ranges, such as when you break down all the ages of adults in a census into categories of 18–35, 36–50, 51–65, and 65+.

```
function buttonClick(datapoint) {                              ←——  Our new buttonClick
    var maxValue = d3.max(incomingData, function(el) {               function sorts the circles in
        return parseFloat(el[datapoint]);                            our visualization into three
    });                                                              categories with colors
    var colorQuantize = d3.scale.quantize()                          associated with them.
        .domain([0,maxValue]).range(colorbrewer.Reds[3]);     ←——————
    var radiusScale = d3.scale.linear()
        .domain([0,maxValue]).range([2,20]);
    d3.selectAll("g.overallG").select("circle").transition().duration(1000)
        .style("fill", function(p) {
            return colorQuantize(p[datapoint]);
        }).attr("r", function(p) {
            return radiusScale(p[datapoint]);
        });
};
```

The quantize scale sorts the numerical data into as many categories as there are in the range. Because colorbrewer.Reds[3] is an array of three values, the dataset is sorted into three discrete categories, and each category has a different shade of red assigned.

One of the conveniences of using colorbrewer.js dynamically paired to a quantizing scale is that if we adjust the number of colors, for instance, from colorbrewer.Reds[3] (shown in figure 3.17) to colorbrewer.Reds[5], the range of numerical data is represented with five colors instead of three.

Figure 3.17   Automatic quantizing linked with the ColorBrewer 3-red scale produces distinct visual categories in the red family. 🖼

```
function buttonClick(datapoint) {
    var maxValue = d3.max(incomingData, function(el) {
            return parseFloat(el[datapoint ]);
        });
    var colorQuantize = d3.scale.quantize()
            .domain([0,maxValue]).range(colorbrewer.Reds[3]);
    var radiusScale = d3.scale.linear()
            .domain([0,maxValue]).range([2,20]);
        d3.selectAll("g.overallG").select("circle").transition()
            .duration(1000).style("fill", function(p) {
            return colorQuantize(p[datapoint ]);
        }).attr("r", function(p) {
            return radiusScale(p[datapoint ]);
        });
};
```

Color is important, and it can behave strangely on the web. Colorblindness, for instance, is a key accessibility issue that most of the colorbrewer scales address. But even though color use and deployment is complex, smart people have been thinking about color for a while, and D3 takes advantage of that.

3.3   Pregenerated content

It's neither fun nor smart to create all your HTML elements using D3 syntax with nested selections and appending. More importantly, there's an entire ecosystem of tools out there for creating HTML, SVG, and static images that you'd be foolish to ignore just because you're using D3 for your general DOM manipulation and information visualization. Fortunately, it's straightforward and easy to load externally generated resources—like images, HTML fragments, and pregenerated SVG—and tie them into your graphical elements.

3.3.1   Images

In chapter 1, I noted that GIFs, despite their resurgent popularity, aren't useful for a rich interactive site. But that doesn't mean you should get rid of images entirely. You'll find that adding images to your data visualizations can vastly improve them. In SVG, the image element is <image>, and its source is defined using the xlink:href attribute if it's located in your directory structure.

We have files in our images directory that are PNGs of the respective flags of each national team. To add them to our data visualization, select the <g> elements that have the team data already bound to them, and add an SVG image:

Figure 3.18 Our graphical representations of each team now include a small PNG national flag, downloaded from Wikipedia and loaded using an SVG `<image>` element.

```
d3.selectAll("g.overallG").insert("image", "text")
  .attr("xlink:href", function(d) {
      return "images/" + d.team + ".png";
  })
  .attr("width", "45px").attr("height", "20px").attr("x", "-22")
  .attr("y", "-10");
```

To make the images show up successfully, use `insert()` instead of `append()` because that gives us the capacity to tell D3 to insert the images before the text elements. This keeps the labels from being drawn behind the newly added images. Because each image name is the same as the team name of each data point, we can use an inline function to point to that value, combined with strings for the directory and file extension. We also need to define the height and width of the images because SVG images, by default, have no setting for height and width and won't display until these are set. We also need to manually center SVG images—here the x and y attributes are set to a negative value of one-half the respective height and width, which centers the images in their respective circles, as shown in figure 3.18.

You can tie image resizing to the button events, but raster images don't resize particularly well, and so you'll want to use them at fixed sizes.

Infoviz term: chartjunk

Now that you're learning how to add images and icons to everything, let's remember that just because you *can* do something doesn't mean you *should*. When building information visualization, the key aesthetic principle is to avoid cluttering your charts and interfaces with distracting and useless "chartjunk" like unnecessary icons, decoration, or skeuomorphic paneling. Remember, simplicity is force.

The term *chartjunk* comes from Tufte, and in general refers to the kind of generic and useless clip art that typifies PowerPoint presentations. Although icons and images are useful and powerful in many situations, and thus shouldn't be avoided just to maintain an austere appearance, you should always make sure that your graphical representations of data are as uncluttered as you can make them.

3.3.2 *HTML fragments*

We've created traditional DOM elements in this chapter using D3 data-binding for our buttons. If you want to, you can use the D3 pattern of selecting and appending to create complex HTML objects, such as forms and tables, on the fly. But HTML has better authoring tools, and you'll likely be working with designers and other developers who want to use those tools and require that those HTML components be included in your application. For instance, let's build a modal dialog box into which we can put the numbers associated with the teams. Say we want to see the stats on our teams—one of the best ways to do this is to build a dialog box that pops up as you click each team. A modal dialog is another way of referring to that "floating" area that typically only shows up when you click an element. We can write only the HTML we need for the table itself in a separate file.

Listing 3.4 modal.html

```
<table>
    <tr>
        <th>Statistics</th>
    </tr>
    <tr><td>Team Name</td><td class="data"></td></tr>
    <tr><td>Region</td><td class="data"></td></tr>
    <tr><td>Wins</td><td class="data"></td></tr>
    <tr><td>Losses</td><td class="data"></td></tr>
    <tr><td>Draws</td><td class="data"></td></tr>
    <tr><td>Points</td><td class="data"></td></tr>
    <tr><td>Goals For</td><td class="data"></td></tr>
    <tr><td>Goals Against</td><td class="data"></td></tr>
    <tr><td>Clean Sheets</td><td class="data"></td></tr>
    <tr><td>Yellow Cards</td><td class="data"></td></tr>
    <tr><td>Red Cards</td><td class="data"></td></tr>
</table>
```

And now we'll add CSS rules for the table and the div that we want to put it in. As you see in the following listing, we can use the `position` and `z-index` CSS styles because this is a traditional DOM element.

Listing 3.5 Update to d3ia.css

```
#modal {
  position:fixed;
  left:150px;
  top:20px;
  z-index:1;
  background: white;
  border: 1px black solid;
  box-shadow: 10px 10px 5px #888888;
}

tr {
  border: 1px gray solid;
}

td {
  font-size: 10px;
}
td.data {
  font-weight: 900;
}
```

Now that we have the table, all we need to do is add a click listener and associated function to populate this dialog, as well as a function to create a div with ID `"modal"` into which we add the loaded HTML code using the `.html()` function:

```
d3.text("resources/modal.html", function(data) {
    d3.select("body").append("div").attr("id", "modal").html(data);
});

teamG.on("click", teamClick);

function teamClick(d) {
    d3.selectAll("td.data").data(d3.values(d))
        .html(function(p) {
            return p
        });
};
```

Creates a new div with an id corresponding to one in our CSS, and populates it with HTML content from modal.html

Selects and updates the td.data elements with the values of the team clicked

The results are immediately apparent when you reload the page. A div with the defined table in modal.html is created, and when you click it, it populates the div with values from the data bound to the element you click (figure 3.19).

We used `d3.text()` in this case because when working with HTML, it can be more convenient to load the raw HTML code like this and drop it into the `.html()` function of a selected element that you've created. If you use `d3.html()`, then you get HTML nodes that allow you to do more sophisticated manipulation, which you'll see now as we work with pregenerated SVG.

Statistics

Team Name	Germany
Region	UEFA
Wins	5
Losses	0
Draws	2
Points	15
Goals For	16
Goals Against	5
Clean Sheets	3
Yellow Cards	10
Red Cards	1

Netherlands   Spain   Germany   Argentina   Uruguay   Brazil   Ghana   Japan

Figure 3.19 The modal dialog is styled based on the defined style in CSS. It's created by loading the HTML data from modal.html and adding it to the content of a newly created div.

3.3.3   *Pregenerated SVG*

SVG has been around for a while, and there are, not surprisingly, robust tools for drawing SVG, like Adobe Illustrator and the open source tool Inkscape. You'll likely want pregenerated SVG for icons, interface elements, and other components of your work. If you're interested in icons, The Noun Project (http://thenounproject.com/) has an extensive repository of SVG icons, including the football in figure 3.20.

When you download an icon from The Noun Project, you get it in two forms: SVG and PNG. You've already learned how to reference images, and you can do the same with SVG by pointing the `xlink:href` attribute of an `<image>` element at an SVG file. But loading SVG directly into the DOM gives you the capacity to manipulate it like any SVG elements that you create in the browser with D3.

Let's say we decide to replace our boring circles with balls, and we don't want them to be static images because we want to be able to modify their color and shape like other SVG. In that case, we'll need to find a suitable ball icon and download it. In the case of downloads from The Noun Project, this means we'll need to go through the hassle of creating an account, and we'll need to properly attribute the creator of the icon or pay a fee to use the icon without attribution. Regardless of where we get our icon, we might need to modify it before using it in our data visualization. In the case of the football icon in this example, we need to make it smaller and center the icon on the 0,0 point of the canvas. This kind of preparation is going to be different for every icon, depending on how it was originally drawn and saved.

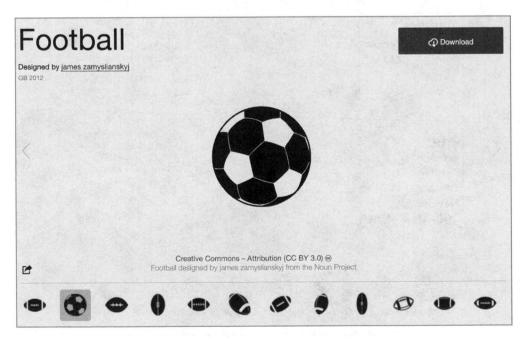

Figure 3.20   An icon for a football created by James Zamyslianskyj and available at http://thenounproject.com/term/football/1907/ from The Noun Project

What we don't want

```
d3.html("resources/icon_1907.svg", function(data) {console.log(data)})
▶ Object {header: function, mimeType: function, responseType: function, response: function, get: function…}
▼ #document-fragment
    <!--?xml version="1.0" encoding="UTF-8" standalone="no"?-->
    ▼ <svg xmlns:dc="http://purl.org/dc/elements/1.1/" xmlns:cc="http://creativecommons.org/ns#" xmlns:rdf=
    "http://www.w3.org/1999/02/22-rdf-syntax-ns#" xmlns:svg="http://www.w3.org/2000/svg" xmlns="http://
    www.w3.org/2000/svg" xmlns:sodipodi="http://sodipodi.sourceforge.net/DTD/sodipodi-0.dtd" xmlns:inkscape=
    "http://www.inkscape.org/namespaces/inkscape" version="1.1" id="Layer_1" x="0px" y="0px" width="100px"
    height="100px" viewBox="0 0 100 100" enable-background="new 0 0 100 100" xml:space="preserve"
    inkscape:version="0.48.2 r9819" sodipodi:docname="icon_1907.svg">
        ▶ <metadata id="metadata73">…</metadata>
        ▶ <defs id="defs71">…</defs>
        <sodipodi:namedview pagecolor="#ffffff" bordercolor="#666666" borderopacity="1" objecttolerance="10"
        gridtolerance="10" guidetolerance="10" inkscape:pageopacity="0" inkscape:pageshadow="2"
        inkscape:window-width="640" inkscape:window-height="480" id="namedview69" showgrid="false"
        inkscape:zoom="2.36" inkscape:cx="50" inkscape:cy="50" inkscape:window-x="0" inkscape:window-y="0"
        inkscape:window-maximized="0" inkscape:current-layer="Layer_1"></sodipodi:namedview>
        <path style="fill-rule:evenodd" inkscape:connector-curvature="0" id="path5" d="m
        -3.1794292,-0.14033119 c -1.445234,-0.432404 -2.9165745,-0.838956 -4.5159127,-1.11750901
        -0.3325407,-1.082785 -0.5479824,-2.1754549 -0.670404,-3.4430128 -0.038273,-0.4030028
        -0.1287581,-0.9289341 -0.044609,-1.2969593 0.11938,-0.5213691 1.3017751,-1.636597 1.6989483,-2.0119726
        0.7728022,-0.7307277 1.4472617,-1.0977391 2.2365389,-1.4307867 0.5936054,-0.2509263 2.0094374,-7.604e-
        4 2.7272394,0.1789434 0.770521,0.1926303 1.434081,0.4972903 1.966856,0.8496009 0.211387,1.0277839
        0.342172,2.102965 0.49222099,3.2638159 0.04537,0.3548452 0.187054,0.8338863 0.133574,1.1180159
        -0.06641,0.3561126 -0.69448299,0.6970175 -1.02829099,0.9836817 -1.057945,0.9078966 -2.123242,1.9285836
        -2.9961608,2.90618261 z" clip-rule="evenodd"></path>
        <path style="fill:#000000" inkscape:connector-curvature="0" id="path7" d="m -3.1786689,-0.13754359
        -0.00152,-2.53e-4 c -1.3752795,-0.4411357 -2.8739937,-0.831606 -4.511153,-1.11750901
        -0.3386237,-1.0977396 -0.5520378,-2.1919302 -0.6726852,-3.4452943 -0.00735,-0.078066
        -0.016982 -0.1612011 -0.026613 -0.246364 -0.0403 -0.3538314 -0.086177 -0.7545531 -0.018249 -1.0513558
```

What we want

Figure 3.21 **An SVG loaded using d3.html() that was created in Inkscape. It consists not only of the graphical <path> elements that make up the SVG but also much data that's often extraneous.**

With the modal table we used earlier, we assumed that we pulled in all the code found in modal.html, and so we could bring it in using d3.text() and drop the raw HTML as text into the .html() function of a selection. But in the case of SVG, especially SVG that you've downloaded, you often want to ignore the verbose settings in the document, which will include its own <svg> canvas as well as any <g> elements that have been not-so-helpfully added. You probably want to deal only with the graphical elements. With our soccer ball, we want to get only the <path> elements. If we load the file using d3.html(), then the results are DOM nodes loaded into a document fragment that we can access and move around using D3 selection syntax. Using d3.html() is the same as using any of the other loading functions, where you designate the file to be loaded and the callback. You can see the results of this command in figure 3.21:

```
d3.html("resources/icon_1907.svg", function(data) {console.log(data);});
```

After we load the SVG into the fragment, we can loop through the fragment to get all the paths easily using the .empty() function of a selection. The .empty() function checks to see if a selection still has any elements inside it and eventually fires true after we've moved the paths out of the fragment into our main SVG. By including .empty() in a while statement, we can move all the path elements out of the document fragment and load them directly onto the SVG canvas.

```
d3.html("resources/icon_1907.svg", loadSVG);
function loadSVG(svgData) {
 while(!d3.select(svgData).selectAll("path").empty()) {
```

The data variable will automatically be passed to loadSVG().

```
    d3.select("svg").node().appendChild(
        d3.select(svgData).select("path").node());
    }
    d3.selectAll("path").attr("transform", "translate(50,50)");
};
```

Notice how we've added a transform attribute to offset the paths so that they won't be clipped in the top-right corner. Instead, you clearly see a football in the top corner of your `<svg>` canvas. Document fragments aren't a normal part of your DOM, so you don't have to worry about accidentally selecting the `<svg>` canvas in the document fragment, or any other elements.

A while loop like this is sometimes necessary, but typically the best and most efficient method is to use `.each()` with your selection. Remember, `.each()` runs the same code on every element of a selection. In this case, we want to select our `<svg>` canvas and append the path to that canvas.

```
function loadSVG(svgData) {
    d3.select(svgData).selectAll("path").each(function() {
        d3.select("svg").node().appendChild(this);
    });
    d3.selectAll("path").attr("transform", "translate(50,50)");
};
```

We end up with a football floating in the top-left corner of our canvas, as shown in figure 3.22.

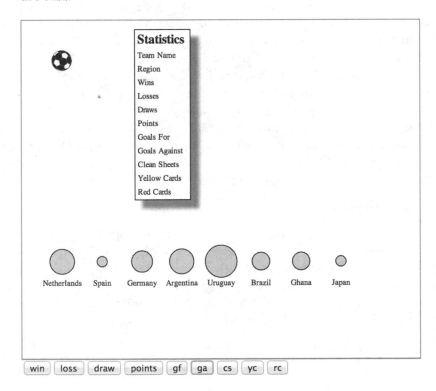

Figure 3.22
A hand-drawn football icon is loaded onto the `<svg>` canvas, along with the other SVG and HTML elements we created in our code.

Netherlands
Spain
Germany
Argentina
Uruguay
Brazil
Ghana
Japan

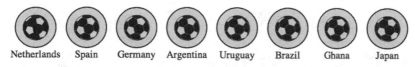

Figure 3.23 Each <g> element has its own set of paths cloned as child nodes, resulting in football icons overlaid on each element.

Loading elements from external data sources like this is useful if you want to move individual nodes out of your loaded document fragment, but if you want to bind the externally loaded SVG elements to data, it's an added step that you can skip. We can't set the `.html()` of a `<g>` element to the text of our incoming elements like we did with the `<div>` when we populated it with the contents of modal.html. That's because SVG doesn't have a corresponding property to innerHTML, and therefore the `.html()` function on a selection of SVG elements has no effect. Instead, we have to clone the paths and append them to each `<g>` element representing our teams:

```
d3.html("resources/icon_1907.svg", loadSVG);
function loadSVG(svgData) {
    d3.selectAll("g").each(function() {
    var gParent = this;
    d3.select(svgData).selectAll("path").each(function() {
          gParent.appendChild(this.cloneNode(true))
      });
    });
};
```

It may seem backwards to select each `<g>` and then select each loaded `<path>`, until you think about how `.cloneNode()` and `.appendChild()` work. We need to take each `<g>` element and go through the `<path>`-cloning process for every path in the loaded icon, which means we use nested `.each()` statements (one for each `<g>` element in our DOM and one for each `<path>` element in the icon). By setting `gParent` to the actual `<g>` node (the `this` variable), we can then append a cloned version of each path in order. The results are soccer balls for each team, as shown in figure 3.23.

We can easily do the same thing using the `<image>` syntax from the first example in this section, but with our SVG elements individually added to each. And now we can style them in the same way as any path element. We could use the national colors for each ball, but we'll settle for making them red, with the results shown in figure 3.24.

```
d3.selectAll("path").style("fill", "darkred")
.style("stroke", "black").style("stroke-width", "1px");
```

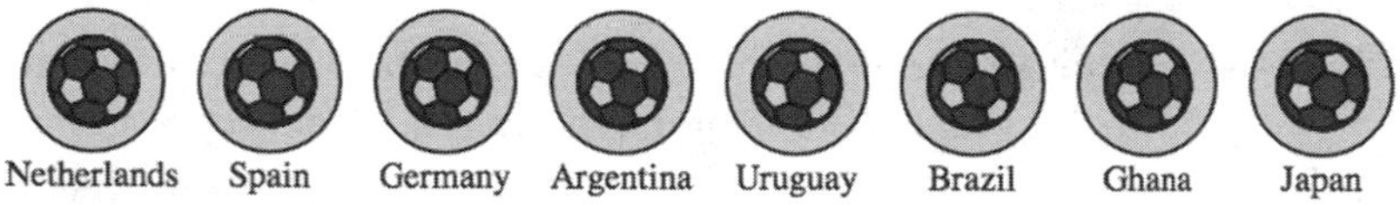

Netherlands
Spain
Germany
Argentina
Uruguay
Brazil
Ghana
Japan

Figure 3.24 Football icons with a fill and stroke set by D3

Figure 3.25   The paths now have the data from their parent element bound to them and respond accordingly when a discrete color scale based on region is applied.

One drawback with this method is that the paths can't take advantage of the D3 .insert() method's ability to place the elements behind the labels or other visual elements. To get around this, we'll need to either append icons to <g> elements that have been placed in the proper order, or use the parentNode and appendChild functions to move the paths around the DOM like we described earlier in this chapter.

The other drawback is that because these paths were added using cloneNode and not selection#append syntax, they have no data bound to them. We looked at rebinding data back in chapter 1. If we select the <g> elements and then select the <path> element, this will rebind data. But we have numerous <path> elements under each <g> element, and selectAll doesn't rebind data. As a result, we have to take a more involved approach to bind the data from the parent <g> elements to the child <path> elements that have been loaded in this manner. The first thing we do is select all the <g> elements and then use .each() to select all the path elements under each <g>. Then, we separately bind the data from the <g> to each <path> using .datum(). What's .datum()? Well, datum is the singular of data, so a piece of data is a datum. The datum function is what you use when you're binding just one piece of data to an element. It's the equivalent of wrapping your variable in an array and binding it to .data(). After we perform this action, we can dust off our old scale from earlier and apply it to our new <path> elements. We can run this code in the console to see the effects, which should look like figure 3.25.

```
d3.selectAll("g.overallG").each(function(d) {
    d3.select(this).selectAll("path").datum(d)
});

var tenColorScale = d3.scale
    .category10(["UEFA", "CONMEBOL", "CAF", "AFC"]);

d3.selectAll("path").style("fill", function(p) {
    return tenColorScale(p.region)
}).style("stroke", "black").style("stroke-width", "2px");
```

Now you have data-driven icons. Use them wisely.

3.4   Summary

Throughout this chapter, we dealt with methods and functionality that typically are glossed over in D3 tutorials, such as the color functions and loading external content like external SVG and HTML. We also saw common D3 functionality, like animated transitions tied to mouse events. Specifically, we covered

- Planning project file structure and placing your D3 code in the context of traditional web development
- External libraries you want to be aware of for D3 applications
- Using transitions and animation to highlight change and interaction
- Creating event listeners for mouse events on buttons and graphical elements
- Using color effectively for categories and numerical data, and being aware of how color is treated in interpolations
- Accessing the DOM element itself from a selection
- Loading external resources, specifically images, HTML fragments, and pregenerated SVG

D3 is a powerful library that can handle much of the needs of an interactive site, but you need to know when to rely on core HTML5 functionality or other libraries when that would be more efficient. Moving forward, we'll transition from the core functions of D3 and get into the higher-level features of the library that allow you to build fully functional charts and chart components. We'll start in the next chapter by looking at generating SVG lines and areas from data as well as preformatted axis components for your charts. We'll also go into more detail about creating complex multipart graphical objects from your data and use those techniques to produce complex examples of information visualization.

Part 2

The pillars of information visualization

The next five chapters provide an exhaustive look into the layouts, components, behaviors, and controls that D3 provides to create the varieties of data visualization you've seen all over the web. In chapter 4 you'll learn how to create line and area charts, deploying D3 axes to make them readable, as well as how to build complex multipart boxplots that encode several different data variables at the same time. Chapter 5 walks through seven different D3 layouts, from the simple pie chart to the exotic Sankey diagram, and shows you how to implement each layout in a few different ways. Chapter 6 focuses entirely on representing network structures, showing you how to visualize them using arc diagrams, adjacency matrices, and force-directed layouts, and introduces several new techniques like SVG markers. Chapter 7 also focuses on a single domain, this time geospatial data, and demonstrates how to leverage D3's incredible geospatial functionality to build different kinds of maps. Chapter 8 shifts to creating more traditional DOM elements using D3 data-binding that result in a spreadsheet and simple image gallery. Whether you're interested in all of these areas or diving deeply into just one, part 2 provides you with the tools to represent any kind of data using advanced data visualization not available in standard charting libraries and applications.

Chart components 4

This chapter covers

- Creating and formatting axis components
- Using line and area generators for charts
- Creating complex shapes consisting of multiple types of SVG elements

D3 provides an enormous library of examples of charts, and GitHub is also packed with implementations. It's easy to format your data to match the existing data used in an implementation and, voilà, you have a chart. Likewise, D3 includes layouts that allow you to create complex data visualizations from a properly formatted dataset. But before you get started with default layouts—which allow you to create basic charts like pie charts, as well as more exotic charts—you should first understand the basics of creating the elements that typically make up a chart and in the process produce charts like those seen in figure 4.1. This chapter focuses on widely used pieces of charts created with D3, such as a labeled axis or a line. It also touches on the formatting, data modeling, and analytical methods most closely tied to creating charts.

Obviously, this isn't your first exposure to charts, because you created a scatterplot and bar chart in chapter 2. This chapter introduces you to components and

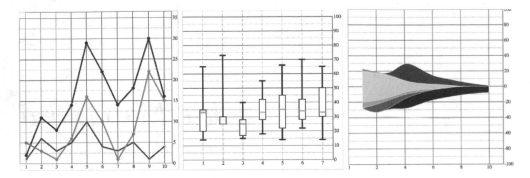

Figure 4.1   The charts we'll create in this chapter using D3 generators and components. From left to right: a line chart, a boxplot, and a streamgraph.

generators. A D3 component, like an axis, is a function for drawing all the graphical elements necessary for an axis. A generator, like `d3.svg.line()`, lets you draw a straight or curved line across many points. The chapter begins by showing you how to add axes to scatterplots as well as create line charts, but before the end you'll create an exotic yet simple chart: the streamgraph. By understanding how D3 generators and components work, you'll be able do more than re-create the charts that other people have made and posted online (many of which they're just re-creating from somewhere else).

A chart (and notice here that I don't use the term *graph* because that's a synonym for *network*) refers to any flat layout of data in a graphical manner. The datapoints, which can be individual values or objects in arrays, may contain categorical, quantitative, topological, or unstructured data. In this chapter we'll use several datasets to create the charts shown in figure 4.1. Although it may seem more useful to use a single dataset for the various charts, as the old saying goes, "Horses for courses," which is to say that different charts are more suitable to different kinds of datasets, as you'll see in this chapter.

4.1   *General charting principles*

All charts consist of several graphical elements that are drawn or derived from the dataset being represented. These graphical elements may be graphical primitives, like circles or rectangles, or more-complex, multipart, graphical objects like the boxplots we'll look at later in the chapter. Or they may be supplemental pieces like axes and labels. Although you use the same general processes you explored in previous chapters to create any of these elements in D3, it's important to differentiate between the methods available in D3 to create graphics for charts.

You've learned how to directly create simple and complex elements with data-binding. You've also learned how to measure your data and transform it for display. Along with these two types of functions, D3 functionality can be placed into three broader categories: generators, components, and layouts, which are shown in figure 4.2 along with a general overview of how they're used.

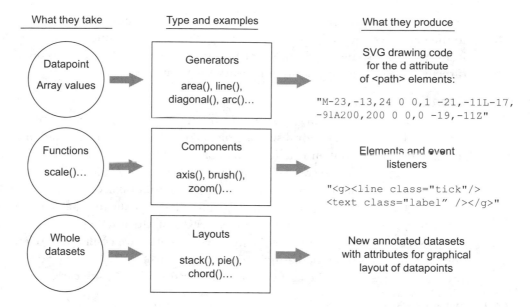

Figure 4.2 The three main types of functions found in D3 can be classified as generators, components, and layouts. You'll see components and generators in this chapter and layouts in the next chapter.

4.1.1 Generators

D3 generators consist of functions that take data and return the necessary SVG drawing code to create a graphical object based on that data. For instance, if you have an array of points and you want to draw a line from one point to another, or turn it into a polygon or an area, a few D3 functions can help you with this process. These generators simplify the process of creating a complex SVG <path> by abstracting the process needed to write a <path> d attribute. In this chapter, we'll look at d3.svg.line and d3.svg.area, and in the next chapter you'll see d3.svg.arc, which is used to create the pie pieces of pie charts. Another generator that you'll see in chapter 5 is d3.svg.diagonal, used for drawing curved connecting lines in dendrograms.

4.1.2 Components

In contrast with generators, which produce the d attribute string necessary for a <path> element, components create an entire set of graphical objects necessary for a particular chart component. The most commonly used D3 component (which you'll see in this chapter) is d3.svg.axis, which creates a bunch of <line>, <path>, <g>, and <text> elements that are needed for an axis based on the scale and settings you provide the function. Another component is d3.svg.brush (which you'll see later), which creates all the graphical elements necessary for a brush selector.

4.1.3 Layouts

In contrast to generators and components, D3 layouts can be rather straightforward, like the pie chart layout, or complex, like a force-directed network layout. Layouts take in one or more arrays of data, and sometimes generators, and append attributes to the data necessary to draw it in certain positions or sizes, either statically or dynamically. You'll see some of the simpler layouts in chapter 5, and then focus on the force-directed network layout and other network layouts in chapter 6.

4.2   *Creating an axis*

Scatterplots, which you worked with in chapters 1 and 2, are a simple and extremely effective charting method for displaying data. For most charts, the x position is a point in time and the y position is magnitude. For example, in chapter 2 you placed your tweets along the x-axis according to when the tweets were made and along the y-axis according to their impact factor. In contrast, a scatterplot places a single symbol on a chart with its xy position determined by quantitative data for that datapoint. For instance, you can place a tweet on the y-axis based on the number of favorites and on the x-axis based on the number of retweets. Scatterplots are common in scientific discourse and have grown increasingly common in journalism and public discourse for presenting data such as the cost compared to the quality of health care.

4.2.1   *Plotting data*

Scatterplots require multidimensional data. Each datapoint needs to have more than one piece of data connected with it, and for a scatterplot that data must be numerical. You need only an array of data with two different numerical values for a scatterplot to work. We'll use an array where every object represents a person for whom we know the number of friends they have and the amount of money they make. We can see if having more or less friends positively correlates to a high salary.

```
var scatterData = [{friends: 5, salary: 22000},
{friends: 3, salary: 18000}, {friends: 10, salary: 88000},
{friends: 0, salary: 180000}, {friends: 27, salary: 56000},
{friends: 8, salary: 74000}];
```

If you think these salary numbers are too high or too low, pretend they're in a foreign currency with an exchange rate that would make them more reasonable.

Representing this data graphically using circles is easy. You've done it several times:

```
d3.select("svg").selectAll("circle")
    .data(scatterData).enter()
    .append("circle").attr("r", 5).attr("cx", function(d,i) {
        return i * 10;
    }).attr("cy", function(d) {
        return d.friends;
    });
```

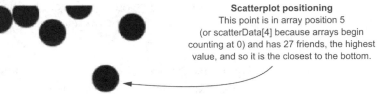

Scatterplot positioning
This point is in array position 5 (or scatterData[4] because arrays begin counting at 0) and has 27 friends, the highest value, and so it is the closest to the bottom.

Figure 4.3   Circle positions indicate the number of friends and the array position of each datapoint.

By designating d.friends for the cy position, we get circles placed with their depth based on the value of the friends attribute. Circles placed lower in the chart represent people in our dataset who have more friends. Circles are arranged from left to right using the old array-position trick you learned earlier in chapter 2. In figure 4.3, you can see that it's not much of a scatterplot.

Next, we need to build scales to make this fit better on our SVG canvas:

```
var xExtent = d3.extent(scatterData, function(d) {
            return d.salary;
        });
var yExtent = d3.extent(scatterData, function(d) {
            return d.friends;
        });
var xScale = d3.scale.linear().domain(xExtent).range([0,500]);
var yScale = d3.scale.linear().domain(yExtent).range([0,500]);
d3.select("svg").selectAll("circle")
        .data(scatterData).enter().append("circle")
        .attr("r", 5).attr("cx", function(d) {
            return xScale(d.salary);
        }).attr("cy", function(d) {
            return yScale(d.friends);
        });
```

The result, in figure 4.4, is a true scatterplot, with points representing people arranged by number of friends along the y-axis and amount of salary along the x-axis.

This chart, like most charts, is practically useless without a way of expressing to the reader what the position of the elements means. One way of accomplishing this is using well-formatted axis labels. Although we could use the same method for binding data and appending elements to create lines and ticks (which are just lines representing equidistant points along an axis) and labels for an axis, D3 provides d3.svg.axis(), which we can use to create these elements based on the scales we used to display the data. After we create an axis function, we define how we want our axis to appear. Then

Figure 4.4 Any point closer to the bottom has more friends, and any point closer to the right has a higher salary. But that's not clear at all without labels, which we're going to make.

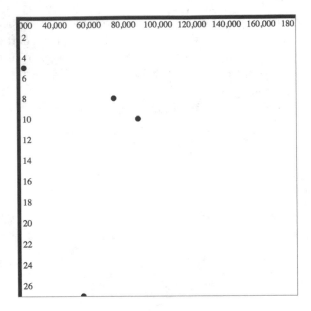

Figure 4.5 The same scatterplot from figure 4.4, but with a pair of labeled axes. The x-axis is drawn in such a way as to obscure one of the points.

we can draw the axis via a selection's .call() method from a selection on a <g> element where we want these graphical elements to be drawn.

```
var yAxis = d3.svg.axis().scale(yScale).orient("right");
d3.select("svg").append("g").attr("id", "yAxisG").call(yAxis);
var xAxis = d3.svg.axis().scale(xScale).orient("bottom");
d3.select("svg").append("g").attr("id", "xAxisG").call(xAxis);
```

Notice that the .call() method of a selection invokes a function with the selection that's active in the method chain, and is the equivalent of writing

```
xAxis(d3.select("svg").append("g").attr("id", "xAxisG"));
```

Figure 4.5 shows a result that's more legible, with the xy positions of the circles denoted by labels in a pair of axes. The labels are derived from the scales that we used to create each axis, and provide the context necessary to interpret this chart.

The axis lines are thick enough to overlap with one of our scatterplot points because the domain of the axis being drawn is a path. Recall from chapter 3 that paths are by default filled in black. We can adjust the display by setting the fill style of those two axis domain paths to "none". Doing so reveals that the ticks for the axes aren't being drawn, because those elements don't have default "stroke" styles applied.

Figure 4.6 demonstrates why we don't see any of our ticks and why we have thick black regions for our axis domains. To improve our axes, we need to style them properly.

4.2.2 *Styling axes*

These elements are standard SVG elements created by the axis function, and they don't have any more or less formatting than any other elements would when first created.

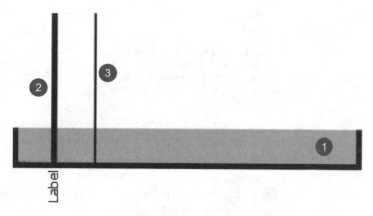

Figure 4.6 Elements of an axis created from `d3.svg.axis` are ① a `<path.domain>` with a size equal to the extent of the axis, ② a `<g.tick.major>` that contains a `<line>` and a `<text>` for each major tick, and ③ a `<line.tick.minor>` for each minor tick (this will only be the case when using the deprecated `tickSubdivide` function in D3 version 3.2 and earlier). Not shown, and invisible, is the `<g>` element that's called and in which these elements are created. In our example, region 1 is filled with black and none of the lines have strokes, because that's the default way that SVG draws `<line>` and `<path>` elements.

This may seem counterintuitive, but SVG is meant to be paired with CSS, so it's better that elements don't have any "helpful" styles assigned to them, or you'd have a hard time overwriting those styles with your CSS. For now, we can set the domain path to `fill:none` and the lines to `stroke: black` using `d3.select()` and `.style()` to see what we're missing, as shown in figure 4.7.

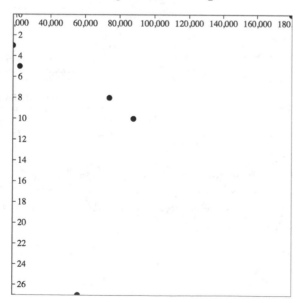

Figure 4.7 If we change the `<path.domain>` fill value to `"none"` and set its and the `<line>` stroke values to `"black"`, we see the ticks and the stroke of `<path.domain>`. It also reveals our hidden datapoint.

```
d3.selectAll("path.domain").style("fill", "none").style("stroke", "black");
d3.selectAll("line").style("stroke", "black");
```

We'll want to be more specific in the future ("line.tick"), because it's likely that whatever we're working on will have more lines than those used in our axes.

We use selectAll because there are two of these paths, one for each axis we called.

If we set the .orient() option of the y-axis to "left" or the .orient() option of the x-axis to "top", is seems like they aren't drawn. This is because they're drawn outside the canvas, like our earlier rectangles. To move our axes around, we need to adjust the .attr("translate") of their parent <g> elements, either when we draw them or later. This is why it's important to assign an ID to our elements when we append them to the canvas. We can move the x-axis to the bottom of this drawing easily:

```
d3.selectAll("#xAxisG").attr("transform","translate(0,500)");
```

Here's our updated code. It uses the .tickSize() function to change the ticks to lines and manually sets the number of ticks using the ticks() function:

```
var scatterData = [{friends: 5, salary: 22000},
        {friends: 3, salary: 18000}, {friends: 10, salary: 88000},
        {friends: 0, salary: 180000}, {friends: 27, salary: 56000},
        {friends: 8, salary: 74000}];

var xScale = d3.scale.linear().domain([0,180000]).range([0,500]);
var yScale = d3.scale.linear().domain([0,27]).range([0,500]);

xAxis = d3.svg.axis().scale(xScale)
        .orient("bottom").tickSize(500).ticks(4);
d3.select("svg").append("g").attr("id", "xAxisG").call(xAxis);

yAxis = d3.svg.axis().scale(yScale)
        .orient("right").ticks(16).tickSize(500);
d3.select("svg").append("g").attr("id", "yAxisG").call(yAxis);

d3.select("svg").selectAll("circle")
        .data(scatterData).enter()
        .append("circle").attr("r", 5)
        .attr("cx", function(d) {return xScale(d.salary);})
        .attr("cy", function(d) {return yScale(d.friends);});
```

Creates a pair of scales to map the values in our dataset to the canvas

Uses method chaining to create an axis and explicitly set its orientation, tick size, and number of ticks

Appends a <g> element to the canvas, and calls the axis from that <g> to create the necessary graphics for the axis

The effect all these functions is uninspiring, as shown in figure 4.8.

Let's examine the elements created by the axis code and shown in figure 4.8 as a giant black square. The <g> element that we created with the ID of "xAxisG" contains <g> elements that each have a line and text:

```
<g class="tick major" transform="translate(0,0)" style="opacity: 1;">
    <line x2="6" y2="0"></line>
    <text x="9" y="0" dy=".32em" style="text-anchor: start;">0</text>
</g>
```

Figure 4.8 Setting axis ticks to the size of your canvas also sets `<path.domain>` to the size of your canvas. Because paths are, by default, filled with black, the result is illegible.

Notice that the `<g>` element has been created with classes, so we can style the child elements (our line and our label) using CSS, or select them with D3. This is necessary if we want our axes to be displayed properly, with lines corresponding to the labeled points. Why? Because along with lines and labels, the axis code has drawn the `<path.domain>` to cover the entire region contained by the axis elements. This domain element needs to be set to `"fill: none"`, or we'll end up with a big black square. You'll also see examples where the tick lines are drawn with negative lengths to create a slightly different visual style. For our axis to make sense, we could continue to apply inline styles by using `d3.select` to modify the styles of the necessary elements, but instead we should use CSS, because it's easier to maintain and doesn't require us to write styles on the fly in JavaScript. The following listing shows a short CSS style sheet that corresponds to the elements created by the axis function.

Listing 4.1 ch4stylesheet.css

```
<style>
line {
  shape-rendering: crispEdges;
  stroke: #000;
}

path.domain {
  fill: none;
  stroke: black;
}
</style>
```

This applies to all our lines, which includes the major lines that we'd otherwise need to reference with "g.major > line".

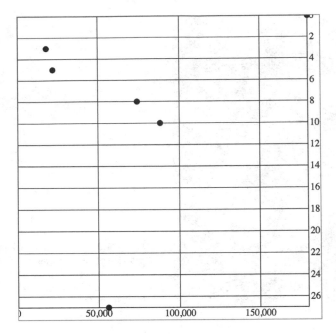

Figure 4.9   With `<path.domain>` fill set to "none" and CSS settings also corresponding to the tick `<line>` elements, we can draw a rather attractive grid based on our two axes.

With this in place, we get something a bit more legible, as shown in figure 4.9.

Take a look at the elements created by the `axis()` function in figure 4.9, and see in figure 4.10 how the CSS classes are associated with those elements.

As you create more-complex information visualization, you'll get used to creating your own elements with classes referenced by your style sheet. You'll also learn where

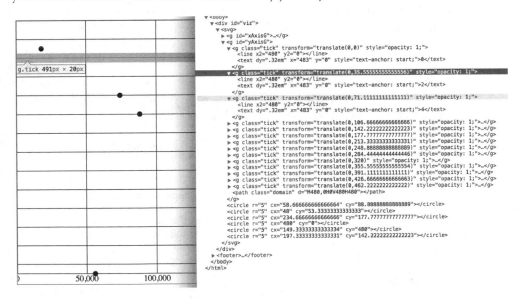

Figure 4.10   The DOM shows how tick `<line>` elements are appended along with a `<text>` element for the label to one of a set of `<g.tick.major>` elements corresponding to the number of ticks.

D3 components create elements in the DOM and how they're classed so that you can style them properly.

4.3 *Complex graphical objects*

Using circles or rectangles for your data won't work with some datasets, for example, if an important aspect of your data has to do with distribution, like user demographics or statistical data. Often, the distribution of data gets lost in information visualization, or is only noted with a reference to standard deviation or other first-year statistics terms that indicate the average doesn't tell the whole story. One particularly useful way of representing data that has a distribution (such as a fluctuating stock price) is the use of a boxplot in place of a traditional scatterplot. The boxplot uses a complex graphic that encodes distribution in its shape. The box in a boxplot typically looks like the one shown in figure 4.11. It uses quartiles that have been preprocessed, but you could easily use `d3.scale.quartile()` to create your own values from your own dataset.

Take a moment to examine the amount of data that's encoded in the graphic in figure 4.11. The median value is represented as a gray line. The rectangle shows the amount of whatever you're measuring that falls in a set range that represents the majority of the data. The two lines above and below the rectangle indicate the minimum and maximum values. Everything except the information in the gray line is lost when you map only the average or median value at a datapoint.

To build a reasonable boxplot, we'll need a set of data with interesting variation in those areas. Let's assume we want to plot the number of registered visitors coming to our website by day of the week so that we can compare our stats week to week (or so that we can present this info to our boss, or for some other reason). We have the data

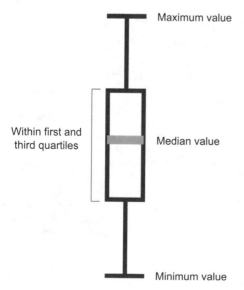

Figure 4.11   **A box from a boxplot consists of five pieces of information encoded in a single shape: (1) the maximum value, (2) the high value of some distribution, such as the third quartile, (3) the median or mean value, (4) the corresponding low value of the distribution, such as the first quartile, and (5) the minimum value.**

for the age of the visitors (based on their registration details) and derived the quartiles from that. Maybe we used Excel, Python, or d3.scale.quartile(), or maybe it was part of a dataset we downloaded. As you work with data, you'll be exposed to common statistical summaries like this and you'll have to represent them as part of your charts, so don't be too intimidated by it. We'll use a CSV format for the information.

The following listing shows our dataset with the number of registered users that visit the site each day, and the quartiles of their ages.

Listing 4.2   boxplots.csv

```
day,min,max,median,q1,q3,number
1,14,65,33,20,35,22
2,25,73,25,25,30,170
3,15,40,25,17,28,185
4,18,55,33,28,42,135
5,14,66,35,22,45,150
6,22,70,34,28,42,170
7,14,65,33,30,50,28
```

When we map the median age as a scatterplot, as in figure 4.12, it looks like there's not too much variation in our user base throughout the week. We do that by drawing scatterplot points for each day at the median age of the visitor for that day. We'll also invert the y-axis so that it makes a bit more sense.

Listing 4.3   Scatterplot of average age

```
    d3.csv("boxplot.csv", scatterplot)

function scatterplot(data) {
    xScale = d3.scale.linear().domain([1,8]).range([20,470]);
    yScale = d3.scale.linear().domain([0,100]).range([480,20]);   ⟵  Scale is inverted, so higher values are drawn higher up and lower values toward the bottom

    yAxis = d3.svg.axis()
        .scale(yScale)
        .orient("right")
        .ticks(8)
        .tickSize(-470);

    d3.select("svg").append("g")
        .attr("transform", "translate(470,0)")   ⟵  Offsets the <g> containing the axis
        .attr("id", "yAxisG")
        .call(yAxis);

    xAxis = d3.svg.axis()
        .scale(xScale)
        .orient("bottom")
        .tickSize(-470)
        .tickValues([1,2,3,4,5,6,7]);   ⟵  Specifies the exact tick values to correspond with the numbered days of the week

    d3.select("svg").append("g")
        .attr("transform", "translate(0,480)")
        .attr("id", "xAxisG")
        .call(xAxis);
```

```
d3.select("svg").selectAll("circle.median")
    .data(data)
    .enter()
    .append("circle")
    .attr("class", "tweets")
    .attr("r", 5)
    .attr("cx", function(d) {return xScale(d.day)})
    .attr("cy", function(d) {return yScale(d.median)})
    .style("fill", "darkgray");
}
```

But to get a better view of this data, we'll need to create a boxplot. Building a box-plot is similar to building a scatterplot, but instead of appending circles for each point of data, you append a <g> element. It's a good rule to always use <g> elements for your charts, because they allow you to apply labels or other important information to your graphical representations. But that means you'll need to use the transform attribute, which is how <g> elements are positioned on the canvas. Elements appended to a <g> base their coordinates off of the coordinates of their parent. When applying x and y attributes to child elements, you need to set them relative to the parent <g>.

Rather than selecting all the <g> elements and appending child elements one at a time, as we did in earlier chapters, we'll use the .each() function of a selection, which allows us to perform the same code on each element in a selection, to create the new elements. Like any D3 selection function, .each() allows you to access the bound data, array position, and DOM element. Earlier on, in chapter 1, we achieved the same functionality by using selectAll to select the <g> elements and directly append <circle>

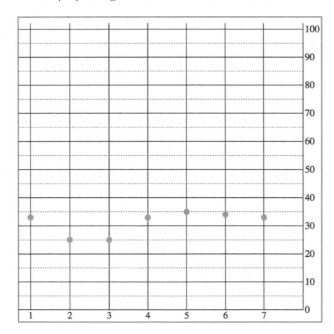

Figure 4.12   The median age of visitors (y-axis) by day of the week (x-axis) as represented by a scatterplot. It shows a slight dip in age on the second and third days.

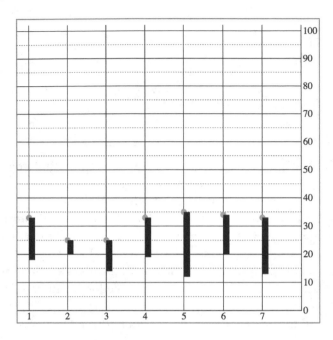

Figure 4.13 The `<rect>` elements represent the scaled range of the first and third quartiles of visitor age. They're placed on top of a gray `<circle>` in each `<g>` element, which is placed on the chart at the median age. The rectangles are drawn, as per SVG convention, from the `<g>` down and to the right.

and `<text>` elements. That's a clean method, and the only reasons to use `.each()` to add child elements are if you prefer the syntax, you plan on doing complex operations involving each data element, or you want to add conditional tests to change whether or what child elements you're appending. You can see how to use `.each()` to add child elements in action in the following listing, which takes advantage of the scales we created in listing 4.3 and draws rectangles on top of the circles we've already drawn.

Listing 4.4   Initial boxplot drawing code

```
d3.select("svg").selectAll("g.box")
    .data(data).enter()
    .append("g")
    .attr("class", "box")
    .attr("transform", function(d) {
        return "translate(" + xScale(d.day) +"," + yScale(d.median) + ")";
    }).each(function(d,i) {
        d3.select(this)
        .append("rect")
        .attr("width", 20)
        .attr("height", yScale(d.q1) - yScale(d.q3));
    });
```

The d and i variables are declared in the .each() anonymous function, so each time we access it, we get the data bound to the original element.

Because we're inside the .each(), we can select(this) to append new child elements.

The new rectangles indicating the distribution of visitor ages, as shown in figure 4.13, are not only offset to the right, but also showing the wrong values. Day 7, for instance, should range in value from 30 to 50, but instead is shown as ranging from 13 to 32. We know it's doing that because that's the way SVG draws rectangles. We have to update our code a bit to make it accurately reflect the distribution of visitor ages:

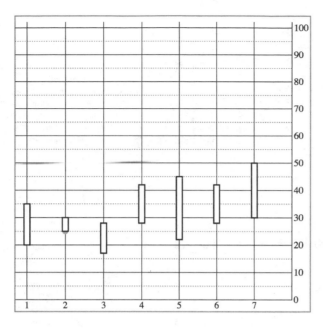

Figure 4.14 The `<rect>` elements are now properly placed so that their top and bottom correspond with the visitor age between the first and third quartiles of visitors for each day. The circles are completely covered, except for the second rectangle where the first quartile value is the same as the median age, and so we can see half the gray circle peeking out from underneath it.

```
...
.each(function(d,i) {
    d3.select(this)
        .append("rect")
        .attr("width", 20)
        .attr("x", -10)
        .attr("y", yScale(d.q3) - yScale(d.median))
        .attr("height", yScale(d.q1) - yScale(d.q3))
        .style("fill", "white")
        .style("stroke", "black");
});
```

Sets a negative offset of half the width to center a rectangle horizontally → `.attr("x", -10)`

The height of the rectangle is equal to the difference between its ql and q3 values, which means we need to offset the rectangle by the difference between the middle of the rectangle (the median) and the high end of the distribution—q3. ← `.attr("y", yScale(d.q3) - yScale(d.median))`

We'll use the same technique we used to create the chart in figure 4.14 to add the remaining elements of the boxplot (described in detail in figure 4.15) by including several append functions in the `.each()` function. They all select the parent `<g>` element created during the data-binding process and append the shapes necessary to build a boxplot.

Listing 4.5 The `.each()` function of the boxplot drawing five child elements

```
...
.each(function(d,i) {
    d3.select(this)
        .append("line")
        .attr("class", "range")
        .attr("x1", 0)
        .attr("x2", 0)
        .attr("y1", yScale(d.max) - yScale(d.median))
        .attr("y2", yScale(d.min) - yScale(d.median))
```

Draws the line from the min to the max value ← `.attr("y1", yScale(d.max) - yScale(d.median))`

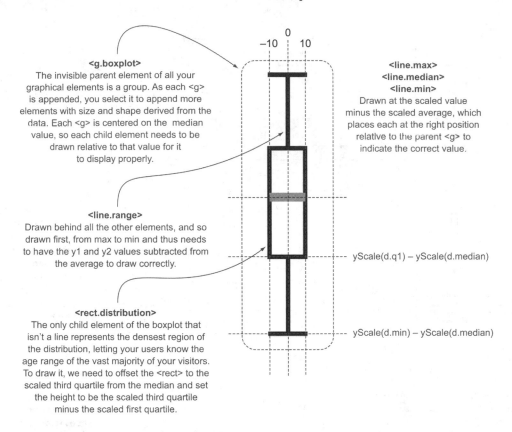

<g.boxplot>
The invisible parent element of all your graphical elements is a group. As each <g> is appended, you select it to append more elements with size and shape derived from the data. Each <g> is centered on the median value, so each child element needs to be drawn relative to that value for it to display properly.

<line.max>
<line.median>
<line.min>
Drawn at the scaled value minus the scaled average, which places each at the right position relative to the parent <g> to indicate the correct value.

<line.range>
Drawn behind all the other elements, and so drawn first, from max to min and thus needs to have the y1 and y2 values subtracted from the average to draw correctly.

<rect.distribution>
The only child element of the boxplot that isn't a line represents the densest region of the distribution, letting your users know the age range of the vast majority of your visitors. To draw it, we need to offset the <rect> to the scaled third quartile from the median and set the height to be the scaled third quartile minus the scaled first quartile.

yScale(d.q1) – yScale(d.median)

yScale(d.min) – yScale(d.median)

Figure 4.15 How a boxplot can be drawn in D3. Pay particular attention to the relative positioning necessary to draw child elements of a <g>. The 0 positions for all elements are where the parent <g> has been placed, so that <line.max>, <rect.distribution>, and <line.range> all need to be drawn with an offset placing their top-left corner above this center, whereas <line.min> is drawn below the center and <line.median> has a 0 y-value, because our center is the median value.

```
        .style("stroke", "black")
        .style("stroke-width", "4px");

    d3.select(this)
        .append("line")
        .attr("class", "max")
        .attr("x1", -10)
        .attr("x2", 10)
        .attr("y1", yScale(d.max) - yScale(d.median))
        .attr("y2", yScale(d.max) - yScale(d.median))
        .style("stroke", "black")
        .style("stroke-width", "4px");

    d3.select(this)
        .append("line")
        .attr("class", "min")
        .attr("x1", -10)
        .attr("x2", 10)
```

The top bar of the min-max line

```
                  .attr("y1", yScale(d.min) - yScale(d.median))
                  .attr("y2", yScale(d.min) - yScale(d.median))
                  .style("stroke", "black")
                  .style("stroke-width", "4px");

              d3.select(this)
                  .append("rect")
                  .attr("class", "range")
                  .attr("width", 20)
                  .attr("x", -10)
                  .attr("y", yScale(d.q3) - yScale(d.median))
                  .attr("height", yScale(d.q1) - yScale(d.q3))
                  .style("fill", "white")
                  .style("stroke", "black")
                  .style("stroke-width", "2px");

              d3.select(this)
                  .append("line")
                  .attr("x1", -10)
                  .attr("x2", 10)
                  .attr("y1", 0)
                  .attr("y2", 0)
                  .style("stroke", "darkgray")
                  .style("stroke-width", "4px");
});
```

The bottom bar of the min-max line

The offset so that the rectangle is centered on the median value

Median line doesn't need to be moved, because the parent <g> is centered on the median value

Listing 4.6 fulfills the requirement that we should also add an x-axis to remind us which day each box is associated with. This takes advantage of the explicit `.tick-Values()` function you saw earlier. It also uses negative `tickSize()` and the corresponding offset of the <g> that we use to call the axis function.

Listing 4.6 Adding an axis using `tickValues`

A negative tickSize draws the lines above the axis, but we need to make sure to offset the axis by the same value.

```
var xAxis = d3.svg.axis().scale(xScale).orient("bottom")
.tickSize(-470)
.tickValues([1,2,3,4,5,6,7]);
    d3.select("svg").append("g")
.attr("transform", "translate(0,470)")
.attr("id", "xAxisG").call(xAxis);
d3.select("#xAxisG > path.domain").style("display", "none");
```

Offsets the axis to correspond with our negative tickSize

Setting specific tickValues forces the axis to only show the corresponding values, which is useful when we want to override the automatic ticks created by the axis.

We can hide this, because it has extra ticks on the ends that distract our readers.

The end result of all this is a chart where each of our datapoints is represented, not by a single circle, but by a multipart graphical element designed to emphasize distribution.

The boxplot in figure 4.16 encodes not just the median age of visitors for that day, but the minimum, maximum, and distribution of the age of the majority of visitors. This expresses in detail the demographics of visitorship clearly and cleanly. It doesn't include the number of visitors, but we could encode that with color, make it available

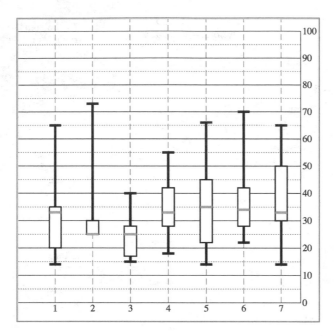

Figure 4.16   Our final boxplot chart. Each day now shows not only the median age of visitors but also the range of visiting ages, allowing for a more extensive examination of the demographics of site visitorship.

on a click of each boxplot, or make the width of the boxplot correspond to the number of visitors.

We looked at boxplots because a boxplot allows you to explore the creation of multipart objects while using lines and rectangles. But what's the value of a visualization like this that shows distribution? It encodes a graphical summary of the data, providing information about visitor age for the site on Wednesday, such as, "Most visitors were between the ages of 18 and 28. The oldest was 40. The youngest was 15. The median age was 25." It also allows you to quickly perform visual queries, checking to see if the median age of one day was within the majority of visitor ages of another day.

We'll stop exploring boxplots, and take a look at a different kind of complex graphical object: an interpolated line.

4.4   *Line charts and interpolations*

You create line charts by drawing connections between points. A line that connects points, and the shaded regions inside or outside the area constrained by the line, tell a story about the data. Although a line chart is technically a static data visualization, it's also a representation of change, typically over time.

We'll start with a new dataset in listing 4.7 that better represents change over time. Let's imagine we have a Twitter account and we've been tracking the number of tweets, favorites, and retweets to determine at what time we have the greatest response to our social media. Although we'll ultimately deal with this kind of data as JSON, we'll want to start with a comma-delimited file, because it's the most efficient for this kind of data.

Listing 4.7 tweetdata.csv

```
day,tweets,retweets,favorites
1,1,2,5
2,6,11,3
3,3,0,1
4,5,2,6
5,10,29,16
6,4,22,10
7,3,14,1
8,5,7,7
9,1,35,22
10,4,16,15
```

First we pull this CSV in using d3.csv() as we did in chapter 2, and then we create circles for each datapoint. We do this for each variation on the data, with the .day attribute determining x position and the other datapoint determining y position. We create the usual x and y scales to draw the shapes in the confines of our canvas. We also have a couple of axes to frame our results. Notice that we differentiated between the three datatypes by coloring them differently.

Listing 4.8 Callback function to draw a scatterplot from tweetdata

```
d3.csv("tweetdata.csv", lineChart);
function lineChart(data) {

    xScale = d3.scale.linear().domain([1,10.5]).range([20,480]);      ⟵    Our scales,
    yScale = d3.scale.linear().domain([0,35]).range([480,20]);             as usual,
                                                                           have margins
                                                                           built in.

    xAxis = d3.svg.axis()
        .scale(xScale)
        .orient("bottom")                                           Fixes the ticks of the
        .tickSize(480)                                              x-axis to correspond
        .tickValues([1,2,3,4,5,6,7,8,9,10]);              ⟵        to the days

    d3.select("svg").append("g").attr("id", "xAxisG").call(xAxis);

    yAxis = d3.svg.axis()
        .scale(yScale)
        .orient("right")
        .ticks(10)
        .tickSize(480);

    d3.select("svg").append("g").attr("id", "yAxisG").call(yAxis);

    d3.select("svg").selectAll("circle.tweets")
        .data(data)
        .enter()
        .append("circle")
        .attr("class", "tweets")                          Each of these uses
        .attr("r", 5)                                     the same dataset, but
        .attr("cx", function(d) {return xScale(d.day)})   bases the y position
        .attr("cy", function(d) {return yScale(d.tweets)})  on tweets, retweets,
        .style("fill", "black");                     ⟵    and favorites values,
                                                          respectively.
```

```
d3.select("svg").selectAll("circle.retweets")
    .data(data)
    .enter()
    .append("circle")
    .attr("class", "retweets")
    .attr("r", 5)
    .attr("cx", function(d) {return xScale(d.day)})
    .attr("cy", function(d) {return yScale(d.retweets)})
    .style("fill", "lightgray");

d3.select("svg").selectAll("circle.favorites")
    .data(data)
    .enter()
    .append("circle")
    .attr("class", "favorites")
    .attr("r", 5)
    .attr("cx", function(d) {return xScale(d.day)})
    .attr("cy", function(d) {return yScale(d.favorites)})
    .style("fill", "gray");
};
```

The graphical results of this code, as shown in figure 4.17, which take advantage of the CSS rules we defined earlier, aren't easily interpreted.

4.4.1   *Drawing a line from points*

By drawing a line that intersects each point of the same category, we can compare the number of tweets, retweets, and favorites. We can start by drawing a line for tweets using d3.svg.line(). This line generator expects an array of points as data, and we'll need to tell the generator what values constitute the x and y coordinates for each

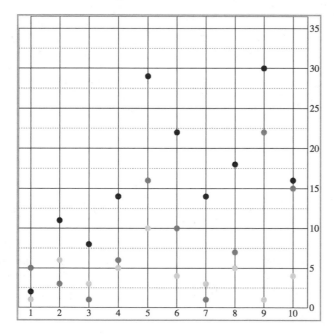

Figure 4.17   A scatterplot showing the datapoints for 10 days of activity on Twitter, with the number of tweets in light gray, the number of retweets in dark gray, and the number of favorites in black

point. By default, this generator expects a two-part array, where the first part is the x value and the second part is the y value. We can't use that, because our x value is based on the day of the activity and our y value is based on the amount of activity.

The .x() accessor function of the line generator needs to point at the scaled day value, while the .y() accessor function needs to point to the scaled value of the appropriate activity. The line function itself takes the entire dataset that we loaded from tweet-data, and returns the SVG drawing code necessary for a line between the points in that dataset. To generate three lines, we use the dataset three times, with a slightly different generator for each. We not only need to write the generator function and define how it accesses the data it uses to draw the line, but we also need to append a <path> to our canvas and set its d attribute to equal the generator function we defined.

Listing 4.9   New line generator code inside the callback function

```
var tweetLine = d3.svg.line()
   .x(function(d) {
       return xScale(d.day);
   })
   .y(function(d) {
   return yScale(d.tweets);
   });

d3.select("svg")
   .append("path")
   .attr("d", tweetLine(data))
   .attr("fill", "none")
   .attr("stroke", "darkred")
   .attr("stroke-width", 2);
```

Defines an accessor for data like ours; in this case we take the day attribute and pass it to xScale first

This accessor does the same for the number of tweets.

The appended path is drawn according to the generator with the loaded tweetdata passed to it.

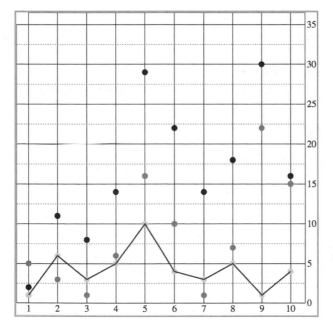

Figure 4.18   The line generator takes the entire dataset and draws a line where the x,y position of every point on the canvas is based on its accessor. In this case, each point on the line corresponds to the day, and tweets are scaled to fit the x and y scales we created to display the data on the canvas.

We draw the line above the circles we already drew, and the line generator produces the plot shown in figure 4.18.

4.4.2   *Drawing many lines with multiple generators*

If we build a line constructor for each datatype in our set and call each with its own path, as shown in the following listing, then you can see the variation over time for each of your datapoints. Listing 4.10 demonstrates how to build those generators with our dataset, and figure 4.19 shows the results of that code.

Listing 4.10   Line generators for each tweetdata

```
var tweetLine = d3.svg.line()
    .x(function(d) {
        return xScale(d.day)
    })
    .y(function(d) {
        return yScale(d.tweets)
    });

var retweetLine = d3.svg.line()
    .x(function(d) {
        return xScale(d.day)
    })
    .y(function(d) {
        return yScale(d.retweets)
    });

var favLine = d3.svg.line()
    .x(function(d) {
        return xScale(d.day);
    })
    .y(function(d) {
        return yScale(d.favorites);
    });

d3.select("svg")
    .append("path")
    .attr("d", tweetLine(data))
    .attr("fill", "none")
    .attr("stroke", "darkred")
    .attr("stroke-width", 2);

d3.select("svg")
    .append("path")
    .attr("d", retweetLine(data))
    .attr("fill", "none")
    .attr("stroke", "gray")
    .attr("stroke-width", 3);

d3.select("svg")
    .append("path")
    .attr("d", favLine(data))
    .attr("fill", "none")
    .attr("stroke", "black")
    .attr("stroke-width", 2);
```

A more efficient way to do this would be to define one line generator, and then modify the .y() accessor on the fly as we call it for each line. But it's easier to see the functionality this way.

Notice how only the y accessor is different between each line generator.

Each line generator needs to be called by a corresponding new <path> element .

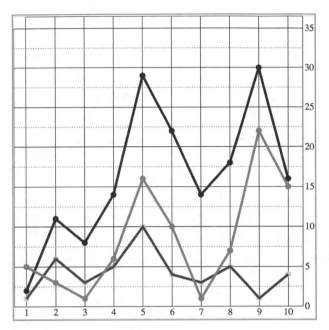

Figure 4.19 **The dataset is first used to draw a set of circles, which creates the scatterplot from the beginning of this section. The dataset is then used three more times to draw each line.**

4.4.3 *Exploring line interpolators*

D3 provides a number of interpolation methods with which to draw these lines, so that they can more accurately represent the data. In cases like tweetdata, where you have discrete points that represent data accurately and not samples, then the default "linear" method shown in figure 4.19 is appropriate. But in other cases, a different interpolation method for the lines, like the ones shown in figure 4.20, may be appropriate. Here's the same data but with the `d3.svg.line()` generator using different interpolation methods:

```
tweetLine.interpolate("basis");
retweetLine.interpolate("step");
favLine.interpolate("cardinal");
```

We can add this code right after we create our line generators and before we call them to change the interpolate method, or we can set .interpolate() as we're defining the generator.

What's the best interpolation?

Interpolation modifies the representation of data. Experiment with this drawing code to see how the different interpolation settings show different information than other interpolators. Data can be visualized in different ways, all correct from a programming perspective, and it's up to you to make sure the information you're visualizing reflects the actual phenomena.

Data visualization deals with the visual representation of statistical principles, which means it's subject to all the dangers of the misuse of statistics. The interpolation of lines is particularly vulnerable to misuse, because it changes a clunky-looking line into a smooth, "natural" line.

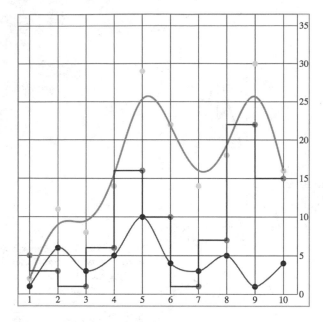

Figure 4.20   Light gray: "basis" interpolation; dark gray: "step" interpolation; black: "cardinal" interpolation

4.5   *Complex accessor functions*

All of the previous chart types we built were based on points. The scatterplot is points on a grid, the boxplot consists of complex graphical objects in place of points, and line charts use points as the basis for drawing a line. In this and earlier chapters, we've dealt with rather staid examples of information visualization that we might easily create in any traditional spreadsheet. But you didn't get into this business to make Excel charts. You want to wow your audience with beautiful data, win awards for your aesthetic *je ne sais quoi,* and evoke deep emotional responses with your representation of change over time. You want to make streamgraphs like the one in figure 4.21.

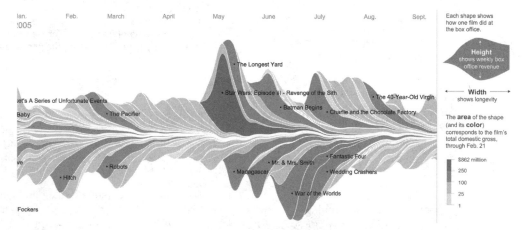

Figure 4.21   Behold the glory of the streamgraph. Look on my works, ye mighty, and despair! (figure from *The New York Times*, February 23, 2008; http://mng.bz/rV7M)

The streamgraph is a sublime piece of information visualization that represents variation and change, like the boxplot. It may seem like a difficult thing to create, until you start to put the pieces together. Ultimately, a streamgraph is what's known as a *stacked chart*. The layers accrete upon each other and adjust the area of the elements above and below, based on the space taken up by the components closer to the center. It appears organic because that accretive nature mimics the way many organisms grow, and seems to imply the kinds of emergent properties that govern the growth and decay of organisms. We'll interpret its appearance later, but first let's figure out how to build it.

The reason we're looking at a streamgraph is because it's not that exotic. A streamgraph is a stacked graph, which means it's fundamentally similar to your earlier line charts. By learning how to make it, you can better understand another kind of generator, `d3.svg.area()`. The first thing you need is data that's amenable to this kind of visualization. Let's follow the *New York Times*, from which we get the streamgraph in figure 4.21, and work with the gross earnings for six movies over the course of nine days. Each datapoint is therefore the amount of money a movie made on a particular day.

Listing 4.11   movies.csv

```
day,movie1,movie2,movie3,movie4,movie5,movie6
1,20,8,3,0,0,0
2,18,5,1,13,0,0
3,14,3,1,10,0,0
4,7,3,0,5,27,15
5,4,3,0,2,20,14
6,3,1,0,0,10,13
7,2,0,0,0,8,12
8,0,0,0,0,6,11
9,0,0,0,0,3,9
10,0,0,0,0,1,8
```

To build a streamgraph, you need to get more sophisticated with the way you access data and feed it to generators when drawing lines. In our earlier example, we created three different line generators for our dataset, but that's terribly inefficient. We also used simple functions to draw the lines. But we'll need more than that to draw something like a streamgraph. Even if you think you won't want to draw streamgraphs (and there are reasons why you may not, which we'll get into at the end of this section), the important thing to focus on when you look at listing 4.11 is how you use accessors with D3's line and, later, area generators.

Listing 4.12   The callback function to draw movies.csv as a line chart

```
var xScale = d3.scale.linear().domain([ 1, 8 ]).range([ 20, 470 ]);
var yScale = d3.scale.linear().domain([ 0, 100 ]).range([ 480, 20 ]);

for (x in data[0]) {
    if (x != "day") {
```

◁── Iterates through our data attributes with a `for` loop, where x is the name of each column from our data ("day", "movie1", "movie2", and so on), which allows us to dynamically create and call generators

Instantiates a line generator for each movie

```
var movieArea = d3.svg.line()
    .x(function(d) {
        return xScale(d.day);
    })
    .y(function(d) {
        return yScale(d[x]);
    })
    .interpolate("cardinal");

d3.select("svg")
    .append("path")
    .style("id", x + "Area")
    .attr("d", movieArea(data))
    .attr("fill", "none")
    .attr("stroke", "black")
    .attr("stroke-width", 3)
    .style("opacity", .75);

    };
};
```

Every line uses the day column for its x value.

Dynamically sets the y-accessor function of our line generator to grab the data from the appropriate movie for our y variable

The line-drawing code produces a cluttered line chart, as shown in figure 4.22. As you learned in chapter 1, lines and filled areas are almost exactly the same thing in SVG. You can differentiate them by a *Z* at the end of the drawing code that indicates the shape is closed, or the presence or absence of a "fill" style. D3 provides d3.svg.line and d3.svg.area generators to draw lines or areas. Both of these constructors produce <path> elements, but d3.svg.area provides helper functions to bound the lower end of your path to produce areas in charts. This means we need to define a .y0()

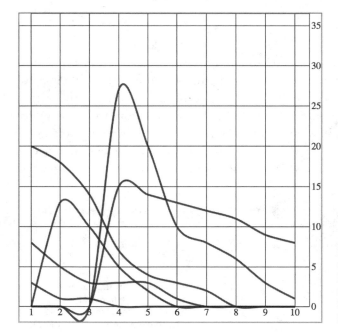

Figure 4.22   Each movie column is drawn as a separate line. Notice how the "cardinal" interpolation creates a graphical artifact, where it seems like some movies made negative money.

accessor that corresponds to our y accessor and determines the shape of the bottom of our area. Let's see how d3.svg.area() works.

Listing 4.13 Area accessors

```
for (x in data[0]) {
   if (x != "day") {

var movieArea = d3.svg.area()
    .x(function(d) {
        return xScale(d.day);
    })
    .y(function(d) {
        return yScale(d[x]);
    })
    .y0(function(d) {          ◁─┐   This new accessor provides us with the
        return yScale(-d[x]);        ability to define where the bottom of the
    })                               path is. In this case, we start by making
    .interpolate("cardinal");        the bottom equal to the inverse of the
                                     top, which mirrors the shape.
d3.select("svg")
    .append("path")
    .style("id", x + "Area")
    .attr("d", movieArea(data))
    .attr("fill", "darkgray")
    .attr("stroke", "lightgray")
    .attr("stroke-width", 2)
    .style("opacity", .5);

   };
};
```

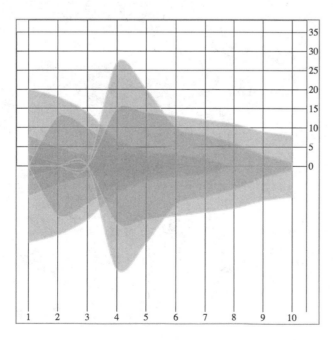

Figure 4.23 By using an area generator and defining the bottom of the area as the inverse of the top, we can mirror our lines to create an area chart. Here they're drawn with semitransparent fills, so that we can see how they overlap.

Should you always draw filled paths with d3.svg.area?

No. Counterintuitively, you should use `d3.svg.line` to draw filled areas. To do so, though, you need to append *Z* to the created `d` attribute. This indicates that the path is closed.

Open path	Closed path changes	Explanation
| ```
movieArea = d3.svg.line()
    .x(function(d) {
      return xScale(d.day)
    })
    .y(function(d) {
      return yScale(d[x])
    })
    .interpolate("cardinal");
``` | | You write the constructor for the line-drawing code the same regardless of whether you want a line or shape, filled or unfilled. |
| ```
d3.select("svg")
    .append("path")
    .attr("d", movieArea(data))
    .attr("fill", "none")
    .attr("stroke", "black")
    .attr("stroke-width", 3);
``` | ```
d3.select("svg")
    .append("path")
    .attr("d", movieArea(data)
          + "Z")
    .attr("fill", "none")
    .attr("stroke", "black")
    .attr("stroke-width", 3);
``` | When you call the constructor, you append a `<path>` element. You specify whether the line is "closed" by concatenating a *Z* to the string created by your line constructor for the `d` attribute of the `<path>`.

When you add a *Z* to the end of an SVG `<path>` element's `d` attribute, it draws a line connecting the two end points. |
| | | |
| ```
d3.select("svg")
    .append("path")
    .attr("d", movieArea(data))
    .attr("fill", "none")
    .attr("stroke", "black")
    .attr("stroke-width", 3);
``` | ```
d3.select("svg")
    .append("path")
    .attr("d", movieArea(data)
          + "Z")
    .attr("fill", "gray")
    .attr("stroke", "black")
    .attr("stroke-width", 3);
``` | You may think that only a closed path could be filled, but the fill of a path is the same whether or not you close the line by appending *Z*.

The area of a path filled is always the same, whether it's closed or not. |
| | | |
```

> You use `d3.svg.line` when you want to draw most shapes and lines, whether filled or unfilled, or closed or open. You should use `d3.svg.area()` when you want to draw a shape where the bottom of the shape can be calculated based on the top of the shape as you're drawing it. It's suitable for drawing bands of data, such as that found in a stacked area chart or streamgraph.

By defining the `y0` function of `d3.svg.area`, we've mirrored the path created and filled it as shown in figure 4.23, which is a step in the right direction. Notice that we're presenting inaccurate data now, because the area of the path is twice the area of the data. We want our areas to draw one on top of the other, so we need `.y0()` to point to a complex stacking function that makes the bottom of an area equal to the top of the previously drawn area. D3 comes with a stacking function, `.stack()`, which we'll look at later, but for the purpose of our example, we'll write our own.

Listing 4.14 Callback function for drawing stacked areas

Creates a color ramp that corresponds to the six different movies

We won't draw a line for the day value of each object, because this is what provides us with our x coordinate.

```
var fillScale = d3.scale.linear()
            .domain([0,5])
            .range(["lightgray","black"]);
var n = 0;
for (x in data[0]) {
    if (x != "day") {
        var movieArea = d3.svg.area()
            .x(function(d) {
                return xScale(d.day)
            })
            .y(function(d) {
                return yScale(simpleStacking(d,x))
            })
            .y0(function(d) {
                return yScale(simpleStacking(d,x) - d[x]);
            })
            .interpolate("basis")

        d3.select("svg")
            .append("path")
            .style("id", x + "Area")
            .attr("d", movieArea(data))
            .attr("fill", fillScale(n))
            .attr("stroke", "none")
            .attr("stroke-width", 2)
            .style("opacity", .5);
        n++;
    };
};
function simpleStacking( incomingData, incomingAttribute) {
    var newHeight = 0;
    for (x in incomingData) {
        if (x != "day") {
            newHeight += parseInt(incomingData[x]);
            if (x == incomingAttribute) {
```

Each movie corresponds to one iteration through the for loop, so we'll increment *n* to use in the color ramp. We could also create an ordinal scale assigning a color for each movie.

A d3.svg.area() generator for each iteration through the object that corresponds to one of our movies using the day value for the x coordinate, but iterating through the values for each movie for the y coordinates

Draws a path using the current constructor. We'll have one for each attribute not named "day". Give it a unique ID based on which attribute we're drawing an area for. Fill the area with a color based on the color ramp we built.

Finishes the for loop, increments to the next attribute in the object, and increments *n* to color the next area

This function takes the incoming bound data and the name of the attribute and loops through the incoming data, adding each value until it reaches the current named attribute. As a result, it returns the total value for every movie during this day up to the movie we've sent.

```
                break;
            }
        }
    }
    return newHeight;
};
```

The stacked area chart in figure 4.24 is already complex. To make it a proper stream-graph, the stacks need to alternate. This requires a more complicated stacking function.

Listing 4.15   A stacking function that alternates vertical position of area drawn

```
...
var movieArea = d3.svg.area().x(function(d) {            We can create whatever
                return xScale(d.day)                     complex accessor function we
        })                                               want for our generators.
.y(function(d) {
                return yScale(alternatingStacking(d,x,"top"))
        })
.y0(function(d) {
                return yScale(alternatingStacking(d,x,"bottom"));
        }).interpolate("basis");
...
function alternatingStacking(incomingData,incomingAttribute,topBottom)
{
var newHeight = 0;                          We need the data, and we also need to know whether
var skip = true;                            we're drawing the top or bottom of the area, which
for (x in incomingData) {                   alternates as we move through the dataset.
        if (x != "day") {
            if (x == "movie1" || skip == false) {
                newHeight += parseInt(incomingData[x]);      Skips the first movie (our
                if (x == incomingAttribute) {                center), and then skips
                    break;                                   every other movie to get
                }                                            the alternating pattern
                if (skip == false) {
                    skip = true;                    Stops when we
                } else {                            reach this
                    n%2 == 0 ? skip = false : skip = true;   movie, which
                }                                   gives us the
            } else {                                baseline
                skip = false;
            }
        }
    }
    if(topBottom == "bottom") {                 The height is negative for
        newHeight = -newHeight;                 areas on the bottom side
    }                                           of the streamgraph, and
    if (n > 1 && n%2 == 1 && topBottom == "bottom") {   positive for those on the
        newHeight = 0;                          top side.
    }
    if (n > 1 && n%2 == 0 && topBottom == "top") {
        newHeight = 0;
    }
    return newHeight;
};
```

Always skips day, because that's just our x position

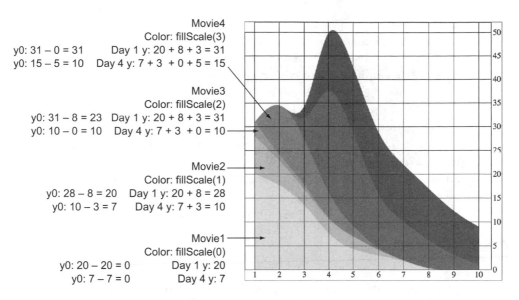

Movie4
Color: fillScale(3)
y0: 31 − 0 = 31   Day 1 y: 20 + 8 + 3 = 31
y0: 15 − 5 = 10   Day 4 y: 7 + 3 + 0 + 5 = 15

Movie3
Color: fillScale(2)
y0: 31 − 8 = 23 Day 1 y: 20 + 8 + 3 = 31
y0: 10 − 0 = 10   Day 4 y: 7 + 3 + 0 = 10

Movie2
Color: fillScale(1)
y0: 28 − 8 = 20   Day 1 y: 20 + 8 = 28
y0: 10 − 3 = 7   Day 4 y: 7 + 3 = 10

Movie1
Color: fillScale(0)
y0: 20 − 20 = 0   Day 1 y: 20
y0: 7 − 7 = 0   Day 4 y: 7

Figure 4.24   Our stacked area code represents a movie by drawing an area, where the bottom of that area equals the total amount of money made by any movies drawn earlier for that day.

The streamgraph in figure 4.25 has some obvious issues, but we're not going to correct them. For one thing, we're over-representing the gross of the first movie by drawing it at twice the height. If we wanted to, we could easily make the stacking function account for this by halving the values of that first area. Another issue is that the areas being drawn are different from the areas being displayed, which isn't a problem when our data visualization is going to be read from only one perspective and not multiple perspectives.

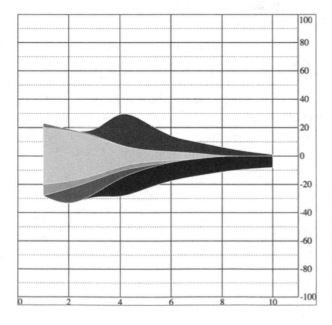

Figure 4.25   A streamgraph that shows the accreted values for movies by day. The problems of using different interpolation methods are clear. The basis method here shows some inaccuracies, and the difficulty of labeling the scale is also apparent.

But the purpose of this section is to focus on building complex accessor functions to create, from scratch, the kinds of data visualization you've seen and likely thought of as exotic. Let's assume this data is correct and take a moment to analyze the effectiveness of this admittedly attractive method of visualizing data. Is this really a better way to show movie grosses than a simpler stacked graph or line chart? That depends on the scale of the questions being addressed by the chart. If you're trying to discover overall patterns of variation in movie grosses, as well as spot interactions between them (for instance, seeing if a particularly high-grossing-over-time movie interferes with the opening of another movie), then it may be useful. If you're trying to impress an audience with a complex-looking chart, it would also be useful. Otherwise, you'll be better off with something simpler than this. But even if you only build less-visually impressive charts, you'll still use the same techniques we've gone over in this section.

4.6   *Summary*

In this chapter you've learned the basics of creating charts:

- Integrating generators and components with the selection and binding process
- Learning about D3 components and the axis component to create chart elements like an x-axis and a y-axis
- Interpolating graphical elements, such as lines or areas from point data, using D3 generators
- Creating complex SVG objects that use the <g> element's ability to create child shapes, which can be drawn based on the bound dataset, using .each()
- Exploring the representation of multidimensional data using boxplots
- Combining and extending these methods to implement a sophisticated charting method, the streamgraph, while learning how such charts may outstrip their audience's ability to successfully interpret such data

These skills and methods will help you to better understand the D3 layouts, which we'll explore in more detail in the following chapters. The incredible breadth of data visualization techniques possible with D3 is based on the fundamental similarity between different methods of displaying data, at the visual level, at the functional level, and at the data level. By understanding how the processes work and how they can be combined to create more interactive and rich representation, you'll be better equipped to choose and deploy the right one for your data.

5

Layouts

This chapter covers

- Histogram and pie chart layouts
- Simple tweening
- Tree, circle pack, and stack layouts
- Sankey diagrams and word clouds

D3 contains a variety of functions, referred to as *layouts*, that help you format your data so that it can be presented using a popular charting method. In this chapter we'll look at several different layouts so that you can understand general layout functionality, learn how to deal with D3's layout structure, and deploy one of these layouts (some of which are shown in figure 5.1) with your data.

In each case, as you'll see with the following examples, when a dataset is associated with a layout, each of the objects in the dataset has attributes that allow for drawing the data. Layouts don't draw the data, nor are they called like components or referred to in the drawing code like generators. Rather, they're a preprocessing step that formats your data so that it's ready to be displayed in the form you've chosen. You can update a layout, and then if you rebind that altered data to your graphical objects, you can use the D3 enter/update/exit syntax you encountered in chapter 2 to update your layout. Paired with animated transitions, this can provide you with the framework for an interactive, dynamic chart.

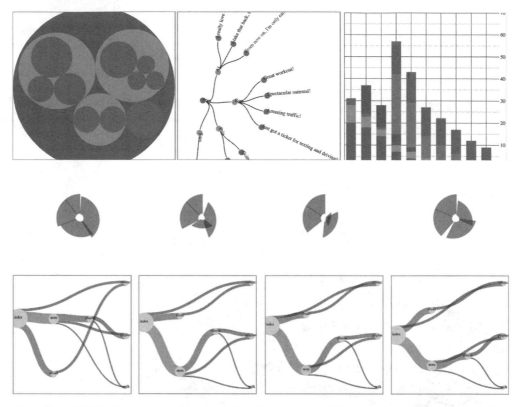

Figure 5.1   Multiple layouts are demonstrated in this chapter, including the circle pack (section 5.3), tree (section 5.4), stack (section 5.5), and Sankey (section 5.6.1), as well as tweening to properly animate shapes like the arcs in pie charts (section 5.2.3).

This chapter gives an overview of layout structure by implementing popular layouts such as the histogram, pie chart, tree, and circle packing. Other layouts such as the chord layout and more exotic ones follow the same principles and should be easy to understand after looking at these. We'll get started with a kind of chart you've already worked with, the bar chart or histogram, which has its own layout that helps abstract the process of building this kind of chart.

5.1   *Histograms*

Before we get into charts that you'll need layouts for, let's take a look at a chart that we easily made without a layout. In chapter 2 we made a bar chart based on our Twitter data by using `d3.nest()`. But D3 has a layout, `d3.layout.histogram()`, that bins values automatically and provides us with the necessary settings to draw a bar chart based on a scale that we've defined. Many people who get started with D3 think it's a charting library, and that they'll find a function like `d3.layout.histogram` that creates a bar chart in a `<div>` when it's run. But D3 layouts don't result in charts; they result in the settings necessary for charts. You have to put in a bit of extra work for charts, but you have enormous flexibility (as you'll see in this and later chapters) that allows you to make diagrams and charts that you can't find in other libraries.

Listing 5.1 shows the code to create a histogram layout and associate it with a particular scale. I've also included an example of how you can use interactivity to adjust the original layout and rebind the data to your shapes. This changes the histogram from showing the number of tweets that were favorited to the number of tweets that were retweeted.

Listing 5.1 Histogram code

```
d3.json("tweets.json", function(error, data) { histogram(data.tweets) });

function histogram(tweetsData) {

    var xScale = d3.scale.linear().domain([ 0, 5 ]).range([ 0, 500 ]);
    var yScale = d3.scale.linear().domain([ 0, 10 ]).range([ 400, 0 ]);

    var xAxis = d3.svg.axis().scale(xScale).ticks(5).orient("bottom");

    var histoChart = d3.layout.histogram();
    histoChart.bins([ 0, 1, 2, 3, 4, 5 ]).value(function(d) {
        return d.favorites.length;
    });

    histoData = histoChart(tweetsData);

    d3.select("svg").selectAll("rect").data(histoData).enter()
            .append("rect").attr("x", function(d) {
                return xScale(d.x);
            }).attr("y", function(d) {
                return yScale(d.y);
            }).attr("width", xScale(histoData[0].dx) - 2)
            .attr("height", function(d) {
                return 400 - yScale(d.y);
            }).on("click", retweets);

    d3.select("svg").append("g").attr("class", "x axis")
            .attr("transform", "translate(0,400)").call(xAxis);

    d3.select("g.axis").selectAll("text").attr("dx", 50);

    function retweets() {
        histoChart.value(function(d) {
            return d.retweets.length;
        });

        histoData = histoChart(tweetsData);

        d3.selectAll("rect").data(histoData)
                .transition().duration(500).attr("x", function(d) {
                    return xScale(d.x)
                }).attr("y", function(d) {
                    return yScale(d.y)
                }).attr("height", function(d) {
                    return 400 - yScale(d.y);
                });
    };

};
```

Creates a new layout function — `var histoChart = d3.layout.histogram();`

Determines the values the histogram bins for

The value the layout is binning for from the datapoint

Formats the data — `histoData = histoChart(tweetsData);`

Formatted data is used to draw the bars

Centers the axis labels under the bars

Changes the value being measured

Binds and redraws the new data

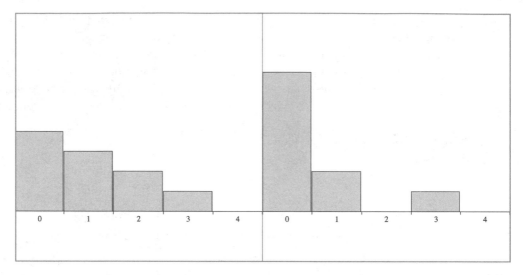

Figure 5.2   The histogram in its initial state (left) and after we change the measure from favorites to retweets (right) by clicking on one of the bars.

You're not expected to follow the process of using the histogram to create the results in figure 5.2. You'll get into that as you look at more layouts throughout this chapter. Notice a few general principles: first, a layout formats the data for display, as I pointed out in the beginning of chapter 4. Second, you still need the same scales and components that you needed when you created a bar chart from raw data without the help of a layout. Third, the histogram is useful because it automatically bins data, whether it's whole numbers like this or it falls in a range of values in a scale. Finally, if you want to dynamically change a chart using a different dimension of your data, you don't need to remove the original. You just need to reformat your data using the layout and rebind it to the original elements, preferably with a transition. You'll see this in more detail in your next example, which uses another type of chart: pie charts.

5.2   *Pie charts*

One of the most straightforward layouts available in D3 is the pie layout, which is used to make pie charts like those shown in figure 5.3. Like all layouts, a pie layout can be created, assigned to a variable, and used as both an object and a function. In this section you'll learn how to create a pie chart and transform it into a ring chart. You'll also learn how to use tweening to properly transition it when you change its data source. After you create it, you can pass it an array of values (which I'll refer to as a dataset), and it will compute the necessary starting and ending angles for each of those values to draw a pie chart. When we pass an array of numbers as our dataset to a pie layout in the console as in the following code, it doesn't produce any kind of graphics but rather results in the response shown in figure 5.4:

```
var pieChart = d3.layout.pie();
var yourPie = pieChart([1,1,2]);
```

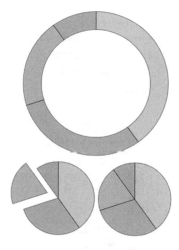

Figure 5.3   The traditional pie chart (bottom right) represents proportion as an angled slice of a circle. With slight modification, it can be turned into a donut or ring chart (top) or an exploded pie chart (bottom left).

Our `pieChart` function created a new array of three objects. The `startAngle` and `endAngle` for each of the data values draw a pie chart with one piece from 0 degrees to pi, the next from pi to 1.5 pi, and the last from 1.5 pi to 2 pi. But this isn't a drawing, or SVG code like the line and area generators produced.

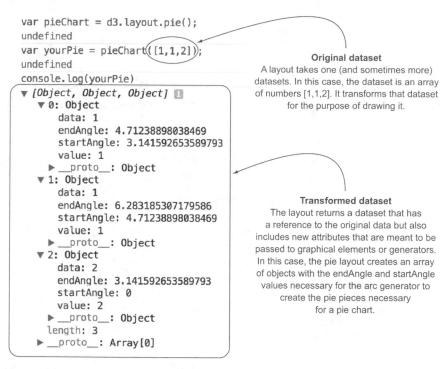

```
var pieChart = d3.layout.pie();
undefined
var yourPie = pieChart([1,1,2]);
undefined
console.log(yourPie)
▼ [Object, Object, Object] 
  ▼ 0: Object
      data: 1
      endAngle: 4.71238898038469
      startAngle: 3.141592653589793
      value: 1
    ▶ __proto__: Object
  ▼ 1: Object
      data: 1
      endAngle: 6.283185307179586
      startAngle: 4.71238898038469
      value: 1
    ▶ __proto__: Object
  ▼ 2: Object
      data: 2
      endAngle: 3.141592653589793
      startAngle: 0
      value: 2
    ▶ __proto__: Object
    length: 3
  ▶ __proto__: Array[0]
```

Original dataset
A layout takes one (and sometimes more) datasets. In this case, the dataset is an array of numbers [1,1,2]. It transforms that dataset for the purpose of drawing it.

Transformed dataset
The layout returns a dataset that has a reference to the original data but also includes new attributes that are meant to be passed to graphical elements or generators. In this case, the pie layout creates an array of objects with the endAngle and startAngle values necessary for the arc generator to create the pie pieces necessary for a pie chart.

Figure 5.4   A pie layout applied to an array of [1,1,2] shows objects created with a start angle, end angle, and value attribute corresponding to the dataset, as well as the original data, which in this case is a number.

5.2.1   *Drawing the pie layout*

These are settings that need to be passed to a generator to make each of the pieces of our pie chart. This particular generator is d3.svg.arc, and it's instantiated like the generators we worked with in chapter 4. It has a few settings, but the only one we need for this first example is the outerRadius() function, which allows us to set a dynamic or fixed radius for our arcs:

Gives our arcs and resulting pie chart a radius of 100 px ⊳

```
var newArc = d3.svg.arc();
newArc.outerRadius(100);
console.log(newArc(yourPie[0]));
```

◁ **Returns the d attribute necessary to draw this arc as a <path> element:**
"M6.123031769111886e-15,100A100,100 0 0,1 -100,1.2246063538223773e-14L0,0Z"

Now that you know how the arc constructor works and that it works with our data, all we need to do is bind the data created by our pie layout and pass it to <path> elements to draw our pie chart. The pie layout is centered on the 0,0 point in the same way as a circle. If we want to draw it at the center of our canvas, we need to create a new <g> element to hold the <path> elements we'll draw and then move the <g> to the center of the canvas:

```
d3.select("svg")
    .append("g")
    .attr("transform","translate(250,250)")
    .selectAll("path")
    .data(yourPie)
    .enter()
    .append("path")
    .attr("d", newArc)
    .style("fill", "blue")
    .style("opacity", .5)
    .style("stroke", "black")
    .style("stroke-width", "2px");
```

◁ **Appends a new <g> and moves it to the middle of the canvas so that it'll be easier to see the results**

Binds the array that was created using the pie layout, not our original array or the pie layout itself ⊳

◁ **Each path drawn based on that array needs to pass through the newArc function, which sees the startAngle and endAngle attributes of the objects and produces the commensurate SVG drawing code.**

Figure 5.5 shows our pie chart. The pie chart layout, like most layouts, grows more complicated when you want to work with JSON object arrays rather than number

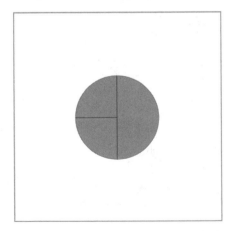

Figure 5.5   A pie chart showing three pie pieces that subdivide the circle between the values in the array [1,1,2].

arrays. Let's bring back our tweets.json from chapter 2. We can nest and measure it to transform it from an array of tweets into an array of Twitter users with their number of tweets computed:

```
var nestedTweets = d3.nest()
    .key(function (el) {
       return el.user;
    })
    .entries(incData);
nestedTweets.forEach(function (el) {
    el.numTweets = el.values.length;
    el.numFavorites = d3.sum(el.values, function (d) {
        return d.favorites.length;
    });
    el.numRetweets = d3.sum(el.values, function (d) {
        return d.retweets.length;
    });
});
```

> **Gives the total number of favorites by summing the favorites array length of all the tweets**

> **Gives the total number of retweets by doing the same for the retweets array length**

5.2.2 Creating a ring chart

If we try to run `pieChart(nestedTweets)` like with the earlier array illustrated in figure 5.4, it will fail, because it doesn't know that the numbers we should be using to size our pie pieces come from the `.numTweets` attribute. Most layouts, pie included, can define where the values are in your array by defining an accessor function to get to those values. In the case of nestedTweets, we define `pieChart.value()` to point at the numTweets attribute of the dataset it's being used on. While we're at it, let's set a value for our arc generator's `innerRadius()` so that we create a donut chart instead of a pie chart. With those changes in place, we can use the same code as before to draw the pie chart in figure 5.6:

```
pieChart.value(function(d) {
                return d.numTweets;
            });
newArc.innerRadius(20)
yourPie = pieChart(nestedTweets);
```

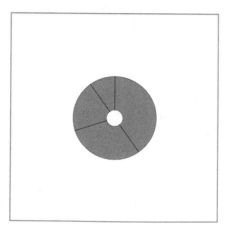

Figure 5.6   A donut chart showing the number of tweets from our four users represented in the `nestedTweets` dataset

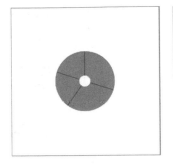 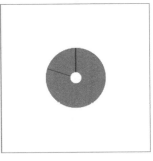

Figure 5.7   **The pie charts representing, on the left, the total number of favorites and, on the right, the total number of retweets**

5.2.3   *Transitioning*

You'll notice that for each value in nestedTweets, we totaled the number of tweets, and also used d3.sum() to total the number of retweets and favorites (if any). Because we have this data, we can adjust our pie chart to show pie pieces based not on the number of tweets but on those other values. One of the core uses of a layout in D3 is to update the graphical chart. All we need to do is make changes to the data or layout and then rebind the data to the existing graphical elements. By using a transition, we can see the pie chart change from one form to the other. Running the following code first transforms the pie chart to represent the number of favorites instead of the number of tweets. The next block causes the pie chart to represent the number of retweets. The final forms of the pie chart after running that code are shown in figure 5.7.

```
pieChart.value(function(d) {
        return d.numFavorites
});
d3.selectAll("path").data(pieChart(nestedTweets))
        .transition().duration(1000).attr("d", newArc);

pieChart.value(function(d) {return d.numRetweets});
d3.selectAll("path").data(pieChart(nestedTweets))
        .transition().duration(1000).attr("d", newArc);
```

Although the results are what we want, the transition can leave a lot to be desired. Figure 5.8 shows snapshots of the pie chart transitioning from representing the number of tweets to representing the number of favorites. As you'll see by running the code

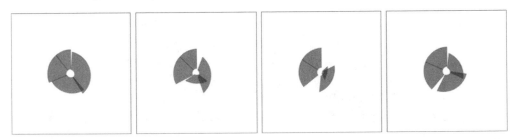

Figure 5.8   **Snapshots of the transition of the pie chart representing the number of tweets to the number of favorites. This transition highlights the need to assign key values for data binding and to use tweens for some types of graphical transition, such as that used for arcs.**

and comparing these snapshots, the pie chart doesn't smoothly transition from one state to another but instead distorts quite significantly.

The reason you see this wonky transition is because, as you learned earlier, the default data-binding key is array position. When the pie layout measures data, it also sorts it in order from largest to smallest, to create a more readable chart. But when you recall the layout, it re-sorts the dataset. The data objects are bound to different pieces in the pie chart, and when you transition between them graphically, you see the effect shown in figure 5.8. To prevent this from happening, we need to disable this sort:

```
pieChart.sort(null);
```

The result is a smooth graphical transition between `numTweets` and `numRetweets`, because the object position in the array remains unchanged, and so the transition in the drawn shapes is straightforward. But if you look closely, you'll notice that the circle deforms a bit because the default `transition()` behavior doesn't deal with arcs well. It's not transitioning the degrees in our arcs; instead, it's treating each arc as a geometric shape and transitioning from one to another.

This becomes obvious when you look at the transition from either of those versions of our pie chart to one that shows `numFavorites`, because some of the objects in our dataset have 0 values for that attribute, and one of them changes size dramatically. To clean this all up and make our pie chart transition properly, we need to change the code. Some of this you've already dealt with, like using key values for your created elements and using them in conjunction with exit and update behavior. But to make our pie pieces transition in a smooth graphical manner, we need to extend our transitions to include a custom tween to define how an arc can grow or shrink graphically into a different arc.

Listing 5.2 Updated binding and transitioning for pie layout

```
pieChart.value(function(d) {                          Updates the function that
           return d.numRetweets;                      defines the value for which
       });                                             we're drawing arcs

d3.selectAll("path").data(pieChart(nestedTweets.filter(function(d) {
                            return d.numRetweets > 0;
       })),                                            Binds only the
           function (d) {                              objects that have
               return d.data.key;                      values, instead of
           }                                           the entire array
)
.exit()                            Removes the
.remove();                         elements that have no
                                   corresponding data
d3.selectAll("path").data(pieChart(nestedTweets.filter(function(d) {
           return d.numRetweets > 0;
       })),
   function (d) {
           return d.data.key}
)
```

User id becomes our key value; this same key value needs to be used in the initial enter() behavior

```
.transition()
.duration(1000)
.attrTween("d", arcTween);
```

            **Calls a tween on
the d attribute**

```
    function arcTween(a) {
       var i = d3.interpolate(this._current, a);
       this._current = i(0);
     return function(t) {
     return newArc(i(t));
     };
  }
```

        **Uses the arc generator to tween
the arc by calculating the shape
of the arc explicitly**

The result of the code in listing 5.2 is a pie chart that cleanly transitions the individual arcs or removes them when no data corresponds to the pie pieces. You'll see more of `attrTween` and `styleTween`, as well as a deeper investigation of easing and other transition properties, in later chapters.

We could label each pie piece `<path>` element, color it according to a measurement or category, or add interactivity. But rather than spend a chapter creating the greatest pie chart application you've ever seen, we'll move on to another kind of layout that's often used: the circle pack.

5.3 *Pack layouts*

Hierarchical data is amenable to an entire family of layouts. One of the most popular is circle packing, shown in figure 5.9. Each object is placed graphically inside the

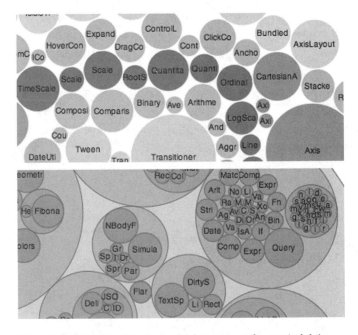

**Figure 5.9 Pack layouts are useful for representing nested data.
They can be flattened (top), or they can visually represent hierarchy
(bottom). (Examples from Bostock, https://github.com/mbostock/
d3/wiki/Pack-Layout.)**

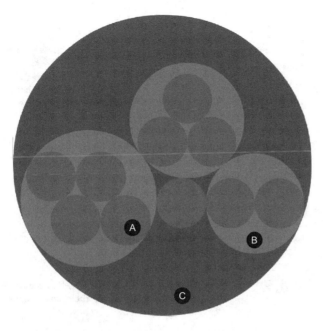

Figure 5.10 Each tweet is represented by a green circle (A) nested inside an orange circle (B) that represents the user who made the tweet. The users are all nested inside a blue circle (C) that represents our "root" node.

hierarchical parent of that object. You can see the hierarchical relationship. As with all layouts, the pack layout expects a default representation of data that may not align with the data you're working with. Specifically, pack expects a JSON object array where the child elements in a hierarchy are stored in a children attribute that points to an array. In examples of layout implementations on the web, the data is typically formatted to match the expected data format. In our case, we would format our tweets like this:

```
{id: "All Tweets", children: [
{id: "Al's Tweets", children: [{id: "tweet1"}, {id: "tweet2"}]},
{id: "Roy's Tweets", children: [{id: "tweet1"}, {id: "tweet2"}]}
...
```

But it's better to get accustomed to adjusting the accessor functions of the layout to match our data. This doesn't mean we don't have to do any data formatting. We still need to create a root node for circle packing to work (what's referred to as "All Tweets" in the previous code). But we'll adjust the accessor function .children() to match the structure of the data as it's represented in nestedTweets, which stores the child elements in the values attribute. In the following listing, we also override the .value() setting that determines the size of circles and set it to a fixed value, as shown in figure 5.10.

Listing 5.3 Circle packing of nested tweets data

```
var nestedTweets = d3.nest().key(function (el) {
        return el.user;
    }).entries(incData);

var packableTweets = {id: "All Tweets", values: nestedTweets};
```

Puts the array that d3.nest creates inside a "root" object that acts as the top-level parent

```
var depthScale = d3.scale.category10([0,1,2]);
var packChart = d3.layout.pack();
packChart.size([500,500])
    .children(function(d) {
            return d.values;
    })
    .value(function(d) {
            return 1;
    });

d3.select("svg")
    .selectAll("circle")
    .data(packChart(packableTweets))
    .enter()
    .append("circle")
    .attr("r", function(d) {return d.r;})
    .attr("cx", function(d) {return d.x;})
    .attr("cy", function(d) {return d.y;})
    .style("fill", function(d) {return depthScale(d.depth);})
    .style("stroke", "black")
    .style("stroke", "2px");
```

Creates a color scale to color each depth of the circle pack differently

Sets the size of the circle-packing chart to the size of our canvas

Sets the pack accessor function for child elements to look for "values", which matches the data created by d3.nest

Binds the results of packChart transforming packableTweets

Creates a function that returns 1 when determining the size of leaf nodes

Radius and xy coordinates are all computed by the pack layout

Gives each node a depth attribute that we can use to color them distinctly by depth

Notice that when the pack layout has a single child (as in the case of Sam, who only made one tweet), the size of the child node is the same as the size of the parent. This can visually seem like Sam is at the same hierarchical level as the other Twitter users who made more tweets. To correct this, we can modify the radius of the circle. That accounts for its depth in the hierarchy, which can act as a margin of sorts:

```
.attr("r", function(d) {return d.r - (d.depth * 10)})
```

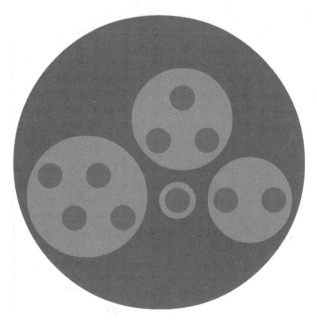

Figure 5.11   An example of a fixed margin based on hierarchical depth. We can create this by reducing the circle size of each node based on its computed "depth" value.

If you want to implement margins like those shown in figure 5.11 in the real world, you should use something more sophisticated than just the depth times 10. That scales poorly with a hierarchical dataset with many levels or with a crowded circle-packing layout. If there were one or two more levels in this hierarchy, our fixed margin would result in negative radius values for the circles, so we should use a `d3.scale.linear()` or other method to set the margin. You can also use the pack layout's built-in `.padding()` function to adjust the spacing between circles at the same hierarchical level.

I glossed over the `.value()` setting on the pack layout earlier. If you have some numerical measurement for your leaf nodes, then you can use that measurement to set their size using `.value()` and therefore influence the size of their parent nodes. In our case, we can base the size of our leaf nodes (tweets) on the number of favorites and retweets each has received (the same value we used in chapter 4 as our "impact factor"). The results in figure 5.12 reflect this new setting.

```
.value(function(d) {return d.retweets.length + d.favorites.length + 1})   ◁─┐
```
Adds 1 so that tweets with no retweets or favorites still have a value greater than zero and are displayed

Layouts, like generators and components, are amenable to method chaining. You'll see examples where the settings and data are all strung together in long chains. As with the pie chart, you could assign interactivity to the nodes or adjust the colors, but this chapter focuses on the general structure of layouts. Notice that circle packing is quite similar to another hierarchical layout known as *treemaps*. Treemaps pack space more effectively because they're built out of rectangles, but they can be harder to read. The next layout is another hierarchical layout, known as a *dendrogram*, that more explicitly draws the hierarchical connections in your data.

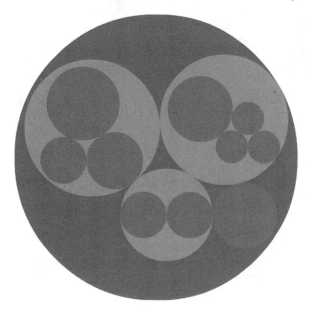

Figure 5.12 A circle-packing layout with the size of the leaf nodes set to the impact factor of those nodes

5.4   *Trees*

Another way to show hierarchical data is to lay it out like a family tree, with the parent nodes connected to the child nodes in a dendrogram (figure 5.13).

The prefix *dendro* means "tree," and in D3 the layout is `d3.layout.tree`. It follows much the same setup as the pack layout, except that to draw the lines connecting the

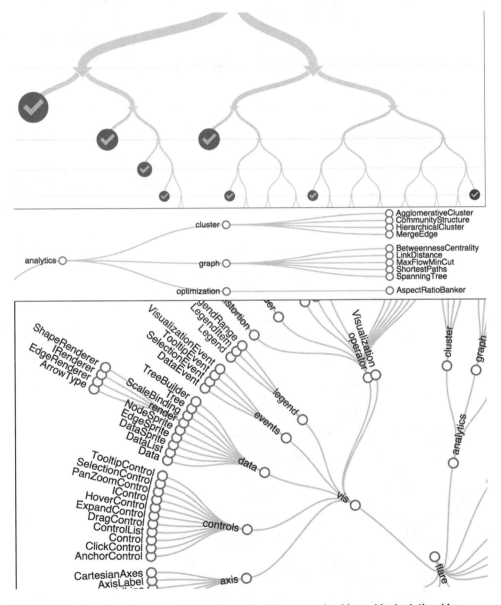

Figure 5.13   Tree layouts are another useful method for expressing hierarchical relationships and are often laid out vertically (top), horizontally (middle), or radially (bottom). (Examples from Bostock.)

nodes, we need a new generator, `d3.svg.diagonal`, which draws a curved line from one point to another.

Listing 5.4 Callback function to draw a dendrogram

```
var treeChart = d3.layout.tree();
treeChart.size([500,500])
        .children(function(d) {return d.values});

var linkGenerator = d3.svg.diagonal();
```
Creates a diagonal generator with the default settings

```
d3.select("svg")
    .append("g")
    .attr("id", "treeG")
    .selectAll("g")
    .data(treeChart(packableTweets))
    .enter()
    .append("g")
    .attr("class", "node")
    .attr("transform", function(d) {
            return "translate(" +d.x+","+d.y+")"
    });
```
Creates a parent <g#treeG> to put all these elements in

This time we'll create <g> elements so we can label them.

Like the pack layout, the tree layout computes the XY coordinates of each node.

Uses packableTweets and depthScale from the previous example

```
d3.selectAll("g.node")
    .append("circle")
    .attr("r", 10)
    .style("fill", function(d) {return depthScale(d.depth)})
    .style("stroke", "white")
    .style("stroke-width", "2px");
```
A little circle representing each node that we color with the same scale we used for the circle pack

```
d3.selectAll("g.node")
    .append("text")
    .text(function(d) {return d.id || d.key || d.content})
```
A text label for each node, with the text being either the id, key, or content attribute, whichever the node has

```
d3.select("#treeG").selectAll("path")
    .data(treeChart.links(treeChart(packableTweets)))
    .enter().insert("path","g")
    .attr("d", linkGenerator)
    .style("fill", "none")
    .style("stroke", "black")
    .style("stroke-width", "2px");
```
The .links function of the layout creates an array of links between each node that we can use to draw these links.

Just like all the other generators

Our dendrogram in figure 5.14 is a bit hard to read. To turn it on its side, we need to adjust the positioning of the <g> elements by flipping the x and y coordinates, which orients the nodes horizontally. We also need to adjust the `.projection()` of the diagonal generator, which orients the lines horizontally:

```
linkGenerator.projection(function (d) {return [d.y, d.x]})

...

    .append("g")

...

    .attr("transform", function(d) {return "translate(" +d.y+","+d.x+")"});
```

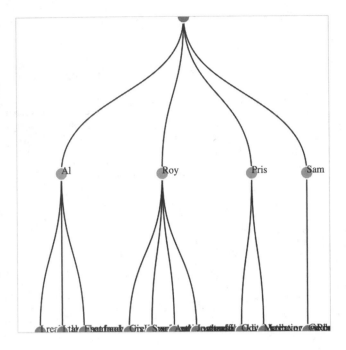

Figure 5.14   A dendrogram laid out vertically using data from tweets.json. The level 0 "root" node (which we created to contain the users) is in blue, the level 1 nodes (which represent users) are in orange, and the level 2 "leaf" nodes (which represent tweets) are in green.

The result, shown in figure 5.15, is more legible because the text isn't overlapping on the bottom of the canvas. But critical aspects of the chart are still drawn off the canvas. We only see half of the root node and the leaf nodes (the blue and green circles) and can't read any of the labels of the leaf nodes, which represent our tweets.

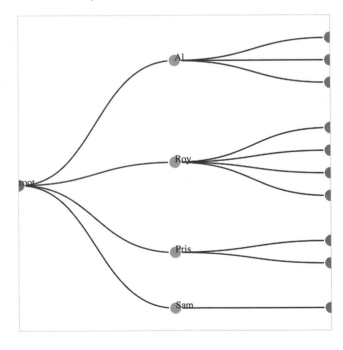

Figure 5.15   The same dendrogram as figure 5.14 but laid out horizontally.

We could try to create margins along the height and width of the layout as we did earlier. Or we could provide information about each node as a information box that opens when we click it, as with the soccer data. But a better option is to give the user the ability to drag the canvas up and down and left and right to see more of the visualization.

To do this, we use the D3 zoom behavior, `d3.behavior.zoom`, which creates a set of event listeners. A behavior is like a component, but instead of creating graphical objects, it creates events (in this case for drag, mousewheel, and double-click) and ties those events to the element that calls the behavior. With each of these events, a zoom object changes its `.translate()` and/or `.scale()` values to correspond to the traditional dragging and zooming interaction. You'll use these changed values to adjust the position of graphical elements in response to user interaction. Like a component, the zoom behavior needs to be called by the element to which you want these events attached. Typically, you call the zoom from the base `<svg>` element, because then it fires whenever you click anything in your graphical area. When creating the zoom component, you need to define what functions are called on *zoomstart, zoom,* and *zoomend,* which correspond (as you might imagine) to the beginning of a zoom event, the event itself, and the end of the event, respectively. Because zoom fires continuously as a user drags the mouse, you may want resource-intensive functions only at the beginning or end of the zoom event. You'll see more complicated zoom strategies, as well as the use of scale, in chapter 7 when we look at geospatial mapping, which uses zooming extensively.

As with other components, to start a zoom component you create a new instance and set any attributes of it you may need. In our case, we only want the default zoom component, with the `zoom` event triggering a new function, `zoomed()`. This function changes the position of the `<g>` element that holds our chart and allows the user to drag it around:

Keys the "zoom" event to the zoomed() function

Creates a new zoom component

Calls our zoom component with the SVG canvas

```
treeZoom = d3.behavior.zoom();
treeZoom.on("zoom", zoomed);
d3.select("svg").call(treeZoom);

function zoomed() {
  var zoomTranslate = treeZoom.translate();
  d3.select("g.treeG").attr("transform",
      "translate("+zoomTranslate[0]+","+zoomTranslate[1]+")")
};
```

Transform attribute changes to reflect the zoom behavior

Updating the `<g>` to set it to the same translate setting of the zoom component updates the position of the `<g>` and all its child elements.

Now we can drag and pan our entire chart left and right and up and down. In figure 5.16, we can finally read the text of the tweets by dragging the chart to the left. The ability to zoom and pan gives you powerful interactivity to enhance your charts. It may seem odd that you learned how to use something called *zoom* and haven't even dealt with

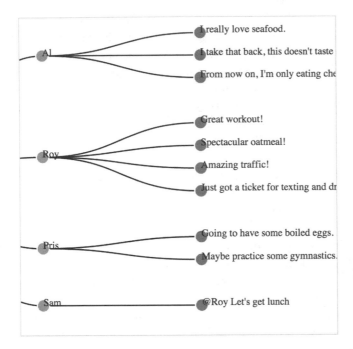

Figure 5.16   The dendrogram, when dragged to the left, shows the labels for the tweets.

zooming in and out, but panning tends to be more universally useful with charts like these, while changing scale becomes a necessity when dealing with maps.

We have other choices besides drawing our tree from top to bottom and left to right. If we tie the position of each node to an angle, and use a diagonal generator subclass created for radial layouts, we can draw our tree diagrams in a radial pattern:

```
var linkGenerator = d3.svg.diagonal.radial()
    .projection(function(d) { return [d.y, d.x / 180 * Math.PI]; });
```

To make this work well, we need to reduce the size of our chart, because the radial drawing of a tree layout in D3 uses the size to determine the maximum radius, and is drawn out from the 0,0 point of its container like a `<circle>` element:

```
treeChart.size([200,200])
```

With these changes in place, we need only change the positioning of the nodes to take rotation into account:

```
.attr("transform", function(d) { return "rotate(" + (d.x - 90) +
    ")translate(" + d.y + ")"; })
```

Figure 5.17 shows the results of these changes.

The dendrogram is a generic way of displaying information. It can be repurposed for menus or information you may not think of as traditionally hierarchical. One example (figure 5.18) is from the work of Jason Davies, who used the dendrogram functionality in D3 to create word trees.

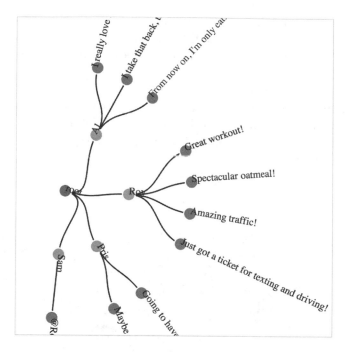

Figure 5.17 The same dendrogram laid out in a radial manner. Notice that the `<g>` elements are rotated, so their child `<text>` elements are rotated in the same manner.

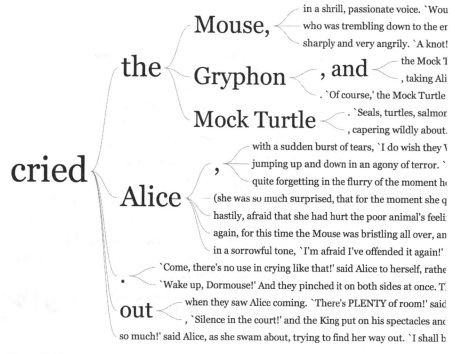

Figure 5.18 Example of using a dendrogram in a word tree by Jason Davies (http://www.jasondavies.com/wordtree/).

Hierarchical layouts are common and well understood by readers. This gives you the option to emphasize the nested container nature of a hierarchy, as we did with the circle pack layout, or the links between parent and child elements, as with the dendrogram.

5.5   *Stack layout*

You saw the effects of the stack layout in the last chapter when we created a streamgraph, an example of which is shown in figure 5.19. We began with a simple stacking function and then made it more complex. As I pointed out then, D3 actually implements a stack layout, which formats your data so that it can be easily passed to d3.svg.area to draw a stacked graph or streamgraph.

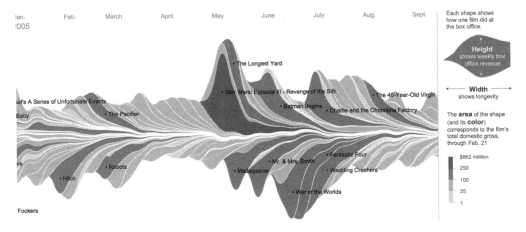

Figure 5.19   The streamgraph used in a *New York Times* piece on movie grosses (figure from *The New York Times*, February 23, 2008; http://mng.bz/rV7M)

To implement this, we'll use the area generator in tandem with the stack layout in listing 5.5. This general pattern should be familiar to you by now:

1 Process the data to match the requirements of the layout.
2 Set the accessor functions of the layout to align it with the dataset.
3 Use the layout to format the data for display.
4 Send the modified data either directly to SVG elements or paired with a generator like d3.svg.diagonal, d3.svg.arc, or d3.svg.area.

The first step is to take our original streamdata.csv data and transform it into an array of movies objects that each have an array of values at points that correspond to the thickness of the section of the streamgraph that they represent.

Listing 5.5   Stack layout example

```
d3.csv("movies.csv", function(error,data) {dataViz(data)});

  function dataViz(incData) {
    expData = incData;
    stackData = [];
```

```
var xScale = d3.scale.linear().domain([0, 10]).range([0, 500]);
var yScale = d3.scale.linear().domain([0, 100]).range([500, 0]);
var movieColors = d3.scale
    .category10(["movie1","movie2","movie3","movie4","movie5","movie6"]);
var stackArea = d3.svg.area()
    .interpolate("basis")
    .x(function(d) { return xScale(d.x); })
    .y0(function(d) { return yScale(d.y0); })
    .y1(function(d) { return yScale(d.y0 + d.y); });
for (x in incData[0]) {
  if (x != "day") {
    var newMovieObject = {name: x, values: []};
    for (y in incData) {
      newMovieObject.values.push({
          x: parseInt(incData[y]["day"]) ,
          y: parseInt(incData[y][x])
      });
    };
    stackData.push(newMovieObject);
  };
};
stackLayout = d3.layout.stack()
    .offset("silhouette")
    .order("inside-out")
    .values(function(d) { return d.values; });

d3.select("svg").selectAll("path")
    .data(stackLayout(stackData))
    .enter().append("path")
    .style("fill", function(d) {return movieColors(d.name);})
    .attr("d", function(d) { return stackArea(d.values); });
};
```

We want to skip the day column, because, in this case, the day becomes our x value.

For each movie, we create an object with an empty array named "values".

Fill the "values" array with objects that list the x coordinate as the day and the y coordinate as the amount of money made by a movie on that day.

After the initial dataset is reformatted, the data in the object array is structured so that the stack layout can deal with it:

```
[
{"name":"movie1","values":[{"x":1,"y":20},{"x":2,"y":18},{"x":3,"y":14},{"x":
    4,"y":7},{"x":5,"y":4},{"x":6,"y":3},{"x":7,"y":2},{"x":8,"y":0},{"x":9,
    "y":0},{"x":10,"y":0}]},
{"name":"movie2","values":[{"x":1,"y":8},{"x":2,"y":5},{"x":3,"y":3},{"x":4,"
    y":3},{"x":5,"y":3},{"x":6,"y":1},{"x":7,"y":0},{"x":8,"y":0},{"x":9,"y"
    :0},{"x":10,"y":0}]}
...
```

The x value is the day, and the y value is the amount of money made by the movie that day, which corresponds to thickness. As with other layouts, if we didn't format our data this way, we'd need to adjust the `.x()` and `.y()` accessors to match our data names for those values. One of the benefits of formatting our data to match the expected data model of the layout is that the layout function is very simple:

```
stackLayout = d3.layout.stack()
.values(function(d) { return d.values; });
```

Function chains on the newly created stack() layout function

After our `stackLayout` function processes our dataset, we can get the results by running `stackLayout(stackData)`. The layout creates x, y, and y0 functions corresponding to the top and bottom of the object at the x position. If we use the stack layout to create a streamgraph, then it requires a corresponding area generator:

```
var stackArea = d3.svg.area()
.x(function(d) { return xScale(d.x); })
.y0(function(d) { return yScale(d.y0); })
.y1(function(d) { return yScale(d.y0 + d.y); });
```

> **Usually at some point you need to pass the data to a scale function to fit it to the screen.**

After we have our data, layout, and area generator in order, we can call them all as part of the selection and binding process. This gives a set of SVG `<path>` elements the necessary shapes to make our chart:

```
d3.select("svg").selectAll("path")
    .data(stackLayout(stackData))
    .enter()
    .append("path")
    .style("fill", function(d) {return movieColors(d.name);})
    .attr("d", function(d) { return stackArea(d.values); });
```

> **The data being bound is stackData processed by stackLayout().**

> **A color scale that associates a unique color with each object in the array**

> **The area generator takes the values from our data processed by the layout to get the SVG drawing code.**

The result, as shown in figure 5.20, isn't a streamgraph but rather a stacked area chart, which isn't that different from a streamgraph, as you'll soon find out.

The stack layout has an `.offset()` function that determines the relative positions of the areas that make up the chart. Although we can write our own offset functions to create exotic charts, this function recognizes a few keywords that achieve the typical effects we're looking for. We'll use the `silhouette` keyword, which centers the drawing

Figure 5.20   The stack layout default settings, when tied to an area generator, produce a stacked area chart like this one.

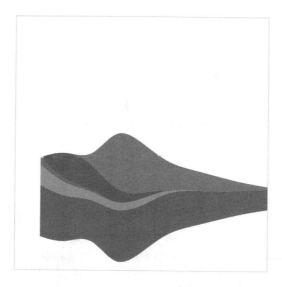

Figure 5.21   The streamgraph effect from a stack layout with basis interpolation for the areas and using the `silhouette` and `inside-out` settings for the stack layout. This is similar to our hand-built example from chapter 4 and shows the same graphical artifacts from the basis interpolation.

of the stacked areas around the middle. Another function useful for creating stream-graphs is the `.order()` function of a stack layout, which determines the order in which areas are drawn, so that you can alternate them like in a streamgraph. We'll use `inside-out` because that produces the best streamgraph effect. The last change is to the area constructor, which we'll update to use the `basis` interpolator because that gave the best look in our earlier streamgraph example:

```
stackLayout.offset("silhouette").order("inside-out");
stackArea.interpolator("basis");
```

This results in a cleaner streamgraph than our example from chapter 4, and is shown in figure 5.21.

The last time we made a streamgraph, we explored the question of whether it was a useful chart. It *is* useful, for various reasons, not least of which is because the area in the chart corresponds graphically to the aggregate profit of each movie.

But sometimes a simple stacked bar graph is better. Layouts can be used for various types of charts, and the stack layout is no different. If we restore the `.offset()` and `.order()` back to the default settings, we can use the stack layout to create a set of rectangles that makes a traditional stacked bar chart:

```
stackLayout = d3.layout.stack()
    .values(function(d) { return d.values; });

var heightScale = d3.scale.linear()
    .domain([0, 70])
    .range([0, 480]);

d3.select("svg").selectAll("g.bar")
    .data(stackLayout(stackData))
    .enter()
    .append("g")
```

```
          .attr("class", "bar")
          .each(function(d) {

             d3.select(this).selectAll("rect")
                .data(d.values)
                .enter()
                .append("rect")
                .attr("x", function(p) { return xScale(p.x) - 15; })
                .attr("y", function(p) { return yScale(p.y + p.y0); })
                .attr("height", function(p) { return heightScale(p.y); })
                .attr("width", 30)
                .style("fill", movieColors(d.name));
          });
```

In many ways, the stacked bar chart in figure 5.22 is much more readable than the streamgraph. It presents the same information, but the y-axis tells us exactly how much money a movie made. There's a reason why bar charts, line charts, and pie charts are the standard chart types found in your spreadsheet. Streamgraph, stacked bar charts, and stacked area charts are fundamentally the same thing, and rely on the stack layout to format your dataset to draw it. Because you can deploy them equally easily, your decision whether to use one or the other can be based on user testing rather than your ability to create awesome dataviz.

The layouts we've looked at so far, as well as the associated methods and generators, have broad applicability. Now we'll look at a pair of layouts that don't come with D3 that are designed for more specific kinds of data: the Sankey diagram and the word cloud. Even though these layouts aren't as generic as the layouts included in the core D3 library that we've looked at, they have some prominent examples and can come in handy.

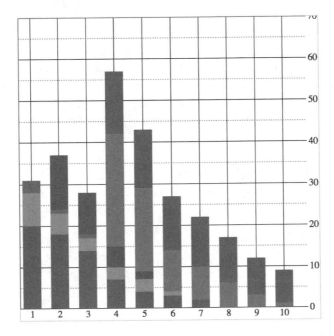

Figure 5.22   A stacked bar chart using the stack layout to determine the position of the rectangles that make up each day's stacked bar

5.6   *Plugins to add new layouts*

The examples we've touched on in this chapter are a few of the layouts that come with the core D3 library. You'll see a few more in later chapters, and we'll focus specifically on the force layout in chapter 6. But layouts outside of core D3 may also be useful to you. These layouts tend to use specifically formatted datasets or different terminology for layout functions.

5.6.1   *Sankey diagram*

The Sankey diagram provides you with the ability to map flow from one category to another. It's the kind of diagram used in Google Analytics (figure 5.23) to show event flow or user flow from one part of your website to another. Sankey diagrams consist of two types of objects: nodes and edges. In this case, the nodes are the web pages or events, and the edges are the traffic between them. This differs from the hierarchical data you worked with before, because nodes can have many overlapping connections.

The D3 version of the Sankey layout is a plugin written by Mike Bostock a couple of years ago, and you can find it at https://github.com/d3/d3-plugins along with other interesting D3 plugins. The Sankey layout has a couple of examples and sparse documentation—one of the drawbacks of noncore layouts. Another minor drawback is that they don't always follow the patterns of the core layouts in D3. To understand the Sankey layout, you need to examine the format of the data, the examples, and the code itself.

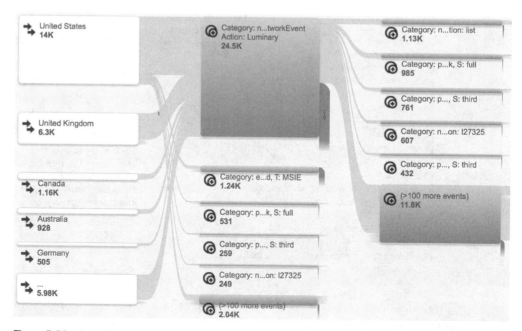

Figure 5.23   Google Analytics uses Sankey diagrams to chart event and user flow for website visitors.

D3 PLUGINS The core d3.js library that you download comes with quite a few layouts and useful functions, but you can find even more at https://github.com/d3/d3-plugins. Besides the two noncore layouts discussed in this chapter, we'll look at the geo plugins in chapter 7 when we deal with maps. Also available is a fisheye distortion lens, a canned boxplot layout, a layout for horizon charts, and more exotic plugins for Chernoff faces and implementing the superformula.

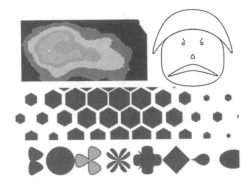

The data is a JSON array of nodes and a second JSON array of links. Get used to this format, because it's the format of most of the network data we'll use in chapter 6. For our example, we'll look at the traffic flow in a website that sells milk and milk-based products. We want to see how visitors move through the site from the homepage to the store page to the various product pages. In the parlance of the data format we need to work with, the nodes are the web pages, the links are the visitors who go from one page to another (if any), and the value of each link is the total number of visitors who move from that page to the next.

Listing 5.6   sitestats.json

```
{
    "nodes":[
        {"name":"index"},              ←  Each entry in this
        {"name":"about"},                 array represents
        {"name":"contact"},               a web page.
        {"name":"store"},
        {"name":"cheese"},
        {"name":"yoghurt"},
        {"name":"milk"}
    ],
    "links":[
        {"source":0,"target":1,"value":25},    ←  Each entry in this array
        {"source":0,"target":2,"value":10},       represents the number of
        {"source":0,"target":3,"value":40},       times someone navigated
        {"source":1,"target":2,"value":10},       from the "source" page to
        {"source":3,"target":4,"value":25},       the "target" page.
        {"source":3,"target":5,"value":10},
        {"source":3,"target":6,"value":5},
        {"source":4,"target":6,"value":5},
        {"source":4,"target":5,"value":15}
    ]
}
```

The nodes array is clear—each object represents a web page. The links array is a bit more opaque, until you realize the numbers represent the array position of nodes in the node array. So when links[0] reads "source": 0, it means that the source is nodes[0], which is the index page of the site. It connects to nodes[1], the about page, and indicates that 25 people navigated from the home page to the about page. That defines our flow—the flow of traffic through a site.

The Sankey layout is initialized like any layout:

```
var sankey = d3.sankey()
  .nodeWidth(20)
  .nodePadding(200)
  .size([460, 460])
  .nodes(data.nodes)
  .links(data.links)
  .layout(200);
```

Where to start and stop drawing the flows between nodes

The number of times to run the layout to optimize placement of flows

The distance between nodes vertically; a lower value creates longer bars representing our web pages

Until now, you've only seen .size(). It controls the graphical extent that the layout uses. The rest you'd need to figure out by looking at the example, experimenting with different values, or reading the sankey.js code itself. Most of it will quickly make sense, especially if you're familiar with the .nodes() and .links() convention used in D3 network visualizations. The .layout() setting is pretty hard to understand without diving into the code, but I'll explain that next.

After we define our Sankey layout as in listing 5.7, we need to draw the chart by selecting and binding the necessary SVG elements. In this case, that typically consists of <rect> elements for the nodes and <path> elements for the flows. We'll also add <text> elements to label the nodes.

Listing 5.7 Sankey drawing code

```
var intensityRamp = d3.scale.linear()
  .domain([0,d3.max(data.links, function(d) {
                    return d.value;
}) ])
  .range(["black", "red"]);

d3.select("svg").append("g")
  .attr("transform", "translate(20,20)").attr("id", "sankeyG");

d3.select("#sankeyG").selectAll(".link")
  .data(data.links)
  .enter().append("path")
  .attr("class", "link")
  .attr("d", sankey.link())
  .style("stroke-width", function(d) { return d.dy; })
  .style("stroke-opacity", .5)
  .style("fill", "none")
  .style("stroke", function(d){ return intensityRamp(d.value); })
  .sort(function(a, b) { return b.dy - a.dy; })
  .on("mouseover", function() {
          d3.select(this).style("stroke-opacity", .8);
  })
  .on("mouseout", function() {
      d3.selectAll("path.link").style("stroke-opacity", .5)
});
```

Offsets the parent <g> of the entire chart

Sankey layout's .link() function is a path generator

Note that layout expects us to use a thick stroke and not a filled area.

Sets the stroke color using our intensity ramp, black to red indicating weak to strong

Emphasizes the link when we mouse over it by making it less transparent

```
d3.select("#sankeyG").selectAll(".node")
    .data(data.nodes)
    .enter().append("g")
    .attr("class", "node")
    .attr("transform", function(d) {
        return "translate(" + d.x + "," + d.y + ")";
    });

d3.selectAll(".node").append("rect")
    .attr("height", function(d) { return d.dy; })
    .attr("width", 20)
    .style("fill", "pink")
    .style("stroke", "gray");

d3.selectAll(".node").append("text")
    .attr("x", 0)
    .attr("y", function(d) { return d.dy / 2; })
    .attr("text-anchor", "middle")
    .text(function(d) { return d.name; });
```

◁—— **Calculates node position as x and y coordinates on our data**

The implementation of this layout has some interactivity, as shown in figure 5.24. Diagrams like these, with wavy paths overlapping other wavy paths, need interaction to make them legible to your site visitor. In this case, it differentiates one flow from another.

With a Sankey diagram like this at your disposal, you can track the flow of goods, visitors, or anything else through your organization, website, or other system. Although you could expand on this example in any number of ways, I think one of the most useful is also one of the simplest. Remember, layouts aren't tied to particular shape elements. In some cases, like with the flows in the Sankey diagram, you'll have a

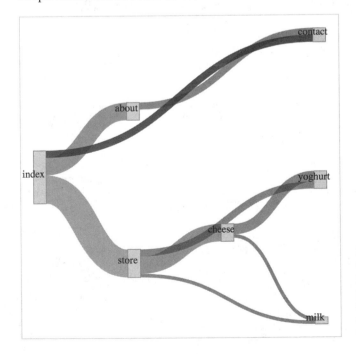

Figure 5.24   A Sankey diagram where the number of visitors is represented in the color of the path. The flow between index and contact has an increased opacity as the result of a mouseover event.

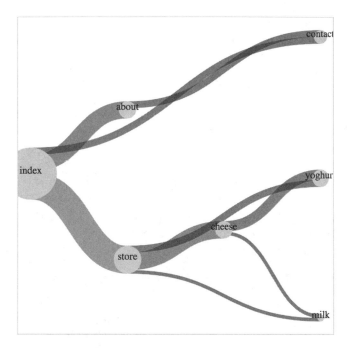

Figure 5.25 A squid-like Sankey diagram

hard time adapting the layout data to any element other than a <path>, but the nodes don't need to be <rect> elements. If we adjust our code, we can easily make nodes that are circles:

```
sankey.nodeWidth(1);

d3.selectAll(".node").append("circle")
    .attr("height", function(d) { return d.dy; })
    .attr("r", function(d) { return d.dy / 2; })
    .attr("cy", function(d) { return d.dy / 2; })
    .style("fill", "pink")
    .style("stroke", "gray");
```

Don't shy away from experimenting with tweaks to traditional charting methods. Using circles instead of rectangles, like in figure 5.25, may seem frivolous, but it may be a better fit visually, or it may distinguish your Sankey from all the boring sharp-edged Sankeys out there. In the same vein, don't be afraid of leveraging D3's capacity for information visualization to teach yourself how a layout works. You'll remember that d3.layout.sankey has a layout() function, and you might discover the operation of that function by reading the code. But there's another way for you to see how this function works: by using transitions and creating a function that updates the .layout() property dynamically, you can see what this function does to the chart graphically.

VISUALIZING ALGORITHMS Although you may think of data visualization as all the graphics in this book, it's also simultaneously a graphical representation of the methods you used to process the data. In some cases, like the Sankey diagram here or the force-directed network visualization you'll see in the next chapter, the algorithm used to sort and arrange the graphical elements is front and center. After you have a layout that displays properly, you can play with the settings and update the elements like you've done with the Sankey diagram to better understand how the algorithm works visually.

First we need to add an onclick function to make the chart interactive, as shown in listing 5.8. We'll attach this function to the <svg> element itself, but you could just as easily add a button like we did in chapter 3.

The moreLayouts() function does two things. It updates the sankey.layout() property by incrementing a variable and setting it to the new value of that variable. It also selects the graphical elements that make up your chart (the <g> and <path> elements) and redraws them with the updated settings. By using transition() and delay(), you'll see the chart dynamically adjust.

Listing 5.8   Visual layout function for the Sankey diagram

```
var numLayouts = 1;
d3.select("svg").on("click", moreLayouts);       Initializes the sankey
sankey.layout(numLayouts);                    ◁──  with only a single
                                                     layout pass
function moreLayouts() {
  numLayouts += 20;                          ◁──
  sankey.layout(numLayouts);

                                              We choose 20 passes because it
  d3.selectAll(".link")                       shows some change without
  .transition()                               requiring us to click too much.
  .duration(500)
  .attr("d", sankey.link())          ◁──   Because the layout updates the
                                           dataset, we just have to call the
  d3.selectAll(".node")                    drawing functions again and they
  .transition()                            automatically update.
  .duration(500)
  .attr("transform", function(d) {
        return "translate(" + d.x + "," + d.y + ")";
  });
}
```

Figure 5.26   The Sankey layout algorithm attempts to optimize the positioning of nodes to reduce overlap. The chart reflects the position of nodes after (from left to right) 1 pass, 20 passes, 40 passes, and 200 passes.

The end result is a visual experience of the effect of the `.layout()` function. This function specifies the number of passes that `d3.layout.sankey` makes to determine the best position of the lines representing flow. You can see some snapshots of this in figure 5.26 showing the lines sort out and get out of each other's way. This kind of position optimization is a common technique in information visualization, and drives the force-directed network layout that you'll see in chapter 6. In the case of our Sankey example, even one pass of the layout provides good positioning. That's because this is a simple dataset, and it stabilizes quickly. As you can see as you click your chart and in figure 5.26, the layout doesn't change much with progressively higher numbers of passes in the `layout()` setting.

It should be clear by this example that when you update the settings of the layout, you can also update the visual display of the layout. You can use animations and transitions by simply calling the elements and setting their drawing code or position to reflect the changed data. You'll see much more of this in later chapters.

5.6.2 Word clouds

One of the most popular information visualization charts is also one of the most maligned: the word cloud. Also known as a tag cloud, the word cloud uses text and text size to represent the importance or frequency of words. Figure 5.27 shows a

Figure 5.27 A word or tag cloud uses the size of a word to indicate its importance or frequency in a text, creating a visual summary of text. These word clouds were created by the popular online word cloud generator Wordle (www.wordle.net).

thumbnail gallery of 15 word clouds derived from text in a species biodiversity database. Oftentimes, word clouds rotate the words to set them at right angles or jumble them at random angles to improve the appearance of the graphics. Word clouds, like streamgraphs, receive criticism for being hard to read or presenting too little information. But both are surprisingly popular with audiences.

I created these word clouds using my data with the popular Java applet Wordle, which provides an easy UI and a few aesthetic customization choices. Wordle has flooded the internet with word clouds because it lets anyone create visually arresting but problematic graphics by dropping text onto a page. This caused much consternation among data visualization experts, who think word clouds are evil because they embed no analysis in the visualization and only highlight superficial data such as the quantity of words in a blog post.

But word clouds aren't evil. First of all, they're popular with audiences. But more than that, words are remarkably effective graphical objects. If you can identify a numerical attribute that indicates the significance of a word, then scaling the size of a word in a word cloud relays that significance to your reader.

So let's start by assuming we have the right kind of data for a word cloud. Fortunately, we do: the top twenty words used in this chapter, with the number of each word.

Listing 5.9   worddata.csv

```
text,frequency
layout,63
function,61
data,47
return,36
attr,29
chart,28
array,24
style,24
layouts,22
values,22
need,21
nodes,21
pie,21
use,21
figure,20
circle,19
we'll,19
zoom,19
append,17
elements,17
```

To create a word cloud with D3, you have to use another layout that isn't in the core library, created by Jason Davies (who created the sentence trees using the tree layout shown in figure 5.17). You'll also need to implement an algorithm written by Jonathan Feinberg (http://static.mrfeinberg.com/bv_ch03.pdf). The layout, `d3.layout.cloud()`, is available on GitHub at https://github.com/jasondavies/d3-cloud. It requires that you define what attribute will determine word size and what size you want the word cloud to lay out for.

Unlike most other layouts, cloud() fires a custom event "end" that indicates it's done calculating the most efficient use of space to generate the word cloud. The layout then passes to this event the processed dataset with the position, rotation, and size of the words. We can then run the cloud layout without ever referring to it again, and we don't even need to assign it to a variable, as we do in the following listing. If we plan to reuse the cloud layout and adjust the settings, we assign it to a variable like with any other layout.

Listing 5.10 Creating a word cloud with d3.layout.cloud

Uses a scale rather than raw values for the font →

```
var wordScale=d3.scale.linear().domain([0,75]).range([10,160]);

d3.layout.cloud()
  .size([500, 500])
  .words(data)
  .fontSize(function(d) { return wordScale(d.frequency); })
  .on("end", draw)
  .start();

function draw(words) {

  var wordG = d3.select("svg").append("g")
    .attr("id", "wordCloudG")
    .attr("transform","translate(250,250)");

  wordG.selectAll("text")
    .data(words)
    .enter()
    .append("text")
    .style("font-size", function(d) { return d.size + "px"; })
    .style("opacity", .75)
    .attr("text-anchor", "middle")
    .attr("transform", function(d) {
        return "translate(" + [d.x, d.y] + ")rotate(" + d.rotate + ")";
    })
    .text(function(d) { return d.text; });
};
```

Assigns data to the cloud layout using .words()

Sets the size of each word using our scale

The cloud layout needs to be initialized; when it's done it fires "end" and runs whatever function "end" is associated with.

We've assigned draw() to "end", which automatically passes the processed dataset as the words variable.

Translation and rotation are calculated by the cloud layout.

This code creates an SVG <text> element that's rotated and placed according to the code. None of our words are rotated, so we get the staid word cloud shown in figure 5.28.

It's simple enough to define rotation, and we only need to set some rotation value in the cloud layout's .rotate() function:

```
randomRotate=d3.scale.linear().domain([0,1]).range([-20,20]);

d3.layout.cloud()
  .size([500, 500])
  .words(data)
  .rotate(function() {return randomRotate(Math.random())} )
```

This scale takes a random number between 0 and 1 and returns an angle between -20 degrees and 20 degrees.

Sets the rotation for each word

```
.fontSize(function(d) { return wordScale(d.frequency); })
.on("end", draw)
.start();
```

At this point, we have your traditional word cloud (figure 5.29), and we can tweak the settings and colors to create anything you've seen on Wordle. But now let's take a look at why word clouds get such a bad reputation. We've taken an interesting dataset, the most common words in this chapter, and, other than size them by their frequency, done little more than place them on screen and jostle them a bit. We have different channels for expressing data visually, and in this case the best channels that we have, besides size, are color and rotation.

With that in mind, let's imagine that we have a keyword list for this book, and that each of these words is in a glossary in the back of the book. We'll place those keywords

Figure 5.28   A word cloud with words that are arranged horizontally

Figure 5.29   A word cloud using the same worddata.csv but with words slightly perturbed by randomizing the rotation property of each word

in an array and use them to highlight the words in our word cloud that appear in the glossary. The code in the following listing also rotates shorter words 90 degrees and leaves the longer words unrotated so that they'll be easier to read.

Listing 5.11   Word cloud layout with key word highlighting

Our array of keywords →

```
var keywords = ["layout", "zoom", "circle", "style", "append", "attr"]

d3.layout.cloud()
    .size([500, 500])
    .words(data)
    .rotate(function(d) { return d.text.length > 5 ? 0 : 90; })
    .fontSize(function(d) { return wordScale(d.frequency); })
    .on("end", draw)
    .start();

function draw(words) {

    var wordG = d3.select("svg").append("g")
        .attr("id", "wordCloudG").attr("transform","translate(250,250)");

    wordG.selectAll("text")
        .data(words)
        .enter()
        .append("text")
        .style("font-size", function(d) { return d.size + "px"; })
        .style("fill", function(d) {
            return (keywords.indexOf(d.text) > -1 ? "red" : "black");
        })
        .style("opacity", .75)
        .attr("text-anchor", "middle")
        .attr("transform", function(d) {
            return "translate(" + [d.x, d.y] + ") rotate(" + d.rotate + ")";
        })
        .text(function(d) { return d.text; });
};
```

← **The rotate function rotates by 90 degrees every word with five or fewer characters.**

If the word appears in the keyword list, color it red; otherwise, color it black. →

Figure 5.30   This word cloud highlights keywords and places longer words horizontally and shorter words vertically.

The word cloud in figure 5.30 is fundamentally the same, but instead of using color and rotation for aesthetics, we used them to encode information in the dataset. You can read about more controls over the format of your word cloud, including selecting fonts and padding, in the layout's documentation at https://www.jasondavies.com/wordcloud/about/.

Layouts like the word cloud aren't suitable for as wide a variety of data as some other layouts, but because they're so easy to deploy and customize, you can combine them with other charts to represent the multiple facets of your data. You'll see this kind of synchronized chart in chapter 9.

5.7   *Summary*

In this chapter, we took an in-depth look at D3 layout structure and experimented with several datasets. In doing so, you learned how to use layouts not just to draw one particular chart, but also variations on that chart. You also experimented with interactivity and animation.

In particular, we covered

- Layout structure and functions common to D3 core layouts
- Arc and diagonal generators for drawing arcs and connecting links
- How to make pie charts and donut charts using the pie layout
- Using tweens to better animate the graphical transition for arc segments (pie pieces)
- How to create circle-packing diagrams and format them effectively using the pack layout
- How to create vertical, horizontal, and radial dendrograms using the tree layout
- How to create stacked area charts, streamgraphs, and stacked bar charts using the stack layout
- How to use noncore D3 layouts to build Sankey diagrams and word clouds

Now that you understand layouts in general, in the next chapter we'll focus on how to represent networks. We'll spend most of our time working with the force-directed layout, which has much in common with general layouts but is distinguished from them because it's designed to be interactive and animated. Because the chapter deals with network data, like the kind you used for the Sankey layout in this chapter, you'll also learn a few tips and tricks for processing and measuring networks.

Network visualization

Network analysis and network visualization are more common now with the growth of online social networks like Twitter and Facebook, as well as social media and linked data in what was known as Web 2.0. Network visualizations like the kind you'll see in this chapter, some of which are shown in figure 6.1, are particularly interesting because they focus on how things are related. They represent systems more accurately than the traditional flat data seen in more common data visualizations.

This chapter focuses on representing networks, so it's important that you understand network terminology. In general, when dealing with networks you refer to the things being connected (like people) as *nodes* and the connections between them (such as being a friend on Facebook) as *edges* or *links*. You may hear nodes referred to as *vertices*, because that's where the edges join. Although it may seem useful to have a figure with nodes and edges labeled, one of the lessons from this chapter is that there is no one way to represent a network. Networks may also be referred to as

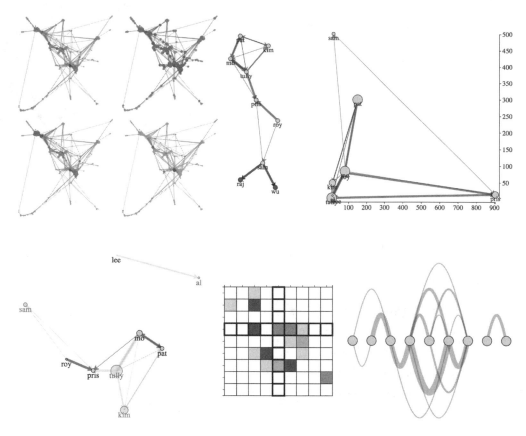

Figure 6.1   Along with explaining the basics of network analysis (section 6.2.3), this chapter includes laying out networks using xy positioning (section 6.2.5), force-directed algorithms (section 6.2), adjacency matrices (section 6.1.2), and arc diagrams (section 6.1.3).

graphs, because that's what they're called in mathematics. Finally, the importance of a node in a network is typically referred to as *centrality.* There's more, but that should be enough to get you started.

Networks aren't just a data format; they're a perspective on data. When you work with network data, you typically try to discover and display patterns of the network or of parts of the network, and not of individual nodes in the network. Although you may use a network visualization because it makes a cool graphical index, like a mind map or a network map of a website, in general you'll find that the typical information visualization techniques are designed to showcase network structure, and not individual nodes.

6.1   *Static network diagrams*

Network data is different from hierarchical data. Networks present the possibility of many-to-many connections, like the Sankey layout from chapter 5, whereas in hierarchical data a node can have many children but only one parent, like the tree and pack layouts from chapter 5. A network doesn't have to be a social network. This format can represent many different structures, such as transportation networks and linked open data. In this chapter we'll look at four common forms for representing networks: as data, as adjacency matrices, as arc diagrams, and using force-directed network diagrams.

In each case, the graphical representation will be quite different. For instance, in the case of a force-directed layout, we'll represent the nodes as circles and the edges as lines. But in the case of the adjacency matrix, nodes will be positioned on x- and y-axes and the edges will be filled squares. Networks don't have a default representation, but the examples you'll see in this chapter are the most common.

6.1.1 Network data

Although you can store networks in several data formats, the most straightforward is known as the *edge list*. An edge list is typically represented as a CSV like that shown in listing 6.1, with a source column and a target column, and a string or number to indicate which nodes are connected. Each edge may also have other attributes, indicating the type of connection or its strength, the time period when the connection is valid, its color, or any other information you want to store about a connection. The important thing is that only the source and target columns are necessary.

In the case of directed networks, the source and target columns indicate the direction of connection between nodes. A directed network means that nodes may be connected in one direction but not in the other. For instance, you could follow a user on Twitter, but that doesn't necessarily mean that the user follows you. Undirected networks still typically have the columns listed as "source" and "target," but the connection is the same in both directions. Take the example of a network made up of connections indicating people have shared classes. Then if I'm in a class with you, you're likewise in a class with me. You'll see directed and weighted networks represented throughout this chapter.

Listing 6.1 edgelist.csv

```
source,target,weight
sam,pris,1
roy,pris,5
roy,sam,1
tully,pris,5
tully,kim,3
tully,pat,1
tully,mo,3
kim,pat,2
kim,mo,1
mo,tully,7
mo,pat,1
mo,pris,1
pat,tully,1
pat,kim,2
pat,mo,5
lee,al,3
```

Our network also has a weight value for the connections, which indicates the strength of connections. In our case, our edge list represents how many times the source favorited the tweets of the target. Sam favorited one tweet made by Pris, and Roy favorited 5 tweets made by Pris, and so on. This is a *weighted network* because the edges have a value. It's a *directed network* because the edges have direction. Therefore, we have a *weighted directed network*, and we need to account for both weight and direction in our network visualizations.

Technically, you only need an edge list to create a network, because you can derive a list of nodes from the unique values in the edge list. This is done by traditional network analysis software packages like Gephi. Although you can derive a node list with JavaScript, it's more common to have a corresponding node list that provides more information about the nodes in your network, like we have in the following listing.

Listing 6.2   nodelist.csv

```
id,followers,following
sam,17,500
roy,83,80
pris,904,15
tully,7,5
kim,11,50
mo,80,85
pat,150,300
lee,38,7
al,12,12
```

Because these are Twitter users, we have more information about them based on their Twitter stats, in this case, the number of followers and the number of people they follow. As with the edge list, it's not necessary to have more than an ID. But having access to more data gives you the chance to modify your network visualization to reflect the node attributes.

How you represent a network depends on its size and the nature of the network. If a network doesn't represent discrete connections between similar things, but rather the flow of goods or information or traffic, then you could use a Sankey diagram like we did in chapter 5. Recall that the data format for the Sankey is exactly the same as what we have here: a table of nodes and a table of edges. The Sankey diagram is only suitable for specific kinds of network data. Other chart types, such as an adjacency matrix, are more generically useful for network data.

Before we get started with code to create a network visualizations, let's put together a CSS page so that we can set color based on class and use inline styles as little as possible. Listing 6.3 gives the CSS necessary for all the examples in this chapter. Keep in mind that we'll still need to set some inline styles when we want the numerical value of an attribute to relate to the data bound to that graphical element, for example, when we base the stroke-width of a line on the strength of that line.

Listing 6.3   networks.css

```css
.grid {
    stroke: black;
    stroke-width: 1px;
    fill: red;
}
.arc {
    stroke: black;
    fill: none;
}
.node {
    fill: lightgray;
    stroke: black;
    stroke-width: 1px;
}
circle.active {
    fill: red;
}
path.active {
    stroke: red;
}
```

6.1.2   *Adjacency matrix*

As you see more and more networks represented graphically, it seems like the only way to represent a network is with a circle or square that represents the node and a line (whether straight or curvy) that represents the edge. It may surprise you that one of the most effective network visualizations has no connecting lines at all. Instead, the *adjacency matrix* uses a grid to represent connections between nodes.

The principle of an adjacency matrix is simple: you place the nodes along the x-axis and then place the same nodes along the y-axis. If two nodes are connected, then the corresponding grid square is filled; otherwise, it's left blank. In our case, because it's a directed network, the nodes along the y-axis are considered the source and the nodes along the x-axis are considered the target, as you'll see in a few pages. Because our network is also weighted, we'll use saturation to indicate weight, with lighter colors indicating a weaker connection and darker colors indicating a stronger connection.

The only problem with building an adjacency matrix in D3 is that it doesn't have an existing layout, which means you have to build it by hand like we did with the bar chart, scatterplot, and boxplot. Mike Bostock has an impressive example at http://bost.ocks.org/mike/miserables/, but you can make something that's functional without too much code, which we'll do with the function in listing 6.4. In doing so, though, we need to process the two JSON arrays that are created from our CSVs and format the data so that it's easy to work with. This is close to writing our own layout, something we'll do in chapter 10, and a good idea generally.

Listing 6.4   The adjacency matrix function

```
function adjacency() {
  queue()
  .defer(d3.csv, "nodelist.csv")
  .defer(d3.csv, "edgelist.csv")
  .await(function(error, file1, file2) {
          createAdjacencyMatrix(file1, file2);
  });

  function createAdjacencyMatrix(nodes,edges) {
    var edgeHash = {};
    for (x in edges) {
      var id = edges[x].source + "-" + edges[x].target;
      edgeHash[id] = edges[x];
    };
    matrix = [];
    for (a in nodes) {
      for (b in nodes) {
        var grid =
          {id: nodes[a].id + "-" + nodes[b].id,
             x: b, y: a, weight: 0};
        if (edgeHash[grid.id]) {
          grid.weight = edgeHash[grid.id].weight;
        };
        matrix.push(grid);
      };
    };

    d3.select("svg")
      .append("g")
      .attr("transform", "translate(50,50)")
      .attr("id", "adjacencyG")
      .selectAll("rect")
      .data(matrix)
      .enter()
      .append("rect")
      .attr("class", "grid")
      .attr("width", 25)
      .attr("height", 25)
      .attr("x", function (d) {return d.x * 25})
      .attr("y", function (d) {return d.y * 25})
      .style("fill-opacity", function (d) {return d.weight * .2;})

    var scaleSize = nodes.length * 25;
    var nameScale = d3.scale.ordinal()
        .domain(nodes.map(function (el) {return el.id}))
        .rangePoints([0,scaleSize],1);

    var xAxis = d3.svg.axis()
        .scale(nameScale).orient("top").tickSize(4);
    var yAxis = d3.svg.axis()
        .scale(nameScale).orient("left").tickSize(4);
    d3.select("#adjacencyG").append("g").call(yAxis);
    d3.select("#adjacencyG").append("g").call(xAxis)
        .selectAll("text")
```

We need to load two datasets before we can get started, and queue lets us move the asynchronous loaders into a synchronous format.

A hash allows us to test if a source-target pair has a link.

Creates all possible source-target connections

Sets the xy coordinates based on the source-target array positions

If there's a corresponding edge in our edge list, give it that weight.

Creates an ordinal scale from the node IDs

Used for ordinal values

Both axes use the same scale.

```
                    .style("text-anchor", "end")
                    .attr("transform", "translate(-10,-10) rotate(90)");
            };
        };
```

Rotates the text on the y-axis

A few new things are going on here. For one, we're using a new scale: d3.scale.ordinal, which takes an array of distinct values and allows us to place them on an axis like we do with the names of our nodes in this example. We need to use a scale function that you haven't seen before, rangePoints, which creates a set of bins for each of our values for display on an axis or otherwise. It does this by associating each of those unique values with a numerical position within the range given. Each point can also have an offset declared in the second, optional variable. The other new piece of code uses queue.js, which we need because we're loading two CSV files and we don't want to run our function until those two CSVs are loaded. We're building this matrix array of objects that may seem obscure. But if you examine it in your console, you'll see, as in figure 6.2, it's just a list of every possible connection and the strength of that connection, if it exists.

Figure 6.3 shows the resulting adjacency matrix based on the node list and edge list.

You'll notice in many adjacency matrices that the square indicating the connection from a node to itself is always filled. In network parlance this is a *self-loop*, and it occurs when a node is connected to itself. In our case, it would mean that someone

```
[▼ Object 🆔           , ▼ Object 🆔           , ▼ Object 🆔           ,
    id: "sam-sam"          id: "sam-roy"          id: "sam-pris"
    weight: 0              weight: 0              weight: "1"
    x: "0"                 x: "1"                 x: "2"
    y: "0"                 y: "0"                 y: "0"
  ▶ __proto__: Object    ▶ __proto__: Object    ▶ __proto__: Object
 ▼ Object 🆔           , ▼ Object 🆔           , ▼ Object 🆔           ,
    id: "sam-tully"        id: "sam-kim"          id: "sam-mo"
    weight: 0              weight: 0              weight: 0
    x: "3"                 x: "4"                 x: "5"
    y: "0"                 y: "0"                 y: "0"
  ▶ __proto__: Object    ▶ __proto__: Object    ▶ __proto__: Object
 ▼ Object 🆔           , ▼ Object 🆔           , ▼ Object 🆔           ,
    id: "sam-pat"          id: "sam-lee"          id: "sam-al"
    weight: 0              weight: 0              weight: 0
    x: "6"                 x: "7"                 x: "8"
    y: "0"                 y: "0"                 y: "0"
  ▶ __proto__: Object    ▶ __proto__: Object    ▶ __proto__: Object
 ▼ Object 🆔           , ▼ Object 🆔           , ▼ Object 🆔           ,
    id: "roy-sam"          id: "roy-roy"          id: "roy-pris"
    weight: "1"           weight: 0              weight: "5"
    x: "0"                 x: "1"                 x: "2"
    y: "1"                 y: "1"                 y: "1"
  ▶ __proto__: Object    ▶ __proto__: Object    ▶ __proto__: Object
 ▼ Object 🆔           , ▼ Object 🆔           , ▼ Object 🆔           ,
    id: "roy-tully"        id: "roy-kim"          id: "roy-mo"
    weight: 0              weight: 0              weight: 0
    x: "3"                 x: "4"                 x: "5"
    y: "1"                 y: "1"                 y: "1"
  ▶ __proto__: Object    ▶ __proto__: Object    ▶ __proto__: Object
 ▶ Object ,  ▶ Object ,  ▶ Object ,  ▶ Object ,  ▶ Object ,  ▶ Object
 ,  ▶ Object ,  ▶ Object ,  ▶ Object ,  ▶ Object ,  ▶ Object ,  ▶ Object ,
```

Figure 6.2 The array of connections we're building. Notice that every possible connection is stored in the array. Only those connections that exist in our dataset have a weight value other than 0. Notice, also, that our CSV import creates the weight value as a string.

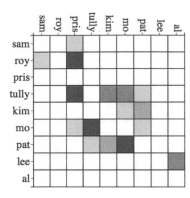

Figure 6.3 A weighted, directed adjacency matrix where lighter red indicates weaker connections and darker red indicates stronger connections. The source is on the y-axis, and the target is on the x-axis. The matrix shows that Roy favorited tweets by Sam but Sam didn't favorite any tweets by Roy.

favorited their own tweet, and fortunately no one in our dataset is a big enough loser to do that.

If we want, we can add interactivity to help make the matrix more readable. Grids can be hard to read without something to highlight the row and column of a square. It's simple to add highlighting to our matrix. All we have to do is add a mouseover event listener that fires a gridOver function to highlight all rectangles that have the same x or y value:

```
d3.selectAll("rect.grid").on("mouseover", gridOver);

    function gridOver(d,i) {
        d3.selectAll("rect").style("stroke-width", function (p) {
    return p.x == d.x || p.y == d.y ? "3px" : "1px"});
};
```

Now you can see in figure 6.4 how moving your cursor over a grid square highlights the row and column of that grid square.

6.1.3 Arc diagram

Another way to graphically represent networks is by using an arc diagram. An arc diagram arranges the nodes along a line and draws the links as arcs above and/or below that line. Again, there isn't a layout available for arc diagrams, and there are even fewer examples, but the principle is rather simple after you see the code. We build

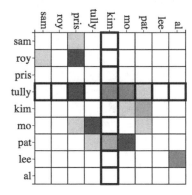

Figure 6.4 Adjacency highlighting column and row of the grid square. In this instance, the mouse is over the Tully-to-Kim edge. You can see that Tully favorited tweets by four people, one of whom was Kim, and that Kim only had tweets favorited by one other person, Pat.

another pseudo-layout like we did with the adjacency matrix, but this time we need to process the nodes as well as the links.

Listing 6.5   Arc diagram code

```
function arcDiagram() {
  queue()
  .defer(d3.csv, "nodelist.csv")
  .defer(d3.csv, "edgelist.csv")
  .await(function(error, file1, file2) {
      createArcDiagram(file1, file2);
  });
}

function createArcDiagram(nodes,edges) {
    var nodeHash = {};
    for (x in nodes) {
      nodeHash[nodes[x].id] = nodes[x];
      nodes[x].x = parseInt(x) * 40;
    };
    for (x in edges) {
      edges[x].weight = parseInt(edges[x].weight);
      edges[x].source = nodeHash[edges[x].source];
      edges[x].target = nodeHash[edges[x].target];
    };

    linkScale = d3.scale.linear()
        .domain(d3.extent(edges, function (d) {return d.weight}))
        .range([5,10])

    var arcG = d3.select("svg").append("g").attr("id", "arcG")
        .attr("transform", "translate(50,250)");

    arcG.selectAll("path")
      .data(edges)
      .enter()
      .append("path")
      .attr("class", "arc")
      .style("stroke-width", function(d) {return d.weight * 2;})
      .style("opacity", .25)
      .attr("d", arc)
    arcG.selectAll("circle")
      .data(nodes)
      .enter()
      .append("circle")
      .attr("class", "node")
      .attr("r", 10)
      .attr("cx", function (d) {return d.x;})
    function arc(d,i) {
      var draw = d3.svg.line().interpolate("basis");
      var midX = (d.source.x + d.target.x) / 2;
      var midY = (d.source.x - d.target.x) * 2;
      return draw([[d.source.x,0],[midX,midY],[d.target.x,0]])
    };
  };
};
```

Creates a hash that associates each node JSON object with its ID value

Sets each node with an x position based on its array position

Replaces the string ID of the node with a pointer to the JSON object

Draws the links using the arc function

Draws the nodes as circles at each node's x position

Draws a basis-interpolated line from the source node to a computed middle point above them to the target node

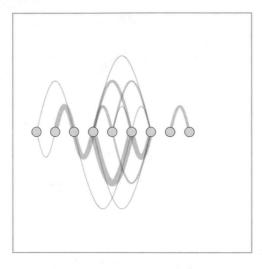

Figure 6.5   An arc diagram, with connections between nodes represented as arcs above and below the nodes. Arcs above the nodes indicate the connection is from left to right, while arcs below the nodes indicate the source is on the right and the target is on the left.

Notice that the edges array that we build uses a hash with the ID value of our edges to create object references. By building objects that have references to the source and target nodes, we can easily calculate the graphical attributes of the `<line>` or `<path>` element we're using to represent the connection. This is the same method used in the force layout that we'll look at later in the chapter. The result of the code is your first arc diagram, shown in figure 6.5.

With abstract charts like these, you're getting to the point where interactivity is no longer optional. Even though the links follow rules, and you're not dealing with too many nodes or edges, it can be hard to make out what is connected to what and how. You can add useful interactivity by having the edges highlight the connecting nodes on mouseover. You can also have the nodes highlight connected edges on mouseover by adding two new functions as shown in the following listing, with the results in figure 6.6.

Listing 6.6   Arc diagram interactivity

```
d3.selectAll("circle").on("mouseover", nodeOver);
d3.selectAll("path").on("mouseover", edgeOver);

function nodeOver(d,i) {
   d3.selectAll("circle").classed("active", function (p) {
            return p == d ? true : false;
   });

   d3.selectAll("path").classed("active", function (p) {
       return p.source == d || p.target == d ? true : false;
   });
};

function edgeOver(d) {
   d3.selectAll("path").classed("active", function(p) {
       return p == d ? true : false;
   });
```

Makes a selection of all nodes to set the class of the node being hovered over to "active"

Any edge where the selected node shows up as source or target renders as red

```
d3.selectAll("circle").style("fill",function(p) {
    return p == d.source ? "blue" : p == d.target ? "green" : "lightgray";
  });
};
```

> This nested if checks to see if a node is the source, which is set to blue, or if it's the target and set to green, or if it's neither and set to gray.

If you're interested in exploring arc diagrams further and want to use them for larger datasets, you'll also want to look into hive plots, which are arc diagrams arranged on spokes. We won't deal with hive plots in this book, but there's a plugin layout for hive plots that you can see at https://github.com/d3/d3-plugins/tree/master/hive. Both the adjacency matrix and arc diagram benefit from the control you have over sorting and placing the nodes, as well as the linear manner in which they're laid out. The next method for network visualization, which is our focus for the rest of the chapter, uses entirely different principles for determining how and where to place nodes and edges.

6.2 Force-directed layout

The force layout gets its name from the method by which it determines the most optimal graphical representation of a network. Like the word cloud and the Sankey diagram from chapter 5, the force() layout dynamically updates the positions of its elements to find the best fit. Unlike those layouts, it does it continuously in real time rather than as a preprocessing step before rendering. The principle behind a force layout is the interplay between three forces, shown in figure 6.7. These forces push nodes away from each other, attract connected nodes to each other, and keep nodes from flying out of sight.

In this section, you'll learn how force-directed layouts work, how to make them, and some general principles from network analysis that will help you better understand them. You'll also learn how to add and remove nodes and edges, as well as adjust the settings of the layout on the fly.

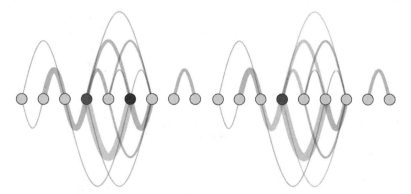

Figure 6.6   Mouseover behavior on edges (left), with the edge being moused over in pink, the source node in blue, and the target node in green. Mouseover behavior on nodes (right), with the node being moused over in red and the connected edges in pink.

Repulsion

All nodes push each other away. Sometimes this force is set to be based on an attribute of a node. Larger nodes can be given more space by setting their repulsion higher, or they can act as anchors by setting their repulsion lower. In D3, this is defined using .charge().

Canvas Gravity

Nodes are pulled toward the layout center to keep the interplay of forces from pushing them out of sight. In D3, this is defined using.gravity().

Attraction

Nodes that are connected to each other are pulled toward each other. Sometimes, this force is based on the strength of connection, so that more strongly connected nodes are closer. In D3, this is defined using .linkDistance() and .linkStrength().

Figure 6.7   The forces in a force-directed algorithm: repulsion, gravity, and attraction. Other factors, such as hierarchical packing and community detection, can also be factored into force-directed algorithms, but these features are the most common. Forces are approximated for larger networks to improve performance.

6.2.1 *Creating a force-directed network diagram*

The `force()` layout you see initialized in listing 6.7 has some settings you've already seen before. The most obvious is `size()`, which uses an array containing the width and height of our layout region to calculate the necessary force settings. The `nodes()` and `links()` settings are the same as for the Sankey layout in chapter 5. They take, as you'd expect, arrays of data that correspond to the nodes and links. We're creating our own source and target references in our links array, just like we did with the arc diagram, and that's the formatting that `force()` expects. It also accepts integer values where the integer values correspond to the array position of a node in the nodes array, like the formatting of data for the Sankey diagram links array from chapter 5. As you can see in the following listing, the one setting that's new is `charge()`, which determines how much each node pushes away other nodes. There's also a new event listener, `"tick"`, that needs to get associated with a tick function that updates the position of your nodes and edges.

> **Listing 6.7   Force layout function**

```
function forceDirected() {
    queue()
    .defer(d3.csv, "nodelist.csv")
    .defer(d3.csv, "edgelist.csv")
```

```
.await(function(error, file1, file2) {
        createForceLayout(file1, file2);
});

function createForceLayout(nodes,edges) {
   var nodeHash = {};
   for (x in nodes) {
     nodeHash[nodes[x].id] = nodes[x];
   };
   for (x in edges) {
     edges[x].weight = parseInt(edges[x].weight);
     edges[x].source = nodeHash[edges[x].source];
     edges[x].target = nodeHash[edges[x].target];
   };

  var weightScale = d3.scale.linear()
     .domain(d3.extent(edges, function(d) {return d.weight;}))
     .range([.1,1]);

  var force = d3.layout.force().charge(-1000)      ◁──  How much each node
     .size([500,500])                                    pushes away each other;
     .nodes(nodes)                                       if set to a positive value,
     .links(edges)                                       nodes attract each other
     .on("tick", forceTick);         ◁──  "tick" events are fired
                                           continuously, running the
                                           associated function.
d3.select("svg").selectAll("line.link")
   .data(edges, function (d) {return d.source.id + "-" + d.target.id;})   ◁──
   .enter()
   .append("line")
   .attr("class", "link")                              Key values for
   .style("stroke", "black")                           your nodes and
   .style("opacity", .5)                               edges will help
   .style("stroke-width", function(d) {return d.weight});   when we
var nodeEnter = d3.select("svg").selectAll("g.node")       update the
   .data(nodes, function (d) {return d.id})               network later.
   .enter()
   .append("g")
   .attr("class", "node");

nodeEnter.append("circle")
   .attr("r", 5)
   .style("fill", "lightgray")
   .style("stroke", "black")
   .style("stroke-width", "1px");      Initializing the network
nodeEnter.append("text")                starts firing "tick" events
   .style("text-anchor", "middle")      and calculates the degree
   .attr("y", 15)                       centrality of nodes.
   .text(function(d) {return d.id;});

force.start();                ◁──          The tick function
                                            updates the edge-
function forceTick() {                      drawing code and
  d3.selectAll("line.link")                 node-drawing code
     .attr("x1", function (d) {return d.source.x;})   ◁──  based on the newly
     .attr("x2", function (d) {return d.target.x;})        calculated node
     .attr("y1", function (d) {return d.source.y;})        positions.
     .attr("y2", function (d) {return d.target.y;});
```

```
    d3.selectAll("g.node")
        .attr("transform", function (d) {
            return "translate("+d.x+","+d.y+")";
        })
    };

};
};
```

The animated nature of the force layout is lost on the page, but you can see in figure 6.8 general network structure that's less prominent in an adjacency matrix or arc diagram. It's readily apparent that four nodes (Mo, Tully, Kim, and Pat) are all connected to each other (forming what in network terms is called a *clique*), and three nodes (Roy, Pris, and Sam) are more peripheral. Over on the right, two nodes (Lee and Al) are connected only to each other. The only reason those nodes are still onscreen is because the layout's gravity pulls unconnected pieces toward the center.

The thickness of the lines corresponds to the strength of connection. But although we have edge strength, we've lost the direction of the edges in this layout. You can tell that the network is directed only because the links are drawn as semitransparent, so you can see when two links of different weights overlap each other. We need to use some method to show if these links are to or from a node. One way to do this is to turn our lines into arrows using SVG markers.

6.2.2   *SVG markers*

Sometimes you want to place a symbol, such as an arrowhead, on a line or path that you've drawn. In that case, you have to define a marker in your svg:defs and then associate that marker with the element on which you want it to draw. You can define your marker statically in HTML, or you can create it dynamically like any SVG element,

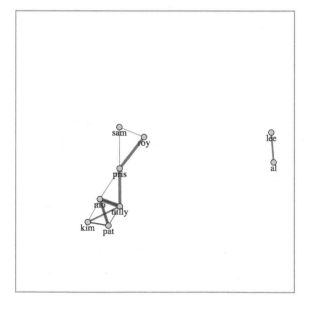

Figure 6.8   A force-directed layout based on our dataset and organized graphically using default settings in the force layout

as we'll do next. The marker we define can be any sort of SVG shape, but we'll use a path because it lets us draw an arrowhead. A marker can be drawn at the start, end, or middle of a line, and has settings to determine its direction relative to its parent element.

Listing 6.8   Marker definition and application

```
var marker = d3.select("svg").append('defs')
    .append('marker')
    .attr("id", "Triangle")
    .attr("rcfX", 12)
    .attr("refY", 6)
    .attr("markerUnits", 'userSpaceOnUse')    ◁─┐
    .attr("markerWidth", 12)
    .attr("markerHeight", 18)
    .attr("orient", 'auto')
    .append('path')
    .attr("d", 'M 0 0 12 6 0 12 3 6');
d3.selectAll("line").attr("marker-end", "url(#Triangle)");  ◁─┘
```

The default setting for markers bases their size off the stroke-width of the parent, which in our case would result in difficult-to-read markers.

A marker is assigned to a line by setting the marker-end, marker-start, or marker-mid attribute to point to the marker.

With the markers defined in listing 6.9, you can now read the network (as shown in figure 6.9) more effectively. You see how the nodes are connected to each other, and you can spot which nodes have reciprocal ties with each other (where nodes are connected in both directions). Reciprocation is important to identify, because there's a big difference between people who favorite Katy Perry's tweets and people whose tweets are favorited by Katy Perry (the current Twitter user with the most followers). Direction of edges is important, but you can represent direction in other ways, such as using curved edges or edges that grow fatter on one end than the other. To do something like that, you'd need to use a <path> rather than a <line> for the edges like we did with the Sankey layout or the arc diagram.

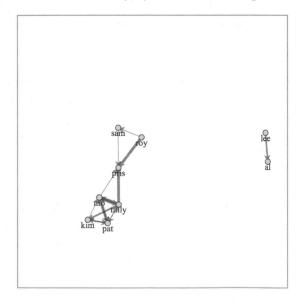

Figure 6.9   Edges now display markers (arrowheads) indicating the direction of connection. Notice that all the arrowheads are the same size.

If you've run this code on your own, your network probably looks a little different than what's shown in figure 6.9. That's because network visualizations created with force-directed layouts are the result of the interplay of forces, and, even with a small network like this, that interplay can result in different positions for nodes. This can confuse users, who think that these variations indicate different networks. One way around this is to generate a network using a force-directed layout and then fix it in place to create a network basemap. You can then apply any later graphical changes to that fixed network. The concept of a basemap comes from geography, and in network visualization refers to the use of the same layout with differently sized and/or colored nodes and edges. It allows readers to identify regions of the network that are significantly different according to different measures. You can see this concept of a basemap in use in figure 6.10, which shows how one network can be measured in multiple ways.

> **Infoviz term: hairball**
>
> Network visualizations are impressive, but they can also be so complex that they're unreadable. For this reason, you'll encounter critiques of networks that are too dense to be readable. These network visualizations are often referred to as *hairballs* due to extensive overlap of edges that make them resemble a mass of unruly hair.
>
> If you think a force-directed layout is hard to read, you can pair it with another network visualization, such as an adjacency matrix, and highlight both as the user navigates either visualization. You'll see techniques for pairing visualizations like this in chapter 11.

The force-directed layout provides the added benefit of seeing larger structures. Depending on the size and complexity of your network, they may be enough. But you may need to represent other network measurements when working with network data.

6.2.3   *Network measures*

Networks have been studied for a long time—at least decades and, if you consider graph theory in mathematics, centuries. As a result, you may encounter a few terms and measures when working with networks. This is only meant to be a brief overview. If you want to learn more about networks, I would suggest reading the excellent introduction to networks and network analysis by S. Weingart, I. Milligan, and S. Graham at http://www.themacroscope.org/?page_id=337.

EDGE WEIGHT

You'll notice that our dataset contains a "weight" value for each link. This represents the strength of the connection between two nodes. In our case, we assume that the more favorites, the stronger a connection that one Twitter user has. We drew thicker lines for a higher weight, but we can also adjust the way the force layout works based on that weight, as you'll see next.

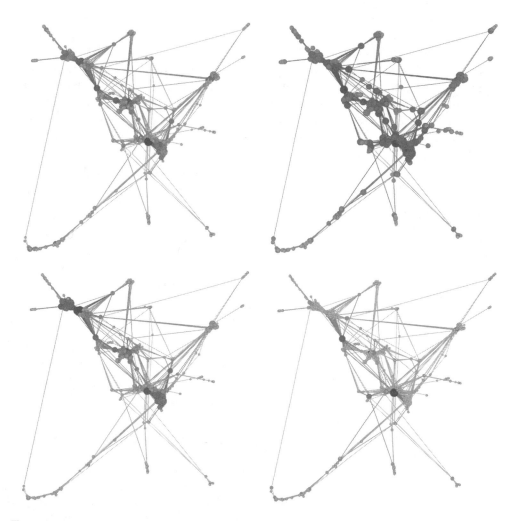

Figure 6.10 The same network measured using degree centrality (top left), closeness centrality (top right), eigenvector centrality (bottom left), and betweenness centrality (bottom right). More-central nodes are larger and bright red, whereas less-central nodes are smaller and gray. Notice that although some nodes are central according to all measures, their relative centrality varies, as does the overall centrality of other nodes.

CENTRALITY

Networks are representations of systems, and one of the things you want to know about the nodes in a system is which ones are more important than the others, referred to as *centrality*. Central nodes are considered to have more power or influence in a network. There are many different measurements of centrality, a few of which are shown in figure 6.10, and different measures more accurately assess centrality in different network types. One measure of centrality is computed by D3's force() layout: degree centrality.

DEGREE

Degree, also known as *degree centrality*, is the total number of links that are connected to a node. In our example data, Mo has a degree of 6, because he's the source or target of 6 links. Degree is a rough measure of the importance of a node in a network, because you assume that people or things with more connections have more power or influence in a network. Weighted degree is used to refer to the total value of the connections to a node, which would give Mo a value of 18. Further, you can differentiate degree into *in degree* and *out degree*, which are used to distinguish between incoming and outgoing links, and which for Mo's case would be 4 and 2, respectively.

Every time you start the force() layout, D3 computes the total number of links per node, and updates that node's weight attribute to reflect that. We'll use that to affect the way the force layout runs. For now, let's add a button that resizes the nodes based on their weight attribute:

```
d3.select("#controls").append("button")
    .on("click", sizeByDegree).html("Degree Size");

function sizeByDegree() {
   force.stop();
   d3.selectAll("circle")
      .attr("r", function(d) {return d.weight * 2;});
};
```

Figure 6.11 shows the value of the degree centrality measure. Although you can see and easily count the connections and nodes in this small network, being able to spot at a glance the most and least connected nodes is extremely valuable. Notice that we're counting links in both directions, so that even though Tully is connected to

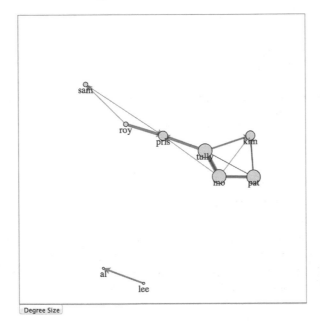

Figure 6.11 Sizing nodes by weight indicates the number of total connections for each node by setting the radius of the circle equal to the weight times 2.

more people, he's the same size as Mo and Pat, who are connected as many times but to fewer people.

CLUSTERING AND MODULARITY

One of the most important things to find out about a network is whether any communities exist in that network and what they look like. This is done by looking at whether some nodes are more connected to each other than to the rest of the network, known as *modularity*. You can also look at whether nodes are interconnected, known as *clustering*. Cliques, mentioned earlier, are part of the same measurement, and *clique* is a term for a group of nodes that are fully connected to each other.

Notice that this interconnectedness and community structure is supposed to arise visually out of a force-directed layout. You see the four highly connected users in a cluster and the other users farther away. If you'd prefer to measure your networks to try to reveal these structures, you can see an implementation of a community detection algorithm implemented by David Mimno with D3 at http://mimno.infosci.cornell .edu/community/. This algorithm runs in the browser and can be integrated with your network quite easily to color your network based on community membership.

6.2.4   *Force layout settings*

When we initialized our force layout, we started out with a charge setting of -1000. Charge and a few other settings give you more control over the way the force layout runs.

CHARGE

Charge sets the rate at which nodes push each other away. If you don't set charge, then it has a default setting of -30. The reason we set charge to -1000 was because the default settings for charge with our network would have resulted in a tiny network onscreen (see figure 6.12).

Figure 6.12   The layout of our network with the default charge, which displays the nodes too closely together to be easily read

Along with setting fixed values for charge, you can use an accessor function to base the charge values on an attribute of the node. For instance, you could base the charge on the weight (the degree centrality) of the node so that nodes with many connections push nodes away more, giving them more space on the chart.

Negative charge values represent repulsion in a force-directed layout, but you could set them to positive if you wanted your nodes to exert an attractive force. This would likely cause problems with a traditional network visualization but may come in handy for a more complicated visualization.

GRAVITY

With nodes pushing each other, the only thing to stop them from flying off the edge of your chart is what's known as *canvas gravity*, which pulls all nodes toward the center of the layout. When gravity isn't specifically set, it defaults to .1. Figure 6.13 shows the results of increasing or decreasing the gravity (from our original `charge(-1000)` setting).

Gravity, unlike charge, doesn't accept an accessor function and only accepts a fixed setting.

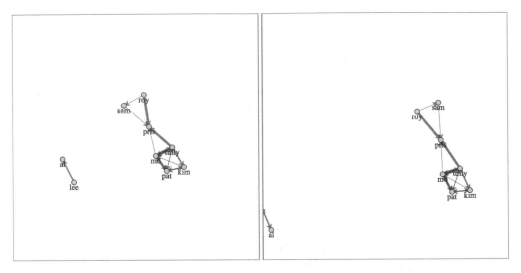

Figure 6.13   Increasing the gravity to .2 (left) pulls the two components closer to the center of the layout area. Decreasing the gravity to .05 (right) allows the small component to drift offscreen.

LINKDISTANCE

Attraction between nodes is determined by setting the `link-Distance` property, which is the optimal distance between connected nodes. One of the reasons we needed to set our charge so high was because the `linkDistance` defaults to 20. If we set it to 50, then we can reduce the charge to -100 and produce the results in figure 6.14.

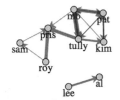

Figure 6.14   With `linkDistance` adjusted, our network becomes much more readable.

Setting your `linkDistance` parameter too high causes your network to fold back in on itself, which you can identify by the presence of prominent triangles in the network visualization. Figure 6.15 shows this folding occur with `linkDistance` set to 200.

You can set `linkDistance` to be a function and associate it with edge weight so that edges with higher or lower weight values have lower or higher distance settings. A better way to achieve that effect is to use `linkStrength`.

LINKSTRENGTH

A force layout is a physical simulation, meaning it uses physical metaphors to arrange the network to its optimal graphical shape. If your network has stronger and weaker

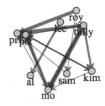

Figure 6.15   Distortion based on high `linkDistance` makes it look like Pris is connected to Pat and otherwise clusters nodes together despite their being unrelated.

links, like our example does, then it makes sense to have those edges exert stronger and weaker effects on the controlling nodes. You can achieve this by using `link-Strength`, which can accept a fixed setting but can also take an accessor function to base the strength of an edge on an attribute of that edge:

```
force.linkStrength(function (d) {return weightScale(d.weight);});
```

Figure 6.16 dramatically demonstrates the results, which reflect the weak nature of some of the connections.

6.2.5 Updating the network

When you create a network, you want to provide your users with the ability to add or remove nodes to the network, or drag them around. You may also want to adjust the various settings dynamically rather than changing them when you first create the force layout.

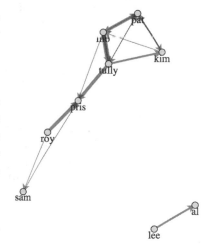

Figure 6.16 **By basing the strength of the attraction between nodes on the strength of the connections between nodes, you see a dramatic change in the structure of the network. The weaker connections between x and y allow that part of the network to drift away.**

STOPPING AND RESTARTING THE LAYOUT

The force layout is designed to "cool off" and eventually stop after the network is laid out well enough that the nodes no longer move to new positions. When the layout has stopped like this, you'll need to restart it if you want it to animate again. Also, if you've made any changes to the force settings or want to add or remove parts of the network, then you'll need to stop it and restart it.

FORCE.STOP()

You can turn off the force interaction by using `force.stop()`, which stops running the simulation. It's good to stop the network when there's an interaction with a component elsewhere on your web page or some change in the styling of the network.

FORCE.START()

To begin or restart the animation of the layout, use `force.start()`. You've already seen `.start()`, because we used it in our initial example to get the force layout going.

FORCE.RESUME()

If you haven't made any changes to the nodes or links in your network and you want the network to start moving again, you can use `force.resume()`. It resets a cooling parameter, which causes the force layout to start moving again.

FORCE.TICK()

Finally, if you want to move the layout forward one step, you can use `force.tick()`. Force layouts can be resource-intensive, and you may want to use one for just a few seconds rather than let it run continuously.

FORCE.DRAG()

With traditional network analysis programs, the user can drag nodes to new positions. This is implemented using the behavior force.drag(). A behavior is like a component in that it's called by an element using .call(), but instead of creating SVG elements, it creates a set of event listeners.

In the case of force.drag(), those event listeners correspond to dragging events that give you the ability to click and drag your nodes around while the force layout runs. You can enable dragging on all your nodes by selecting them and calling force.drag() on that selection:

```
d3.selectAll("g.node").call(force.drag());
```

FIXED

When a force layout is associated with nodes, each node has a boolean attribute called fixed that determines whether the node is affected by the force during ticks. One effective interaction technique is to set a node as fixed when the user interacts with it. This allows users to drag nodes to a position on the canvas so they can visually sort the important nodes. To differentiate fixed nodes from unfixed nodes, we'll also have the function give fixed nodes a thicker "stroke-width". The effect of dragging some of our nodes is shown in figure 6.17.

```
d3.selectAll("g.site").on("click", fixNode);

function fixNode(d) {
    d3.select(this).select("circle").style("stroke-width", 4);
    d.fixed = true;
};
```

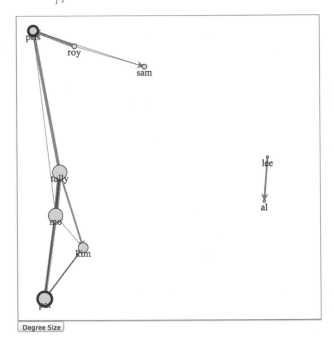

Figure 6.17   The node representing Pat has been dragged to the bottom-left corner and fixed in position, while the node representing Pris has been dragged to the top-left corner and fixed in position. The remaining unfixed nodes have taken their positions based on the force-directed layout.

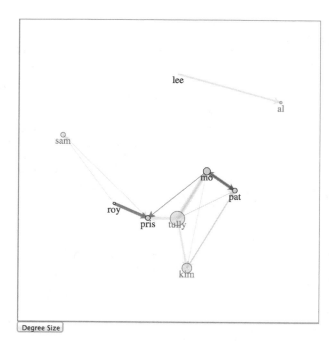

Degree Size

Figure 6.18 The network has been filtered to only show nodes with more than 20 followers, after clicking the Degree Size button. Notice that Lee, with no connections, has a degree of 0 and so the associated circle has a radius of 0, rendering it invisible. This catches two processes in midstream, the transition of nodes from full to 0 opacity and the removal of edges.

6.2.6 Removing and adding nodes and links

When dealing with networks, you may want to filter the networks or give the user the ability to add or remove nodes. To filter a network, you need to `stop()` it, remove any nodes and links that are no longer part of the network, rebind those arrays to the force layout, and then `start()` the layout.

This can be done as a filter on the array that makes up your nodes. For instance, we may want to only see the network of people with more than 20 followers, because we want to see how the most influential people are connected.

But that's not enough, because we would still have links in our layout that reference nodes that no longer exist. We'll need a more involved filter for our links array. By using the `.indexOf` function of an array, though, we can easily create our filtered links by checking to see if the source and target are both in our filtered nodes array. Because we used key values when we first bound our arrays to our selection in listing 6.8, we can use the `selection.exit()` behavior to easily update our network. You can see how to do this in the following listing and the effects in figure 6.18.

Listing 6.9 Filtering a network

```
function filterNetwork() {
    force.stop();
    var originalNodes = force.nodes();          ◄┐ Accesses the current array
    var originalLinks = force.links();           │  of nodes and array of links
    var influentialNodes = originalNodes.filter(function (d) {  └─ associated with the force layout
        return d.followers > 20;
    });
```

```
    var influentialLinks = originalLinks.filter(function (d) {
            return influentialNodes.indexOf(d.source) > -1 &&
                    influentialNodes.indexOf(d.target) > -1;
    });

    d3.selectAll("g.node")
        .data(influentialNodes, function (d) {return d.id})
        .exit()
        .transition()
        .duration(4000)
        .style("opacity", 0)
        .remove();

    d3.selectAll("line.link")
    .data(influentialLinks, function (d) {
                return d.source.id + "-" + d.target.id;
    })
    .exit()
    .transition()
    .duration(3000)
    .style("opacity", 0)
    .remove();

    force
        .nodes(influentialNodes)
        .links(influentialLinks);

    force.start();
};
```

> **Makes an array of links only out of those that reference existing nodes** ⟵

> **By setting a transition on the .exit(), it applies the transition only to those nodes being removed and waits until the transition is finished to remove them** ⟵

Because the force algorithm is restarted after the filtering, you can see how the shape of the network changes with the removal of so many nodes. That animation is important because it reveals structural changes in the network.

Putting more nodes and edges into the network is easy, as long as you properly format your data. You stop the force layout, add the properly formatted nodes or edges to the respective arrays, and rebind the data as you've done in the past. If, for instance, we want to add an edge between Sam and Al as shown in figure 6.19, we need to stop the force layout like we did earlier, create a new datapoint for that edge, and add it to the array we're using for the links. Then we rebind the data and append a new line element for that edge before we restart the force layout.

Listing 6.10   A function for adding edges

```
function addEdge() {
    force.stop();
    var oldEdges = force.links();
    var nodes = force.nodes();
    newEdge = {source: nodes[0], target: nodes[8], weight: 5};
    oldEdges.push(newEdge);
    force.links(oldEdges);
    d3.select("svg").selectAll("line.link")
    .data(oldEdges, function(d) {
                return d.source.id + "-" + d.target.id;
    })
```

```
    .enter()
    .insert("line", "g.node")
    .attr("class", "link")
    .style("stroke", "red")
    .style("stroke-width", 5)
    .attr("marker-end", "url(#Triangle)");

    force.start();
};
```

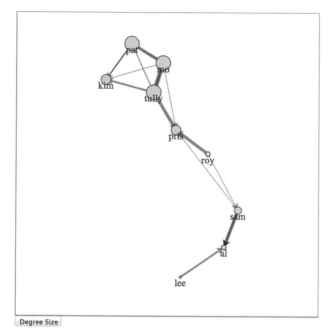

Figure 6.19   Network with a new edge added. Notice that because we re-initialized the force layout, it correctly recalculated the weight for Al.

If we want to add new nodes as shown in figure 6.20, we'll also want to add edges at the same time, not because we have to, but because otherwise they'll float around in space and won't be connected to our current network. The code and process, which you can see in the following listing, should look familiar to you by now.

Listing 6.11   Function for adding nodes and edges

```
function addNodesAndEdges() {
    force.stop();
    var oldEdges = force.links();
    var oldNodes = force.nodes();
    var newNode1 = {id: "raj", followers: 100, following: 67};
    var newNode2 = {id: "wu", followers: 50, following: 33};
    var newEdge1 = {source: oldNodes[0], target: newNode1, weight: 5};
    var newEdge2 = {source: oldNodes[0], target: newNode2, weight: 5};
    oldEdges.push(newEdge1,newEdge2);
    oldNodes.push(newNode1,newNode2);
    force.links(oldEdges).nodes(oldNodes);
```

```
d3.select("svg").selectAll("line.link")
    .data(oldEdges, function(d) {
    return d.source.id + "-" + d.target.id
})
.enter()
.insert("line", "g.node")
.attr("class", "link")
.style("stroke", "red")
.style("stroke-width", 5)
.attr("marker-end", "url(#Triangle)");

var nodeEnter = d3.select("svg").selectAll("g.node")
    .data(oldNodes, function (d) {
        return d.id
    }).enter()
    .append("g")
    .attr("class", "node")
    .call(force.drag());

nodeEnter.append("circle")
    .attr("r", 5)
    .style("fill", "red")
    .style("stroke", "darkred")
    .style("stroke-width", "2px");

nodeEnter.append("text")
    .style("text-anchor", "middle")
    .attr("y", 15)
    .text(function(d) {return d.id;});

    force.start();
};
```

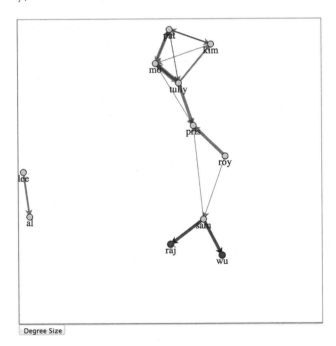

Figure 6.20   Network with two
new nodes added (Raj and Wu),
both with links to Sam

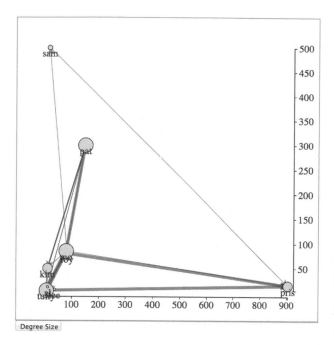

Figure 6.21 When the network is represented as a scatterplot, the links increase the visual clutter. It provides a useful contrast to the force-directed layout, but can be hard to read on its own.

6.2.7 *Manually positioning nodes*

The force-directed layout doesn't move your elements. Instead, it calculates the position of elements based on the x and y attributes of those elements in relation to each other. During each tick, it updates those x and y attributes. The tick function selects the <line> and <g> elements and moves them to these updated x and y values.

When you want to move your elements manually, you can do so like you normally would. But first you need to stop the force so that you prevent that tick function from overwriting your elements' positions. Let's lay out our nodes like a scatterplot, looking at the number of followers by the number that each node is following. We'll also add axes to make it readable. You can see the code in the following listing and the results in figure 6.21.

Listing 6.12   Moving our nodes manually

```
function manuallyPositionNodes() {
    var xExtent = d3.extent(force.nodes(), function(d) {
            return parseInt(d.followers)
    });
    var yExtent = d3.extent(force.nodes(), function(d) {
            return parseInt(d.following)
    });
    var xScale = d3.scale.linear().domain(xExtent).range([50,450]);
    var yScale = d3.scale.linear().domain(yExtent).range([450,50]);

    force.stop();
    d3.selectAll("g.node")
        .transition()
```

```
            .duration(1000)
            .attr("transform", function(d) {
                return "translate("+ xScale(d.followers)
                        +","+yScale(d.following) +")";
            });

    d3.selectAll("line.link")
        .transition()
        .duration(1000)
        .attr("x1", function(d) {return xScale(d.source.followers);})
        .attr("y1", function(d) {return yScale(d.source.following);})
        .attr("x2", function(d) {return xScale(d.target.followers);})
        .attr("y2", function(d) {return yScale(d.target.following);});

    var xAxis = d3.svg.axis().scale(xScale).orient("bottom").tickSize(4);
    var yAxis = d3.svg.axis().scale(yScale).orient("right").tickSize(4);

    d3.select("svg").append("g").attr("transform",
            "translate(0,460)").call(xAxis);
    d3.select("svg").append("g").attr("transform",
            "translate(460,0)").call(yAxis);

    d3.selectAll("g.node").each(function(d){
        d.x = xScale(d.followers);
        d.px = xScale(d.followers);
        d.y = yScale(d.following);
        d.py = yScale(d.following);
    });

};
```

Notice that you need to update the x and y attributes of each node, but you also need to update the px and py attributes of each node. The px and py attributes are the previous x and y coordinates of the node before the last tick. If you don't update them, then the force layout thinks that the nodes have high velocity, and will violently move them from their new position.

If you didn't update the x, y, px, and py attributes, then the next time you started the force layout, the nodes would immediately return to their positions before you moved them. This way, when you restart the force layout with force.start(), the nodes and edges animate from their current position.

6.2.8   *Optimization*

The force layout is extremely resource-intensive. That's why it cools off and stops running by design. And if you have a large network running with the force layout, you can tax a user's computer until it becomes practically unusable. The first tip to optimization, then, is to limit the number of nodes in your network, as well as the number of edges. A general rule is no more than 100 nodes, unless you know your audience is going to be using the browsers that perform best with SVG, like Safari and Chrome.

But if you have to present more nodes and want to reduce the performance press, you can use force.chargeDistance() to set a maximum distance when computing the repulsive charge for each node. The lower this setting, the less structured the force layout will be, but the faster it will run. Because networks vary so much, you'll have to experiment with different values for `chargeDistance` to find the best one for your network.

6.3   *Summary*

In this chapter you learned several methods for displaying network data, and looked in-depth at the force layouts available for network data in D3. There's no one way to visually represent a network. Now you have multiple methods, and static, dynamic, and interactive variations, with which to work. Specifically, we covered

- Formatting a node and edge list in the manner D3 typically uses
- Building a weighted, directed adjacency matrix and adding interaction to explore it
- Building an interactive weighted, directed arc diagram
- Applying simple techniques to find links to a node
- Building and customizing force-directed layouts
- The basics of network terminology and statistics, such as edge, node, degree, and centrality
- Using accessors to create dynamic forces
- Adding interactivity to update node size based on degree centrality

We focused on network information visualization because our world is awash in network data. In the next chapter, we'll look at another broadly applicable but specific domain: geographic information visualization. Just as you've seen several different ways to represent networks in this chapter, in chapter 7 you'll learn different ways of making maps, including tiled maps, globes, and traditional data-driven polygon maps.

Geospatial information visualization

7

This chapter covers

- Creating points and polygons from GeoJSON and TopoJSON data
- Using Mercator, Mollweide, orthographic, and satellite projections
- Advanced TopoJSON neighbor and merging functionality
- Tiled mapping using `d3.geo.tile`

One of the most common categories of data you'll encounter is geospatial data. This can come in the form of administrative regions like states or counties, points that represent cities or the location of a person when making a tweet, or satellite imagery of the surface of the earth.

In the past, if you wanted to make a web map you needed a specialized library like Google Maps, Leaflet, or OpenLayers. But D3 provides enough core functionality to make any kind of map you've seen on the web (some examples of maps created in this chapter using D3 can be seen in figure 7.1). Because you're already working with D3, you can make that map far more sophisticated and distinctive than the out-of-the-box maps you typically see. The major reason to continue to use

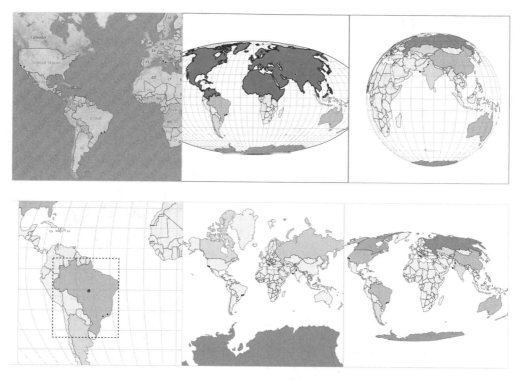

Figure 7.1 Mapping with D3 takes many forms and offers many options, including traditional tile-based maps (section 7.5), cutting-edge TopoJSON operations (section 7.4), globes (section 7.3.1), spatial calculations (section 7.1.4), and data-driven maps (section 7.1) using novel projections (section 7.1.3).

a dedicated library like Google Maps API is because of the added functionality that comes from being in that ecosystem, such as Street View of Google tiles or integrated support for Fusion Tables. But if you're not going to use the ecosystem, then it may be a smarter move to build the map with D3. You won't have to invest in learning a different syntax and abstraction layer, and you'll have the greater flexibility D3 mapping affords.

Because mapmaking and geographic information systems and science (known as GIS and GIScience, respectively) have been in practice for so long, well-developed methods exist for representing this kind of data. D3 has built-in robust functionality to load and display geospatial data. A related library that you'll get to know in this chapter, TopoJSON, provides more functionality for geospatial information visualization.

In this chapter, we'll start by making maps that combine points, lines, and polygons using data from CSV and GeoJSON formatted sources. You'll learn how to style those maps and provide interactive zooming by revisiting d3.zoom() and exploring it in more detail. After that, we'll look at the TopoJSON data format and its built-in functionality that uses topology, and why it provides significantly smaller data files. Finally, you'll learn how to make maps using tiles to show terrain and satellite imagery.

7.1   *Basic mapmaking*

Before you explore the boundaries of mapping possibilities, you need to make a simple map. In D3, the simplest map you can make is a vector map using SVG `<path>` and `<circle>` elements to represent countries and cities. We can bring back cities.csv, which we used in chapter 2, and finally take advantage of its coordinates, but we need to look a bit further to find the data necessary to represent those countries. After we have that data, we can render it as areas, lines, or points on a map. Then we can add interactivity, such as highlighting a region when you move your mouse over it, or computing and showing its center.

Before we get started, though, let's take a look at the CSS for this chapter.

Listing 7.1   ch7.css

```
path.countries {
    stroke-width: 1;
    stroke: black;
    opacity: .5;
    fill: red;
}

circle.cities {
    stroke-width: 1;
    stroke: black;
    fill: white;
}

circle.centroid {
    fill: red;
    pointer-events: none;
}
rect.bbox {
    fill: none;
    stroke-dasharray: 5 5;
    stroke: black;
    stroke-width: 2;
    pointer-events: none;
}

path.graticule {
    fill: none;
    stroke-width: 1;
    stroke: black;
}

path.graticule.outline {
    stroke: black;
}
```

7.1.1   *Finding data*

Making a map requires data, and you have an enormous amount of data available. Geographic data can come in several forms. If you're familiar with GIS, then you'll be familiar with one of the most common forms for complex geodata, the *shapefile*, which is a format developed by Esri and is most commonly found in desktop GIS applications. But the most human-readable form of geodata is latitude and longitude (or xy coordinates like we list in our file) when dealing with points like cities, oftentimes in a CSV. We'll use cities.csv, shown in the following listing. This is the same CSV we measured in chapter 2 that had the locations of eight cities from around the world.

Listing 7.2   cities.csv

```
"label","population","country","x","y"
"San Francisco", 750000,"USA",-122,37
"Fresno", 500000,"USA",-119,36
"Lahore",12500000,"Pakistan",74,31
"Karachi",13000000,"Pakistan",67,24
"Rome",2500000,"Italy",12,41
"Naples",1000000,"Italy",14,40
"Rio",12300000,"Brazil",-43,-22
"Sao Paolo",12300000,"Brazil",-46,-23
```

One thing you'll notice is that the latitudes and longitudes are imprecise. San Francisco, for instance, isn't at 37,-122 but rather 37.783, -122.417. When you plot these cities, they're going to look pretty off as you zoom in. Obviously, you'll want to use more accurate coordinates for your maps, but for this example, which mostly uses maps that are zoomed way out, this should be fine.

If you only have city names or addresses and need to get latitude and longitude, you can take advantage of geocoding services that provide latitude and longitude from addresses. These exist as APIs and are available on the web for small batches. You can see an example of these services maintained by Texas A&M at http://geoservices .tamu.edu/Services/Geocode/.

When dealing with more complex geodata like shapes or lines, you'll necessarily deal with more complex data formats. You'll want to use GeoJSON, which has become the standard for web-mapping data.

GEOJSON

GeoJSON (geojson.org) is, like it sounds, a way of encoding geodata in JSON format. Each *feature* in a *featureCollection* is a JSON object that stores the border of the feature in a *coordinates* array as well as metadata about the feature in a *properties* hash object. For instance, if you wanted to draw a square that went around the island of Manhattan, then it would have corners at [-74.0479, 40.6829], [-74.0479, 40.8820], [-73.9067, 40.8820], and [-73.9067, 40.6829], as shown in figure 7.2. You can easily export shapefiles into GeoJSON using QGIS (a desktop GIS application; qgis.org), PostGIS (a spatial database run on Postgres; postgis.net), GDAL (a library for manipulation of geospatial data; gdal.org), and other tools and libraries.

A rectangle drawn over a geographic feature like this is known as a *bounding box*. It's often represented with only two coordinate pairs: the upper-left and bottom-right corners. But any polygon data, such as the irregular border of a state or coastline, can be represented by an array of coordinates like this. In the following listing, we have a

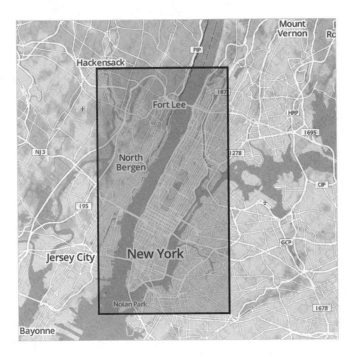

Figure 7.2   A polygon drawn at the coordinates [-74.0479, 40.8820], [-73.9067, 40.8820], [-73.9067, 40.6829], and [-74.0479, 40.6829].

fully compliant GeoJSON `"FeatureCollection"` with only one feature, the simplified borders of the small nation of Luxembourg.

Listing 7.3   GeoJSON example of Luxembourg

```
{
    "type": "FeatureCollection",
    "features": [
        {
            "type": "Feature",
            "id": "LUX",
            "properties": {
                "name": "Luxembourg"
            },
            "geometry": {
                "type": "Polygon",
                "coordinates": [
                    [
                        [
                            6.043073,
                            50.128052
                        ],
                        [
                            6.242751,
                            49.902226
                        ],
                        [
                            6.18632,
                            49.463803
```

```
            ],
            [
                5.897759,
                49.442667
            ],
            [
                5.674052,
                49.529484
            ],
            [
                5.782417,
                50.090328
            ],
            [
                6.043073,
                50.128052
            ]
          ]
        ]
      }
    }
  ]
}
```

We're not going to create our own GeoJSON in this chapter, and unless you get into serious GIS, you may never create your own GeoJSON. Instead, you can get by with downloading existing geodata, and either use it without editing it or edit it in a GIS application and export it. In our examples in this chapter, we'll use world.geojson (available at emeeks.github.io/d3ia/world.geojson), a file that consists of the countries of the world in the same simplified, low-resolution representation that you see in listing 7.4.

PROJECTION

Entire books have been written on creating web maps, and an entire book could be written on using D3.js for crafting maps. Because this is only one chapter, I'll gloss over many deep issues. One of these is projection. In GIS, *projection* refers to the process of rendering points on a globe, like the earth, onto a flat plane, like your computer monitor. You can project geographic data in many different ways for representation on your screen, and in this chapter we'll look at a few different methods.

To start, we'll use one of the most common geographic projections, the Mercator projection, which is used in most web maps. It became the de facto standard because it's the projection used by Google Maps. To use the Mercator projection, you have to include an extension of D3, d3.geo.projection.js, which you'll want for some of the more interesting work you'll do later in the chapter. By defining a projection, you can take advantage of d3.geo.path, which draws geoData onscreen based on your selected projection. After we've defined a projection and have geo.path() ready, the entire code in the following listing is all that we need to draw the map shown in figure 7.3.

Figure 7.3 A map of the world using the default settings for D3's Mercator projection. You can see most of the Western Hemisphere and some of Europe and Africa, but the rest of the world is rendered out of sight.

Listing 7.4 Initial mapping function

```
d3.json("world.geojson", createMap);

function createMap(countries) {
  var aProjection = d3.geo.mercator();
  var geoPath = d3.geo.path().projection(aProjection);
  d3.select("svg").selectAll("path").data(countries.features)
    .enter()
    .append("path")
    .attr("d", geoPath)
    .attr("class", "countries");
};
```

Projection functions have many options that you'll see later.

d3.geo.path() takes properly formatted GeoJSON features and returns SVG drawing code for SVG paths.

d3.geo.path() defaults to albersUSA, which is a projection suitable only for maps of the United States.

Why do you only see part of the world in figure 7.3? Because the default settings of the Mercator projection show only part of the world in your SVG canvas. Each projection has a `.translate()` and `.scale()` that follow the syntax of the transform convention in SVG, but have different effects with different projections.

SCALE

You have to do some tricks to set the right scale for certain projects. For instance, with our Mercator projection if we divide the width of the available space by 2 and divide the quotient by `Math.pi`, then the result will be the proper scale to display the entire world in the available space. Figuring out the right scale for your map and your projection is typically done through experimenting with different values, but it's easier when you include zooming, as you'll see in section 7.2.2.

Different families of projections have different scale defaults. The `d3.geo.albers-Usa` projection defaults to 1070, while `d3.geo.mercator` defaults to 150. As with most D3 functions like this, you can see the default by calling the function without passing it a value:

```
d3.geo.mercator().scale()          ⟵─┐ 150
d3.geo.albersUsa().scale()           ⟵─┐ 1070
```

By adjusting the `translate` and `scale` as in listing 7.5, we can adjust the projection to show different parts of the geodata we're working with—in our case, the world. The result in figure 7.4 shows that we now see the entire world rendered.

Listing 7.5 Simple map with scale and translate settings

```
function createMap(countries) {
    var width = 500;                              ⟵─┐ By defining the size of our SVG as
    var height = 500;                               │ variables, we can refer to them
    var aProjection = d3.geo.mercator()             │ throughout our visualization code.
    .scale(80)
    .translate([width / 2, height / 2]);          ⟵──┐
    var geoPath = d3.geo.path().projection(aProjection);

    d3.select("svg").selectAll("path").data(countries.features)
     .enter()
     .append("path")
     .attr("d", geoPath)
     .attr("class", "countries");
};
```

Moves the center of the projection to the center of our canvas ⟶

Scale values are different for different families of projections; 80 works well in this case.

Figure 7.4 The Mercator-projected world from our data now fitting our SVG area. Notice the enormous distortion in size of regions near the poles, such as Greenland and Antarctica.

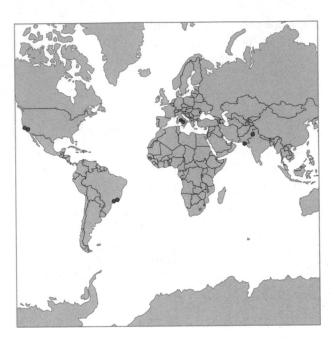

Figure 7.5   Our map with our eight world cities added to it. At this distance, you can't tell how inaccurate these points are, but if you zoom in, you see that both of our Italian cities are actually in the Mediterranean.

7.1.2   *Drawing points on a map*

Projection isn't used only to display areas; it's also used to place individual points. Typically, you think of cities or people as represented not by their spatial footprint (though you do this with particularly large cities) but with a single point on a map, which is sized based on some variable such as population. A D3 projection can be used not only in a geo.path() but also as a function on its own. When you pass it an array with a pair of latitude and longitude coordinates, it returns the screen coordinates necessary to place that point. For instance, if we want to know where to place a point representing San Francisco (roughly speaking, -122 latitude, 37 longitude), then we could simply pass those values to our projection:

```
aProjection([-122,37])          ←⊢  [79.65586500535346,
                                     194.32096033997914]
```

We can use this to add cities to our map along with loading the data from cities.csv, as in the following listing and which you see in figure 7.5.

Listing 7.6   Loading point and polygon geodata

```
queue()
    .defer(d3.json, "world.geojson")
    .defer(d3.csv, "cities.csv")
    .await(function(error, file1, file2) {
            createMap(file1, file2);
    });
```

```
function createMap(countries, cities) {
  var width = 500;
  var height = 500;
  var projection = d3.geo.mercator()
                    .scale(80)
                    .translate([width / 2, height / 2]);
  var geoPath = d3.geo.path().projection(projection);

  d3.select("svg").selectAll("path").data(countries.features)
    .enter()
    .append("path")
    .attr("d", geoPath)
    .style("fill", "gray");

  d3.select("svg").selectAll("circle").data(cities)
    .enter()
    .append("circle")
    .style("fill", "red")
    .attr("class", "cities")
    .attr("r", 3)
    .attr("cx", function(d) {return projection([d.x,d.y])[0]})
    .attr("cy", function(d) {return projection([d.x,d.y])[1]});
};
```

Overrides the fill style so it'll be easier to see your cities

You want to draw the cities over the countries, so you append them second.

Projection returns an array, which means you need to take the [0] value for cx and the [1] value for cy

One thing to note from listing 7.6 is that coordinates are often given in the real world in the order of "latitude, longitude." Because latitude corresponds to the y-axis and longitude corresponds to the x-axis, you have to flip them to provide the x, y coordinates necessary for GeoJSON and D3.

7.1.3 Projections and areas

Depending on what projection you use, the graphical size of your geographic objects will appear different. This is because it's impossible to perfectly display spherical coordinates on a flat surface. Different projections are designed to visually display the geographic area of land or ocean regions, or the measurable distance, or particular shapes. Because we included d3.geo.projection.js, we have access to quite a few more projections to play with, one of which is the Mollweide projection. In the code in listing 7.7, you can see the settings necessary to properly display a Mollweide projection of our geodata. We'll use the calculated area of the countries (the graphical area, not their actual physical area) to color each country. The results are quite distinct from the same code running on our Mercator projection, as shown in figure 7.6. The world as displayed with Mollweide curves the edges, rather than stretching them into a rectangle like Mercator does.

Listing 7.7 Mollweide projected world

```
queue()
  .defer(d3.json, "world.geojson")
  .defer(d3.csv, "cities.csv")
  .await(function(error, file1, file2) {
        createMap(file1, file2);
  });
```

```
function createMap(countries, cities) {

  var width = 500;
  var height = 500;

  var projection = d3.geo.mollweide()
                    .scale(120)
                    .translate([width / 2, height / 2]);

  var geoPath = d3.geo.path().projection(projection);

  var featureSize = d3.extent(countries.features,
                    function(d) {return geoPath.area(d);});

  var countryColor = d3.scale.quantize()
                .domain(featureSize).range(colorbrewer.Reds[7]);

  d3.select("svg").selectAll("path").data(countries.features)
      .enter()
      .append("path")
      .attr("d", geoPath)
      .attr("class", "countries")
      .style("fill", function(d) {
              return countryColor(geoPath.area(d))
      });

  d3.select("svg").selectAll("circle").data(cities)
      .enter()
      .append("circle")
      .attr("class", "cities")
      .attr("r", 3)
      .attr("cx", function(d) {return projection([d.x,d.y])[0]})
      .attr("cy", function(d) {return projection([d.x,d.y])[1]});
};
```

> For a Mollweide projection; shows the entire world

> Measures the features and assigns the size classes to a color ramp

> Colors each country based on its size

Figure 7.6   Mercator (left) dramatically distorts the size of Antarctica so much that no other shape looks as large. In comparison, the Mollweide projection maintains the actual physical area of the countries and continents in your geodata, at the cost of distorting their shape and angle. Notice that `geo.path.area` measures the graphical area and not the actual physical area of the features.

Picking the right projection is never easy, and depends on the goals of the map you're making. If you're working with traditional tile mapping, then you'll probably stick with Mercator. If you're working on the world scale, it's usually best to use an equal-area projection like Mollweide that doesn't distort the visual area of geographic features. But because D3 has so many different projections available, you should experiment to see which best suits the particular map you're creating.

Infoviz term: choropleth map

As you encounter more mapmaking, you'll hear the term *choropleth map* used to refer to a map that encodes data using the color of a region. You can use the existing geographic features, in this case countries, to display statistical data, such as the GDP of a country, its population, or its most widely used language. You can do this in D3 either by getting geodata where the `properties` field has that information or by linking a table of data to your geodata where they both have the same unique ID values in common.

Keep in mind that choropleth maps, although useful, are subject to what's known as the *areal unit problem*, which is what happens when you draw boundaries or select existing features in such a way that they disproportionately represent your statistics. This is the case with gerrymandering, when political districts are drawn in such a way as to create majorities for one political party or another.

7.1.4 *Interactivity*

Much of the geospatial data-related code in D3 comes with built-in functionality that you'll typically need when working with geodata. In addition to determining the area like we did to color our features, D3 has other useful functions. Two that are commonly used in mapping are the ability to quickly calculate the center of a geographic area (known as a *centroid*) and its bounding box, like you see in figure 7.7. In the following listing, you can see how to add mouseover events to the paths we created and draw a circle at the center of each geographic area, as well as a bounding box around it.

Listing 7.8 Rendering bounding boxes with geodata

```
d3.selectAll("path.countries")
.on("mouseover", centerBounds)
    .on("mouseout", clearCenterBounds);

    function centerBounds(d,i) {
      var thisBounds = geoPath.bounds(d);            ⟵ Functions of geo.path
      var thisCenter = geoPath.centroid(d);          ⟵ that give results based on
                                                          the associated projection
      d3.select("svg")
        .append("rect")
        .attr("class", "bbox")                       Bounding box is the top-
        .attr("x", thisBounds[0][0])                 left and bottom-right
        .attr("y", thisBounds[0][1])            ⟵    coordinates as an array
        .attr("width", thisBounds[1][0] - thisBounds[0][0])
```

```
          .attr("height", thisBounds[1][1] - thisBounds[0][1])
            .style("fill", "none")
            .style("stroke-dasharray", "5 5")
            .style("stroke", "black")
            .style("stroke-width", 2)
          .style("pointer-events", "none");

     d3.select("svg")
       .append("circle")
       .attr("class", "centroid")
       .style("fill", "red")
       .attr("r", 5)
       .attr("cx", thisCenter[0]).attr("cy", thisCenter[1])
       .style("pointer-events", "none");
   };
   function clearCenterBounds() {
     d3.selectAll("circle.centroid").remove();
     d3.selectAll("rect.bbox").remove();
   };
```

Centroid is
an array with
the x and y
coordinates
of the center
of a feature

Removes the
shapes when you
mouse off a feature

You've learned the core geo functions that allow you to make maps with D3: `geo` `.projection` and `geo.path`. By using these functions, you can create maps with a distinct look and feel, and provide your users with the ability to interact with them as shapes and as geographic features. D3 provides more functionality, and we'll dive into it now.

7.2 *Better mapping*

To make your maps more readable, you can use built-in features from `d3.geo`: the graticule generator and the zoom behavior. One provides grid lines that make it easier

Figure 7.7 Your interactivity provides a bounding box around each country and a red circle representing its graphical center. Here you see the bounding box and centroid of China. The D3 implementation of a centroid is weighted, so that it's the center of most area, and not just the center of the bounding box.

to read a map, and the other allows you to pan and zoom around your map. Both of these follow the same format and functionality of other behaviors and generators in D3, but are particularly useful for maps.

7.2.1 Graticule

A *graticule* is a grid line on a map. Just as D3 has generators for lines, areas, and arcs, it has a generator for graticules to make your maps more beautiful. The graticule generator creates gridlines (you can specify where and how many, or use the default) and also creates an outline that can provide a useful border. Listing 7.9 shows how to draw a graticule beneath the countries we've already drawn. Instead of `.data` we use `.datum`, which is a convenience function that allows us to bind a single datapoint to a selection so it doesn't need to be in an array. In other words, `.datum(yourDatapoint)` is the same as `.data([yourDatapoint])`.

Listing 7.9 Adding a graticule

```
var graticule = d3.geo.graticule();

d3.select("svg").append("path")
    .datum(graticule)
    .attr("class", "graticule line")
    .attr("d", geoPath)
    .style("fill", "none")
    .style("stroke", "lightgray")
    .style("stroke-width", "1px");

d3.select("svg").append("path")
    .datum(graticule.outline)
    .attr("class", "graticule outline")
    .attr("d", geoPath)
    .style("fill", "none")
    .style("stroke", "black")
    .style("stroke-width", "1px");
```

But how are we drawing so many graticule lines in figure 7.8 from a single datapoint? The `geo.graticule` function creates a feature known as a *multilinestring*. A multilinestring, as you may have figured out, is an array of arrays of coordinates, each corresponding to separate individual components of a feature. Multilinestrings and their counterparts, multipolygons, have always been a part of GIS because countries like the United States or Indonesia are made up of disconnected features such as states and regions, and that information needed to be stored in the data. As a result, when `d3.geo.path` gets a multipolygon or multilinestring, it draws a `<path>` element made up of multiple, disconnected pieces.

7.2.2 Zoom

You dealt with zoom a little bit in chapter 5, when you saw how the zoom behavior can easily allow you to pan a chart around the screen. Now it's time you start zooming with zoom. When we first looked at the zoom behavior, we used it to adjust the `transform`

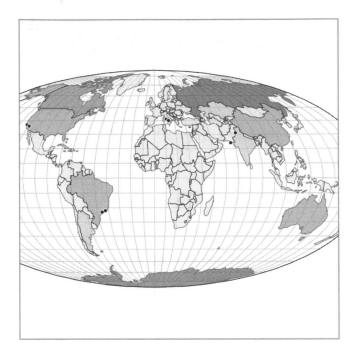

Figure 7.8 Our map with a graticule (in light gray) and a graticule outline (the black border around the edge of the map)

attribute of a <g> element that held our chart. This time, we'll use the scale and translate values of the zoom behavior to update the settings of our projection, which will give us the ability to zoom and pan our map.

Create a zoom behavior and call it from the <svg> element. Whenever you have a drag event on anything in the <svg>, a mousewheel event, or a double-click, then it triggers zoom. When we worked with zoom before, we only dealt with the dragging, which updates the zoom.translate() value and which you can use to update the translate value of whatever element you want to update. This time, we'll also use the zoom.scale() value, which gives us an increasing (when you double-click or roll your mousewheel forward) or decreasing (when you roll your mousewheel backward) value. To use zoom with a projection, we'll want to overwrite the initial zoom.scale() value with the scale value of the projection, and do the same with the zoom translate value. After that, any time we have an event that triggers zoom, we'll use the new values to update our projection, as shown in the following listing and in figure 7.9.

Listing 7.10 Zoom and pan with maps

```
var mapZoom = d3.behavior.zoom()
    .translate(projection.translate())
    .scale(projection.scale())
    .on("zoom", zoomed);

d3.select("svg").call(mapZoom);

function zoomed() {
    projection.translate(mapZoom.translate()).scale(mapZoom.scale());
```

Overwrites the translate and scale of the zoom to match the projection

Whenever the zoom behavior is called, overwrites the projection to match the updated zoom values

```
d3.selectAll("path.graticule").attr("d", geoPath);
  d3.selectAll("path.countries").attr("d", geoPath);

d3.selectAll("circle.cities")
    .attr("cx", function(d) {return projection([d.x,d.y])[0]})
    .attr("cy", function(d) {return projection([d.x,d.y])[1]});
};
```

Also calls the now-updated projection

Any path will be properly redrawn by calling the d3.geo.path associated with the updated projection.

The zoom behavior updates its `.translate()` array in reference to your dragging behavior, and increases or decreases the `.scale()` value in reference to your mousewheel and double-click behavior. Because it's designed to work with SVG transform and D3 geographic projections, `d3.behavior.zoom` is all you need for pan-and-zoom functionality.

Infoviz term: semantic zoom

When you think about zooming in on things, you naturally think about increasing their size. But from working with mapping, you know that you don't just increase the size or resolution as you zoom in; you also change the kind of data that you present to the reader. This is known as *semantic zoom* in contrast to *graphical zoom*. It's most clear when you look at a zoomed-out map and see only country boundaries and a few major cities, but as you zoom in you see roads, smaller cities, parks, and so on.

You should try to use semantic zoom whenever you're letting your user zoom in and out of any data visualization, not just a chart. It allows you to present strategic or global information when zoomed out, and high-resolution data when zoomed in.

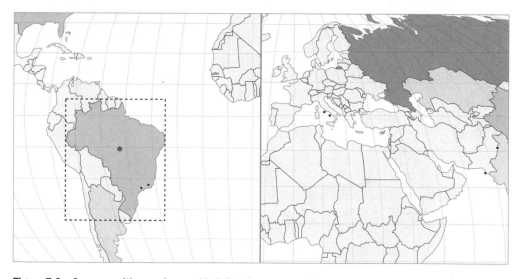

Figure 7.9   Our map with zooming enabled. Panning occurs with the drag behavior and zooming with mousewheel and/or double-clicking. Notice that the bounding box and centroid functions still work, because they're based on our constantly updating projection.

Figure 7.10 Zoom buttons and the effect of pressing Zoom Out five times. Because the zoom buttons modify the zoom behavior's translate and scale, any mouse interaction afterward reflects the updated settings.

The default zoom behavior assumes a user knows that the mousewheel and double-clicking are associated with zooming. But sometimes you want zoom buttons, because you can't assume the user knows that interaction or because you want to constrain or control the zooming process in a more complicated manner. The code in the following listing creates a zoom function and adds the necessary buttons, as seen in figure 7.10.

Listing 7.11 Manual zoom controls for maps

```
function zoomButton(zoomDirection) {
  if (zoomDirection == "in") {
    var newZoom = mapZoom.scale() * 1.5;
    var newX =
      ((mapZoom.translate()[0] - (width / 2)) * 1.5) + width / 2;
    var newY =
      ((mapZoom.translate()[1] - (height / 2)) * 1.5) + height / 2;
  }
  else if (zoomDirection == "out") {
    var newZoom = mapZoom.scale() * .75;
    var newX = ((mapZoom.translate()[0] - (width / 2)) * .75) + width / 2;
    var newY = ((mapZoom.translate()[1] - (height / 2)) * .75) + height / 2;
  }

  mapZoom.scale(newZoom).translate([newX,newY])
  zoomed();
}

d3.select("#controls").append("button").on("click", function (){
                      zoomButton("in") }).html("Zoom In");
```

Calculating the new scale is easy.

Calculating the new translate settings isn't so easy and requires that you recalculate the center.

Redraws the map based on the updated settings

Sets the zoom behavior's scale and translate settings to your new settings

```
d3.select("#controls").append("button").on("click", function (){
                    zoomButton("out")}).html("Zoom Out");
```

With this kind of styling and interactivity in place, you can make a map for most any application. Zooming and panning is important for maps because users expect to be able to zoom in and out, and they also expect the details of the map to change when they do so. In that way, geospatial is one of the most powerful forms of information visualization because users have a high level of literacy when it comes to reading and interacting with maps. But users also expect a map to have certain features and functionality, and when those are missing they think it's broken. Make sure that when you create your map, it either includes this functionality or you have a good reason to leave it out.

7.3 Advanced mapping

We've covered the aspects of creating maps that you'll likely end up using with all your maps. You could explore many variations. You may want to scale your `<circle>` elements based on population, or use `<g>` elements so that you can also provide labels like we did earlier. But if you're making a map, it will probably have polygons and points and take advantage of bounding boxes or centroids, and will likely be tied to a zoom behavior. The exciting thing about D3 is that it lets you explore more complex ways of representing geography, with a little more effort.

7.3.1 Creating and rotating globes

We'll do only one thing in 3D in this entire book, and that's create a globe. We don't need to load three.js or learn WebGL. Instead, we'll take advantage of a trick of one of the geographic projections available in D3: the orthographic projection, which renders geographic data as it would appear from a distant point viewing the entire globe. We need to update our projection to refer to the orthographic projection and have a slightly different scale.

Listing 7.12 Creating a simple globe

```
projection = d3.geo.orthographic()
    .scale(200)
    .translate([width / 2, height / 2])
    .center([0,0]);
```

With this new projection, you can see what looks like a globe in figure 7.11.

To make it rotate, we need to use `d3.mouse`, which returns the current position of the mouse on the SVG canvas. Pair this with event listeners to turn on and off a mouse-move listener on the canvas. This simulates dragging the globe, which we'll use only to rotate it along the x-axis. Because we're introducing new behavior and it's been a while since we looked at the full code, the following listing has the entire code for creating the globe.

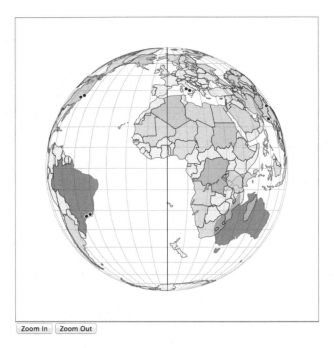

Zoom In   Zoom Out

Figure 7.11   An orthographic projection makes our map look like a globe. Notice that even though the paths for countries are drawn over each other, they're still drawn above the graticules. Also notice that although zooming in and out works, panning doesn't spin the globe but simply moves it around the canvas. The coloration of our countries is once again based on the graphical size of the country.

Listing 7.13   A draggable globe in D3

```
    queue()
    .defer(d3.json, "world.geojson")
    .defer(d3.csv, "cities.csv")
    .await(function(error, file1, file2) { createMap(file1, file2); });

function createMap(countries, cities) {
  …code to set up orthographic projection…
  var mapZoom =
    d3.behavior.zoom().translate(projection.translate()).scale(projection.sc
    ale()).on("zoom", zoomed);
  d3.select("svg").call(mapZoom);

  var rotateScale = d3.scale.linear()
  .domain([0, width])
  .range([-180, 180]);

  d3.select("svg").on("mousedown", startRotating).on("mouseup",
    stopRotating);

  function startRotating() {
  d3.select("svg").on("mousemove", function() {
var p = d3.mouse(this);
projection.rotate([rotateScale(p[0]), 0]);
  zoomed();
});
  }

  function stopRotating() {
    d3.select("svg").on("mousemove", null);
}
}
```

Dragging globe requires an explicit mousemove event listener triggered by mousedown

End of dragging requires clearing the mousemove listener

```
function zoomed() {
  var currentRotate = projection.rotate()[0];
  projection.scale(mapZoom.scale());
  d3.selectAll("path.graticule").attr("d", geoPath);
  d3.selectAll("path.countries").attr("d", geoPath);

  d3.selectAll("circle.cities")
  .attr("cx", function(d) {return projection([d.y,d.x])[0]})
  .attr("cy", function(d) {return projection([d.y,d.x])[1]})
  .style("display", function(d) {return parseInt(d.y) + currentRotate <
  90 && parseInt(d.y) + currentRotate > -90 ? "block" : "none"})
}
```

…code to add manual zoom and zoom buttons…

…code to draw graticule, countries and cities…

…code to create and clear center and bounding box…
```
}
```

A plugin by Jason Davies known as `d3.geo.zoom` (https://www.jasondavies.com/maps/rotate/) abstracts this functionality.

But this map still has the problem of a graphical artifact from the graticule outline, which must be removed when drawing globes. Another problem is seeing through the globe to the other side. This might be a fine idea, if it didn't also muddle the SVG drawing code so that the shapes are drawn poorly when they get near the border (notice how poorly Antarctica looks in figure 7.12). Also, our cities are drawn above the paths, even when they're ostensibly on the other side of the world (for example, Karachi).

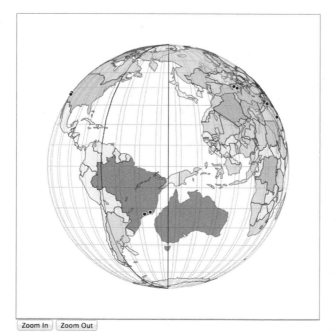

Figure 7.12   A globe with a transparent surface. You can see Australia through the globe because the projection doesn't by default clip this. Cities are drawn at the correct coordinates but are uniformly drawn above the features because the `<circle>` elements are drawn on top of the `<path>` elements in the DOM.

The path drawing can be handled with the `clipAngle` property of the projection, which clips any paths drawn with that projection if they fall outside of a particular angle from its center. This can be useful to show only small parts of your dataset for performance or display purposes. Here's how it looks in our new projection code:

```
projection = d3.geo.orthographic()
    .scale(200)
    .translate([width / 2, height / 2])
    .clipAngle(90);
```

This won't work for the circles we're using for our cities, because `clipAngle` only applies to data that's created by `d3.geo.path()`. For the circles, we have to ensure that they're only displayed if they fall within that clip angle. Taking this into account, we can pass a test in the zoomed function to determine whether a city should be displayed based on its coordinates.

Listing 7.14   Hiding cities on the other side of a rotated globe

```
function zoomed() {
    var currentRotate = projection.rotate()[0];
    projection.scale(mapZoom.scale());
    d3.selectAll("path.graticule").attr("d", geoPath);
    d3.selectAll("path.countries").attr("d", geoPath);

    d3.selectAll("circle.cities")
        .attr("cx", function(d) {return projection([d.x,d.y])[0]})
        .attr("cy", function(d) {return projection([d.x,d.y])[1]})
        .style("display", function(d) {
            return parseInt(d.y) + currentRotate < 90 &&        ◁──
                    parseInt(d.y) + currentRotate > -90 ?
                    "block" : "none";
        });
};
```

> If this city's y position is within 90 degrees of the current rotation of the globe, then display it; otherwise, hide it.

Figure 7.13   Our rotating and properly clipped globe

You may think you're done, but there's one related issue to address now. You draw all the countries when the globe is first initialized, but many of them are clipped, and so your geo.path.area() function, which determines the area as the shape is drawn, has even worse issues than the Mercator projection had. For instance, in figure 7.13, Australia is colored as if it had an area similar to Madagascar. Fortunately, D3 also includes d3.geo.area(), which determines the spherical area of a shape corresponding to its geographic area, as in figure 7.14.

We could rewrite the draw code to use d3.geo.area, but instead let's recolor our existing globe. But how do we get the data? Until now, we've assumed that the data array was exposed somewhere our functions could get to, but what if it's outside our current scope? In this case, we can use selectAll.data() and get an array of data associated with whatever we select (which includes undefined elements if we select HTML elements that aren't bound with data). You'll see this in action more in the next chapter.

```
var featureData = d3.selectAll("path.countries").data();

var realFeatureSize =
d3.extent(featureData, function(d) {return d3.geo.area(d)});

var newFeatureColor =
d3.scale.quantize().domain(realFeatureSize).range(Reds[7]);

d3.selectAll("path.countries")
.style("fill", function(d) {return newFeatureColor(d3.geo.area(d))});
```

The spherical area of a shape as measured by d3.geo.area() is given in steradians, and so it's only a roughly proportionate area. If you want the actual square kilometers of a country or other shape, you'll still need to calculate that in a GIS package like QGIS, or get that information from another source.

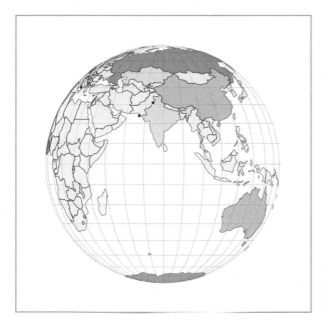

Figure 7.14 Our globe with countries colored by their geographic area, rather than their graphical area

This globe still has some issues. Because you don't update the `projection.center()`, and you base the rotation off the current position of the mouse, it resets any time you drag the globe. You also don't clip the cities when you first draw them. Further, you can make a D3 globe drag in any of the three directions you can rotate a normal globe. But if you're looking for that level of functionality, then you're better off exploring the many and robust examples available online (such as those of Jason Davies at http://jasondavies.com/maps/voronoi/capitals/). Instead, we'll look at another exotic way of representing geodata, the satellite projection.

7.3.2   *Satellite projection*

Isometric views of the world are powerful tools for storytelling. Imagine you had to create a map related to how the Middle East has a changing view of Europe. By crafting a satellite view looking out over the Mediterranean from the Middle East as shown in figure 7.15, you invite your map reader to see a distant Europe from a geographical perspective in the Middle East.

This is a projection just like the orthographic, Mercator, and Mollweide projections we previously used, but, as you see in the following listing, it has specific settings for scale and rotate. It also uses new settings, tilt and distance, to determine the angle of the satellite projection.

Listing 7.15   Satellite projection settings

```
projection = d3.geo.satellite()
    .scale(1330)
    .translate([250,250])
    .rotate([-30.24, -31, -56])      The angle of the
    .tilt(30)                        perspective on the
    .distance(1.199)                 geographic features
    .clipAngle(45);
                                                          The distance of the
                                                          surface from your
                                                          perspective
```

Figure 7.15   A satellite projection of data from the Middle East facing Europe

Tilt is the angle of the perspective on the data, while distance is the percentage of the radius of the earth (so 1.119 is 11.9% of the radius of the earth above the earth). How do you come up with such exact settings? You have two options. The first is to understand how to describe a tilted projection like this mathematically. If you have a degree in math or geography, you can look into literature for calculating this. If, like me, you don't have that kind of background, then I would suggest building a tool, using the code we explored in this chapter, to adjust the rotation, tilt, distance, and scale settings interactively. That's how I did it, and you can play with my satellite projection tool here: http://bl.ocks.org/emeeks/10173187.

Recall my advice for understanding how the Sankey layout works. Use information visualization to visualize how the functions work so that you can better understand them and find the right settings. Otherwise, you're going to need to take a course in GIS or wait for someone to write *D3.js Mapping in Action*.

Now we'll shift gears away from visualization and back to geodata structure to explore a library that was developed by Mike Bostock and is intimately tied to D3 mapping: TopoJSON.

7.4 *TopoJSON data and functionality*

TopoJSON (https://github.com/mbostock/topojson) is, fundamentally, three different things. First of all, it's a data standard for geographic data, and an extension of GeoJSON. Secondly, it's a library that runs in node.js to create TopoJSON-formatted files from GeoJSON files. Thirdly, it's a library that runs in JavaScript that processes TopoJSON-formatted files to create the data objects necessary to render them with libraries like D3. You won't deal with the second form at all, and you'll only examine the first in a cursory manner as you learn about rendering TopoJSON data, merging it, and using it to find a feature's neighbors.

7.4.1 *TopoJSON the file format*

The difference between GeoJSON files and TopoJSON files is that while GeoJSON records for each feature an array of longitude and latitude points that describe a point, line, or polygon, TopoJSON stores for each feature an array of arcs. An arc is any distinct segment of a line shared by one or more features in your dataset. The shared border between the United States and Mexico is a single arc that's referred to in the arcs array of the feature for the United States and the arcs array of the feature for Mexico.

Because most datasets have shared segments, TopoJSON often produces significantly smaller datasets. This is part of its appeal. Another part is that if you know what segments are shared, then you can do interesting things with the data, like easily calculating the neighboring features or the shared border, or merging features.

TopoJSON stores the arcs as a reference to a particular arc in a master list of arcs that defines the coordinates of that arc. You need the Topojson.js library included in any website you're using to create maps with TopoJSON, because it changes TopoJSON into a format that D3 can read and create graphics from.

7.4.2   *Rendering TopoJSON*

Because TopoJSON stores its data in a format different from the GeoJSON structure that's expected by d3.geo.path(), we need to include Topojson.js and use it to process TopoJSON data to produce GeoJSON features. This is rather straightforward and can be done in a call to our new datafile, as shown in the following listing. Figure 7.16 shows the properly formatted features in your console.

> **Listing 7.16   Loading TopoJSON**

```
queue()
    .defer(d3.json, "world.topojson")
    .defer(d3.csv, "cities.csv")
    .await(function(error, file1, file2) { createMap(file1, file2); });

function createMap(file1, file2) {

    var worldFeatures = topojson.feature(file1, file1.objects.countries)   ◁─┐
    console.log(worldFeatures);
};
```

Notice that our TopoJSON file has a property "objects", which all TopoJSON files have, but "countries" is specific to this file and might be "rivers" or "land" or other property names in other files.

Now that it's in the format we want, we can send it to our existing code and draw this array of features like we did with the features we loaded from world.geojson. We replace our earlier countries with the worldFeatures variable declared in listing 7.16. That's all that most people do with TopoJSON, and they're happy for it because TopoJSON data is significantly smaller than GeoJSON data. But because we know the topology of the features in a TopoJSON data file, we do interesting geographic tricks with it.

```
▼ Object {type: "FeatureCollection", features: Array[177]}
  ▼ features: Array[177]
    ▼ [0 … 99]
      ▼ 0: Object
        ▼ geometry: Object
          ▼ coordinates: Array[1]
            ▼ 0: Array[69]
              ▼ 0: Array[2]
                  0: 61.20961209612096
                  1: 35.650872576725774
                  length: 2
                ▶ __proto__: Array[0]
              ▼ 1: Array[2]
                  0: 62.23202232022322
                  1: 35.2705859391594
                  length: 2
                ▶ __proto__: Array[0]
              ▼ 2: Array[2]
                  0: 62.98442984429846
                  1: 35.40429402634027
                  length: 2
                ▶ __proto__: Array[0]
              ▶ 3: Array[2]
              ▶ 4: Array[2]
              ▶ 5: Array[2]
```

Figure 7.16   TopoJSON data formatted using Topojson.feature(). **The data is an array of objects, and it represents geometry as an array of coordinates like the features that come out of a GeoJSON file.**

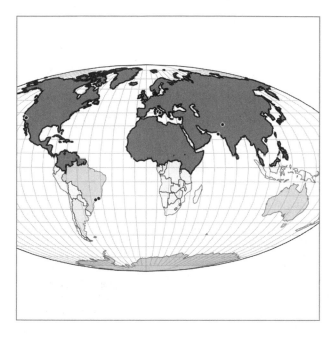

Figure 7.17 The results of merging based on the centroid of a feature. The feature in gray is a single merged feature made up of many separate polygons.

7.4.3 Merging

The TopoJSON library provides you with the capacity to create new features by merging existing features. You can create a new feature for "North America" by merging the countries in North America, or create "The United States in 1912" by merging the states that were part of the United States in 1912. Listing 7.17 shows the code to draw a map using our new TopoJSON data file and merge all the countries that have a center west of 0° longitude. The results, in figure 7.17, show that merging combines not only contiguous features but also separate features into a multipolygon.

Listing 7.17 Rendering and merging TopoJSON

```
queue()
  .defer(d3.json, "world.topojson")
  .defer(d3.csv, "cities.csv")
  .await(function(error, file1, file2) { createMap(file1, file2); });
function createMap(topoCountries, cities) {
  var countries =
    topojson.feature(topoCountries, topoCountries.objects.countries);
  var width = 500;
  var height = 500;
  var projection = d3.geo.mollweide()
    .scale(120)
    .translate([width / 2, height / 2])
    .center([20,0]);

  var geoPath = d3.geo.path().projection(projection);

  var featureSize =
    d3.extent(countries.features, function(d) {return geoPath.area(d)});
```

```
var countryColor = d3.scale.quantize()
        .domain(featureSize).range(colorbrewer.Reds[7]);

var graticule = d3.geo.graticule();

d3.select("svg").append("path")
    .datum(graticule)
    .attr("class", "graticule line")
    .attr("d", geoPath)
    .style("fill", "none")
    .style("stroke", "lightgray")
    .style("stroke-width", "1px");

d3.select("svg").append("path")
    .datum(graticule.outline)
    .attr("class", "graticule outline")
    .attr("d", geoPath)
    .style("fill", "none")
    .style("stroke", "black")
    .style("stroke-width", "1px");

d3.select("svg").selectAll("path.countries")
    .data(countries.features)
    .enter()
    .append("path")
    .attr("d", geoPath)
    .attr("class", "countries")
    .style("fill", function(d) {return countryColor(geoPath.area(d))})
    .style("stroke-width", 1)
    .style("stroke", "black")
    .style("opacity", .5);

d3.select("svg").selectAll("circle").data(cities)
    .enter()
    .append("circle")
    .style("fill", "black")
    .style("stroke", "white")
    .style("stroke-width", 1)
    .attr("r", 3)
    .attr("cx", function(d) {return projection([d.x,d.y])[0];})
    .attr("cy", function(d) {return projection([d.x,d.y])[1];});

mergeAt(0);

function mergeAt(mergePoint) {

    var filteredCountries = topoCountries.objects.countries.geometries
        .filter(function(d) {
            var thisCenter = d3.geo.centroid(
                topojson.feature(topoCountries, d)
            );
            return thisCenter[1] > mergePoint? true : null;
        });

    d3.select("svg").insert("g", "circle")
      .datum(topojson.merge(topoCountries, filteredCountries))
      .insert("path")
      .style("fill", "gray")
      .style("stroke", "black")
```

After processed by Topojson.features, we use exactly the same methods to render the features.

To use geo.centroid, we convert each feature into GeoJSON.

We're working with the TopoJSON dataset.

Our merge function

Results in an array of only the corresponding geometries

Uses datum because merge returns a single multipolygon

```
        .style("stroke-width", "2px")
        .attr("d", geoPath);
    };
};
```

We can adjust the `mergeAt` test slightly to look at the x coordinate or to see features that have greater values of `mergeAt`. As shown in figure 7.18, this creates a single feature in each of four cases: less than or greater than 0° latitude and less than or greater than 0° longitude. Notice in each case that it's a single feature but not a single polygon.

A quick note for those who may want to continue working in topologies: `Topo json.merge` has a sister function, `mergeArcs`, that allows you to merge shapes but keep them in TopoJSON format. Why would you want to maintain arcs? Because then you could continue to use TopoJSON functionality like merging, creating meshes, or finding neighbors of your newly merged features.

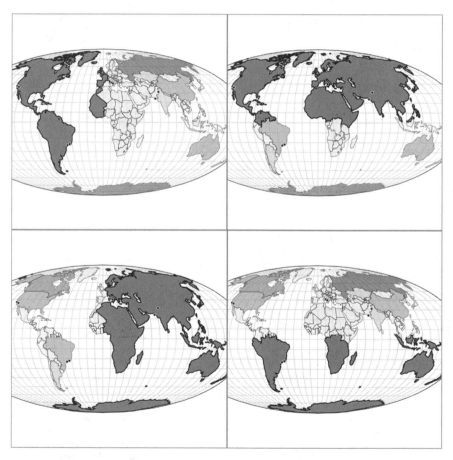

Figure 7.18 By adjusting the merge settings, we can create something like northern, southern, eastern, and western hemispheres as merged features. Notice that because this is based on a centroid, we can see at the bottom left a piece of Eastern Russia as part of our merged feature, along with Antarctica.

7.4.4 *Neighbors*

Because we know when features share arcs, we also know what features neighbor each other. The function `Topojson.neighbors` builds an array of all the features that share a border. We can use this array to easily identify neighboring countries in our dataset using the code in the following listing. The results of the interaction provided by this code are shown in figure 7.19.

> **Listing 7.18 Calculating neighbors and interactive highlighting**

```
    var neighbors =
topojson.neighbors(topoCountries.objects.countries.geometries);   ◁──  Creates an
                                                                        array indicating
    d3.selectAll("path.countries")                                      neighbors by
    .on("mouseover", findNeighbors)                                     their array
    .on("mouseout", clearNeighbors);                                    position

    function findNeighbors (d,i) {            Colors the
d3.select(this).style("fill", "red");        country you
d3.selectAll("path.countries")          ◁──  hover over red
    .filter(function (p,q) {return neighbors[i].indexOf(q) > -1})
    .style("fill", "green")
    };
                                                              Colors all
    function clearNeighbors () {                              countries gray to
d3.selectAll("path.countries").style("fill", "gray");  ◁──   "clear" results
    };
```

Colors all neighbors green

TopoJSON is a powerful new technology that provides tremendous opportunity for web map development. Understanding how it models data and the functionality that it provides are key to creating maps that impress users. As you explore traditional web

Figure 7.19 Hover behavior displaying the neighbors of France using TopoJSON's `neighbor` function. Because Guyana is an overseas department of France, France is considered to be neighbors with Brazil and Suriname. This is because France is represented as a multipolygon in the data, and any neighbors with any of its shapes are returned as neighbors.

tile mapping, you'll see that you can combine more traditional web mapping techniques with the advanced functionality provided by TopoJSON and D3's geo functions to make incredibly sophisticated web maps.

7.5   *Tile mapping with d3.geo.tile*

So far you've made choropleth maps, some of which are simple and others, like the satellite projection or the globe, rather exotic. But none of your maps have terrain, or satellite imagery. That kind of data—*raster* or *image* data—isn't nearly as lightweight as vector data. Think about the size of a picture you take with the camera on your phone, and imagine how large an image must be if you want to give your user the ability to zoom in to any street in the world.

To get around the problem of these massive images, web mapping uses tiles to display satellite and terrain data. A high-resolution satellite image of a city, for instance, would be cut into 256- by 256-px tiles at as many zoom levels as are appropriate and stored on a server in directories indicating the zoom and position of those tiles. It sounds like it might be a lot of work to make tiles, but fortunately, you don't have to, because companies like Mapbox (mapbox.com) provide you with tiles and the tools, like TileMill, to customize them. (Both free and commercial versions are available, depending on how many visitors your site receives.)

If you open up tile.js and take a look at it, you'll see that it's a small file. That's because geotiles are simple. Each tile is a raster image (typically a PNG) that represents one square of the earth somewhere, as you see in figure 7.20. Its filename indicates the

Figure 7.20   Your first tiled map, using pregenerated tiles from Mapbox

geographic location and at what zoom level the image shows. The d3.geo.tile() function (the library to access this function is available at https://github.com/d3/d3-plugins/tree/master/geo/tile) parses that filename and directory structure for us so that we can use these tiles in our map. First, though, we have to calibrate the scale and translate of our projection as well as our zoom behavior.

Listing 7.19   A tile map

```
var width = 500,
    height = 500;

d3.select("svg").append("g").attr("id", "tiles");        ⟵ A group to keep our
                                                            tiles behind any other
var tile = d3.geo.tile()                    ⟵                drawn features
    .size([width, height]);         The function we use
                                    to create your tiles
var projection = d3.geo.mercator()
    .scale(120)
    .translate([width / 2, height / 2]);

var center = projection([12, 42]);

var path = d3.geo.path()
    .projection(projection);

var zoom = d3.behavior.zoom()
    .scale(projection.scale() * 2 * Math.PI)
    .translate([width - center[0], height - center[1]])
    .on("zoom", redraw);

d3.select("svg").call(zoom);
    redraw();
                                    The dataset we
                                    use to create
function redraw() {                 the images
    var tiles = tile                ⟵
        .scale(zoom.scale())
        .translate(zoom.translate())();         Generates proper
                                            transform settings based
    var image = d3.select("#tiles")           on the current zoom
        .attr("transform",
        "scale(" + tiles.scale + ") translate(" + tiles.translate + ")")  ⟵
        .selectAll("image")
        .data(tiles, function(d) { return d; });    ⟵  Binds the tiles data to
                                                        svg:image elements
    image.exit()
        .remove();
                                              ⟵ Appends new ones
    image.enter().append("image")
        .attr("xlink:href",
            function(d) { return "http://" +
            ["a", "b", "c", "d"][Math.random() * 4 | 0] +
            ".tiles.mapbox.com/v3/examples.map-zgrqqx0w/" +
            d[2] + "/" + d[0] + "/" + d[1] + ".png"; })   ⟵  Path to the tiles is
        .attr("width", 1)                                     generated by tile.js for
        .attr("height", 1)                                    services like Mapbox
        .attr("x", function(d) { return d[0]; })
        .attr("y", function(d) { return d[1]; });
};
```

Removes any that are offscreen ⟶ (annotation for `image.exit()`)

Figure 7.21   A tile map overlaid with the point and polygon data we worked with throughout this chapter

We'll want to add our points and polygons to this map. The code to do that isn't very different from the code you saw in listing 7.19 and the code we've been working with throughout the chapter. We'll use the same data, but add a function on the display styling of the countries to make half of them disappear. You can see the results in figure 7.21.

Listing 7.20   A tile map with vector data overlaid

```
queue()
    .defer(d3.json, "world.topojson")
    .defer(d3.csv, "cities.csv")
    .await(function(error, file1, file2) {
                        createMap(file1, file2); });

function createMap(topoCountries, cities){

var countries =
    topojson.feature(topoCountries, topoCountries.objects.countries);

var width = 500,
    height = 500;

d3.select("svg").append("g").attr("id", "tiles");

var tile = d3.geo.tile()
    .size([width, height]);
```

```
var projection = d3.geo.mercator()
    .scale(120)
    .translate([width / 2, height / 2]);

var center = projection([12, 42]);

var path = d3.geo.path()
    .projection(projection);

  var featureSize = d3.extent(countries.features, function(d) {
                    return path.area(d);
                    });
  var countryColor = d3.scale.quantize()
                    .domain(featureSize)
                    .range(colorbrewer.Reds[7]);

var zoom = d3.behavior.zoom()
    .scale(projection.scale() * 2 * Math.PI)
    .translate([width - center[0], height - center[1]])
    .on("zoom", redraw);

    d3.select("svg").call(zoom);
    redraw();

d3.select("svg").selectAll("path.countries").data(countries.features)
    .enter()
    .append("path")
    .attr("d", path)
    .attr("class", "countries")
    .style("fill", function(d) {return countryColor(path.area(d))})
    .style("stroke-width", 1)
    .style("stroke", "black")
    .style("opacity", .5)

    d3.select("svg").selectAll("circle").data(cities)
              .enter()
            .append("circle")
              .attr("class", "cities")
              .attr("r", 3)
              .attr("cx", function(d) {
                    return projection([d.x,d.y])[0];
              })
            .attr("cy", function(d) {
    return projection([d.x,d.y])[1];
});

    function redraw() {
      var tiles = tile
      .scale(zoom.scale())
      .translate(zoom.translate())
      ();

      var image = d3.select("#tiles")
      .attr("transform", "scale(" + tiles.scale + ")translate(" +
          tiles.translate + ")")
      .selectAll("image")
      .data(tiles, function(d) { return d; });
```

```
image.exit()
.remove();

image.enter().append("image")
.attr("xlink:href", function(d) { return "http://" +
    ["a", "b", "c", "d"][Math.random() * 4 | 0] +
    ".tiles.mapbox.com/v3/examples.map-zgrqqx0w/" + d[2] +
    "/" + d[0] + "/" + d[1] + ".png"; })
.attr("width", 1)
.attr("height", 1)
.attr("x", function(d) { return d[0]; })
.attr("y", function(d) { return d[1]; });

projection
.scale(zoom.scale() / 2 / Math.PI)
.translate(zoom.translate());

d3.selectAll("path.countries")
.attr("d", path);

        d3.selectAll("circle").attr("cx", function(d) {
                return projection([d.x,d.y])[0];
            })
            .attr("cy", function(d) {
                return projection([d.x,d.y])[1];
            });
    };
};
```

◄── **Note that we're not taking zoom.scale() directly like we did before, but processing it to get the properly formatted scale for our Mercator projection.**

7.6   *Further reading for web mapping*

As I said in the beginning of this chapter, the things you can do with D3's mapping capabilities would fill an entire book. Following are a few other capabilities we didn't cover in this chapter.

7.6.1   *Transform zoom*

The method we used for our zoom behavior in this chapter is known as *projection zoom* and recalculates mathematically the shape of features based on a change in scale and translation. But if you're using a projection that's flat like Mercator, then you can achieve faster performance by tying the change in scale and translate of the zoom behavior to your features' SVG transform. One issue you'll run into is that font size and stroke width are affected by SVG transform, and so you'll need to adjust those settings on the fly.

7.6.2   *Canvas drawing*

The .context function d3.geo.path allows you to easily draw your vector data to a <canvas> element, which can dramatically improve speed in certain cases. It also allows you to use .toDataURL() to dynamically create a PNG for users to save or share on social media.

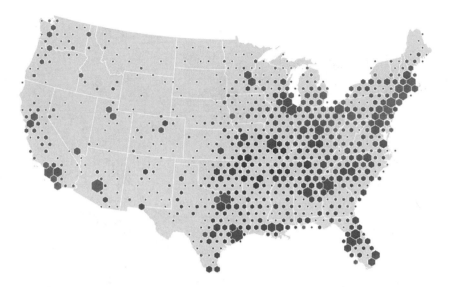

Figure 7.22   An example of hexbinning by Mike Bostock showing the locations of WalMart stores in the United States (available at http://bl.ocks.org/mbostock/4330486).

7.6.3   Raster reprojection

Jason Davies and Mike Bostock have both provided examples of reprojecting, not just vector data, but the tile data used in tile maps (see bl.ocks.org/mbostock/ and www.jasondavies.com/maps/raster/satellite/). You can use this to show a satellite-projected terrain map, or a terrain map with the Mollweide projection we used earlier.

7.6.4   Hexbins

The `d3.hexbin` plugin allows you to easily create hexbin overlays for your maps like that seen in figure 7.22. This can be effective when you have quantitative data in point form and you want to aggregate it by area.

7.6.5   Voronoi diagrams

As with hexbins, if you only have point data and want to create area data from it, you can use the `d3.geom.voronoi` function to derive polygons from points like the kind seen in figure 7.23.

7.6.6   Cartograms

Distorting the area or length of a geographic object to show other information creates a *cartogram*. For example, you could distort the streets of your city based on the time it takes to drive along them, or make the size of countries on a world map bulge or shrink based on population. Although no simple functions exist to create cartograms, examples of how to create them in D3 include one created by Jason Davies (http://www.jasondavies.com/maps/dorling-world/), one created by Mike Bostock (http://bl.ocks.org/mbostock/4055908), and the cost cartogram I built (orbis.stanford.edu).

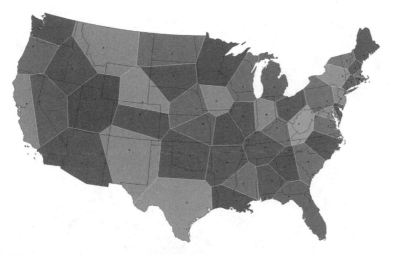

Figure 7.23   An example of a Voronoi diagram used to split the United States into polygons based on the closest state capital (available at http://www.jasondavies.com/maps/voronoi/us-capitals/).

7.7   *Summary*

In this chapter, we've covered the incredible breadth of geospatial information visualization capabilities present in D3. Maps are a core aspect of information visualization, and the creation of rich interactive websites and D3's geo functions allow you to make maps that are much richer than the pushpin web maps that you typically see on the web. To make those maps, we walked through a massive amount of functions and concepts, including

- Understanding the GeoJSON spatial data format
- Creating simple maps
- Creating map components like graticules
- Computing geospatial attributes like centroids and bounding boxes
- Giving the user rich interactive panning and zooming
- Using different projections
- Creating globes
- Rendering TopoJSON and using it to merge features and find neighbors
- Creating tile maps with TopoJSON overlays.

In the next chapter, you'll start using D3 selections and data-binding to create galleries and tables using traditional DOM elements.

Traditional DOM manipulation with D3

This chapter covers

- Making spreadsheets with data
- Drawing graphics with HTML5 canvas
- Building image galleries with data
- Populating drop-down lists with data-binding

Many introductions to D3 start with sizing `<div>` elements to create a bar chart. They figure you're a web developer and that you won't be as intimidated by a div as you'd be by an SVG rectangle. This book even begins by creating a set of `<p>` elements in chapter 1, the first time you saw data-binding in action. But then these tutorials (and this book) quickly transition into the creation of SVG elements, with an emphasis on the graphical display of information. This is at odds with traditional web development, which focuses on the presentation of blocks of text, images, buttons, lists, and so on. As a result, it seems like D3 is for data visualization, but somehow not for manipulating traditional DOM elements like paragraphs, divs, and lists (like those seen in figure 8.1). The benefit of using D3 to create these kinds of elements is that you can use D3 transitions, data-binding, and other functionality to make a more interactive and dynamic website.

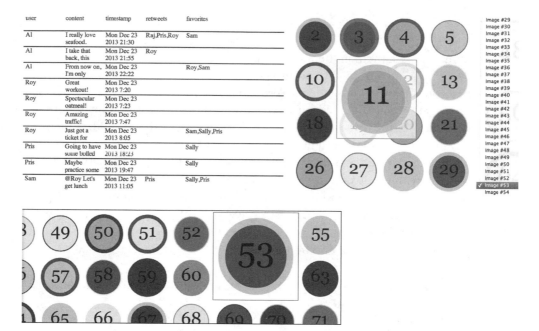

Figure 8.1 The traditional DOM-based pieces that are created in this chapter are a spreadsheet (section 8.2) and an image gallery (section 8.4), with interactivity based on a data-driven drop-down list (section 8.4.2) and images drawn using HTML5 canvas (8.3).

The principles at work in D3 not only *can* be used for traditional DOM elements, but in many cases *should* be used that way. In this chapter, we'll use D3 to create a spreadsheet as well as an image gallery. We'll also explore how to use HTML5 canvas to draw and save images. This won't include an exhaustive example of canvas, because that's beyond the scope of the book, but it'll give you the fundamentals to deploy it in tandem with D3 in your applications. In each case, we'll use D3 data-binding, transitions, and selections the same way we did to make charts, but instead make more traditional HTML elements.

By using the same datasets and functions to deal with your DOM elements as you do with your SVG elements, you make it easier to tie them together and reduce the amount of syntax you need to learn to deploy rich sites. In later chapters, you'll see these different methods of presenting information working in together in tandem.

8.1 Setup

As you may expect, we need to make a few changes to the files we're working with, now that we're going to do coding that resembles more traditional web development. In one case, this means simplifying, because our HTML page loses the `<svg>` element necessary for representing SVG graphics, but in another sense it means making things more complex. Although we used CSS primarily for graphical changes with SVG, we need to use it for more than that when working with traditional DOM elements.

8.1.1 CSS

You use more CSS when you work with traditional DOM elements, because if you want to manipulate them in the way you manipulate SVG elements, you typically need to set them up a bit differently; for instance, if you want to place HTML elements precisely like you do with SVG elements. Also, most of the graphical aspects of these elements aren't set with attributes like in SVG, but with styles (we covered the difference between styles, attributes, and properties back in chapter 1). This shouldn't be a surprise for anyone who's had experience working with CSS, because it's usually the case in the complex examples and under the hood when you use JavaScript libraries. For example, if you look at the CSS of various libraries that provide autocomplete or more sophisticated UI elements, you'll see that they typically combine JavaScript with a variety of styles assigned to complex CSS selectors. In the following listing you'll see the style sheet we'll use for this chapter. Some of these elements, like `<img.infinite>`, you won't see until the end of the chapter.

> **Listing 8.1 Style sheet for chapter 8**

```
tr {
  border: 1px gray solid;
}

td {
  border: 2px black solid;
}

div.table {
  position:relative;
}
div.data {
  position: absolute;
  width: 90px;
  padding: 0 5px;
}

div.head {
  position: absolute;
}

div.datarow {
  position: absolute;
  width: 100%;
  border-top: 2px black solid;
  background: white;
  height: 35px;
  overflow: hidden;
}

div.gallery {
  position: relative;
}

img.infinite {
  position: absolute;
```

```
    background: rgba(255,255,255,0);
    border-width: 1px;
    border-style: solid;
    border-color: rgba(0,0,0,0);
}
```

8.1.2 HTML

The HTML is pretty simple: a single `<div>` with the ID value of `"traditional"` in your `<body>` element, as shown in the following listing. You still need a reference to d3.js, but otherwise it's a Spartan HTML page. You'll either modify or add new elements to that div for every example.

Listing 8.2 chapter8.html

```
<!doctype html>
<html>
<script src="d3.v3.min.js" type="text/JavaScript"></script>
<body>
<div id="traditional">
</div>
</body>
</html>
```

8.2 Spreadsheet

Let's assume we want to take the tweets data that we've been working with throughout the book and present it as a spreadsheet. It may help to first think of spreadsheets as a kind of information visualization. They have an x-axis (columns) and a y-axis (rows) and visual channels to express information (not only color applied to text and cells but also position and font styling). This is especially true of large spreadsheets, because they also use aggregated functions to tally results.

8.2.1 Making a spreadsheet with table

The easiest way to make a spreadsheet is to use the HTML `<table>` element and data-binding to create rows and cells. As we've done previously, we create key values by using `d3.keys` on one of the entries in our dataset, which will be the venerable tweets.json. After we bind the dataset to the table, we need to create individual cells. We can accomplish this by taking each JSON object and applying `d3.entries()` to it, which turns an object into an array of key-value pairs perfectly suited for D3 data-binding.

Listing 8.3 Spreadsheet example

```
d3.json("tweets.json",function(error,data) {
                createSpreadsheet(data.tweets)});

    function createSpreadsheet(incData) {

        var keyValues = d3.keys(incData[0]);
```

This won't work if your objects have differing numbers of attributes, but usually that's not the case.

```
d3.select("#traditional")
         .append("table");

d3.select("table")
   .append("tr")
   .attr("class", "head")
   .selectAll("th")
   .data(keyValues)                    ←─┐  Creates our header
   .enter()                              │  row from our keys
   .append("th")
   .html(function (d) {return d;});

d3.select("table")
   .selectAll("tr.data")
   .data(incData).enter()              ←─┐  Creates each
   .append("tr")                         │  row for a tweet
   .attr("class", "data");

d3.selectAll("tr")
   .selectAll("td")
   .data(function(d) {return d3.entries(d)})  ←─┐  Creates each cell
   .enter()                                      │  for an entry in
   .append("td")                                 │  each datapoint
   .html(function (d) {return d.value});
};
```

The result of listing 8.3 is a decent tabular presentation of our tweets data, as shown in figure 8.2. Notice that the arrays have been transformed into comma-delimited strings.

It's a simple task to take data and bind it to create traditional DOM elements in the same way we bound data to create SVG elements. We could have created an `<ol>` element and appended `<li>` elements to it from our dataset just as easily. We can also use D3's `.on` function to assign event listeners to highlight cells or rows by changing their background or font color. But rather than do that with a spreadsheet built using `<table>`, we'll build another spreadsheet entirely out of `<div>` elements.

user	content	timestamp	retweets	favorites
Al	I really love seafood.	Mon Dec 23 2013 21:30 GMT-0800 (PST)	Raj,Pris,Roy	Sam
Al	I take that back, this doesn't taste so good.	Mon Dec 23 2013 21:55 GMT-0800 (PST)	Roy	
Al	From now on, I'm only eating cheese sandwiches.	Mon Dec 23 2013 22:22 GMT-0800 (PST)		Roy,Sam
Roy	Great workout!	Mon Dec 23 2013 7:20 GMT-0800 (PST)		
Roy	Spectacular oatmeal!	Mon Dec 23 2013 7:23 GMT-0800 (PST)		
Roy	Amazing traffic!	Mon Dec 23 2013 7:47 GMT-0800 (PST)		
Roy	Just got a ticket for texting and driving!	Mon Dec 23 2013 8:05 GMT-0800 (PST)		Sam,Sally,Pris
Pris	Going to have some boiled eggs.	Mon Dec 23 2013 18:23 GMT-0800 (PST)		Sally
Pris	Maybe practice some gymnastics.	Mon Dec 23 2013 19:47 GMT-0800 (PST)		Sally
Sam	@Roy Let's get lunch	Mon Dec 23 2013 11:05 GMT-0800 (PST)	Pris	Sally,Pris

Figure 8.2 **A tabular display of the data found in tweets.json using `<table>`, `<tr>`, and `<td>` elements**

8.2.2 *Making a spreadsheet with divs*

Why use <div> elements? Because we're going to start moving our cells and rows around however we want, and by the time we override all the styles that make a table and its constituent elements work, we're better off starting fresh with a div. By setting the <div> position to absolute, we can use D3 transitions to move them around in the same way we moved SVG around in our earlier examples. We need to apply a bit more CSS to make the <div> elements take up the right amount of space, whereas *<table>* does that for us, but the added flexibility is worth it. A quick note for those of you who, like me, always forget the one crazy rule of positioning DOM elements: elements set to position:relative need to have a parent set to position:relative or position:absolute. We'll create a parent <div> (div.table) with position:relative to hold the <div> elements that make up our table.

Listing 8.4   A spreadsheet made of divs

```
d3.json("tweets.json",function(error,data) {
    createSpreadsheet(data.tweets)}};

    function createSpreadsheet(incData) {

        var keyValues = d3.keys(incData[0]);

        d3.select("#traditional")
        .append("div")
        .attr("class", "table");             ◁─┐  It's a <div.table>,
                                               │  not a <table>.
        d3.select("div.table")
        .append("div")
        .attr("class", "head")
        .selectAll("div.data")
        .data(keyValues)                     ◁── Same as before
        .enter()
        .append("div")
        .attr("class", "data")
        .html(function (d) {return d})
        .style("left", function(d,i) {return (i * 100) + "px";}); ◁─┐ Instead of x/y
        d3.select("div.table")                                     │ or transform,
        .selectAll("div.datarow")                                  │ HTML elements
        .data(incData, function(d) {return d.content})             │ have top/
        .enter()                                                   │ bottom/left/
        .append("div")                                             │ right
        .attr("class", "datarow")
        .style("top", function(d,i) {return (40 + (i * 40)) + "px";});

        d3.selectAll("div.datarow")
        .selectAll("div.data")
        .data(function(d) {return d3.entries(d)})
        .enter()
        .append("div")
        .attr("class", "data")
        .html(function (d) {return d.value})
        .style("left", function(d,i,j) {return (i * 100) + "px";});
    };
```

user	content	timestamp	retweets	favorites
Al	I really love seafood.	Mon Dec 23 2013 21:30	Raj,Pris,Roy	Sam
Al	I take that back, this	Mon Dec 23 2013 21:55	Roy	
Al	From now on, I'm only	Mon Dec 23 2013 22:22		Roy,Sam
Roy	Great workout!	Mon Dec 23 2013 7:20		
Roy	Spectacular oatmeal!	Mon Dec 23 2013 7:23		
Roy	Amazing traffic!	Mon Dec 23 2013 7:47		
Roy	Just got a ticket for	Mon Dec 23 2013 8:05		Sam,Sally,Pris
Pris	Going to have some boiled	Mon Dec 23 2013 18:23		Sally
Pris	Maybe practice some	Mon Dec 23 2013 19:47		Sally
Sam	@Roy Let's get lunch	Mon Dec 23 2013 11:05	Pris	Sally,Pris

Figure 8.3   Our improved spreadsheet built with `<div>` elements. You can see how each div is the same width. Because of our overflow settings, it displays as much of the text as it can.

This code has some obvious oversimplifications. As shown in figure 8.3, it doesn't make much sense to have each column the same width. Although we could create a method for measuring the maximum size of the text in that field, that's not where we'll go in this chapter. I want to show a general overview of manipulating elements like these rather than create the ultimate D3 spreadsheet.

8.2.3   Animating our spreadsheet

It's time now to add interactivity to the static chart shown in figure 8.3. One traditional interaction technique applied to spreadsheets is the ability to sort them. We can do that with our spreadsheet by sorting the data and rebinding it to the cells, just like we did previously with SVG elements. By tying this to the same `transition()` behavior we used before, we can also animate that sorting.

Listing 8.5   Sorting functions

```
d3.select("#traditional").insert("button", ".table")
        .on("click", sortSheet).html("sort");
d3.select("#traditional").insert("button", ".table")
        .on("click", restoreSheet).html("restore");

function sortSheet() {
    var dataset = d3.selectAll("div.datarow").data();
    dataset.sort(function(a,b) {
        var a = new Date(a.timestamp);
        var b = new Date(b.timestamp);
```

Simple controls for our spreadsheet

Casts as date and sorts the array so that earlier tweets are lower in the array

```
              return a>b ? 1 : (a<b ? -1 : 0);
    });

    d3.selectAll("div.datarow")
           .data(dataset, function(d) {return d.content})
           .transition()
           .duration(2000)
           .style("top", function(d,i) {return (40 + (i * 40)) + "px";});
};
function restoreSheet() {
    d3.selectAll("div.datarow")
           .transition()
           .duration(2000)
           .style("top", function(d,i) {return (40 + (i * 40)) + "px"});
    };
```

	user	content	timestamp	retweets	favorites
sort restore					
	Roy	Great workout!	Mon Dec 23 2013 7:20		
	Roy	Spectacular oatmeal!	Mon Dec 23 2013 7:23		
	Roy	Amazing traffic!	Mon Dec 23 2013 7:47		
	Roy	Just got a ticket for back, this	Mon Dec 23 2013 8:05 2013 21:55		Sam,Sally,Pris
	Pris	Going to have	Mon Dec 23		Sally
	Sam	@Roy Let's get lunch	Mon Dec 23 2013 11:05	Pris	Sally,Pris
	Pris	Maybe practice some	Mon Dec 23 2013 19:47		Sally

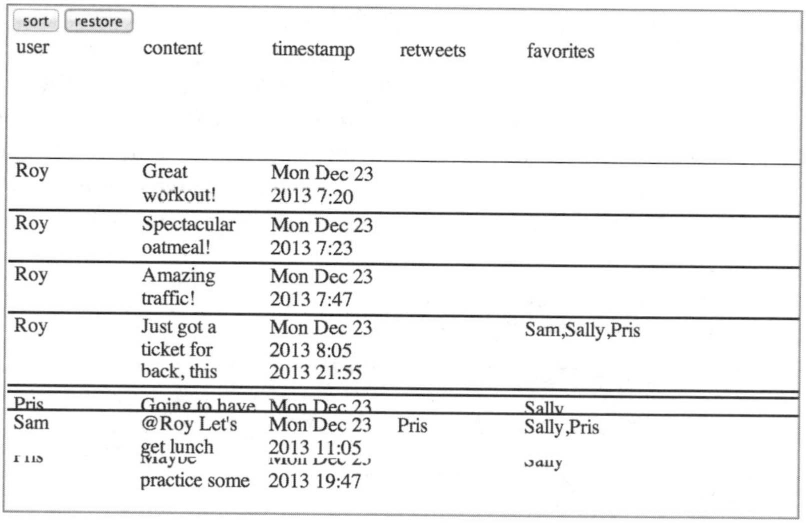

Figure 8.4 The rows of your spreadsheet in the middle of the sort function.

We have a spreadsheet with sortable rows that float over and under each other after we click the sorting button. Figure 8.4 shows that animation caught in an intermediate state. If we want to sort the columns, though, we need to do something slightly different.

Listing 8.6 Column sorting

```
d3.select("#traditional").insert("button", ".table")
          .on("click", sortColumns).html("sort columns ");
d3.select("#traditional").insert("button", ".table")
          .on("click", restoreColumns).html("restore columns");

function sortColumns() {
    d3.selectAll("div.datarow")
          .selectAll("div.data")
          .transition()
          .duration(2000)
```

```
    .style("left", function(d,i,j) {
        return (Math.abs(i - 4) * 100) + "px";
    });
};

function restoreColumns() {
  d3.selectAll("div.datarow")
    .selectAll("div.data")
    .transition()
    .duration(2000)
    .style("left", function(d,i,j) {
        return (i * 100) + "px";
    });
};
```

There you have it—a sortable animated spreadsheet that, if you catch it in midtransition as I have in figure 8.5, is rather messy. It's animated, interactive, and data-driven with no SVG at all. Rather than adding more interactivity to our spreadsheet, we'll switch gears and focus on a second kind of traditional component of a web page: image galleries. But before we get to that, we'll need some images. Instead of loading them from external files, we'll draw our own PNGs using HTML5 canvas, an API made for drawing static images. We're not going to dive deep into canvas, but just use it to create circles with numbers on them to stand in for whatever images we might put in a gallery.

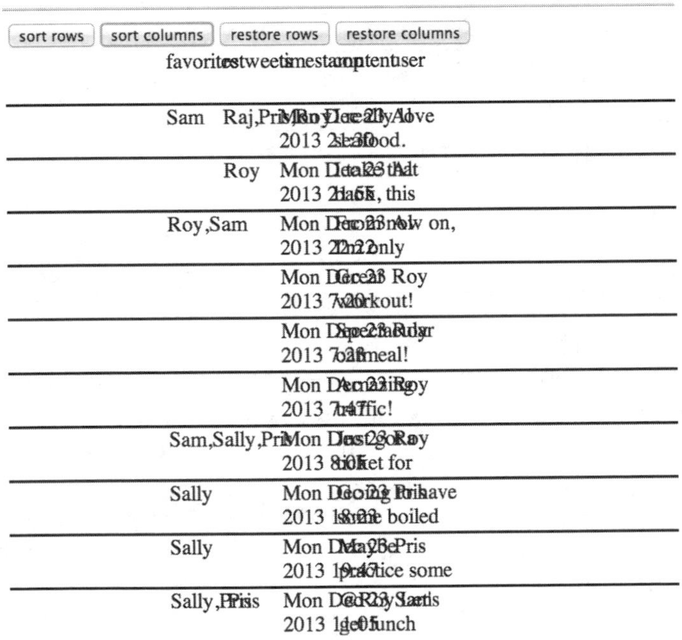

Figure 8.5 Sorting columns in our sheet. Because we didn't define a background value for the divs, the text floats over itself. In this screenshot, you can see that I've added all the buttons for sorting and restoring columns and divs.

8.3 *Canvas*

We won't use canvas too much here, but you should recognize that, although the canvas drawing syntax like that in listing 8.7 is different from SVG, it's something you could easily tie to D3. You may do that because you want to create images like we're doing here. Or you may use canvas because you can achieve greatly improved performance if you're dealing with large datasets. A number of online examples use canvas instead of SVG for D3 (especially with maps like the one at http://bl.ocks.org/mbostock/3783604, but also the implementation of a Voronoi diagram in canvas at http://bl.ocks.org/mbostock/6675193). But for our purposes, we don't need much code to create our image.

We'll use canvas to draw circles with numbers in them. We'll do this so we can have a set of images that we can use for our gallery. Your gallery probably has a set of images in a directory or called from an API, but because we don't have that here, we'll create them on the fly. At the same time, you'll get a sense of the functionality of the canvas API in regard to how it can be used alongside D3.

8.3.1 Drawing with canvas

The first thing we'll draw with canvas won't use much D3 code. What little it does use, such as d3.select() and .node(), could easily be replaced with native JavaScript. Later, when we start drawing many different images, and pass those images on to other elements, you'll see the kind of D3 functionality you've grown used to.

Listing 8.7 Canvas drawing code

```
d3.select("#traditional")
  .append("canvas")
  .attr("height", 500)
  .attr("width", 500);

var context = d3.select("canvas").node().getContext("2d");

context.strokeStyle = "black";
context.lineWidth = 2;
context.fillStyle = "red";
context.beginPath();
context.arc(250,250,200,0,2*Math.PI);
context.fill();
context.stroke();

context.textAlign = "center";
context.font="200px Georgia";
context.fillStyle = "black";
context.textAligh = "center";
context.fillText("1",250,250);
```

The result is the circle in figure 8.6. You'll notice a few important differences from the code we used earlier. First, we hardly use D3 in this example. We could easily have skipped it entirely by using the built-in selectors in core JavaScript. Second, we draw with canvas, not on an `<svg>`

Figure 8.6 A circle and text drawn using HTML5 canvas

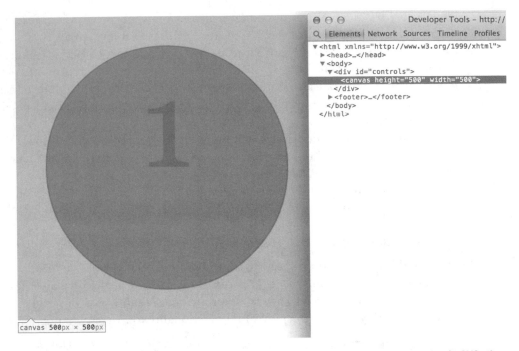

Figure 8.7   Any graphics created in canvas are stored as a bitmap or raster image. Unlike in SVG, the individual shapes are no longer accessible or modifiable after being drawn.

element, but on a <canvas> element that needs to be created in the DOM. Third, canvas has a syntax distinct from SVG.

But there's one more major difference between the graphics created using canvas and the graphics created using SVG. You can see it if you inspect that circle, as shown in figure 8.7. Anything drawn in canvas is drawn to a bitmap, so you don't have an individual text or circle element that you could assign an event listener to, or whose appearance or text content you can later modify. It's also not vector-based, so if you try to zoom the image, you'll see the pixilation you're familiar with from zooming photos and other raster imagery. Because HTML5 canvas doesn't create separate DOM elements, it benefits from higher performance when dealing with large amounts of those graphical elements. But you lose the flexibility of SVG.

8.3.2   *Drawing and storing many images*

We want images because our plan is to build an image gallery, but the canvas element in the DOM doesn't act like the kind of image that you're accustomed to dealing with in web development. You can't right-click and save it, or open it in a new window in its current form. But the <canvas> element includes a .toDataURL() function that provides a string designed to be the src attribute of an <img> element. You can see in the following listing the results of .toDataURL() when applied to one of your drawn circles. This is only the first three lines—the actual value would go on like this for nine pages.

Listing 8.8 Sample `toDataURL()` output

```
data:image/png;base64,iVBORw0KGgoAAAANSUhEUgAAAfQAAAH0CAYAAADL1t+KAAAgAElEQVR
4Xu2dC3xV1ZX/171B1JJggNoSsSSY+QrWiQnB4dCoEH7Tgg4dVdNRCWg3SqQVm+i99TIfQmc7UPkbU
9sNDW0KVWluFYYClFu9FdAW99AALWWUE2sCtWCgQQfkdz73+smV1NIyyH3sc89ae//258MnK0f/
```

In our new example in the following listing, we create 100 circles of varying colors with varying borders. We then use `.toDataURL` to create an array of values that can be bound to `<img>` elements to create our first gallery of one hundred images.

Listing 8.9 Drawing 100 circles with canvas

```
imageArray = [];
    d3.select("#traditional").append("canvas")
                .attr("height", 500).attr("width", 500);

    var context = d3.select("canvas").node().getContext("2d");
    context.textAlign = "center";
    context.font="200px Georgia";
    colorScale = d3.scale.quantize().domain([0,1])
                        .range(colorbrewer.Reds[7]);                    ◁─┐  These scales
                                                                           │  are designed
                                                                           │  for random
    lineScale = d3.scale.quantize().domain([0,1]).range([10,40]); ◁──┘  numbers to
    for (var x=0;x<100;x++) {                                              create random
        context.clearRect(0,0,500,500);                                   graphics.
        context.strokeStyle = colorScale(Math.random());
        context.lineWidth = lineScale(Math.random());        ◁─┐  Draws a
        context.fillStyle = colorScale(Math.random());          │  randomly colored
        context.beginPath();                                    │  circle 100 times
        context.arc(250,250,200,0,2*Math.PI);
        context.fill();
        context.stroke();

        context.fillStyle = "black";
        context.fillText(x,250,280);
        var dataURL = d3.select("canvas").node().toDataURL();  ◁─┐  Gets the data URL
        imageArray.push({x: x, url: dataURL});                    │  for each drawing
    }                                                             │  and pushes it into
    d3.select("#traditional")                                     │  an array
    .append("div").attr("class", "gallery")
    .selectAll("img").data(imageArray)
    .enter().append("img")                      ◁─┐  Uses that array to
    .attr("src", function(d) {return d.url})       │  create 100 images
    .style("height", "50px")
    .style("float", "left");       ◁─  <img> elements have automatic resizing, so the
                                       width of the image automatically adjusts to scale
                                       the image to this height without distorting.
```

As shown in figure 8.8, each of our slightly different circles is turned into a PNG and assigned to an `<img>` element. We can also use `toDataURL()` to create JPEGs by specifying that format, but by default it creates PNGs. Because they're `<img>` elements now, they resize automatically. Even though we only specified the height of the images, the `<img>` element by default proportionately scaled the width of the image so that it wouldn't distort. Because of the `float:left` setting on those elements, they easily fill

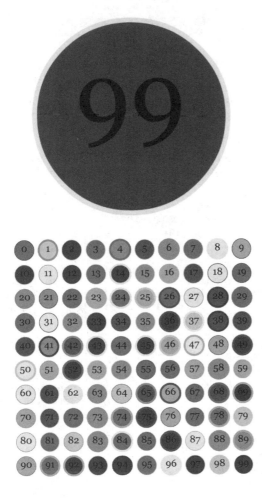

Figure 8.8   The final canvas-drawn circle (top) remains in our `<canvas>` element, and every variation according to the settings as an image in a div (bottom).

the div we created for them. And because it's an `<img>`, we can do anything with these that we normally could with an image on a web page, including save them or open them in a new tab.

That's not much of an image gallery, though. We'll continue to expand on this code in the next section, and also make something a bit more interesting by taking advantage of the interaction and animation techniques we've already used.

8.4   *Image gallery*

You've spent time learning canvas so that you could make image elements for a gallery. When spec'ing out an image gallery, keep in mind a few features that everyone wants. First, you want more control over where you place images. Instead of using float, we'll do the same thing we did with the spreadsheet divs in section 8.2.2 and use `position:absolute` along with `top:` and `left:` to place them like our div cells and rows or the SVG elements that we used in previous chapters. You also want images to cleanly fit the space you provide, and you want those images to grow or shrink if the user changes the size of the window.

For all these examples, we'll use the same method described in listing 8.9 to create the `imageArray` dataset that we'll use. The figures in this chapter will have slight variation from the results of running this code, because we randomly generate some of the visual elements. We can create our first gallery with surprisingly little code.

Listing 8.10   Resizing eight-image gallery

Resizes automatically to fit any number of images per row →

```
imgPerLine = 8;
d3.select("canvas").remove();
d3.select("#traditional")
   .append("div").attr("class", "gallery")
   .selectAll("img").data(imageArray).enter().append("img")
   .attr("class", "infinite")
   .attr("src", function(d) {return d.data;});

redrawGallery();

function redrawGallery() {
    var newWidth = parseFloat(d3.select("div.gallery")
       .node().clientWidth);
    var imageSize = newWidth / imgPerLine;
    function imgX(x) {
      return Math.floor(x / imgPerLine) * imageSize;
    };
    function imgY(x) {
      return Math.floor(x%imgPerLine * imageSize);
    };
    d3.selectAll("img")
       .style("width", newWidth / imgPerLine)
       .style("top", function(d) {return imgX(d.x)})
       .style("left", function(d) {return imgY(d.x)})
};

window.onresize = function(event) {
   redrawGallery();
};
```

Deletes the canvas element because it's not needed anymore ←

Placement code in a separate function for ease of use with dynamic updates ←

Size based on the parent div width ←

x and y based on custom accessor functions ←

Resizes the gallery whenever the page is resized ←

As shown in figure 8.9, this produces a scrollable div with eight images per line. The images not only scale to fit the div, but rescale as you adjust your browser window.

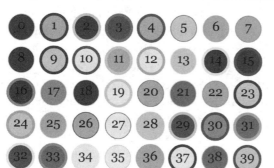

Figure 8.9   Automatically scaled-to-fit images that pack eight images per row

The `imgX` and `imgY` functions create an object for each image that stores an x value. This should remind you of D3 layout accessor functions. We'll build something more involved like this in chapter 9 and dive into writing layouts in chapter 10, but for this example we won't try to create an image gallery layout.

8.4.1   *Interactively highlighting DOM elements*

From here, we can add interactivity, such as making an image expand on mouseover. The process is rather simple.

Listing 8.11   Expand image on mouseover

```
function highlightImage(d) {
    var newWidth = parseFloat(d3.select("div.gallery")
                              .node().clientWidth);
    var imageSize = newWidth / 8;                        ◁─────  We have to recalculate
    d3.select(this).transition().duration(500)                  the width, because that
        .style("width", imageSize * 2)                          value isn't accessible in
        .style("background", "rgba(255,255,255,1)")             this function.
        .style("border-color", "rgba(0,0,0,1)");
    this.parentNode.appendChild(this)                   ◁─────  Moves the image up
                                                                the DOM to ensure
};                                                              it's drawn above the
                                                                images around it
function dehighlightImage(d) {
    var newWidth = parseFloat(d3.select("div.gallery")
                   .node().clientWidth);
    var imageSize = newWidth / 8;
    d3.select(this).transition().duration(500)
            .style("width", imageSize)
            .style("background", "rgba(255,255,255,0)")
            .style("border-color", "rgba(0,0,0,0)");    ◁─────  We don't move the
                                                                image back in the
};                                                              DOM, because it
                                                                can't overlap when
d3.selectAll("img")                                             it's reduced in size.
        .on("mouseover", highlightImage)
        .on("mouseout", dehighlightImage);
```

If you're a savvy web developer, you've probably spotted an artifact from working with SVG in the code above. It's the `appendChild` trick that we need to use to make SVG elements draw in front of each other. We're using relative and absolute positioned DOM elements, so we don't need this, because CSS has a z-index that allows elements to be drawn in front of each other. But I wanted to keep `appendChild` to remind you that working with traditional DOM elements has benefits that SVG elements don't.

Another reason to use the DOM rather than a z-index for positioning is to highlight the array position value in the accessor functions in D3. You may think that the array position corresponds to the array position of a datapoint in the original JavaScript array that we bound to the selection, but it doesn't. It corresponds to the array position of the DOM element in the selection. When you start to use `append-Child` to shift elements up and down the DOM, you change that array value. When we first created `imageArray`, we set the x value equal to the original array position, and

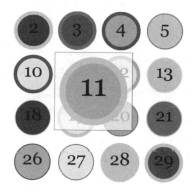

Figure 8.10 One of our gallery images in mid-transition. A border and background are added for UX purposes—the transparent regions of a PNG still register mouse2 events, and so the user should be reminded of the effective region for mouseover events. ▨

didn't use array position to place the individual gallery images. This is why redraw-Gallery keeps drawing images in the right place, even after we start shifting images around in the DOM by mousing over them.

When you run the code in listing 8.11, D3's transitions are smart enough to process the rgba string designating a transparent background, as shown in figure 8.10. In some cases, like the next example, you may have to use D3's tweening capabilities to make sure that a DOM element interpolates properly. It probably doesn't follow the rules that make shape and color transitions work so easily. Still, with color and simple size transitions, you can use exactly the same code for <div> elements that we used with <rect> and <circle> elements, unless you're trying to transition to "height:auto" or some other nonnumerical value.

8.4.2 Selecting

Our final example adds a drop-down list to select a particular image and scroll the gallery to the row that holds that image. To do so, we need to populate the <select> element with choices that correspond to our images, and write a function that scrolls the gallery to the correct line. If you know how a <select> element works (it has a bunch of <option> elements nested underneath it in the DOM), you should guess how to do this with D3 using imageArray as your data. But creating the scrolling function is a bit more involved because we need to write a custom tween to scroll the <div> element that contains our gallery.

Listing 8.12 Zoom to a specific image from a select input

```
function zoomTo() {
  var selectValue = d3.select("select").node().value;        ◁─── Gets the selected
  var newWidth = parseFloat(d3.select("div.gallery")              image value
                            .node().clientWidth);
  var imageSize = newWidth / 8;
  var scrollTarget = Math.floor(selectValue / 8) * imageSize;  ◁─── Calculates
                                                                     where that
  d3.selectAll("img")                                                image is
      .filter(function(d) { return d.x == selectValue; })
      .transition().duration(2000).style("width", imageSize * 2)
```

```
            .style("background", "rgba(255,255,255,1)")
            .style("border-color", "rgba(0,0,0,1)");
    var selectedNode = d3.selectAll("img")
                .filter(function(d) {return d.x == selectValue}).node();

    selectedNode.parentNode.appendChild(selectedNode);

    d3.select("div.gallery").transition().duration(2000)
            .tween("scrollTween", scrollTopTween(scrollTarget));

    function scrollTopTween(scrollTo) {
        return function() {
            var i = d3.interpolateNumber(this.scrollTop, scrollTo);
            return function(t) { this.scrollTop = i(t); };
        };
    };
};

d3.select("div.gallery").style("height", "50%")
            .style("overflow","scroll").style("border", "2px black solid");

d3.select("#traditional").append("select")
    .on("change", zoomTo)
    .selectAll("option")
    .data(d3.selectAll("img").data()).enter()
    .append("option")
    .attr("value", function(d) {return d.x;})
    .html(function(d) {return "Image #" +d.x;});
```

> ⟵ **Zooms that image in the same way we did with mouseover**

> ⟵ **Brings that image forward in the DOM**

> ⟵ **Scrolls the div with a tween**

> ⟵ **Continuously updates the div's scrollTop attribute to be a value between its current scrollTop and the calculated location of the selected image**

This produces a gallery like that in figure 8.11. If we wanted to deploy this gallery, we'd need to do some cleaning up. But the purpose of this chapter is to demonstrate how you can use D3 functionality to work with bitmaps, divs, and other traditional materials of web design. Notice that we'll need to adjust some of our workflows and syntax and also integrate CSS more, but buttons, images, and paragraphs can be

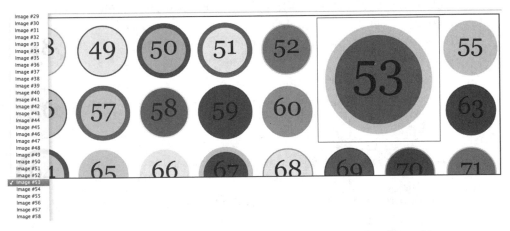

Figure 8.11 Selecting an image from the list scrolls the div to the proper location and increases its size.

data-driven and have the same kind of graphical and interactive sophistication as the geometric shapes you'll work with more often.

I tend to use D3 for my traditional DOM elements not only because of the flexibility, but because it uses the same syntax and abstractions. As a result, it's easy to do things like create a view of data as a bulleted list to go along with a map.

8.5 Summary

In this chapter, you saw the potential of using D3 to create dynamic content with traditional DOM elements. You can embed your more traditional SVG-based data visualization in a web page that's equally dynamic, or create dynamic web pages that don't have any SVG at all. Specifically, this chapter focused on

- Using D3 to create and manipulate traditional DOM elements like <table>, <select>, <div>, and <img>
- Creating interactive and dynamic spreadsheets and galleries
- Getting a taste of the HTML5 canvas API
- Taking a closer look at tweening and transitions

In chapter 9 you'll see how you can tie together multiple visualizations and traditional DOM elements with custom events to create your first interactive data-driven application that will examine tweets using multiple views into the data. Although we haven't combined traditional DOM elements and SVG data visualization in this chapter, you'll see that in the next chapter as we put sparklines in our spreadsheets and divs in our tree diagrams.

Part 3

Advanced techniques

The final three chapters and chapter 12 (online) are focused on moving beyond small-scale and one-off data visualization to create interactive applications and the reusable code they require. Chapter 9 ties together multiple views into data using different layouts with brush-based filtering to produce a data dashboard. Chapter 10 focuses on the structure of components and layouts in D3 by walking you through the creation of a simple grid layout and legend component. Chapter 11 tackles the problem of representing thousands of datapoints graphically onscreen while maintaining performance and interactivity. Chapter 12 (online only: www.manning.com/meeks/) shows how to use D3's built-in functionality in a touch and mobile environment, while exploring the concept of responsive data visualization. Part 3 and chapter 12 give you the skills necessary to build your own framework or application on top of D3, with high performance in a mobile or big data environment.

Composing interactive applications

This chapter covers

- Linking multiple charts
- Automatically resizing graphics based on screen size change
- Creating and using brush controls
- Implementing time scales

Throughout this book, you've seen how data can be measured and transformed to produce charts highlighting one or another aspect of the data. Even though you've used the same dataset in different layouts and with different methods, you haven't presented different charts simultaneously. In this chapter, you'll learn how to tie multiple views of your data together. This type of application is typically referred to as a *dashboard* in data visualization terminology (an example of which will be built in this chapter, as shown in figure 9.1). You'll need to create and manage multiple <svg> elements as well as implement the brush component, which allows you to easily select part of a dataset. You'll also need to more clearly understand data-binding so that you can coordinate the interactivity.

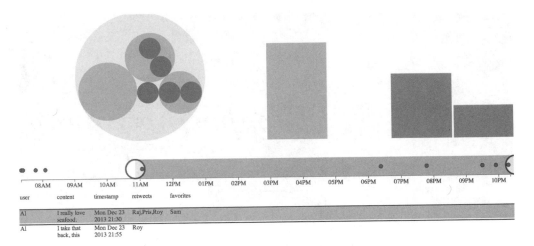

Figure 9.1   Throughout this chapter, we'll build toward this fully operational data dashboard, first creating the individual chart elements (section 9.1), then adding interactivity (section 9.2), and finally adding a brush to filter the data by time (section 9.3).

Infoviz term: dashboard

Multiple charts combined into a single application have been around since the 1970s and were traditionally associated with decision support systems. Dashboards provide the kind of multiple views into a dataset that you'll see in this chapter, and are often the selling point of charting libraries like NVD3.

Although they're typically presented as several charts sharing screen space, the principles of data dashboards can also be applied to web mapping and text-based applications through modal pop-ups or any website that provides several different charts simultaneously. In those cases, the act of highlighting datapoints may be a response to the scrolling of text or zooming in on a map, rather than mousing over a data visualization element.

To get started, we need to design the interface that we want. Designs can be rough sketches or detailed sets of user requirements. Figure 9.2 shows a simple sketch that combines several of the charts we used in previous chapters. Each of these could represent the same dataset from tweets.json, but in a different manner. With a data dashboard, we want to provide a user with multiple perspectives of the data as well as the ability to drill down into the data and see individual datapoints. We'll use a circle pack like we used in chapter 5 so that users can differentiate tweeters and their tweets, a bar chart for raw number of tweets, and a spreadsheet like the one in chapter 8 so that users can view the content of individual tweets. We also want to let users slice and dice their data, so later we'll add that functionality with a brush. Both the bar chart and circle packing require that we use d3.nest(), whereas the spreadsheet takes the unchanged object array.

Figure 9.2   A sketch of a dashboard, showing a circle pack, bar chart, and spreadsheet that display our data

From the sketch, you can easily imagine interaction possibilities and changes that you may want to see based on user activity; for instance, highlighting which elements in each chart correspond to elements in other charts, or giving more detail on a particular element based on a click.

9.1   *One data source, many perspectives*

By the time you're done with this section, you'll have created the data dashboard shown in figure 9.3, and added interactivity and dynamic filtering to it.

To make this all work, we need an HTML page that has the divs and other elements that we'll use.

> **Listing 9.1   HTML for our dashboard**

```
<!doctype html>
<html>
<script src="d3.v3.min.js" type="text/JavaScript"></script>
<body onload="dashboard()" >
<svg id="leftSVG" class="svgDash"></svg>
<svg id="rightSVG"  class="svgDash"></svg>
<div id="spreadsheet"></div>
</body>
</html>
```

We also need to set up our CSS to split the page into the required three regions: two SVG canvases (one for the circle packing layout and one for the bar chart) and one div element for the spreadsheet. In the following listing, you can see the initial CSS for our dashboard.

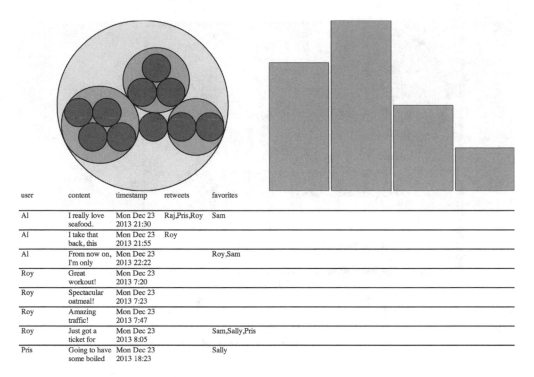

user	content	timestamp	retweets	favorites
Al	I really love seafood.	Mon Dec 23 2013 21:30	Raj,Pris,Roy	Sam
Al	I take that back, this	Mon Dec 23 2013 21:55	Roy	
Al	From now on, I'm only	Mon Dec 23 2013 22:22		Roy,Sam
Roy	Great workout!	Mon Dec 23 2013 7:20		
Roy	Spectacular oatmeal!	Mon Dec 23 2013 7:23		
Roy	Amazing traffic!	Mon Dec 23 2013 7:47		
Roy	Just got a ticket for	Mon Dec 23 2013 8:05		Sam,Sally,Pris
Pris	Going to have some boiled	Mon Dec 23 2013 18:23		Sally

Figure 9.3   What our data dashboard will ultimately look like

---

Listing 9.2   Dashboard CSS

```
body,html {
    width: 100%;
    height: 100%;
}
.svgDash {
    width: 50%;
    height: 50%;
    background: #fcfcfc;
}
#spreadsheet {
    width: 100%;
    height: 50%;
    overflow:auto;
    background: #fcfcfc;
}

circle.pack {
    stroke: black;
    stroke-width: 2px;
}

rect.bar {
    fill: gray;
```

> ◁ **Mozilla browsers require us to set the width and height of our body and HTML elements to 100% for SVG to size properly.**

```
    stroke: black;
    stroke-width: 1px;
}
```

We can use percentages of the screen because an SVG element can be displayed as a percentage just like div elements. But the elements drawn in the SVG won't scale to fit the SVG automatically. Instead, we'll bind functionality to `window.onresize` to redraw our visual elements (as shown in listing 9.3). We could also use the viewport attribute of an SVG element to automatically resize the graphics, but we'll want more fine-grained control of our graphics when creating data visualization applications (recall the distinction between graphical and semantic zoom discussed in chapter 7).

9.1.1 Data dashboard basics

Before we redraw anything, we need to load our data and add our charts. We'll accomplish that by calling the `startup` function on the successful completion of d3.json loading the venerable tweets.json file we worked with in chapter 5.

Listing 9.3 General dashboard function

```
function dashboard() {
  window.onresize = function(event) {         Whenever the user
    redraw();                                  adjusts the screen, we
  };                                           want to redraw the charts.

  d3.json("tweets.json",function(error,data) {startup(data.tweets)});

  function startup(incData) {
    createSpreadsheet(incData, "#spreadsheet");     The spreadsheet takes
                                                    the array of tweets.
    var nestedTweets = d3.nest()
      .key(function (el) {return el.user})
      .entries(incData);

    packableTweets = {id: "root", values: nestedTweets};
                                                        The bar chart
    createBar(nestedTweets, "#rightSVG");              takes the
    createPack(packableTweets, "#leftSVG");            nested tweets.
    redraw();
  };                  Without calling redraw (shown    The circle pack takes
};                    in section 9.1.5), we wouldn't   the nested tweets in
                      see any of our SVG graphics.     a root node.
```

We'll get to `redraw()` in listing 9.8 after we first look at each individual chart, so that you can see everything that's happening on startup.

Each chart has its own function accessing the raw or processed dataset, as shown in listing 9.3. By using the same nested array for our packable tweets and our bar chart, we can determine if the data bound to SVG elements in each chart is the same. It's critical that you use the same array for both, and not use `d3.nest` twice to create an array that contains the same data but isn't the same array. That's because `d3.nest` creates new nested user elements ("Al", "Pris", "Sam", "Roy") that are treated differently (even though they have the same attributes) than another set of nested user elements created by another iteration of d3.nest.

This is easier to understand in practice. The code in listing 9.4 shows two uses of d3.nest to create the same nested structure with the same data. But when you check to see if one element in the first array is the same as an element in the second array, you see that they're different objects, even though they look the same.

Listing 9.4   Comparing nested data

```
var nestedTweets = d3.nest()
    .key(function (el) {return el.user})
    .entries(incData);

var nestedTweets2 = d3.nest()                 ◄──  Seems to be a duplicate
    .key(function (el) {return el.user})            of nestedTweets but is a
    .entries(incData);                              different object

packableTweets = {id: "root", values: nestedTweets};

nestedTweets.value[0] == nestedTweets2.value[0]       ◄──  True
nestedTweets[0] == nestedTweets2[0]                   ◄──  False
packableTweets.values[0] == nestedTweets[0]           ◄──  True
packableTweets.values[0] == nestedTweets2[0]          ◄──  False
```

Keeping this in mind, we create the chart function in listing 9.3 to pass datasets that have shared elements. Because the objects are shared, we can identify which graphics (whether a circle or rectangle or line of a spreadsheet) refer to the same object.

9.1.2   *Spreadsheet*

The first chart we'll create is the same spreadsheet we made in chapter 8, except without any of the sorting buttons. It takes the object array as it appears in tweets.json, which we can pass straight to our createSpreadsheet function in the following listing. I'm not going to dwell on the individual charting functions like this, which are explained in more detail in earlier chapters.

Listing 9.5   The spreadsheet code

```
function createSpreadsheet(incData, targetDiv) {

  var keyValues = d3.keys(incData[0]);

  d3.select(targetDiv)
  .append("div")
  .attr("class", "table");

  d3.select("div.table")
  .append("div")
  .attr("class", "head row")
  .selectAll("div.data")
  .data(keyValues)
  .enter()
  .append("div")
```

```
   .attr("class", "data")
   .html(function (d) {return d})
   .style("left", function(d,i) {return (i * 100) + "px";});

   d3.select("div.table")
   .selectAll("div.datarow")
   .data(incData, function(d) {return d.content}).enter()
   .append("div")
   .attr("class", "datarow row")
   .style("top", function(d,i) {return (40 + (i * 40)) + "px";});

   d3.selectAll("div.datarow")
   .selectAll("div.data")
   .data(function(d) {return d3.entries(d);})
   .enter()
   .append("div")
   .attr("class", "data")
   .html(function (d) {return d.value})
   .style("left", function(d,i,j) {return (i * 100) + "px";});

};
```

Notice that `createSpreadsheet` uses a variable `targetDiv` that's passed to each select function. This is in contrast to earlier implementations where the CSS selector was explicitly declared in the code. This way the functions could be reused for different pages.

9.1.3 Bar chart

The second chart we'll add to our dashboard is a bar chart, which requires that we nest the data so that we can count tweets. Because we'll redraw the graphical elements in a separate function, you'll see in the following listing that the code doesn't declare any graphical aspects of the rectangles that make up our bar chart.

> **Listing 9.6 Bar chart code**

```
function createBar(incData,targetSVG) {

   d3.select(targetSVG).selectAll("rect").data(incData)
   .enter()
   .append("rect")
   .attr("class", "bar");
};
```

When we use the redraw function later, we'll use D3 functions that you haven't seen before to draw this chart more effectively and dynamically.

9.1.4 Circle pack

You learned how to make a circle pack chart in chapter 5. Listing 9.7 shows how we can deploy similar code to lay the groundwork for adding our circle pack chart to our dashboard. As with the bar chart, we don't declare any of the graphical channels that we expect to change if the page is resized, which means we only declare fill and stroke.

Listing 9.7   Circle pack code

```
function createPack(incData,targetSVG) {

    var depthScale = d3.scale.quantize()
        .domain([0,1,2]).range(colorbrewer.Reds[3]);

    packChart = d3.layout.pack();
    packChart.size([100,100])
        .children(function(d) {return d.values;})
        .value(function(d) {return 1;});

    d3.select(targetSVG)
        .append("g")
        .attr("transform", "translate(0,0)")
        .selectAll("circle")
        .data(packChart(incData))
        .enter()
        .append("circle")
        .attr("class", "pack")
        .style("fill", function(d) {return depthScale(d.depth);});

};
```

> This could be anything; we'll redraw and recall the layout to do so in the redraw function.

9.1.5   *Redraw: resizing based on screen size*

The redraw function creates the visual elements of your charts based on the current size of the screen. Without the redraw function, your charts wouldn't display, because the circles in the circle pack have no xy information and the bars in your bar chart have no height or width. This may seem counterintuitive, but it's better to have your chart-drawing code in one place for easy maintainability. If you're going to constantly update a chart, as we're doing with our dashboard, then there's no reason at all to draw the elements (or set their graphical channels) when you first append them to the SVG canvas. By decoupling the preparation of the dataset from their drawing, you're doing the same thing that layout functions are designed to do in D3: not draw things, but process them for drawing. You can then call the redraw function, as shown in the following listing, not only when the screen resizes but whenever a change to filters or data warrants it. For example, we can filter the tweets to a certain period of time, which we'll do in section 9.3, "Brushing."

Listing 9.8   The `redraw` function

```
function redraw() {
    var leftSize = canvasSize("#leftSVG");
    packChart.size(leftSize)

    d3.select("#leftSVG")
        .selectAll("circle")
        .data(packChart(packableTweets))
        .attr("r", function(d) {return d.r;})
        .attr("cx", function(d) {return d.x;})
        .attr("cy", function(d) {return d.y;});
```

> The pack layout creates new data based on the adjusted size of the SVG.

We need to calculate a scale dynamically based on the bar chart data to resize it.

```
var rectNumber = d3.select("#rightSVG")
    .selectAll("rect").size();
var rectData = d3.select("#rightSVG").selectAll("rect").data();
var rectMax = d3.max(rectData, function(d) {return d.values.length});

var rightSize = canvasSize("#rightSVG");

barXScale = d3.scale.ordinal()
    .domain(rectData.map(function(d){return d.key}))
    .rangeBands([0, rightSize[0]]);

barYScale = d3.scale.linear()
    .domain([0, rectMax])
    .range([rightSize[1],0]);

d3.select("#rightSVG")
    .selectAll("rect")
    .attr("x", function(d,i) {return barXScale(d.key) + 5})
    .attr("width", function() {return barXScale.rangeBand() - 5})
    .attr("y", function(d) {return barYScale(d.values.length)})
    .attr("height", function(d) {
        return rightSize[1] - barYScale(d.values.length);
    });

function canvasSize(targetElement) {
    var height = parseFloat(d3.select(targetElement)
                    .node().clientHeight);
    var width = parseFloat(d3.select(targetElement).node().clientWidth);
    return [width,height];
};

};
```

x scale from an ordinal scale based on the "key" value created by d3.nest ←

y scale from the maximum length of the "values" array created by d3.nest ←

Width and x position with a 5-pixel margin ▷

Calculate the current size of the SVG element in pixels ←

We use the `rangeBands` function of `d3.scale.ordinal()` to efficiently create a reusable bar chart. `rangeBands` divides the given width into equal areas, which is useful for a bar chart. You may be tempted to use the bare object array as your domain, but `rangeBands` uses the string version of the domain objects, which results in `"[object object]"` rather than unique identifiers for each object. Instead, we'll create a mapping of our array based on the key values (the names of each tweet creator) to use as our domain. For the range array of the ordinal scale, we'll use the current width of the svg element where it's being used, which we calculate using `canvasSize()`.

Our redraw function finally produces graphics for a screenshot. With this code, the charts respond to changes in screen size, as demonstrated by the various versions in figure 9.4.

I didn't make any redraw functions for the spreadsheet, because it's a more involved process that follows the same principles. But now that we have a dashboard that loads the data into different views and resizes automatically, it's time to wire the views together to make it interactive.

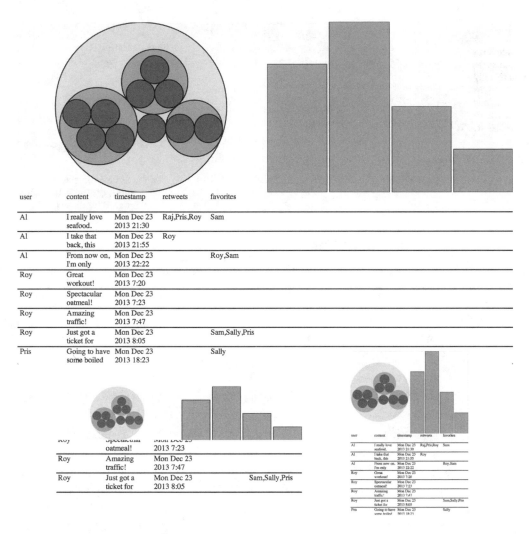

Figure 9.4   The charts automatically resize when the screen is resized. The bar chart is stretched to fit, while the circle pack chart is recalculated to fit the space as best as possible.

9.2   *Interactivity: hover events*

First, we'll highlight a row on the spreadsheet when hovering over the corresponding circles in the circle pack. You do this by checking the circle elements to see if the bound data is the same as the data bound to the spreadsheet elements. If you're using the same data to create multiple charts, as we do in this example, then this is the most straightforward method to use. But if you're loading data from multiple sources, but that data refers to the same things, then you'll need to use a unique ID for this test, such as an employee identification number or a user ID. Because both the divs and the circles hold the same data, binding the same event listener to each, as in listing 9.9, results in cross-highlighting, as shown in figure 9.5.

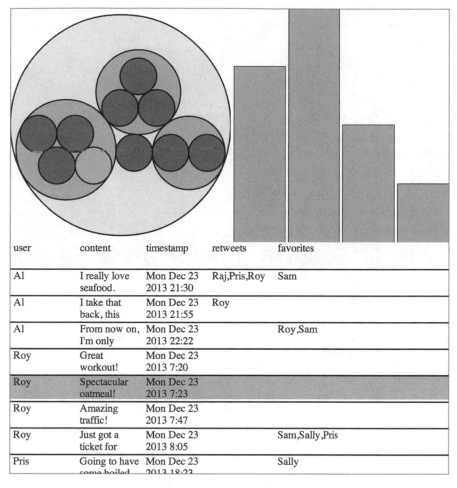

user	content	timestamp	retweets	favorites
Al	I really love seafood.	Mon Dec 23 2013 21:30	Raj,Pris,Roy	Sam
Al	I take that back, this	Mon Dec 23 2013 21:55	Roy	
Al	From now on, I'm only	Mon Dec 23 2013 22:22		Roy,Sam
Roy	Great workout!	Mon Dec 23 2013 7:20		
Roy	Spectacular oatmeal!	Mon Dec 23 2013 7:23		
Roy	Amazing traffic!	Mon Dec 23 2013 7:47		
Roy	Just got a ticket for	Mon Dec 23 2013 8:05		Sam,Sally,Pris
Pris	Going to have some boiled	Mon Dec 23 2013 18:23		Sally

Figure 9.5 Hovering over a circle or data row highlights the element moused over and the corresponding element data row or circle that represents the same datapoint.

Listing 9.9 Row-highlighting code

```
d3.selectAll("div.datarow,circle.pack")
        .on("mouseover", hover)
        .on("mouseout", mouseOut);

    function hover(hoverD) {
        d3.selectAll("circle.pack")
                .filter(function (d) {return d == hoverD;})
                .style("fill", "#94B8FF");
        d3.selectAll("div.datarow")
                .filter(function (d) {return d == hoverD;})
                .style("background", "#94B8FF");
    };
```

CSS syntax to select both div.datarow and circle.pack

Filters the selection to return only the matching elements and changes their background or fill to light blue

```
function mouseOut() {
    d3.selectAll("circle.pack")
            .style("fill", function(d) {
                    return depthScale(d.depth);
            });
    d3.selectAll("div.datarow").style("background", "white");
};
```

> Restores fill and
> background color
> on mouseout

Now we'll tie the bar chart in. Recall that because of our nesting function, each bar in the bar chart corresponds to one of the level 1 hierarchical circles. Therefore, we can update our hover behavior to do the same thing we did with the spreadsheet rows and check to see if one bound datapoint is the same as the other, with the results seen in figure 9.6.

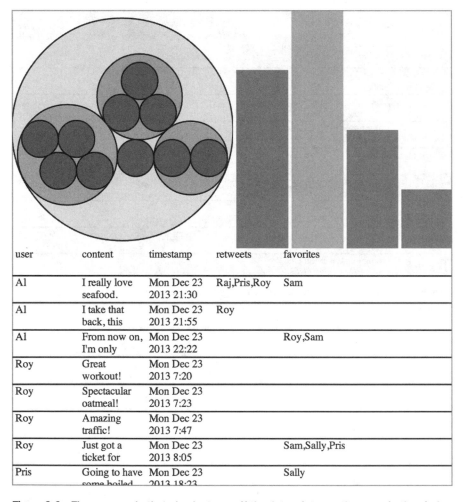

user	content	timestamp	retweets	favorites
Al	I really love seafood.	Mon Dec 23 2013 21:30	Raj,Pris,Roy	Sam
Al	I take that back, this	Mon Dec 23 2013 21:55	Roy	
Al	From now on, I'm only	Mon Dec 23 2013 22:22		Roy,Sam
Roy	Great workout!	Mon Dec 23 2013 7:20		
Roy	Spectacular oatmeal!	Mon Dec 23 2013 7:23		
Roy	Amazing traffic!	Mon Dec 23 2013 7:47		
Roy	Just got a ticket for	Mon Dec 23 2013 8:05		Sam,Sally,Pris
Pris	Going to have some boiled	Mon Dec 23 2013 18:23		Sally

Figure 9.6   The same code that checks to see if the datapoints are the same in the circle pack chart as in the spreadsheet can be used to identify nested data parents, as long as the data comes from the same `d3.nest` operation.

Listing 9.10   Highlighting nested data elements

```
function hover(hoverD) {
  d3.selectAll("circle").filter(function (d) {return d == hoverD})
      .style("fill", "#94B8FF");
  d3.selectAll("div.datarow").filter(function (d) {return d == hoverD})
      .style("background", "#94B8FF");
      d3.selectAll("rect.bar").filter(function(d) {
                    return d.values.indexOf(hoverD) > -1;
          }).style("fill", "#94B8FF");
  };
```

But we also want to check if the group of tweets represented in each bar contains the
data point represented by the element being hovered over (whether a circle or
spreadsheet row). We'll use JavaScript's built-in indexOf function of an array to test
the rect.bar elements to see if they contain one of these tweets. We'll also do the
same in reverse to highlight the data rows that appear in a level 1 circle of the circle
pack or one of the bars in the bar chart. The new, improved functions are shown in
the following listing, and the results are shown in figure 9.7.

Listing 9.11   Improved highlighting functions

```
d3.selectAll("div.datarow,circle.pack,rect.bar")
    .on("mouseover", hover)
    .on("mouseout", mouseOut);

function hover(hoverD) {
    var nestArray = hoverD.values || [];
    d3.selectAll("circle.pack")
      .filter(function (d) {return d == hoverD;})
      .style("fill", "#94B8FF");

    d3.selectAll("rect.bar")
    .filter(function (d) {
          return d == hoverD || d.values.indexOf(hoverD) > -1;
    })
    .style("fill", "#94B8FF");

    d3.selectAll("div.datarow")
    .filter(function (d) {
          return d == hoverD || nestArray.indexOf(d) > -1;
    })
    .style("background", "#94B8FF");
};

function mouseOut() {
    d3.selectAll("circle")
    .style("fill", function(d) {return depthScale(d.depth)});

    d3.selectAll("rect").style("fill", "gray").style("stroke-width", 0);
    d3.selectAll("div.datarow").style("background", "white");
};
```

> **Not every element we mouseover will have a values array, so we need to create an empty array so the indexOf check doesn't fail.**

> **Highlight any rectangle that either shares the same datapoint or has the datapoint in its values array**

> **Highlight any row that shares the same datapoint or is in the values array of the called data**

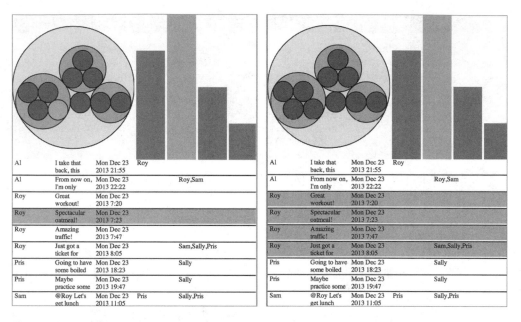

Figure 9.7   Cross-highlighting in action. The same code provides both results shown if we mouseover an individual data row or level 2 circle (right), highlighting the corresponding bar on the bar chart that represents that nested data. It also highlights the data rows that correspond to the nested elements in the data for the level 1 circles or bars when we mouseover those (left).

Obviously, the same principles could be applied to click events, or you could reintroduce the modal pop-up we used in chapter 3 to expose more functionality. But rather than add more interactivity, I'll switch gears and introduce a new control: the brush.

9.3   Brushing

The brush component, d3.svg.brush(), is like the axis component because it creates SVG elements when called (typically by a <g> element). But it's also like the zoom behavior because brush has interactions that update a data element that you can use for interactivity. Brushes are valuable interactive components that allow users to intuitively slice up their data. For our dashboard, we'll add a brush that lets users show tweets only from particular times of the day. You not only need to learn how to use the brush component and understand the brush events that come with the component, but also, because we'll base our activity on when tweets are made, you need to understand D3's built-in scale for dealing with time: d3.time.scale.

9.3.1   Creating the brush

A brush in D3 takes a scale and creates a region where the user can select part of that scale by clicking and dragging. First, we need a new div into which we'll place our brush, and so we need to update our page to include a #brush div in between our chart divs and our spreadsheet div.

Listing 9.12   HTML for our dashboard with a brush

```
<!doctype html>
<html>
<script src="d3.v3.min.js" type="text/JavaScript"></script>
<body onload="dashboard()" >
<svg id="leftSVG" class="svgDash"s"></svg>
<svg id="rightSVG"  class="svgDash"></svg>
<div id="brush"></div>
<div id="spreadsheet"></div>
</body>
</html>
```

This requires that we add a reference in the CSS to our new div and slightly adjust the #spreadsheet div to take up less room.

Listing 9.13   Brush div CSS changes

```
#brush {
    overflow: auto;
    width: 100%;
    height: 20%;
}
#spreadsheet {
    overflow: auto;
    width: 100%;
    height: 30%;
}
```

Because we need a scale to build a brush, we'll start by making a new scale that suits our tweet data: d3.time.scale. This scale is designed to take JavaScript Date datatypes and deal with them like the more common d3.scale.linear. To populate the domain of our new scale, we need to find the earliest and latest times of each tweet. We do this by using d3.extent and built-in JavaScript array mapping functionality to create an array of Date datatypes from the string representation of the times of each tweet.

A brush is an interactive collection of components that allows a user to drag one end of the brush to designate an extent, or to move that extent to a different range. Typical brush aspects are explained in figure 9.8. In this chapter we only create a brush that allows selection along the x-axis, but if you want to see a brush that selects along the x- and y-axes, you can check out chapter 11, where we use it to select points laid out on an xy plane.

It's also helpful to create an axis to go along with our brush. The brush is created as a region of interactivity, and clicking on that region produces a rectangle in response. But before any interaction, the area looks blank. By including an axis, we inform the user of the range attached to this brush. Our new axis needs more particular formatting because we're using a time scale.

After that, we'll create a brush and assign the time scale to the brush's .x() function. We can also create brushes that are vertical or allow for selecting a region by setting the .y() function. We'll assign an event listener that listens for the custom

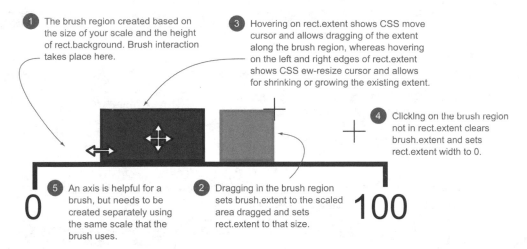

Figure 9.8 Components of a brush

event "brush" to call the function brushed(). Code to create the brush is shown in listing 9.14, while code for the actual behavior when the brush is used is explained in listing 9.15. The "brush" event happens any time the user drags the mouse along the brush region after clicking on the region.

Listing 9.14 Brush creation and function

```
function createBrush(incData) {

    var timeRange = d3.extent(incData.map(function(d) {
                return new Date(d.timestamp);
            })
    );

    var timeScale = d3.time.scale().domain(timeRange).range([10,990]);

    var timeBrush = d3.svg.brush()
                    .x(timeScale)
                    .extent(timeRange)
                    .on("brush", brushed);

    var timeAxis = d3.svg.axis()
        .scale(timeScale)
        .orient('bottom')
        .ticks(d3.time.hours, 2)
        .tickFormat(d3.time.format('%I%p'));

    var brushSVG = d3.select("#brush")
        .append("svg").attr("height", "100%").attr("width", "100%");

    brushSVG.append("g")
        .attr("transform", "translate(0,100)")
        .attr("id", "brushAxis").call(timeAxis);

    brushSVG.append("g").attr("transform", "translate(0,50)")
            .attr("id", "brushG").call(timeBrush)
            .selectAll("rect").attr("height", 50);
```

We'll make our brush dynamically resize later.

Gives us latest and earliest times of tweets

Fires the brushed() function on every "brush" event

Shows a tick for every two hours, and formats it to only show hour and AM/PM

Our axis

Our brush

Immediately calls the created rect elements and makes them 50 px high

```
function brushed() {
    // brushed code
  };

};
```

In particular, we use d3.time.hours in the ticks() function to create an axis with ticks every two hours. We then use d3.time.format in the tickFormat() function to show only the hour and whether it's A.M. or P.M.

The brushed() function (listing 9.15) that we previously defined in the create-Brush function gets the current extent of the brush using its built-in function and compares that extent to the two datasets we used for our circle pack chart and bar chart. It then adjusts the size of the bars in the bar chart or the visibility of the circles in the circle pack based on whether the corresponding data falls within the range of the current extent.

Listing 9.15 The brushed function

```
function brushed() {
    var e = timeBrush.extent();                ←── Gets the current
                                                     extent of the brush
        d3.selectAll("circle.pack")
            .filter(function(d){return d.depth == 2})   ←── Hides any depth 2
            .style("display", function (d) {                circles not tweeted
                return new Date(d.timestamp) >= e[0] &&     within the current
                    new Date(d.timestamp) <= e[1] ? "block" : "none";   extent
            });

        var rightSize = canvasSize("#rightSVG");

        d3.select("#rightSVG")
          .selectAll("rect")
          .attr("x", function(d,i) {return barXScale(d.key) + 5})
          .attr("width", function() {return barXScale.rangeBand() - 5})
          .attr("y", function(d) {return barYScale(filteredLength(d))})
          .style("stroke", "black")
          .attr("height", function(d) {
              return rightSize[1] - barYScale(filteredLength(d));
          });
      function filteredLength(d) {
          var filteredValues = d.values.filter(function (p) {
            return Date(p.timestamp) >= e[0] && new Date(p.timestamp) <= e[1];
          });
          return filteredValues.length;
      };
  };
```

Redraws the bar chart to reflect only tweets within the current extent

This brush allows users to designate a block of time during the day that the tweets are made. It shows only those level 2 circles on the circle pack that correspond to tweets that were made during that time. It also adjusts the bar chart to show totals for the tweets made during that time. Figure 9.9 shows three different brushed regions and the corresponding changes to the circle pack chart and bar chart.

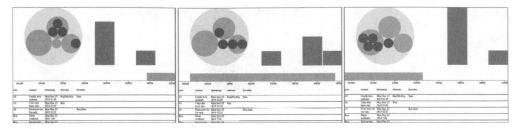

Figure 9.9   The results of our `brushed()` function showing level 2 circle visibility and bar chart changes based on the changing extent of our brush

9.3.2 *Making our brush more user friendly*

The addition of an axis makes a brush more comprehensible to a user than a blank space that happens to show a different cursor on mouseover. But brushing isn't a common user activity, and you should do a couple things to make brushes more user friendly. One common thing is to add a set of handles on each end of the brush to signify that the brush is resizable from those ends. The areas that allow for resizing (and that trigger the `ew-resize` cursor) are on both ends of the brush. They can be seen by selecting the SVG rect elements in use by the brush and changing their visibility style as well as their fill:

```
d3.selectAll("g.resize > rect").style("visibility", "visible").style("fill",
"red")
```

The result, shown in figure 9.10, is that our invisible resizing regions are now visible and distinct from the rest of the brush. This may be fine, but typically, handles are, if you'll pardon the pun, handled differently.

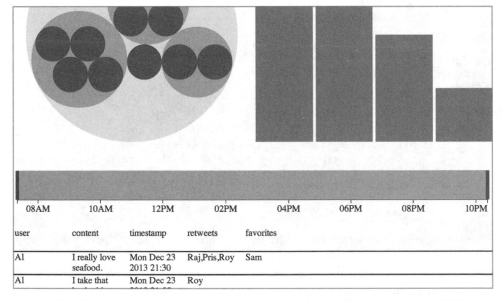

Figure 9.10   The `rect` elements in the resizing areas on each end of the brush are now visible and filled red.

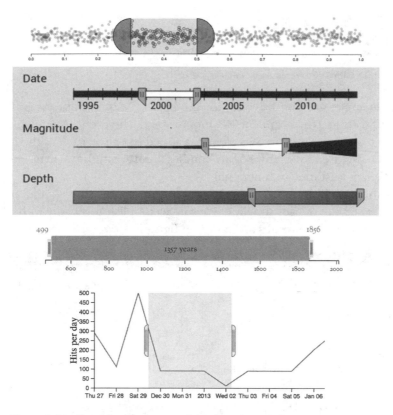

Figure 9.11   Brush handles on a variety of brushes, such as (from top) an example by Mike Bostock, a CS project exploring earthquake frequency, the Kindred Britain search brush, and dc.js.[1]

D3.js examples use a variety of brush handles, from semicircles to beveled rectangles, as shown in figure 9.11. But you can do more than give a brush handles; for example, you can provide feedback about whether there's any data that overlaps with the brushed region. You'll see that as soon as you make handles for your brush.

Our handles won't be quite as exciting as these. Instead, we'll add semitransparent circles on each end, which results in a brush with handles like that shown in figure 9.12:

```
d3.selectAll("g.resize").append("circle")
    .attr("r", 25)
    .attr("cy",25)
    .style("fill", "white")
    .style("stroke", "black")
    .style("stroke-width", "4px")
    .style("opacity", .75);
```

---

[1] See these examples at the following URLs: Brush Handles by Mike Bostock (http://bl.ocks.org/mbostock/ 4349545); earthquake visualization by Andrew Lee (http://vis.berkeley.edu/courses/cs294-10-fa13/wiki/ index.php/A3-AndrewLee); Kindred Britain search brush (http://kindred.stanford.edu); dc.js (http://dc-js.github.io/dc.js/).

Figure 9.12   A brush with SVG circles as handles

Notice that the circles are also listening for the brush resizing event (as you can tell because the ew-resize cursor appears on mouseover). The event listener is assigned to the g.resize element, and any SVG elements added to that g (such as the circles we just appended) also fire that event. So our handles are not only attractive, they're also functional. Well, at least they're functional.

The next thing we'll do to improve the usability of our brush is to add an indication of where tweets fall on our timeline. We can accomplish this easily with the code in the following listing. The results are shown in figure 9.13.

Listing 9.16   Tweets on a timeline

```
var tweets = d3.selectAll("div.datarow").data();        ◁──── If our data is still
                                                                exposed elsewhere, we
d3.select("#brushG")                                            could just use that.
    .selectAll("circle.timeline")
    .data(tweets)
    .enter()
    .append("circle")
    .style("fill","red").style("stroke", "black")               We don't want the
    .style("stroke-width", "1px")                               circles to interrupt
    .style("pointer-events","none")          ◁──────            brush interaction.
    .attr("class","timeline").attr("r", 5).attr("cy", 25)
    .attr("cx", function(d) {return timeScale(new Date(d.timestamp))})
```

Places the circles at their timestamp scaled location

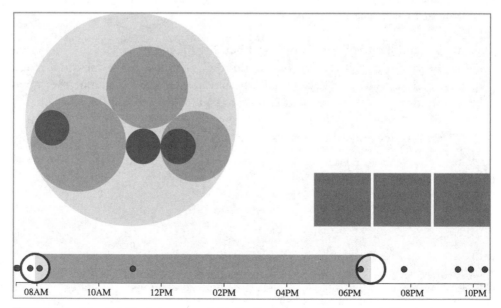

Figure 9.13   A brush with circles appended indicating when tweets occurred

We could do more with upgrading the brush UI elements, such as making the timeline circles highlight and dim if they fall in the brush range. But instead let's look more closely at the brush events fired by the brush control.

9.3.3 Understanding brush events

Activity on the brush region fires three separate custom events: `"brush"`, `"brush-start"`, and `"brushend"`. You've probably figured them out based on their names, but for clarity, `"brushstart"` is fired when you mousedown on the brush region, `"brush"` is fired continuously as you drag your mouse after `"brushstart"` and before mouseup, and `"brushend"` is fired on mouseup. In most implementations of a brush, it makes sense to wire it up so that whatever function you want applied with user activity only happens on the `"brush"` event. But you may have functions that are more expensive, such as redrawing an entire map or querying a database. In that case you could use `"brushstart"` to cause a visual change in your map (turning elements gray or transparent) and wait until `"brushend"` to run more heavy-duty activity.

9.3.4 Redrawing components

Our entire application responsively resizes whenever we change the dimensions of our browser window. But our brush doesn't resize. It was drawn at a particular size when we created it, and runs off the screen if we make the width too small or looks puny if we make the width too large.

It may seem like you need to delete the graphical elements of the brush and recreate it whenever you redraw your other visual elements. Fortunately, D3 components like axis and brush can be recalled by the containing element to resize them. All you need to do is include in your redraw code the code in the following listing, which now includes reference to the axis and brush components we earlier created.

Listing 9.17 Component redrawing

```
var timeTickScale = d3.scale.linear()
    .domain([0,1000])
    .rangeRound([10,1])
    .clamp(true);

var bExtent = timeBrush.extent();

timeScale.range([10,rightSize[0] + leftSize[0] - 10]);
timeAxis.scale(timeScale)
    .ticks(d3.time.hours, timeTickScale((rightSize[0] + leftSize[0])));
timeBrush.x(timeScale);

d3.select("#brushAxis").call(timeAxis);
d3.select("#brushG").call(timeBrush.extent(bExtent));

d3.select("#brushG").selectAll("circle.timeline")
    .attr("cx", function(d) {return timeScale(new Date(d.timestamp))});
```

Gets the current brush extent → `var bExtent = timeBrush.extent();`

We need to dynamically determine the number of ticks on our axis based on available screen space.

Sets the current range of timeScale to the width of the two SVGs minus margins

Updates timeAxis to the current scale and ticks

Updates timeBrush as well

Updates the position of the timeline circles

Calls both from their respective containers, passing the original extent to make the brush refresh

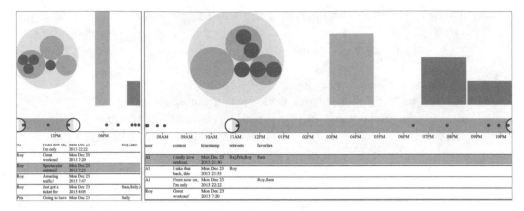

Figure 9.14   Two different sizes of our application showing that the axis and brush, as well as axis ticks and brush timeline circles, update based on screen size

As shown in figure 9.14, we now have an axis and brush and datapoints on the brush that all update as the screen is resized.

We'll stop there. You could replace any of the charts with one of the charts we looked at earlier, such as a pie chart, network visualization, or map. Controls like the brush can be powerful, but it's also important to make such controls accessible to your users.

9.4   *Summary*

In this chapter you learned how to create an interactive dashboard with multiple chart types and brush-based filtering. Specifically, you learned about

- Formatting HTML for multiple SVG canvases
- How to bind the same dataset to multiple charts to allow for easy cross-highlighting
- Decoupling chart creation from drawing to enable a redraw function for a responsive page
- How to implement the time scale
- How to implement the brush control
- Making the brush more useful for users
- Making components and controls like axis and brush responsive to screen resizing

In the next chapter, we'll focus on creating components like the axis component, and layouts like pie or pack. Learning how to create components and layouts will give you a better understanding of how D3 works while giving you the tools to make better, more reusable code in the future.

Writing layouts and components

10

This chapter covers

- Writing a custom legend component
- Writing a custom grid layout
- Adding functionality to make layout and component settings customizable
- Adding interactivity to components

Throughout this book, we've dealt with D3 components and layouts. In this chapter we'll write them. After you've created your own layout and your own component, you'll more clearly understand the structure and function of layouts. You'll also be able to use that layout, and other layouts that you create on your own later, in the charts that you build with D3.

In this chapter we'll create a custom layout that places a dataset on a grid. For most of the chapter, we'll use our tweets dataset, but the advantage of a layout is that the particular dataset doesn't matter. The purpose of this chapter isn't to create a grid, but rather to help you understand how layouts work. We'll create a grid layout because it's simple and allows us to focus on layout structure rather than the particulars of any data visualization layout. We'll follow that up by extending the layout so it can have a set size that we can change. You'll also see how the layout annotates the dataset we send so that individual datapoints can be drawn as circles or rectangles. A grid isn't the most useful or sexy layout, but it can teach you the basics of layouts. After that, we'll build a legend component that tells users the meaning of the color of our elements. We'll do this by basing the graphical components of the legend on the scale we've used to color our chart elements.

10.1 Creating a layout

Recall from chapter 5 that a layout is a function and an object that modifies a dataset for graphical representation. Here, we'll build that function. Later, we'll give it the capacity to modify the settings of the layout in the same manner that built-in D3 layouts operate.

You'll see this in more detail later, but first we need to create an object that returns the function that processes our data. After we create this function, we'll use it to implement the calls that a layout needs. In the following listing, you can see the function and a test where we instantiate it and pass it data.

> **Listing 10.1   d3.layout.grid.js**

```
d3.layout.grid = function() {
    function processGrid(data) {
        console.log(data)
    }
    return processGrid;
}

var grid = d3.layout.grid();        Prints [1,2,3,4,5]
grid([1,2,3,4,5]);              ◁   to the console
```

That's not an exciting layout, but it works. We don't need to name our layout d3.layout.x or any other particular name, but using that namespace makes it more readable in the future. Before we start working on the functions that will create our grid, we have to define what this layout does. We know we want to put the data on a grid, but what else do we want? Here's a simple spec:

- We want to have a default arrangement of that grid, say, equal numbers of rows and columns.
- We also want to let the user define the number of rows or columns.
- We want the grid to be laid out over a certain size.
- We also need to allow the user to define the size of the grid.

That's a good start. First we need to initialize all the variables that this grid needs to access to make it happen. We also need to define getter and setter functions to let the user access those variables, because we want to keep them scoped to the d3.layout.grid function. The first thing we can do is update the processGrid function to look like it does in listing 10.2. It takes an array of objects and updates them with x and y data based on grid positions. We derive the size of the grid from the number of data objects sent to processGrid. It turns out this isn't a difficult mathematical problem. We take the square root of the number of datapoints and round it up to the nearest whole number to get the right number of rows and columns for our grid. This makes sense when you think about how a grid is a set of rows and columns that allows you to place a cell on one of those rows and columns for each datapoint. The number of rows times columns needs to be at least the number of cells (the number of datapoints). If we decide to have the same number of rows as columns, then it's that number squared.

Listing 10.2 Updated `processGrid` function

```
function processGrid(data) {
    var rows = Math.ceil(Math.sqrt(data.length));          ⟵ Calculates the number
    var columns = rows;                                         of rows/columns

    var cell = 0;                                          ⟵ Initializes a variable to
                                                             walk through the dataset
    for (var i = 0; i < rows; i++) {
        for (var j = 0; j < columns; j++) {               ⟵ Loops through the
            if (data[cell]) {                                  rows and columns
                data[cell].x = j;
                data[cell].y = i;                         ⟵ This assumes the data consists
                cell++;                                       of an array of objects.
            }
            else {                                        Sets the current datapoint to
                break;                                    corresponding row and column
            }
        }
    }                                          Increments the
                                               datapoint variable
    return data;
}
```

To test our nascent grid layout, we can load tweets.json and pass it to grid. The grid function displays the graphical elements onscreen based on their computed grid position. In the following listing, you can see how we'd pass data from tweets.json to our grid layout.

Listing 10.3 Using our grid layout

```
d3.json("tweets.json", function(error, data) {
})                                                        A scale to
                                                          fit our grid
function makeAGrid(data) {                                onto our
    var scale = d3.scale.linear().domain([0,5]).range([100,400]);  ⟵ SVG canvas
    var grid = d3.layout.grid();
    var griddedData = grid(data.tweets);
    d3.select("svg").selectAll("circle")
        .data(griddedData)
        .enter()                                          Sets circles to a scaled
        .append("circle")                                 position based on the
        .attr("cx", function(d) {return scale(d.x);})     ⟵ layout's calculated x
                                                          and y values
```

```
    .attr("cy", function(d) {return scale(d.y);})
    .attr("r", 20)
    .style("fill", "pink");
}
```

The results in figure 10.1 show how the grid function has correctly appended x and y coordinates to draw the tweets as circles on a grid.

The benefit of building this as a layout is that if we add more data to it, it automatically adjusts and allows us to use transitions to animate that adjustment. To do this, we need more data. Listing 10.4 includes a few lines to create data that represents our new tweets. We also use the .concat() function of an array in native JavaScript that, when given the state shown in figure 10.1, should produce the results in figure 10.2.

Listing 10.4   Update the grid with more elements

```
var fakeTweets = [];
for (var x = 0;x < 12;x++) {
    var tweet = {id: x, content: "Fake Tweet #" + x};    ◁─── Creates 12 new
    fakeTweets.push(tweet);                                    fake tweets
}

var doubledArray = data.tweets.concat(fakeTweets);    ◁─── Combines the
var newGriddedData = grid(doubledArray);                   original dataset with
                                                           our new dataset
d3.select("svg").selectAll("circle")
    .data(newGriddedData)
    .enter()
    .append("circle")
    .attr("cx", 0)               ◁─── Adds any new
    .attr("cy", 0)                    tweets at 0,0
    .attr("r", 20)
    .style("fill", "darkred");

d3.select("svg").selectAll("circle")
    .transition()                                         ◁─── Moves all tweets (old
    .duration(1000)                                            and new) to their newly
    .attr("cx", function(d) {return scale(d.x)})               computed positions
    .attr("cy", function(d) {return scale(d.y)})
```

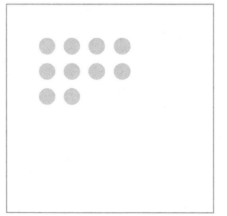

Figure 10.1   The results of our `makeAGrid` function that uses our new `d3.layout.grid` to arrange the data in a grid. In this case, our data consists of 10 tweets that are each represented as a pink circle laid out on a grid.

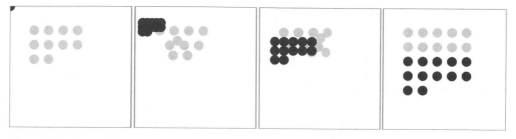

Figure 10.2 The grid layout has automatically adjusted to the size of our new dataset. Notice that our new elements are above the old elements, but our layout has changed in size from a 4 x 4 grid to a 5 x 5 grid, causing the old elements to move to their newly calculated position.

The results in figure 10.2 show snapshots of the animation from the old position to the new position of the circles.

Calculating a scale based on what you know to be the grid size results in an inefficient piece of code. That wouldn't be useful if someone put in a different dataset. Instead, when designing layouts you'll want to provide functionality so that the layout size can be declared, and then any adjustments necessary happen within the code of the layout that processes data. To do this, we need to add a scoped size variable and then add a function to our `processGrid` function to allow the user to change that size variable. Sending a variable sets the value, and sending no variable returns the value. We achieve this by checking for the presence of arguments using the `arguments` object in native JavaScript. The updated function is shown in the following listing.

Listing 10.5 `d3.layout.grid` with size functionality

```
d3.layout.grid = function() {
var gridSize = [0,10];                                    Initializes the variable
                                                         with a default value
    var gridXScale = d3.scale.linear();
var gridYScale = d3.scale.linear();                      Creates two scales but
function processGrid(data) {                              doesn't define their
                                                         range or domain
      var rows = Math.ceil(Math.sqrt(data.length));
        var columns = rows;

      gridXScale.domain([1,columns]).range([0,gridSize[0]]);   Defines the
        gridYScale.domain([1,rows]).range([0,gridSize[1]]);    range and
        var cell = 0;                                          domain each
                                                               time the
      for (var i = 1; i <= rows; i++) {                        layout is called
        for (var j = 1; j <= columns; j++) {
          if (data[cell]) {
            data[cell].x = gridXScale(j);
            data[cell].y = gridYScale(i);          Applies the scaled
            cell++;                                values as x and y
          }
          else {
            break;
          }
        }
      }
    }
```

```
    return data;
  }
  processGrid.size = function(newSize) {
        if (!arguments.length) return gridSize;

      gridSize = newSize;
      return this;
  }

  return processGrid;
}
```

Getter/setter
function for
layout size

You can see the updated grid layout in action by slightly changing our code for calling
the layout, as shown in the following listing. We set the size, and when we create our
circles, we use the x and y values directly instead of using scaled values.

```
var grid = d3.layout.grid();
grid.size([400,400]);
var griddedData = grid(data.tweets);

d3.select("svg")
  .append("g")
  .attr("transform", "translate(50,50)")
  .selectAll("circle").data(griddedData)
  .enter()
  .append("circle")
  .attr("cx", function(d) {return d.x})
  .attr("cy", function(d) {return d.y})
  .attr("r", 20)
  .style("fill", "pink");

var fakeTweets = [];
for (var x = 0;x<12;x++) {
    var tweet = {id: x, content: "Fake Tweet #" + x};
    fakeTweets.push(tweet);
}

var doubledArray = data.tweets.concat(fakeTweets);
var newGriddedData = grid(doubledArray);

d3.select("g").selectAll("circle").data(newGriddedData)
  .enter()
  .append("circle")
  .attr("cx", 0)
  .attr("cy", 0)
  .attr("r", 20)
  .style("fill", "darkred");

d3.select("g").selectAll("circle")
  .transition()
  .duration(1000)
  .attr("cx", function(d) {return d.x})
  .attr("cy", function(d) {return d.y})
  .each("end", resizeGrid1);
```

Sets layout
size

Position circles
with their x/y
values

At the end of the
transition, calls
resizeGrid1

This code refers to a `resizeGrid1()` function, shown in the following listing, that's chained to a `resizeGrid2()` function. These functions use the ability to update the size setting on our layout to update the graphical display of the elements created by the layout.

Listing 10.7   The `resizeGrid1()` function

```
function resizeGrid1() {
  grid.size([200,200]);                    ←  Changes the size,
  grid(doubledArray);                         reapplies the layout, and
                                              updates the display
  d3.select("g").selectAll("circle")
    .transition()
    .duration(1000)
    .attr("cx", function(d) {return d.x})
    .attr("cy", function(d) {return d.y})
    .each("end", resizeGrid2);
};

function resizeGrid2() {                   ┐ Again, with a
  grid.size([200,400]);                    ┘ different size
  grid(doubledArray);                      ←

  d3.select("g").selectAll("circle")
    .transition()
    .duration(1000)
    .attr("cx", function(d) {return d.x;})
    .attr("cy", function(d) {return d.y;});
};
```

This creates a grid that fits our defined space perfectly, as shown in figure 10.3, and with no need to create a scale to place the elements.

Figure 10.4 shows a pair of animations where the grid changes in size as we adjust the size setting. The grid changes to fit a smaller or an elongated area. This is done using the transition's `"end"` event. It calls a new function that uses our original grid layout but updates its size and reapplies it to our dataset.

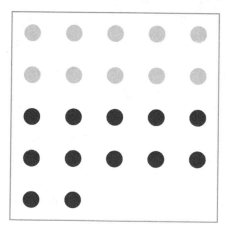

Figure 10.3   The grid layout run on a 400 x 400 size setting

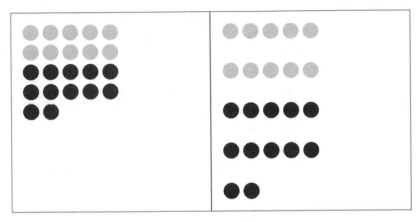

Figure 10.4   The grid layout run in a 200 x 200 size (left) and a 200 x 400 size (right)

Before we move on, it's important that we extend our layout a bit more so that you can better understand how layouts work. In D3 a layout isn't meant to create something as specific as a grid full of circles. Rather *it's supposed to annotate a dataset so you can represent it using different graphical methods.* Let's say we want our layout to also handle squares, which would be a desired feature when dealing with grids.

To handle squares, or more specifically rectangles (because we want them to stretch out if someone uses our layout and sets the height and width to different values), we need the capacity to calculate `height` and `width` values. That's easy to add to our existing layout function.

Listing 10.8   Layout code for calculating height and width of grid cells

```
var gridCellWidth = gridSize[0] / columns;
var gridCellHeight = gridSize[1] / rows;

//other code

  for (var i = 1; i <= rows; i++) {
    for (var j = 1; j <= columns; j++) {
      if (data[cell]) {
        data[cell].x = gridXScale(j);
        data[cell].y = gridYScale(i);
        data[cell].height = gridCellHeight;        ◁─── New code
        data[cell].width = gridCellWidth;
        cell++;
      }
      else {
        break;
      }
    }
  }
}
```

And with that in place, we can call our layout and append `<rect>` elements instead of circle elements. We can update our code as in listing 10.9 to offset the x and y attributes (because `<rect>` elements are drawn from the top left and not from the center like `<circle>` elements) and also apply the width and height values that our layout computes.

Listing 10.9 Appending rectangles with our layout

```
d3.select("g").selectAll("rect")
.transition()
.duration(1000)
.attr("x", function(d) {return d.x - (d.width / 2);})
.attr("y", function(d) {return d.y - (d.height / 2);})
.attr("width", function(d) {return d.width;})
.attr("height", function(d) {return d.height;})
.each("end", resizeGrid1);
```

If we update the rest of our code accordingly, the result is the same animated transition of our layout between different sizes, but now with rectangles that grow and distort based on those sizes, as shown in figure 10.5.

This is a simple example of a layout, and doesn't do nearly as much as the kinds of layouts we've used throughout this book, but even a simple layout like this provides reusable, animatable content. Now we'll look at another reusable pattern in D3, the component, which creates graphical elements automatically.

10.2 Writing your own components

You've seen components in action, particularly the `d3.svg.axis` component. You can also think of the brush as a component, because it creates graphical elements. But it tends to be described as a "control" because it also loads with built-in interactivity.

The component that we'll build is a simple legend. Legends are a necessity when working with data visualization, and they all share some things in common. First, we'll need a more interesting dataset to consider, though we'll continue to use our grid layout. The legend component that we'll create will consist eventually of labeled rectangles, each with a color corresponding to the color assigned to our datapoints by a D3 scale. This way our users can tell, at a glance, which colors correspond to which values in our data visualization.

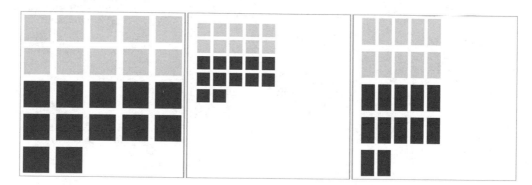

Figure 10.5 The three states of the grid layout using rectangles for the grid cells

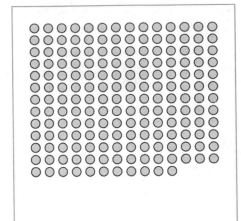

Figure 10.6   The countries of the world as a grid

10.2.1 Loading sample data

Instead of the tweets.json data, we'll use world.geojson, except we'll use the features as datapoints on our custom grid layout from section 10.1 without putting them on a map. Listing 10.10 shows the corresponding code, which produces figure 10.6. You may find it strange to load geodata and represent it not as geographic shapes but in an entirely different way. Presenting data in an untraditional manner can often be a useful technique to draw a user's attention to the patterns in that data.

Listing 10.10   Loading the countries of the world into a grid

```
d3.json("world.geojson ", function(error, data) {
   makeAGrid(data);
 })

function makeAGrid(data) {
  var grid = d3.layout.grid();
  grid.size([300,300]);
  var griddedData = grid(data.features);

  griddedData.forEach(function (country) {          Calculates the area of each
    country.size = d3.geo.area(country);     ◁─── country and appends that
  });                                               to the datapoint

  d3.select("svg")
    .append("g")
    .attr("transform", "translate(50,50)")
    .selectAll("circle")
    .data(griddedData)
    .enter()                                        Appends a circle
    .append("circle")                        ◁─── for each country
    .attr("cx", function(d) {return d.x})
    .attr("cy", function(d) {return d.y})
    .attr("r", 10)
    .style("fill", "lightgray")
```

```
        .style("stroke", "black")
        .style("stroke-width", "1px");
};
```

We'll focus on only one attribute of our data: the size of each country. We'll color the circles according to that size using a quantize scale that puts each country into one of several discrete categories. In our case, we'll use the colorbrewer.Reds[7] array of light-to-dark reds as our bins. The quantize scale will split the countries into seven different groups. In the following listing you can see how to set that up, and figure 10.7 shows the result of our new color scale.

Listing 10.11 Changing the color of our grid

```
var griddedData = d3.selectAll("circle").data();                              ◁──┐
var sizeExtent = d3.extent(griddedData, function (d) {return d.size;});
var countryColor = d3.scale.quantize()
            .domain(sizeExtent).range(colorbrewer.Reds[7]);      Gets the data
d3.selectAll("circle").style("fill", function (d) {              array bound
            return countryColor(d.size);});                      to our circles
```

For a more complete data visualization, we'd want to add labels for the countries or other elements to identify the continent or region of the country. But we'll focus on explaining what the color indicates. We don't want to get bogged down with other details from the data that could be explained, for example, using modal windows, as we did for our World Cup example in chapter 4, or using other labeling methods discussed throughout this book. For our legend to be useful, it needs to account for the different categories of coloration and indicate which color is associated with which band of values. But before we get to that, let's build a component that creates graphical elements when we call it. Remember that the d3.select("#something").call(someFunction) function of a selection is the equivalent of someFunction(d3.select("#something")). With that in mind, we'll create a function that expects a selection and operates on it.

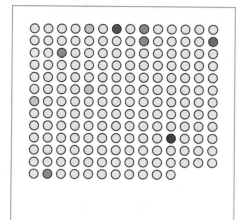

Figure 10.7 Circles representing countries colored by area

Listing 10.12   A simple component

```
d3.svg.legend = function() {

    function legend(gSelection) {
      var testData = [1,2,3,4,5];

      gSelection.selectAll("rect")
          .data(testData)
        .enter()
        .append("rect")
        .attr("height", 20)
        .attr("width", 20)
        .attr("x", function (d,i) {return i *25})
        .style("fill", "red")

      return this;
    }

    return legend;
};
```

→ A component is sent a selection with .call().

→ Appends to that selection a set of rectangles

We can then append a <g> element to our chart and call this component, with the results shown in figure 10.8:

```
var newLegend = d3.svg.legend();

d3.select("svg").append("g")
    .attr("id","legend")
    .attr("transform", "translate(50,400)")
    .call(newLegend);
```

And now that we have the structure of our component, we can add functionality to it, such as allowing the user to define a custom size like we did with our grid layout. We also need to think about where this legend is going to get its data. Following the pattern of the axis component, it would make the most sense for the legend to refer directly to the scale we're using and derive, from that scale, the color and values associated with the color of each band in the scale.

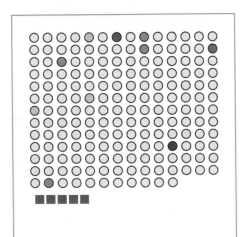

Figure 10.8   The new legend component, when called by a <g> element placed below our grid, creates five red rectangles.

10.2.2 *Linking components to scales*

To do that, we have to write a new function for our legend that takes a scale and derives the necessary range bands to be useful. The scale that we send it will be the same countryColor scale that we use to color our grid circles. Because this is a quantize scale, we'll make our legend component hardcoded to handle only quantize scales. If we wanted to make this a more robust component, we'd need to make it identify and handle the various scales that D3 uses.

Just like all scales have an invert function, they also have the ability to tell you what domain values are mapped to what range values. First, we need to know the range of values of our quantize scale as they appear to the scale. We can easily get that range by using scale.quantize.range():

countryColor.range()   ⟵| ["#fee5d9", "#fcbba1", "#fc9272", "#fb6a4a",
                                     "#ef3b2c", "#cb181d", "#99000d"]

We can pass those values to scale.quantize.invertExtent to get the numerical domain mapped to each color value:

countryColor.invertExtent("#fee5d9")   ⟵| **[0.000006746501002759535,
                                                  0.05946855349777645]**

Armed with these two functions, all we need to do now is give our legend component the capacity to have a scale assigned to it and then update the legend function itself to derive from that scale the dataset necessary for our legend. Listing 10.13 shows both the new d3.legend.scale() function that uses a quantize scale to create the necessary dataset, and the updated legend() function that uses that data to draw a more meaningful set of <rect> elements.

Listing 10.13   Updated `legend` function

```
d3.svg.legend = function() {
      var data = [];                                    Sets a           Initializes an x-axis
      var size = [300,20];                     ⟵|      default size     scale but doesn't set
      var xScale = d3.scale.linear();                                   domain or range  ⟵
      var scale;                                                   |

            function legend(gSelection) {        Calls the function to
                                                 process the scale into    Calculates
            createLegendData(scale);      ⟵|    a data array              the min/max
                                                                          of the scale
      var xMin = d3.min(data, function(d) {return d.domain[0];}); ⟵|     data
      var xMax = d3.max(data, function(d) {return d.domain[1];});
    xScale.domain([xMin,xMax]).range([0,size[0]])        ⟵
                                                          Sets the
    gSelection.selectAll("rect")                          x-axis scale
        .data(data)
        .enter()
        .append("rect")                   Draws rectangles based on
        .attr("height", size[1])    ⟵|    component settings and scale data
```

The scale that will be sent to the component

```
        .attr("width", function (d) {
                return xScale(d.domain[1]) -  xScale(d.domain[0]);
        })
        .attr("x", function (d) {return xScale(d.domain[0]);})
        .style("fill", function(d) {return d.color;});

        return this;
    };
    function createLegendData(incScale) {
        var rangeArray = incScale.range();
        data = [];

        for (var x in rangeArray) {
          var colorValue = rangeArray[x];
          var domainValues = incScale.invertExtent(colorValue);
          data.push({color: colorValue, domain: domainValues})
        }
    };
    legend.scale = function(newScale) {
        if (!arguments.length) return scale;
        scale = newScale;
        return this;
    };

    return legend;
};
```

◁—┐ **Processes the scale into a data array**

◁—┐ **Setter/getter to set the legend's scale**

We call this updated legend and set it up:

```
var newLegend = d3.svg.legend().scale(countryColor);

d3.select("svg").append("g")
    .attr("transform","translate(50,400)")
    .attr("id", "legend").call(newLegend);
```

This new legend now creates a rect for each band in our scale and colors it accordingly, as shown in figure 10.9.

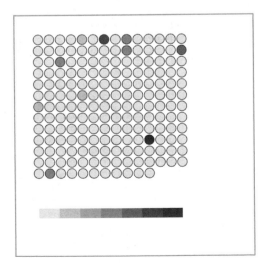

Figure 10.9   The updated legend component is automatically created, with a <rect> element for each band in the quantize scale that's colored according to that band's color.

If we want to add interactivity, it's a simple process because we know that each rect in the legend corresponds to a two-piece array of values that we can use to test the circles in our grid. The following listing shows that function and the call to make the legend interactive.

Listing 10.14 Legend interactivity

```
d3.select("#legend").selectAll("rect").on("mouseover", legendOver);

function legendOver(d) {
    console.log(d)
    d3.selectAll("circle")
        .style("opacity", function(p) {
            if (p.size >= d.domain[0] && p.size <= d.domain[1]) {
                return 1;
            } else {
                return .25;
            }
        });
};
```

Notice that this function isn't defined inside our legend component. Instead, it's defined and called after the legend is created, because after it's created, our legend component is just a set of SVG elements with data bound to it like any other part of our charts. This interactivity allows us to mouseover the legend and see which circles fall in a particular range of values, as shown in figure 10.10.

Finally, before we can call our legend done, we need to add an indication of what those colored bands mean. We could call an axis component and allow that to label the bands, or we can label the break points by appending text elements for each. In our case, because the numbers provided for d3.geo.area are so small, we'll also need to rotate and shrink those labels quite a bit for them to fit on the page. To do this, we can add the code in listing 10.15 to our legend function in d3.svg.legend.

Figure 10.10 The legendOver behavior highlights circles falling in a particular band and deemphasizes the circles not in that band by making them transparent.

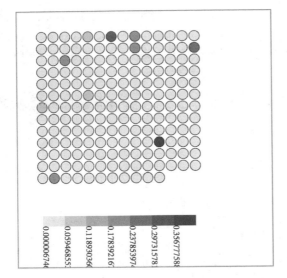

Figure 10.11   Our legend with rudimentary labels

Listing 10.15   Text labels for legend

```
gSelection.selectAll("text")
    .data(data)
    .enter()
    .append("g")
    .attr("transform", function (d) {
        return "translate(" + xScale(d.domain[0]) +"," + size[1] + ")";
    })
    .append("text")
        .attr("transform", "rotate(90)")
        .text(function(d) {return d.domain[0];});
```

> The text element needs to be placed in a g so that it can be translated and then rotated; otherwise, it'll be rotated and then translated, which would place it at the translation relative to its new rotation (taking the text off the page).

As shown in figure 10.11, they aren't the prettiest labels. We could adjust their positioning, font, and style to make them more effective. They also need functions like the grid layout has to define size or other elements of the component.

This is usually the point where I say that the purpose of this chapter is to show you the structure of components and layouts, and that making the most effective layout or component is a long and involved process that we won't get into. But this is an ugly legend. The break points are hard to read, and it's missing pieces that the component needs, such as a title and an explanation of units.

10.2.3 *Adding component labels*

Let's add those features to the legend, and create ways to access them, as shown in listing 10.16. We're using d3.format, which allows us to set a number-formatting rule based on the popular Python number-formatting mini-language (found at https://docs.python.org/release/3.1.3/library/string.html#formatspec).

Listing 10.16 Title and unit attributes of a legend

```
var title = "Legend";
var numberFormat = d3.format(".4n");      These are added right
var units = "Units";                      after var scale inside the
                                          d3.svg.legend function.
//other code

legend.title = function(newTitle) {
  if (!arguments.length) return title;
  title = newTitle;                       All these functions
  return this;                            are added right after
};                                        legend.scale.

legend.unitLabel = function(newUnits) {
  if (!arguments.length) return units;
  units = newUnits;
  return this;
};

legend.formatter = function(newFormatter) {
  if (!arguments.length) return numberFormat;
  numberFormat = newFormatter;
  return this;
};
```

We'll use these new properties in our updated legend drawing code shown in listing 10.17. This new code draws SVG <line> elements at each breakpoint, and foregoes the rotated text in favor of more readable, shortened text labels at each breakpoint. It also adds two new <text> elements, one above the legend that corresponds to the value of the title variable and one at the far right of the legend that corresponds to the units variable.

Listing 10.17 Updated legend drawing code

```
gSelection.selectAll("line")              This follows your existing code
    .data(data)                           to draw the legend <rect>
    .enter()                              elements, and updates the text.
    .append("line")
    .attr("x1", function (d) {return xScale(d.domain[0]);})    Each line is
    .attr("x2", function (d) {return xScale(d.domain[0]);})    drawn at the
    .attr("y1", 0)                                             breakpoint
    .attr("y2", size[1] + 5)                                   and drawn a
    .style("stroke", "black")                                  little lower to
    .style("stroke-width", "2px");                             "point" at the
                                                               breakpoint
gSelection.selectAll("text")                                   value.
    .data(data)
    .enter()
    .append("g")
    .attr("transform", function (d) {
        return "translate(" + (xScale(d.domain[0])) +","
                            + (size[1] + 20) + ")";
    })
    .append("text")
```

```
                       .style("text-anchor", "middle")
                       .text(function(d) {return numberFormat(d.domain[0]);});

          gSelection.append("text")
              .attr("transform", function (d) {
                  return "translate(" + (xScale(xMin)) +"," + (size[1] - 30) + ")";
              })
              .text(title);

          gSelection.append("text")
              .attr("transform", function (d) {
                  return "translate(" + (xScale(xMax)) +"," + (size[1] + 20) + ")";
              })
              .text(units);
```

Anchors your unrotated labels at the midpoint and formats the value according to the set formatter

Adds a fixed, user-defined title above the legend rectangles and at the minimum value position

Adds a fixed, user-defined unit label on the same line as the labels but at the maximum value position

This requires that we set these new values using the code in the following listing before we call the legend.

Listing 10.18   Calling the legend with title and unit setting

```
var newLegend = d3.svg.legend()
    .scale(countryColor)
    .title("Country Size")
    .formatter(d3.format(".2f"))
    .unitLabel("Steradians");

d3.select("svg").append("g").attr("transform", "translate(50,400)")
    .attr("id", "legend")
    .call(newLegend);
```

Sets the legend title and unit labels and formats to reflect the data being visualized

This part is unchanged.

And now, as shown in figure 10.12, we have a label that's eminently more readable, still interactive, and useful in any situation where the data visualization uses a similar scale.

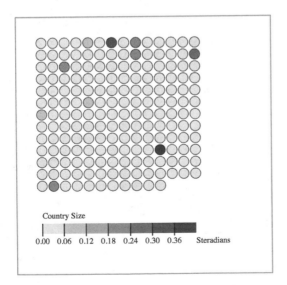

Country Size

0.00 0.06 0.12 0.18 0.24 0.30 0.36   Steradians

Figure 10.12   Our legend with title, unit labels, appropriate number formatting, and additional graphical elements to highlight the breakpoints

By building components and layouts, you better understand how D3 works, but there's another reason why they're so valuable: reusability. You've built a chart using a layout and component (no matter how simple) that you wrote yourself. You could use either in tandem with another layout or component, or on its own, with any data visualization charts you use elsewhere.

Infoviz term: reusable charts

After you've worked with components, layouts, and controls in D3, you may start to wonder if there's a higher level of abstraction available that could combine layouts and controls in a reusable fashion. That level of abstraction has been referred to as a *chart*, and the creation of reusable charts has been of great interest to the D3 community.

This has led to the development of several APIs on top of D3, such as NVD3, D4 (for generic charts), and my own `d3.carto.map` (for web mapping, not surprisingly). It's also led The Miso Project to develop `d3.chart`, a framework for reusable charts. If you're interested in using or developing reusable charts, you may want to check these out:

d3.chart http://misoproject.com/d3-chart/

d3.carto.map https://github.com/emeeks/d3-carto-map

http://visible.io (D4)

http://nvd3.org (NVD3)

You may also try your hand at building more responsive components that automatically update when you call them again, like the axis and brushes we dealt with in the last chapter. Or you may try creating controls like `d3.brush` and behaviors like `d3.behavior.drag`. Regardless of how extensively you follow this pattern, I recommend that you look for instances when your information visualization can be abstracted into layouts and components, and try to create those instead of building another one-off visualization. By doing that, you'll develop a higher level of skill with D3 and fill your toolbox with your own pieces for later work.

10.3 Summary

This chapter showed you how to follow two of the patterns that appear in D3: layouts and components. You learned how to create both of these in a way that you can reuse them and combine them in a single chart:

- Create a general layout structure with getter and setter functions.
- Build the functionality necessary for the layout to modify sent data with attributes for drawing.
- Make a layout dynamically change size based on a size setting.
- Modify sent data to dynamically change the size of individual grid cells.

- Create a general component that can be called by a `<g>` element to create graphical elements.
- Tie that component to scale for its dataset.
- Label the individual pieces of the component with `<text>` elements.

In the next chapter we'll look at a few optimization techniques that you'll find useful for data visualization with large datasets.

Big data visualization

This chapter covers

- Creating large random datasets of multiple types
- Using HTML5 canvas in conjunction with SVG to draw large datasets
- Optimizing geospatial, network, and traditional dataviz
- Working with quadtrees to enhance spatial search performance

This chapter focuses on techniques to create data visualization with large amounts of data. Because it would be impractical to include a few large datasets, we'll also touch on how to create large amounts of sample data to test your code with. You'll use several layouts that you saw earlier, such as the force-directed network layout from chapter 6 and the geospatial map from chapter 7, as well as the brush component from chapter 9, except this time you'll use it to select regions across the x- and y-axes.

This chapter touches on an exotic piece of functionality in D3: the quadtree (shown in figure 11.1). This is an advanced technique we'll use to improve interactivity

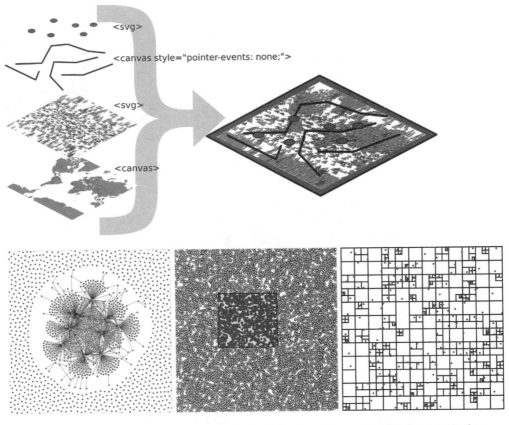

Figure 11.1 This chapter focuses on optimization techniques such as using HTML5 canvas to draw large datasets in tandem with SVG for the interactive elements. This is demonstrated with maps (section 11.1), networks (11.2), and traditional xy data (section 11.3), which uses the D3 quadtree function (section 11.3.2).

and performance. We'll also revisit HTML5 canvas throughout the chapter to see how we can use canvas in tandem with SVG to get the high performance and maintain the interactivity that SVG is so useful for.

We've worked with data throughout this book, but this time, we'll appreciably up the ante by trying to represent a thousand or more datapoints using maps, networks, and charts, which are significantly more resource-intensive than a circle pack chart, a bar chart, or a spreadsheet.

11.1 Big geodata

In chapter 7, you had only 10 cities representing the entire globe. That's not typical: when you're working with geodata, you'll often work with large datasets describing many complex shapes. Fortunately, there's built-in functionality in D3 for drawing that complex data with HTML5 canvas, which dramatically improves performance. For this chapter, we'll need to include a `<canvas>` element in our DOM.

Listing 11.1 bigdata.html

```html
<!doctype html>
<html>
<head>
   <title>Big Data Visualization</title>
   <meta charset="utf-8" />
      <link type="text/css" rel="stylesheet" href="bigdata.css" />
</head>
<body>
<div>
<canvas height="500" width="500"></canvas>
    <div id="viz">
       <svg></svg>
</div>
</div>
<footer>
<script src="d3.v3.min.js" type="text/javascript"></script>
</footer>
</body>
</html>
```

Make sure to set the height and width attributes, not just the style attributes.

To handle our `<canvas>` element, as well as some of the visual elements we'll create in this chapter, we need to account for them in our CSS, as in the following listing. We want our `<canvas>` element to line up with our `<svg>` element so that we can use HTML5 canvas as a background layer to any SVG elements we create.

Listing 11.2 bigdata.css

```css
body, html {
    margin: 0;
   }
canvas {
  position: absolute;
  width: 500px;
  height: 500px;
}
svg {
  position: absolute;
  width:500px;
  height:500px;
}
path.country {
    fill: gray;
    stroke-width: 1;
    stroke: black;
    opacity: .5;
}
path.sample {
    stroke: black;
    stroke-width: 1px;
    fill: red;
    fill-opacity: .5;
}
```

In this chapter we'll draw SVG over canvas, so the canvas element needs to have the same attributes as the SVG element.

Likewise, identical settings for the SVG element

```
line.link {
      stroke-width: 1px;
      stroke: black;
      stroke-opacity: .5;
}
circle.node {
  fill: red;
  stroke: white;
  stroke-width: 1px;
}
circle.xy {
  fill: pink;
  stroke: black;
  stroke-width: 1px;
}
```

11.1.1 Creating random geodata

The first thing we need is a dataset with a thousand datapoints. Rather than using data from a pregenerated file, we'll invent it. One useful function available in D3 is d3.range(), which allows you to create an array of values. We'll use d3.range() to create an array of a thousand values. We'll then use that array to populate an array of objects with enough data to put on a network and on a map. Because we're going to put this data on a map, we need to make sure it's properly formatted geoJSON, as in the following listing, which uses the randomCoords() function to create triangles.

Listing 11.3   Creating sample data

```
var sampleData = d3.range(1000).map(function(d) {          ◁──   d3.range creates
  var datapoint = {};                                   ◁──      an array that we
  datapoint.id = "Sample Feature " + d;                          immediately map
  datapoint.type = "Feature";                                    to an object array.
  datapoint.properties = {};
  datapoint.geometry = {};                                       Each datapoint is an
  datapoint.geometry.type = "Polygon";                           object with the
  datapoint.geometry.coordinates = randomCoords();               necessary attributes to
  return datapoint;                                              be placed on a map.
});

function randomCoords() {                                 ◁──   Draws a triangle
  var randX = (Math.random() * 350) - 175;                       around each
  var randY = (Math.random() * 170) - 85;                        random lat/long
  return [[[randX - 5,randY], [randX,randY - 5],                 coordinate pair
       [randX - 10,randY - 5], [randX - 5,randY]]];
};
```

After we have this data, we can throw it on a map like the one we first created in chapter 7. In the following listing we use the world.geojson file from chapter 7, so that we have some context for where the triangles are drawn.

Listing 11.4   Drawing a map with our sample data on it

```
d3.json("world.geojson", function(data) {createMap(data)});

function createMap(countries) {
  var projection = d3.geo.mercator()
      .scale(100).translate([250,250])

  var geoPath = d3.geo.path().projection(projection);
  var g = d3.select("svg").append("g");

  g.selectAll("path.country")
     .data(countries.features)
     .enter()
     .append("path")
     .attr("d", geoPath)
     .attr("class", "country");

  g.selectAll("path.sample")
     .data(sampleData)
     .enter()
     .append("path")
     .attr("d", geoPath)
     .attr("class", "sample");
};
```

Adjusts the projection and translation of the projection rather than the `<g>` so we can use the projection later to draw to canvas

Although our random triangles will obviously be in different places, our code should still produce something that looks like figure 11.2.

A thousand datapoints isn't very many, even on a small map like this. And in any browser that supports SVG, the data should be able to render quickly and provide you with the kind of functionality, like mouseover and click events, that you may want from your data display. But if you add zoom controls, like you see in listing 11.5 (the same zooming we had in chapter 7), then you'll notice that the performance of

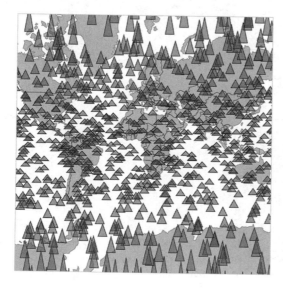

Figure 11.2   Drawing random triangles on a map entirely with SVG

Infoviz term: big data visualization

By the time you read this book, *big data* will probably sound as dated as *Pentium II*, *Rich Internet Application*, or *Buffy Cosplay*. Big data and all the excitement surrounding big data resulted from the broad availability of large datasets that were previously too large to handle. Often, big data is associated with exotic data stores like Hadoop or specialized techniques like GPU supercomputing (along with overpriced consultants).

But what constitutes *big* is in the eye of the beholder. In the domain of data visualization, the representation of big data doesn't typically mean placing thousands (or millions or trillions) of individual datapoints onscreen at once. Rather, it tends to mean demographic, topological, and other traditional statistical analysis of these massive datasets. Counterintuitively, big data visualization often takes the form of pie charts and bar charts. But when you look at traditional practice with presenting data interactively—natively—in the browser, the size of the datasets you're dealing with in this chapter really can be considered "*big.*"

the zooming and panning of the map isn't so great. If you expect your users to be on mobile, then optimization is still a good idea.

Listing 11.5   Adding zoom controls to a map

```
var mapZoom = d3.behavior.zoom().translate(projection.translate())
    .scale(projection.scale()).on("zoom", zoomed);
d3.select("svg").call(mapZoom);

function zoomed() {
    projection
      .translate(mapZoom.translate())
      .scale(mapZoom.scale());

    d3.selectAll("path.sample").attr("d", geoPath);
    d3.selectAll("path.country").attr("d", geoPath);

};
```

We use projection zoom in this example because it'll be easier to draw canvas elements later.

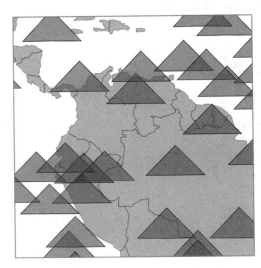

Figure 11.3   Zooming in on the sample geodata around South America

Now we can zoom into our map and pan around, as shown in figure 11.3. If you expect your users to be on browsers that handle SVG very well, like Chrome or Safari, and you don't expect to put more features on a map, then you may not even need to worry about optimization.

But what if you want to build interactive websites that work on all modern browsers? Firefox doesn't have the best SVG performance, and zooming this map in Firefox isn't a pleasant experience. If you change your d3.range() setting from 1000 to 5000, then even browsers that handle SVG well start to slow down.

11.1.2 *Drawing geodata with canvas*

One solution for optimization, which we touched on earlier, is to draw the elements with canvas instead of SVG. That's why we have a canvas element in our sample HTML page for this chapter, and why it's styled in such a way as to be directly underneath our <svg> element. Instead of creating SVG elements using D3's enter syntax, we use the built-in functionality in d3.geo.path to provide a context for HTML5 canvas. In the following listing, you can see how to use that built-in functionality with your existing dataset.

Listing 11.6 Drawing the map with canvas

```
function createMap(countries) {
  var projection = d3.geo.mercator().scale(50).translate([150,100]);
  var geoPath = d3.geo.path().projection(projection);

  var mapZoom = d3.behavior.zoom().translate(projection.translate())
              .scale(projection.scale()).on("zoom", zoomed);

  d3.select("svg").call(mapZoom);

  zoomed();

  function zoomed() {

    projection.translate(mapZoom.translate()).scale(mapZoom.scale());

    var context = d3.select("canvas").node().getContext("2d");
    context.clearRect(0,0,500,500);
    geoPath.context(context);

    context.strokeStyle = "black";
    context.fillStyle = "gray";
    context.lineWidth = "1px";
    for (var x in countries.features) {
      context.beginPath();
  geoPath(countries.features[x]);
      context.stroke()
      context.fill();
    }

    context.strokeStyle = "black";
    context.fillStyle = "rgba(255,0,0,.2)";
    context.lineWidth = "1px";
    for (var x in sampleData) {
```

Styles settings for countries

Always clear the canvas before redrawing it if you're updating it.

Switches geoPath to a context generator with our canvas context

Draws each country feature to canvas

```
        context.beginPath();
        geoPath(sampleData[x]);          ◁──┐  Draws each
        context.stroke();                   │  triangle to
        context.fill();                     │  canvas
      }
   };
};
```

You can see some key differences between listings 11.6 and 11.5. In contrast with SVG, where you can move elements around as well as redraw them, you always have to clear and redraw the canvas to update it. Although it seems this would be slower, performance increases on all browsers, especially those that don't have the best SVG performance, because you don't need to manage hundreds or thousands of DOM elements. The graphical results, as seen in figure 11.4, demonstrate that it's hard to see the difference between SVG and canvas rendering.

11.1.3 *Mixed-mode rendering techniques*

The drawback with using canvas is that you can't easily provide the level of interactivity you may want for your data visualization. Typically, you draw your interactive elements with SVG and your large datasets with canvas. If we assume that the countries we're drawing aren't going to provide any interactivity, but the triangles will, then we can render the triangles as SVG and render the countries as canvas using the code in the following listing. This requires that we initialize two versions of d3.geo.path—one for drawing SVG and one for drawing canvas—and then we use both in our zoomed function.

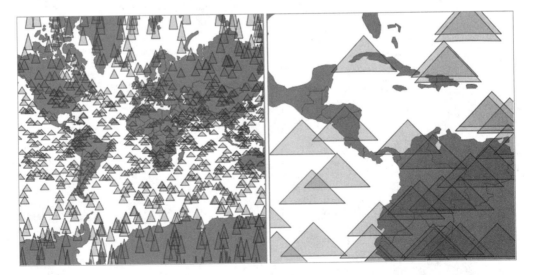

Figure 11.4 Drawing our map with canvas produces higher performance, but slightly less crisp graphics. On the left, it may seem like the triangles are as smoothly rendered as the earlier SVG triangles, but if you zoom in as we've done on the right, you can start to see clearly the slightly pixelated canvas rendering.

Listing 11.7 Rendering SVG and canvas simultaneously

```
function createMap(countries) {
    var projection = d3.geo.mercator().scale(100).translate([250,250]);
    var svgPath = d3.geo.path().projection(projection);
    var canvasPath = d3.geo.path().projection(projection);

    var mapZoom = d3.behavior.zoom()
      .translate(projection.translate())
      .scale(projection.scale())
      .on("zoom", zoomed);

    d3.select("svg").call(mapZoom);

    var g = d3.select("svg");

    g.selectAll("path.sample")
      .data(sampleData)
      .enter()
      .append("path")
      .attr("class", "sample")
      .on("mouseover", function() {d3.select(this).style("fill", "pink")});

    zoomed();

    function zoomed() {
      projection.translate(mapZoom.translate()).scale(mapZoom.scale());

      var context = d3.select("canvas").node().getContext("2d");
      context.clearRect(0,0,500,500);
      canvasPath.context(context);

      context.strokeStyle = "black";
      context.fillStyle = "gray";
      context.lineWidth = "1px";
      for (var x in countries.features) {
        context.beginPath();
        canvasPath(countries.features[x]);
        context.stroke();
        context.fill();
      }
    d3.selectAll("path.sample").attr("d", svgPath);
  };
};
```

> We need to instantiate a different d3.geo.path for canvas and for SVG.

> Updates the map when it's first created

> Draws canvas features with canvasPath

> Draws SVG features with svgPath

This allows us to maintain interactivity, such as the mouseover function on our triangles to change any triangle's color to pink when moused over. This approach maximizes performance by rendering any graphics that have no interactivity using HTML5 canvas instead of SVG. As shown in figure 11.5, the appearance produced using this method is virtually identical to that using canvas only or SVG only.

But what if you have massive numbers of elements and you really do want interactivity on all them, but you also want to give the user the ability to pan and drag? In that case, you have to embrace an extension of this mixed-mode rendering. You render in canvas whenever users are interacting in such a way that they can't interact with other elements. In other words, we need to render the triangles in canvas when the map is

Figure 11.5 Background countries are drawn with canvas, while foreground triangles are drawn with SVG to use interactivity. SVG graphics are individual elements in the DOM and therefore amenable to having click, mouseover, and other event listeners attached to them. 🖱

being zoomed and panned, but render them in SVG when the map isn't in motion and the user is mousing over certain elements.

How do you determine when a zoom event starts and when it finishes? In the past you had to set a timer, check to see if the user was still zooming, and then redraw the elements. But, fortunately, D3 introduced a pair of new events to the zoom control: `"zoomstart"` and `"zoomend"`. These fire, as you may guess, when the zoom event begins and ends, respectively. The following listing shows how you'd initialize a zoom behavior with different functions for these different events.

Listing 11.8 Mixed rendering based on zoom interaction

```
var projection = d3.geo.mercator().scale(100).translate([250,250]);
var svgPath = d3.geo.path().projection(projection);
var canvasPath = d3.geo.path().projection(projection);

 mapZoom = d3.behavior.zoom()
    .translate(projection.translate())
    .scale(projection.scale())
    .on("zoom", zoomed)
    .on("zoomstart", zoomInitialized)          ⟵  Assigns separate
    .on("zoomend", zoomFinished);                  functions for each
                                                   zoom state
d3.select("svg").call(mapZoom);

var g = d3.select("svg").append("g")

g.selectAll("path.sample").data(sampleData)
    .enter()
    .append("path")
```

```
      .attr("class", "sample")
      .on("mouseover", function() {
        d3.select(this).style("fill", "pink");
      });
    zoomFinished();
```

> We have to call zoomFinished (listing 11.9) to draw the canvas countries with SVG triangles.

This allows us to restore our canvas drawing code for triangles to the zoomed function and to move the SVG rendering code out of the zoomed function and into a new zoom-Finished function. We also need to hide the SVG triangles when zooming or panning starts by creating a zoomInitialized function that itself also fires the zoomed function (to draw the triangles we just hid, but in canvas). Finally, our zoomFinished function also contains the canvas drawing code necessary to only draw the countries. The different drawing strategies based on zoom events are shown in table 11.1.

Table 11.1 Rendering action based on zoom event

zoom event	*Countries* rendered as	Triangles rendered as
zoomed	Canvas	Canvas
zoomInitialized	Canvas	Hide SVG
zoomFinished	Canvas	SVG

As you can see in the following listing, this code is inefficient, but I wanted to be explicit about this functionality, because it's a bit convoluted.

Listing 11.9 Zoom functions for mixed rendering

```
function zoomed() {
  projection.translate(mapZoom.translate()).scale(mapZoom.scale());

  var context = d3.select("canvas").node().getContext("2d");
  context.clearRect(0,0,500,500);
  canvasPath.context(context);

  context.strokeStyle = "black";
  context.fillStyle = "gray";
  context.lineWidth = "1px";
  for (var x in countries.features) {
    context.beginPath();
    canvasPath(countries.features[x]);
    context.stroke()
    context.fill();
  }

  context.strokeStyle = "black";
  context.fillStyle = "rgba(255,0,0,.2)";
  context.lineWidth = 1;
  for (var x in sampleData) {
    context.beginPath();
```

> Draws all elements as canvas during zooming

```
        canvasPath(sampleData[x]);
        context.stroke()
        context.fill();
    }
};

function zoomInitialized() {
  d3.selectAll("path.sample")
    .style("display", "none");
  zoomed();
};

function zoomFinished() {
  var context = d3.select("canvas").node().getContext("2d");
  context.clearRect(0,0,500,500);
  canvasPath.context(context)

  context.strokeStyle = "black";
  context.fillStyle = "gray";
  context.lineWidth = "1px";
  for (var x in countries.features) {
    context.beginPath();
    canvasPath(countries.features[x]);
    context.stroke()
    context.fill();
  }

  d3.selectAll("path.sample")
    .style("display", "block")
    .attr("d", svgPath);
};
```

Hides SVG elements when zooming starts

Calls zoomed to draw with canvas the SVG triangles we just hid

Only draws countries with canvas at the end of the zoom

Shows SVG elements when zoom ends

Sets the new position of SVG elements

As a result of this new code, we have a map that uses canvas rendering when users zoom and pan, but SVG rendering when the map is fixed in place and users have the ability to click, mouse over, or otherwise interact with the graphical elements. It's the best of both worlds. The only drawback of this approach is that we have to invest more time making sure our <canvas> element and our <svg> element line up perfectly, and that our opacity, fill colors, and so on are close enough matches that it's not jarring to the user to see the different modes. I haven't done this in the previous code, so that you can see that the two modes are in operation at the same time, and that's reflected in the difference between the two graphical outputs in figure 11.6.

The kind of pixel-perfect alignment necessary to make the transition from one mode to another, as well as the fastidious color matching also required, isn't something I have the space to explain in this book, but you'll need to do both to make the best interactive information visualization. If you look closely at figure 11.6, you'll notice that the canvas element (on the right) is a pixel or so shifted up and to the left, and that's without testing it in other browsers that may have different default settings for <canvas> or <svg> or both.

Finally, using canvas and SVG drawing simultaneously may present a difficulty. Say we want to draw a canvas layer over an SVG layer because we want the canvas layer to

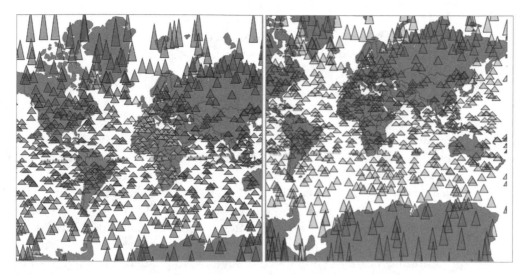

Figure 11.6 The same randomly generated triangles rendered in SVG while the map isn't being zoomed or panned (left) and in canvas while the map is being zoomed or panned (right). Notice that only the SVG triangles have different fill values based on user interaction, because that isn't factored into the canvas drawing code for the triangles on the right.

appear above *some* of our SVG elements visually but below other SVG elements, and we want interactivity on all them. In that case we'd need to sandwich our canvas layer between our SVG layers and set the `pointer-events` style of our canvas layer, as shown in figure 11.7.

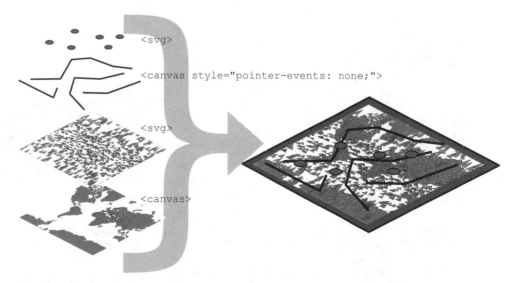

Figure 11.7 Placing interactive SVG elements below a `<canvas>` element requires that you set its `pointer-events` style to `"none"`, even if it has a transparent background, in order to register click events on the `<svg>` element underneath it.

If you add further alternating layers of interactivity but with graphical placement above and below, then you can end up making a <canvas> and <svg> layer cake in your DOM that's hard to manage and also hard to mentally conceptualize.

11.2   *Big network data*

It's great that d3.geo.path has built-in functionality for drawing geodata to canvas, but what about other types of data visualization? One of the most performance-intensive layouts is the force-directed layout that we dealt with in chapter 6. The layout calculates new positions for each node in your network at every tick. When you use SVG, you need to redraw the network constantly. When I first started working with force-directed layouts in D3, I found that any network with more than 100 nodes was too slow to prove useful. That was a problem because larger networks could still have structure that would benefit from interactivity and animation that needed SVG.

In my own work, I looked at how different small D3 applications hosted on gist.github.com share common D3 functions. D3 coders can understand how different information visualization methods use D3 functions commonly associated with other types of information visualization. You can explore this network along with how D3 Meetup users describe themselves at http://emeeks.github.io/introspect/block_block.html.

To explore these connections, I needed to have a method for dealing with over a thousand different examples and thousands of connections between them. You can see some of this network in figure 11.8. I wanted to show how this network changed

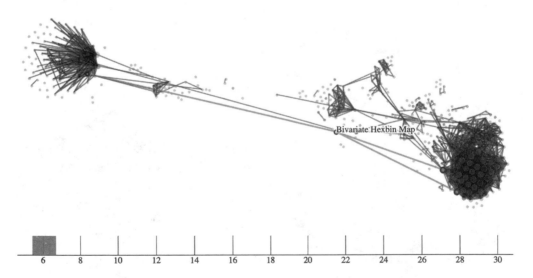

Figure 11.8   A network of D3 examples hosted on gist.github.com that connects different examples to each other by shared functions. Here you can see that the example "Bivariate Hexbin Map" by Mike Bostock (http://bl.ocks.org/mbostock/4330486) shares functions in common with three different examples: "Metropolitan Unemployment," "Marey's Trains II," and "GitHub Users Worldwide." The brush and axis component allows you to filter the network by the number of connections from one block to another.

based on a threshold of shared functions, and I also wanted to provide users with the capacity to click each example to get more details, so I couldn't draw the network using canvas. Instead, I needed to draw the network using the same mixed-rendering method we looked at to draw all those triangles on a map. But in this case I used canvas for the network edges and SVG for the network nodes.

Using bl.ocks.org

Although D3 is suitable for building large, complex interactive applications, you often make a small, single-use interactive data visualization that can live on a single page with limited resources. For these small applications, it's common in the D3 community to host the code on gist.github.com, which is the part of GitHub designed for small applications. If you host your D3 code as a gist, and it's formatted to have an index.html, then you can use bl.ocks.org to share your work with others.

To make your gist work on bl.ocks.org, you need to have the data files and libraries hosted in the gist or accessible through it. Then you can take the alphanumeric identifier of your gist and append it to bl.ocks.org/username/ to serve a working copy for sharing. So, for instance, I have a gist at https://gist.github.com/emeeks/0a4d7cd56e027023bf78 that demonstrates how to do the mixed rendering of a force-directed layout like I described in this chapter. As a result, I can point people to http://bl.ocks.org/emeeks/0a4d7cd56e027023bf78 and they can see the code itself as well as the animated network in action.

Doing this kind of mixed rendering with networks isn't as easy as it is with maps. That's because there's no built-in method to render regular data to canvas as with d3.geo.path. If you want to create a similar large network that combines canvas and SVG rendering, you have to build the function manually. First, though, you need data. This time, instead of sample geodata, listing 11.10 shows how to create sample network data.

Building sample network data is easy: you can create an array of nodes and an array of random links between those nodes. But building a sample network that's not an undifferentiated mass is a little bit harder. In listing 11.10 you can see my slightly sophisticated network generator. It operates on the principle that a few nodes are very popular and most nodes aren't (we've known about this principle of networks since grade school). This does a decent job of creating a network with 3000 nodes and 1000 edges that doesn't look quite like a giant hairball.

Listing 11.10   Generating random network data

```
var linkScale = d3.scale.linear()
        .domain([0,.9,.95,1]).range([0,10,100,1000]);      ◁─┐  This scale makes
                                                              90% of the links to
var sampleNodes = d3.range(3000).map(function(d) {           1% of the nodes.
  var datapoint = {};
  datapoint.id = "Sample Node " + d;
  return datapoint;
})
```

```
var sampleLinks = [];
  var y = 0;
  while (y < 1000) {
    var randomSource = Math.floor(Math.random() * 1000);
    var randomTarget = Math.floor(linkScale(Math.random()));
    var linkObject = {source: sampleNodes[randomSource], target:
        sampleNodes[randomTarget]}
    if (randomSource != randomTarget) {
        sampleLinks.push(linkObject);
    }
    y++;
}
```

The source of each link is purely random.

The target is weighted toward popular nodes.

Don't keep any links that have the same source as target.

With this generator in place, we can instantiate our typical force-directed layout using the code in the following listing, and create a few lines and circles with it.

Listing 11.11   Force-directed layout

```
var force = d3.layout.force()
    .size([500,500])
    .gravity(.5)
    .nodes(sampleNodes)
    .links(sampleLinks)
    .on("tick", forceTick);

d3.select("svg")
    .selectAll("line.link")
    .data(sampleLinks)
    .enter()
    .append("line")
    .attr("class", "link");

d3.select("svg").selectAll("circle.node")
    .data(sampleNodes)
    .enter()
    .append("circle")
    .attr("r", 3)
    .attr("class", "node");

force.start();

function forceTick() {
    d3.selectAll("line.link")
        .attr("x1", function(d) {return d.source.x})
        .attr("y1", function(d) {return d.source.y})
        .attr("x2", function(d) {return d.target.x})
        .attr("y2", function(d) {return d.target.y});

    d3.selectAll("circle.node")
        .attr("cx", function(d) {return d.x})
        .attr("cy", function(d) {return d.y});
};
```

This is all vanilla force-directed layout code like in chapter 6.

For our initial implementation, we render everything in SVG and update the SVG on every tick.

This code should be familiar to you if you've read chapter 6. Generation of random networks is a complex and well-described practice. This random generator isn't going to win any awards, but it does produce a recognizable structure. Typical results are

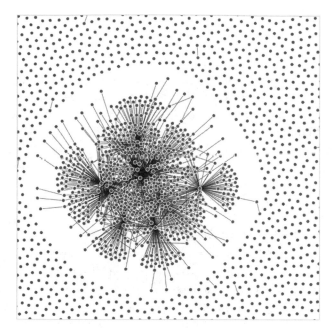

Figure 11.9 A randomly generated network with 3000 nodes and 1000 edges

shown in figure 11.9. What's lost in the static image is the slow and jerky rendering, even on a fast computer using a browser that handles SVG well.

When I first started working with these networks, I thought the main cause of slow-down was calculating the myriad positions for each node on every tick. After all, node position is based on a simulation of competing forces caused by nodes pushing and edges pulling, and something like this, with thousands of components, seems heavy duty. That's not what's taxing the browser, though. Instead, it's the management of so many DOM elements. You can get rid of many of those DOM elements by replacing the SVG lines with canvas lines. Let's change our code so that it doesn't create any SVG `<line>` elements for the links and instead modify our `forceTick` function to draw those links with canvas.

Listing 11.12 Mixed rendering network drawing

```
function forceTick() {
  var context = d3.select("canvas").node()
          .getContext("2d");
  context.clearRect(0,0,500,500);

  context.lineWidth = 1;
  context.strokeStyle = "rgba(0, 0, 0, 0.5)";

  sampleLinks.forEach(function (link) {
    context.beginPath();
    context.moveTo(link.source.x,link.source.y)
    context.lineTo(link.target.x,link.target.y)
    context.stroke();
  });
```

Remember: you always need to clear your canvas.

Draws links as 50% transparent black

Starts each line at the link source coordinates

Draws each link to the link target coordinates

```
d3.selectAll("circle.node")
    .attr("cx", function(d) {return d.x})
    .attr("cy", function(d) {return d.y});
};
```
◁— **Draws nodes as SVG**

The rendering of the network is similar in appearance, as you can see in figure 11.10, but the performance improves dramatically. Using canvas, I can draw 10,000 link networks with performance high enough to have animation and interactivity. The canvas drawing code can be a bit cumbersome (it's like the old LOGO drawing code), but the performance makes it more than worth it.

We could use the same method as with the earlier maps to use canvas during animated periods and SVG when the network is fixed. But we'll move on and look at another method for dealing with large amounts of data: quadtrees.

11.3   *Optimizing xy data selection with quadtrees*

When you're working with a large dataset, one issue is optimizing search and selection of elements in a region. Let's say you're working with a set of data with xy coordinates (anything that's laid out on a plane or screen). You've seen enough examples in this book to know that this may be a scatterplot, points on a map, or any of a number of different graphical representations of data. When you have data like this, you often want to know what datapoints fall in a particular selected region. This is referred to as *spatial search* (and notice that "spatial" in this case doesn't refer to geographic, but rather space in a more generic sense). The quadtree functionality is a spatial version of d3.nest, which we used in chapter 5 and chapter 8 and will use again in chapter 12 (available online only) to create hierarchical data. Following the

Figure 11.10   A large network drawn with SVG nodes and canvas links

theme of this chapter, we'll get started by creating a big dataset of random points and render them in SVG.

11.3.1 Generating random xy data

Our third random data generator doesn't require nearly as much work as the first two did. In the following listing, all we do is create 3000 points with random x and y coordinates.

Listing 11.13   xy data generator

```
sampleData = d3.range(3000).map(function(d) {
  var datapoint = {};
  datapoint.id = "Sample Node " + d;
  datapoint.x = Math.random() * 500;
  datapoint.y = Math.random() * 500;

  return datapoint;
})
d3.select("svg").selectAll("circle")
  .data(sampleData)
  .enter()
  .append("circle")
  .attr("class", "xy")
  .attr("r", 3)
  .attr("cx", function(d) {return d.x})
  .attr("cy", function(d) {return d.y});
```

◁── **Because we know the fixed size of our canvas, we can hardwire this.**

As you may expect, the result of this code, shown in figure 11.11, is a bunch of pink circles scattered randomly all over our canvas.

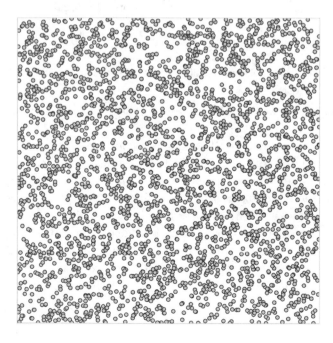

Figure 11.11   3000 randomly placed points represented by pink SVG `<circle>` elements

11.3.2 *xy brushing*

Now we'll create a brush to select some of these points. Recall when we used a brush in chapter 9 that we only allowed brushing along the x-axis. This time, we allow brushing along both x- and y-axes. Then we can drag a rectangle over any part of the canvas. In listing 11.14, you can see how quick and easy it is to add a brush to our canvas. We'll also add a function to highlight any circles in the brushed region. In this example we use d3.scale.identity for our .x() and .y() selectors. All d3.scale.identity does is create a scale where the domain and range are exactly the same. It's useful for times like these when the function operates with a scale but your scale domain directly matches the range of your graphical area.

> **Listing 11.14   xy brushing**

```
var brush = d3.svg.brush()
  .x(d3.scale.identity().domain([0, 500]))      ◁── Because we aren't
  .y(d3.scale.identity().domain([0, 500]))           going to adjust scale
  .on("brush", brushed);                             settings, we can define
                                                     them inline.
d3.select("svg").call(brush)

function brushed() {
  var e = brush.extent();
  d3.selectAll("circle")                             Tests to see if the
    .style("fill", function (d) {                     data is in our
      if (d.x >= e[0][0] && d.x <= e[1][0]             selected area
              && d.y >= e[0][1] && d.y <= e[1][1])  ◁──
      {
        return "darkred";              ◁──   Colors the points
      }                                       in the selected
      else {                                  area dark red
        return "pink";       ◁──   Colors the points
      }                             outside the
    });                             selected area pink
};
```

With this brushing code, we can now see the circles in the brushed region, as shown in figure 11.12.

This works, but it's terribly inefficient. It checks every point on the canvas without using any mechanism to ignore points that might be well outside the selection area. Finding points within a prescribed area is an old problem that has been well explored. One of the tools available to solve that problem quickly and easily is a quadtree. You may ask, what is a quadtree and what should I use it for?

A *quadtree* is a method for optimizing spatial search by dividing a plane into a series of quadrants. You then divide each of those quadrants into quadrants, until every point on that plane falls in its own quadrant. By dividing the xy plane like this, you nest the points you'll be searching in such a way that you can easily ignore entire quadrants of data without testing the entire dataset.

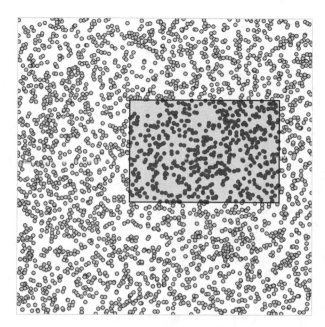

Figure 11.12 Highlighting points in a selected region

Another way to explain a quadtree is to show it. That's what this information visualization stuff is for, right? Figure 11.13 shows the quadrants that a quadtree produces based on a set of point data.

Creating a quadtree with xy data of the kind we have in our dataset is easy, as you can see in listing 11.15. We set the x and y accessors like we do with layouts and other D3 functions.

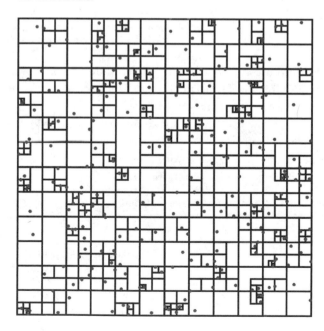

Figure 11.13 A quadtree for points shown in red with quadrant regions stroked in black. Notice how clusters of points correspond to subdivision of regions of the quadtree. Every point falls in only one region, but each region is nested in several levels of parent regions.

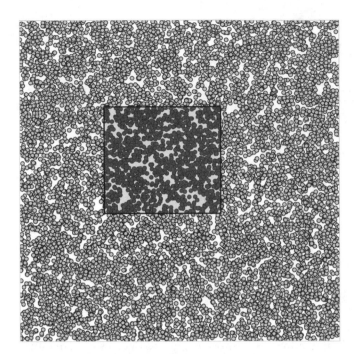

Figure 11.14 Quadtree-optimized selection used with a dataset of 10,000 points

---

Listing 11.15   Creating a quadtree from xy data

Accessors pointed at our data's xy format

```
var quadtree = d3.geom.quadtree()
    .extent([[0,0], [500,500]])          ◁— We need to define the bounding box of
    .x(function(d) {return d.x})              a quadtree as an array of upper-left
    .y(function(d) {return d.y});             and lower-right points.

var quadIndex = quadtree(sampleData);    ◁— After creating a quadtree, we create
                                              the index by passing our dataset to it.
```

After you create a quadtree and use it to create a quadtree index dataset like we did with quadIndex, you can use that dataset's .visit() function for quadtree-optimized searching. The .visit() functionality replaces your test in a new brush function, as shown in listing 11.16. First, I'll show you how to make it work in listing 11.16. Then, I'll show you that it *does* work in figure 11.14, and I'll explain *how* it works in detail. This isn't the usual order of things, I realize, but with a quadtree, it makes more sense if you see the code before analyzing its exact functionality.

Listing 11.16   Quadtree-optimized xy brush selection

```
function brushed() {
  var e = brush.extent();

  d3.selectAll("circle")                              Sets all circles to pink,
      .style("fill", "pink")                          and gives each a selected
      .each(function(d) {d.selected = false})    ◁—  attribute to designate
                                                      which are in our selection
```

Calls .visit()

Checks each point to see if it's inside our brush extent and sets selected to true if it is

```
quadIndex.visit(function(node,x1,y1,x2,y2) {
    if (node.point) {
        if (node.point.x >= e[0][0] && node.point.x <= e[1][0]
            &&node.point.y >= e[0][1] && node.point.y <= e[1][1]) {
            node.point.selected = true;
        }
    }
    return x1 > e[1][0] || y1 > e[1][1] || x2 < e[0][0] || y2 < e[0][1];
})

d3.selectAll("circle")
    .filter(function(d) {
        return d.selected;
    })
    .style("fill", "darkred");
};
```

Checks each node to see if it's a point or a container

Checks to see if this area of the quadtree falls outside our selection

Shows which points were selected

The results are impressive and much faster. In figure 11.14, I increased the number of points to 10,000 and still got good performance. (But if you're dealing with datasets that large, I recommend switching to canvas, because forcing the browser to manage all those SVG elements is going to slow things down.)

How does it work? When you run the `visit` function, you get access to each node in the quadtree, from the most generalized to the more specific. With each node, which we access in listing 11.16 as `node`, you also get the bounds of that node (`x1`, `y1`, `x2`, `y2`). Because nodes in a quadtree can either be the bounding areas or the actual points that generated the quadtree, you have to test if the node is a point and, if it is, you can then test if it's in your brush bounds like we did in our earlier example. The final piece of the `visit` function is where it gets its power, but it's also the most difficult to follow, as you can see in figure 11.15.

The `visit` function looks at every node in a quadtree, unless `visit` returns `true`, in which case it stops searching that particular quadrant and all its child nodes. So you test to see if the node you're looking at (represented as the bounds `x1,y1,x2,y2`) is entirely outside the bounds of your selection area (represented as the bounds `e[0][0],e[0][1],e[1][0],e[1][1]`). You create this test to see if the top of the selection is below the bottom of the node's bounds; if the bottom of the selection is above the top of the node's bounds; if the left side of the selection is to the right of the right side of the node's bounds; or if the right side of the selection is to the left of the left side of the node's bounds. That may seem a bit hard to follow (and sure takes up more time as a sentence than it does as a piece of code), but that's how it works.

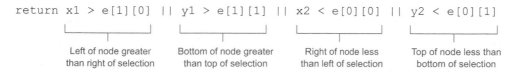

```
return x1 > e[1][0] || y1 > e[1][1] || x2 < e[0][0] || y2 < e[0][1]
```

Left of node greater than right of selection | Bottom of node greater than top of selection | Right of node less than left of selection | Top of node less than bottom of selection

Figure 11.15 The test to see if a quadtree node is outside a brush selection involves four tests to see if it is above, left, right, or below the selection area. If it passes `true` for any of these tests, then the quadtree will stop searching any child nodes.

You can use that `visit` function to do more than optimized search. I've used it to cluster nearby points on a map (http://bl.ocks.org/emeeks/066e20c1ce5008f884eb) and also to draw the bounds of the quadtree in figure 11.13.

11.4 *More optimization techniques*

You can improve the performance of the data visualization of large datasets in many other ways. Here are three that should give you immediate returns: avoid general opacity, avoid general selections, and precalculate positions.

11.4.1 *Avoid general opacity*

Whenever possible, use fill-opacity and stroke-opacity or RGBA color references rather than the element opacity style. General element opacity, the kind of setting you get when you use `"style: opacity"`, can slow down rendering. When you use specific fill or stroke opacity, it forces you to pay more attention to where and how you're using opacity.

So instead of

```
d3.selectAll(elements).style("fill", "red").style("opacity", .5)
```

do this:

```
d3.selectAll(elements).style("fill", "red").style("fill-opacity", .5)
```

11.4.2 *Avoid general selections*

Although it's convenient to select all elements and apply conditional behavior across those elements, you should try to use `selection.filter` with your selections to reduce the number of calls to the DOM. If you look at the code in listing 11.16, you'll see this general selection that clears the selected attribute for all the circles and sets the fill of all the circles to pink:

```
d3.selectAll("circle")
.style("fill", "pink")
.each(function(d) {d.selected = false})
```

Instead, clear the attribute and set the fill color of only those circles that are currently set to the selection. This limits the number of costly DOM calls:

```
d3.selectAll("circle")
.filter(function(d) {return d.selected})
.style("fill", "pink")
.each(function(d) {d.selected = false})
```

If you adjust the code in that example, the performance is further improved. Remember that manipulating DOM elements, even if it's changing a setting like fill, can cause the greatest performance hit.

11.4.3 *Precalculate positions*

You can also precalculate positions and then apply transitions. If you have a complex algorithm that determines an element's new position, first go through the data array and calculate the new position. Then append the new position as data to the data-point of the element. After you've done all your calculations, select and apply a transition based on the calculated new position. When you're calculating complex new positions and applying those calculated positions to a transition of a large selection of elements, you can overwhelm the browser and see jerky animations.

So, instead of

```
d3.selectAll(elements)
.transition()
.duration(1000)
.attr("x", newComplexPosition);
```

do this:

```
d3.selectAll(elements)
.each(function(d) {d.newX = newComplexPosition(d)});

d3.selectAll(elements)
.transition()
.duration(1000)
.attr("x", function(d) {return d.newX});
```

11.5 *Summary*

In this chapter, we looked at a few ways to deal with large datasets, and by necessity touched on methods for generating those datasets. Specifically, we looked at

- Generating random geodata
- Using the `.context` function of `d3.geo.path` to draw map features using canvas
- Using zoom's start and end functionality to render elements in canvas or SVG
- Generating random network data
- Drawing network lines in canvas
- Generating random xy data
- Creating an xy brush
- Highlighting selected features
- Building a quadtree
- Using a quadtree for optimized spatial search

In the next chapter (available as an online supplement), we'll focus on one area where performance tuning is important: data visualization on mobile. You'll see the built-in functionality in D3 for handling touch interfaces and spend time thinking about design principles for interactive data visualization on mobile.

If you want to grow your D3 skill set, I'd suggest starting with bl.ocksplorer (http://bl.ocksplorer.org/), which allows you to find examples of D3 code based on specific

D3 functions. You should also check out the work of Mike Bostock (http://bl.ocks .org/mbostock) and Jason Davies (http://www.jasondavies.com/) to see the cutting edge of data visualization with D3. D3 has an active Google Group (https://groups .google.com/forum/#!forum/d3-js), if you're interested in discussing the internals of the library, and many popular Meetup groups like the Bay Area D3 User Group (http://www.meetup.com/Bay-Area-d3-User-Group/). I find the best place to keep up with D3 is on Twitter, where you can see examples posted with the hashtag #d3js and examples of when things don't quite go right (but are still beautiful) with the hashtag #d3brokeandmadeart.

index